THE PHILOSOPHY OF THE UPANISHADS

THE PHILOSOPHY
OF
THE UPANISHADS

BY
PAUL DEUSSEN

AUTHORIZED ENGLISH TRANSLATION BY
REV. A. S. GEDEN, M.A.

DOVER PUBLICATIONS. INC., NEW YORK

This Dover edition, first published in 1966, is an unabridged and unaltered republication of the work originally published by T. & T. Clark in 1906.

Library of Congress Catalog Card Number: 66-20325

Manufactured in the United States of America
Dover Publications, Inc.
180 Varick Street
New York, N. Y. 10014

PREFACE

Dr. Deussen's treatise on the Upanishads needs no formal introduction or commendation to students of Indian thought who are familiar with the German language. To others I would fain hope that the translation here presented, which appears with the author's sanction, may serve to make known a work of very marked ability and of surpassing interest. As far as my knowledge extends, there is no adequate exposition of the Upanishads available in English. The best was published by Messrs. Trübner more than a quarter of a century ago, and is in many respects out of date. As traced here by the master-hand of the author, the teaching of the ancient Indian seers presents itself in clearest light, and claims the sympathetic study of all lovers of truth.

For the English rendering I am alone responsible. And where I may have failed to catch the precise meaning of the original, or adequately to represent the turn of phrase, I can only ask the indulgence of the reader. Dr. Deussen's style is not easy. And if a more capable hand than mine had been willing to essay the task of translation, I would gladly have resigned my office. With whatsoever care I can hardly hope entirely to have escaped error. But for any indication of oversight or mistake, and any suggestion for improvement, I shall be most grateful. The work has exacted many hours that could be ill spared from a very full life. If however it conduce in any way to a better understanding of the mind and heart of India I shall be amply repaid.

A. S. GEDEN.

RICHMOND,
December 1905.

PREFACE BY THE AUTHOR

THE present work forms the second part of my *General History of Philosophy.* It is however complete in itself; and has for its subject the Philosophy of the Upanishads, the culminating point of the Indian doctrine of the universe. This point had been already reached in Vedic, pre-Buddhist times; and in philosophical significance has been surpassed by none of the later developments of thought up to the present day. In particular the Sâṅkhya system has followed out lines of thought traced for it in the Upanishads, and has emphasized realistic tendencies already found there (*infra*, pp. 239–255). Buddhism also, though of entirely independent origin, yet betrays its indebtedness in essential points to the teaching of the Upanishads, when its main fundamental thought (*nirvâṇam*, the removal of suffering by the removal of *ṭrishṇâ*) meets us expressed in other words (union with Brahman by the removal of *kâma*) in the passage from the Bṛihadâraṇyaka quoted below.[1]

The thoughts of the Vedânta therefore became for India a permanent and characteristic spiritual atmosphere, which pervades all the products of the later literature.

[1] Bṛih. 4. 4. 6, *infra* p. 348.

To every Indian Brâhman to-day the Upanishads are what the New Testament is to the Christian.

So significant a phenomenon deserved and demanded a more comprehensive treatment than it had yet obtained. And my hope is to remove in some measure the cloud which hitherto has obscured this subject, and to exhibit order and consistency in place of the confused mass of contradictory conceptions, which alone had been supposed to exist. If the result is not a uniform and unified system, there is yet found a regular historical development, the key to which is an original, abrupt and daring idealism; and this in its further progress by a twofold concession, on the one hand to traditional beliefs, and on the other to the empirical prepossessions natural to us all, was gradually developed into that which we, adopting Western phraseology if not always in a Western sense, call pantheism, cosmogonism, theism, atheism (Sâṅkhya), and deism (Yoga). Chap. ix., "The Unreality of the Universe" (pp. 226–239), which by its paradoxical title attracts attention and provokes contradiction, or the final survey at the close of the book (p. 396 ff.), may well serve as a first introduction to these oriental teachings.

A remarkable and at first sight perplexing feature in this entire evolution of thought is the persistence with which the original idealism holds its ground, not annulled or set aside by the pantheistic and theistic developments that have grown out of it. On the contrary it remains a living force, the influence of which may be more or less directly traced everywhere, until it is finally abandoned by the Sâṅkhya system. Adopted by the Vedânta it is proclaimed as the only "higher knowledge" (*parâ vidyâ*), and contrasted with all those realistic developments which together with the creation and transmigration doctrines are known as the "lower knowledge" (*aparâ vidyâ*), and are explained as accommodations of the written revelation to the weakness of human understanding. This accommodation theory of the later Vedântist teachers is not wholly baseless, and needs correction only in the one point that this adjustment to the empirical capacity of the intellect (which works within the relations of time, space and causality) was not intentional and conscious, but unconscious. In this shape the idea of accommodation becomes a key which is fitted to unlock the secrets not only of the doctrinal developments of the Upanishads, but of many analogous phenomena in Western philosophy. For the practice of clothing metaphysical intuitions in the forms of empirical knowledge is met with not only in India, but also in Europe from the earliest times. And for that very reason no account would have been taken of it had not Kant demonstrated the incorrectness of the whole procedure, as I hope to show in detail in the later parts of my work.

P. DEUSSEN.

CONTENTS

THE PHILOSOPHY OF THE UPANISHADS:

THE SECOND PERIOD OF INDIAN PHILOSOPHY, OR THE CONTINUANCE AND CLOSE OF THE TIMES OF THE BRÂHMAṆAS

INTRODUCTION TO THE PHILOSOPHY OF THE UPANISHADS

PAGE

THE SYSTEM OF THE UPANISHADS

FIRST PART: THEOLOGY, OR THE DOCTRINE OF BRAHMAN

PAGE

SECOND PART: COSMOLOGY, OR THE DOCTRINE OF THE UNIVERSE

THIRD PART: PSYCHOLOGY, OR THE DOCTRINE OF THE SOUL

THE PHILOSOPHY
OF
THE UPANISHADS

THE

PHILOSOPHY OF THE UPANISHADS

A. INTRODUCTION TO THE PHILOSOPHY OF THE UPANISHADS

I. THE PLACE OF THE UPANISHADS IN THE LITERATURE OF THE VEDA

1. *The Veda and its Divisions*

It will be remembered that our earlier investigations led to a classification of Vedic literature into four principal parts, which correspond to the four priestly offices at the Soma sacrifice; these are the Ṛig, Yajur, Sâma, and Atharvaveda, each of which comprises a Saṁhitâ, a Brâhmaṇa, and a Sûtra. The Brâhmaṇa (in the wider sense of the term) is then further divided by the exponents of the Vedânta into three orders, which as regards their contents are for the most part closely connected with and overlap one another, viz.—Vidhi, Arthavâda, and Vedânta or Upanishad. The following scheme may be helpful in retaining in the memory this primary classification of the Veda:—

I. Ṛigveda.	*A.* Samhitâ.	*a.* Vidhi.
II. Sâmaveda.	*B.* Brâhmana.	*b.* Arthavâda.
III. Yajurveda.	*C.* Sûtra.	*c.* Vedânta. (Upanishad.)
IV. Atharvaveda.		

A further preliminary remark is that each of the above twelve parts of the Veda has been preserved as a rule not separately, but in several often numerous forms, inasmuch as each Veda was taught in different *S'âkhâs* (literally, "branches" of the tree of the Veda), *i.e.* Vedic schools, which in their treatment of the common subject-matter varied so considerably from one another that, in course of time, distinct works were produced, the contents of which nevertheless remained practically the same. In particular, each of the three ancient Vedas (in the case of the fourth the relations are usually different) comprises not one Brâhmaṇa, but several; and similarly there exist for each Veda not one but several Upanishads. On this subject more will be found below.

2. *Brâhmaṇa, Âraṇyaka, Upanishad*

The link between the Upanishad and the Brâhmaṇa with its very different spirit is as a rule not direct, but established ordinarily by means of an *Âraṇyaka* or "forest-book," to the close of which the Upanishad is attached, or in which it is included. The name is given either because (as Oldenberg supposes, *Prol.*, p. 291), on account of its mysterious character it should be imparted to the student not in the village (*grâme*), but outside of it (*araṇye*, in the jungle) (cp. the narrative, Bṛih. 3. 2. 13, and the names *rahasyam*, *upanishad*), or because from the very beginning it was "a Brâhmaṇa appointed for the vow of the anchorite."[1] The contents of the Âraṇyakas perhaps favour rather the latter conception, so far as they consist mainly of all kinds of explanations of the ritual and allegorical speculations therein. This is only what might be expected in the life

[1] *Âraṇyaka-vrata-rûpam brâhmaṇam*, Sâyana ; see Aufrecht, *Einl. zum Ait. Br.*, p. iii., and cp. Deussen, *Upan.*, p. 7.

of the forest as a substitute for the actual sacrificial observances, which for the most part were no longer practicable; and they form a natural transition to the speculations of the Upanishads, altogether emancipated as these are from the limitations of a formal cult. The connecting-link is never wanting where the written tradition of a S'âkhâ has been handed down unbroken (as is not the case with the *Kâṭhaka*, *S'vetâs'vatara*, *Maitrâyaṇîya*), for both the *Aitareyins* and *Kaushîtakins* of the Ṛigveda and the *Taittirîyakas* and *Vâjasaneyins* of the Yajurveda possess together with the Saṁhitâ their Brâhmaṇa with Âraṇyaka and Upanishad. Even then, if in the schools of the Sâmaveda the name Âraṇyaka is not employed, yet there also the introductions to the Upanishads[1] bear throughout the character of Âraṇyakas. This succession of ritual allegorical and philosophical texts, which is really the same in all the S'âkhâs, may be due partly to the order of thought adopted for the purposes of instruction, in which the Saṁhitâ would naturally be followed immediately by the Brâhmaṇa (so far as this was generally taught, cp. Oldenberg, *Prol.*, p. 291); the deep mysterious meaning of the ceremonies would then be unfolded in the Âraṇyaka; and finally the exposition of the Upanishads would close the period of Vedic instruction. As early, therefore, as S'vet. 6. 22 and Muṇḍ. 3. 2. 6, and thenceforward, the Upanishads bore the name *Vedânta* (*i.e.* "end of the Veda"). On the other hand it is not to be denied that the order of the texts within the canon of each S'âkhâ corresponds generally to their historical development, and that the position of the several parts affords an indication of their earlier or later date. If, however, these two factors that determined the arrangement, namely, the tendency to a systematic classification of the material for instruction and the

[1] Chândogya Upan. 1–2, Upanishadbrâh. 1–3.

preservation of the order of chronological development, do actually for the most part coincide in their result, this is very simply explained on the supposition that in the course of time the general interest was transferred from the ritualistic method of treatment to the allegorical, and from that again to the philosophical. Moreover, the separation of the material is by no means strictly carried out, but in all three classes, Brâhmaṇas, Âraṇyakas, and Upanishads, there are found occasionally digressions of a ritual as well as allegorical or philosophical nature. Especially noteworthy, however, and demanding explanation is the circumstance that, apart from this occasional overlapping of the subject-matter, the broad distinctions between Brâhmaṇa Âraṇyaka and Upanishad are by no means always correctly observed; *e.g.*, among the Aitareyins the matter of the Brâhmaṇa extends into the Âraṇyaka, while with the Taittirîyakas the close of the Brâhmaṇa and the beginning of the Âraṇyaka agree throughout, and the dividing line is entirely arbitrary. This state of things is to be explained probably only on the supposition that the entire teaching material of each S'âkhâ formed originally a consecutive whole, and that this whole was first in the later times distinguished into Brâhmaṇa Âraṇyaka and Upanishad, on a principle which did not depend upon the character of the subject-matter alone, but which, though in general correspondence with it, was in fact imposed from without. Such a principle we seem to be able to recognise in the later order of the four *âs'ramas*, by virtue of which it became the duty of every Indian Brâhman first as *brahmac'ârin* to spend a portion of his life with a Brâhman teacher, then as *gṛihastha* to rear a family and to carry out the obligatory sacrifices, in order thereafter as *vânaprastha* to withdraw into the solitude of the forest, and to devote himself to self-discipline and meditation, until finally in extreme old age, purified from all attachment to earth, homeless and without possessions, free from all obligations, he wandered about as *sannyâsin* (*bhikshu*, *parivrâjaka*), awaiting only his spirit's release into the supreme spirit. In the instruction communicated to him the *brahmac'ârin* was put in possession of a rule of conduct for his entire future life. From the Brâhmaṇa he learnt how, as *gṛihastha*, he would have to carry out the ritual of sacrifice with the aid of the officiating priests; the Âraṇyaka, as indeed is implied in the name, belonged to the period of life as *vânaprastha*, during which for the most part meditation took the place of the sacrificial acts; and finally the Upanishad taught theoretically that aloofness from the world which the *sannyâsin* was bound to realise in practice. Therefore it is said of him, that he should "live without the (liturgical) precepts of the Veda," but yet "recite the Âraṇyaka and the Upanishad of all the Vedas."[1] And as ordinarily Âraṇyaka and Upanishad were blended together, so until quite late times, as we shall see, no strict line of demarcation was drawn in most instances between *vânaprastha* and *sannyâsin*.

3. *The Upanishads of the three older Vedas*

As the Brâhmaṇas formed the ritual text-books of the Vedic S'âkhâs, so the Upanishads attached to them were originally nothing more that the text-books of dogma, a fact which accounts especially for the identity in them all of the fundamental thought, which is developed at greater or less length and with the utmost variety. The earliest rise of the S'akhas or Vedic schools, on which this community of the ritual, and with it the philosophical tradition depends, is to be sought in a time in which the contents of the Saṁhitâ were already substantially fixed, and were transmitted from teacher to pupil to be committed to memory.[2]

[1] Âruṇeya-Up. 2.

[2] Cp. Chând. 6. 7. 2.

On the other hand the necessary ritual allegorical and dogmatic explanations were communicated to the pupils extempore, and from these subsequently the oldest Indian prose took its rise. The result was that the common material of instruction, which in its essential features was already determined, received very various modifications, corresponding to the idiosyncrasy of the teacher, not only in regard to execution and mystical interpretation of the particular ceremonies, but also because one laid greater stress on the liturgical, another on the dogmatic teaching. Hence it is that the Upanishads of the individual schools differ so greatly in length. In the course of centuries the originally extempore instruction crystallised into fixed texts in prose, which were committed to memory verbatim by the pupil, while at the same time the divergences between the individual schools became wider. It is therefore quite credible that Indian writers should have been able to enumerate a considerable number of S'âkhâs, in which each Veda was studied. But it is equally intelligible that of these many S'âkhâs the majority disappeared in the struggle for existence, and that for each Veda only a few prominent S'âkhâs with the Upanishads belonging to them have been preserved. We must limit ourselves here for general guidance to a mere enumeration of the eleven extant Upanishads of the three older Vedas, with the remark, however, that in the case of several of these it is doubtful whether they are correctly attributed to the S'âkhâ concerned. A further discussion of this point will be found in the Introductions prefixed to my translations of the sixty Upanishads.

Upanishad.	S'âkhâ.
I. Ṛigveda.	
Aitareya Upanishad.	Aitareyins.
Kaushîtaki Upanishad.	Kaushîtakins.

II. Sâmaveda.	
Chândogya Upanishad.	Tâṇḍins.
Kena (Talavakâra) Upanishad.	Jaiminîyas (Talavakâras).
III. Yajurveda—(*a*) Black.	
Taittirîya Upanishad. / Mahânârâyana Upanishad.	Taittirîyakas.
Kâṭhaka Upanishad.	Kâṭhas.
S'vetâs'vatara Upanishad.	(wanting.)
Maitrâyaṇîya Upanishad	Maitrâyaṇîyas.
(*b*) White.	
Bṛihadâraṇyaka Upanishad. / Îs'â Upanishad.	Vâjasaneyins.

4. *The Upanishads of the Atharvaveda*

The case is entirely different with the numerous Upanishads which have found admission into the Atharvaveda. It is true that several of them trace back their doctrine to S'aunaka or Pippalâda, or even (as the Brahma-Up.) to both together; and according to the tradition communicated by Nârâyana and Colebrooke, not only single treatises, but complete series of Upanishads were attributed to the S'aunakîyas or Pippalâdis. But the contradictions of these accounts, as well as the circumstance that the most diverse Upanishads refer their doctrine to the alleged founders of the Atharvaveda S'âkhâs, S'aunaka and Pippalâda, suggest the conjecture that we should see in this little more than an arbitrary attachment to well-known names of antiquity; just as other Atharva-Upanishads trace back their doctrine to Yâjñavalkhya, to Aṅgiras or Atharvan, or even to Brahma Rudra and Prajâpati. Moreover the names of the Atharva-Upanishads (apart from a few doubtful exceptions, as *Mâṇḍûkya*, *Jâbâla*, *Paiṅgala*, *Shavank*) are no longer, as is the case with the Upanishads of the three older Vedas, formed on the model of the names of the S'âkhâs, but are derived partly from the contents and partly from any accidental circumstance. This proves that in the Atharva-Upanishads we must not expect to find the dogmatic text-books of definite Vedic schools.

Many indications (of which more will be said hereafter) point to the fact that the leading ideas of the Upanishads, the doctrine, namely, of the sole reality of the Âtman, of its evolution as the universe, its identity with the soul, and so forth, although they may have originated from Brâhmans such as Yâjñavalkhya, yet in the earliest times met with acceptance rather in Kshatriya circles[1] than among Brâhmans, engrossed as the latter were in the ritual. It was only later on that they were adopted by the Brâhmans, and interwoven with the ritual on the lines of allegorical interpretation.

Under these circumstances it is very probable that the âtman doctrine, after it had been taken in hand by the S'âkhâs of the three older Vedas, was further prosecuted outside of these schools, and that consequently in course of time works were published, and have been partially at least preserved, which occupy a position as compared with the Upanishads of the Ṛig Sâma and Yajurvedas precisely similar to that of the Saṁhitâ of the Atharvaveda to their Saṁhitâs. And as at an earlier date hymns of various kinds found admittance into this Saṁhitâ, which were partly of too late composition for the older Saṁhitâs, and partly were despised by them ; so now again it was the Atharvaveda which opened its arms to the late born or rejected children of the spirit of âtman research. The consequence of this generosity was that in course of time everything which appeared in the shape of an Upanishad, that is a mystical text,

[1] As an illustration of the different relation of Brâhmans and Kshatriyas to the novel doctrine of the Âtman, Bṛih. 3–4 may be referred to, where Yâjnavalkhya, as exponent of this new doctrine, is met with jealousy and doubt on the side of the Brâhmans, but by the king Janaka with enthusiastic assent. To this question we return later (*infra*, p. 17 ff.).

whether it were the expression merely of the religious philosophical consciousness of a limited circle or even an individual thinker, was credited to the Atharvaveda, or by later collectors was included in it without further hesitation. The regularity with which a given text reappears in the different collections forms, as far as we can see, the sole mark of its canonicity (if we may use the word in such a connection). Guided by this principle we have gathered together in our translation of the "Sixty Upanishads" all those texts which seem to have met with general recognition. Referring then for further details to the Introduction there to the Atharva-Upanishads, we propose here, for the sake of a general survey, merely to enumerate the more important of these works according to the fivefold classification which we have made of them.[1]

I. PURE VEDÂNTA UPANISHADS.—These remain essentially faithful to the old Vedânta doctrine, without laying more definite stress than is already the case in the older Upanishads on its development into the Yoga, Sannyâsa, and Vaishnavite or S'aivite symbolism :—

Muṇḍaka, Pras'na, Mâṇḍûkya (with the Kârikâ);
Garbha, Prâṇâgnihotra, Piṇḍa;
Âtma, Sarvopanishatsâra, Gâruḍa.

II. YOGA UPANISHADS.—These from the standpoint of the Vedânta treat predominantly and exclusively of the apprehension of the Âtman through the Yoga by means of the *moræ* of the syllable *Om* :—

Brahmavidyâ, Kshurikâ, C'ûlikâ;
Nâdabindu, Brahmabindu, Amṛitabindu, Dhyânabindu, Tejobindu;
s'ikhâ, Yogatattva, Haṁsa.

III. SANNYÂSA UPANISHADS.—As a rule these are equally one-sided, and enjoin and describe the life

[1] Following, in reality, Weber's example.

of the Sannyâsin as the practical issue of Upanishad teaching :—

Brahma, Sannyâsa, Âruṇeya, Kaṇṭhas'ruti;
Paramahaṁsa, Jâbâla, Âs'rama.

IV. S'IVA UPANISHADS.—These interpret the popularly worshipped S'iva (Îs'âna, Mahes'vara, Mahâdeva, etc.) as a personification of the Âtman :—

Atharvas'iras, Atharvas'ikhâ, Nîlarudra;
Kâlâgnirudra, Kaivalya.

V. VISHṆU UPANISHADS.—These explain Vishṇu (Nârâyaṇa, Nṛisiṁha, etc.) similarly in the sense of the Upanishad teaching, and regard his various avatâras as impersonations of the Âtman :—

Mahâ, Nârâyaṇa, Âtmabodha;
Nṛisiṁhapûrvatâpanîya, Nṛisiṁhottaratâpanîya;
Râmapûrvatâpanîya, Râmottaratâpanîya.

5. *On the Meaning of the Word Upanishad*

According to S'ankara, the Upanishads were so named because they "destroy" inborn ignorance,[1] or because they "conduct" to Brahman.[2] Apart from these interpretations, justifiable neither on grounds of philology nor of fact, the word Upanishad is usually explained by Indian writers by *rahasyam* (*i.e.* "secret," Anquetil's *secretum tegendum*). Thus it is said, for example, in Nṛisiṁh. 8 four times in succession *iti rahasyam*, instead of the earlier usual form *iti upanishad* (as is found *e.g.* at the close of Taitt. 2 and 3, Mahânâr. 62. 63. 64). In older passages also, where mention is made of Upanishad texts, such expressions are used as *guhyâ' âdes'âḥ*,[3] *paramam guhyam*,[4] *vedaguhya-upanishatsu gûḍham*,[5] *guhyatamam*.[6]

[1] S'ankara on Bṛih. p. 2. 4, Kâṭh. p. 73. 11.
[2] *Id.* on Taitt. p. 9. 5, Muṇḍ. p. 261. 10.
[3] Chând. 3. 5. 2.
[4] Kâṭh. 3. 17, S'vet. 6. 22.
[5] S'vet. 5. 6.
[6] Maitr. 6. 29.

The attempt to maintain secrecy with regard to abstruse and therefore easily misunderstood doctrines has numerous analogies even in the West. To the question why He speaks to them in parables Jesus answers, ὅτι ὑμῖν δέδοται γνῶναι τὰ μυστήρια τῆς βασιλείας τῶν οὐρανῶν, ἐκείνοις δὲ οὐ δέδοται.[1] Pythagoras requires of his pupils μυστικὴ σιωπή, mystical silence. A saying is preserved of Heracleitus, τὰ τῆς γνώσεως βάθη κρύπτειν ἀπιστίη ἀγαθή. Plato finds fault with the art of writing on the ground that it οὐκ ἐπίσταται λέγειν οἷς δεῖ γε καὶ μή.[2] And Schopenhauer demands of his readers as a preliminary condition that they should have grappled with the difficulties of Kant.

The same feeling inspires the warning repeated again and again in the Upanishads, not to impart a certain doctrine to unworthy students.

Ait. Âr. 3. 2. 6. 9 :—"These combinations of letters (according to their secret meaning, their *upanishad*) the teacher shall not impart to anyone who is not his immediate pupil (*antevâsin*), who has not already lived for a year in his house, who does not himself intend to be a teacher."

Chând. 3. 11. 5 :—"Therefore only to his eldest son shall the father as Brahman communicate it (this doctrine), but to no one else, whoever he may be."

Bṛih. 6. 3. 12 :—"This (the mixed drink, *mantha*, and its ritual) shall be communicated to no one, except the son or the pupil."

S'vet. 6. 22 :—"Give it (this supreme secret) to none who is not tranquil, who is not a son or at least a pupil."

Muṇḍ. 3. 2. 11 :—"None may read this who has not observed his vow."

Maitr. 6. 29 :—"This most mysterious secret shall be

[1] Mt. 13. 11. [2] Phaedr. 275, E.

imparted to none who is not a son or a pupil, and who has not yet attained tranquillity."

Nṛisiṁh. 1. 3 :—"But if a woman or a S'ûdra learns the Savitṛi formula, the Lakshmî formula, the Praṇava, one and all go downwards after death. Therefore let these never be communicated to such! If anyone communicates these to them, they and the teacher alike go downwards after death."

Râmap. 84 :—"Give it not (the diagram) to common men."

The same explanation is to be given of the striking feature, which is constantly recurring in the Upanishads, that a teacher refuses to impart any instruction to a pupil who approaches him, until by persistence in his endeavour he has proved his worthiness to receive the instruction. The best known instance of this kind is Nac'iketas in the Kâṭhaka Upanishad, to whom the god of death vouchsafes the desired instruction on the nature of the soul and its fate only after the young man has steadily rejected all attempts to divert him from his wish.[1] Indra deals in a similar way with Pratardana,[2] Raikva with Jânas'ruti,[3] Satyakâma with Upakosala,[4] Pravâhaṇa with Âruṇi,[5] Prajâpati with Indra and Vairoc'ana,[6] Yâjñavalkya with Janaka,[7] S'âkâyanya with Bṛihadratha.[8]

From all this it follows that the universal tendency of antiquity, and of the circle which produced the Upanishads, was in the direction of keeping their contents secret from unfit persons, and that the Indian writers were practically justified in explaining the term *upanishad* by *rahasyam*, "secret." Less easy is it at first sight to understand how the word *upanishad* has

[1] Kâṭh. 1. 20 f. [2] Kaush. 3. 1. [3] Chând. 4. 2.
[4] Chând. 4. 10. 2. [5] Chând. 5. 3. 7, Bṛih. 6. 2. 6.
[6] Chând. 8. 8. 4. [7] Bṛih. 4. 3. 1 f. [8] Maitr. 1. 2.

come to signify "secret meaning, secret instruction, a secret." For *upanishad*, derived as a substantive from the root *sad*, to sit, can only denote a "sitting"; and as the preposition *upa* (near by) indicates, in contrast to *parishad*, *saṁsad* (assembly), a "confidential secret sitting," we must assume, even if actual proof is wanting, that this name for "secret-sitting" was used also in course of time to denote the purpose of this sitting, *i.e.* "secret instruction." Just as the German "college" has been transferred from the idea of "convention" to that of the subject-matter of instruction; so that in such an expression as "to read, to hear, etc. a lecture" the original meaning of *college* (from *colligere*, to collect) is altogether forgotten, as in the case of the Upanishads the original conception of "sitting." Similar instances are quite common, as for example the φυσικαὶ ἀκροάσεις of Aristotle or the διατριβαί of Epictetus no longer signify lectures, conversations, but definite written compositions.

Another explanation of the word *upanishad* has been recently put forward by Oldenberg, according to which *upanishad*, precisely as *upâsanâ*, would have originally meant "adoration," *i.e.* reverential meditation on the Brahman or Âtman.[1] The suggestion deserves attention, but is open to the following objections. (1) The words *upa* + *âs*, "to sit before someone or something (in adoration)," and *upa* + *sad* (*upa* + *ni* + *sad* does not occur in the Upanishads), "to seat oneself before someone (for the purpose of instruction)," are, according to prevailing usage, to be carefully distinguished from one another. Even if in the older texts the linguistic usage was not yet rigorously fixed, yet in the Upanishads (as a glance at Jacob's concordance proves), *upa* + *âs* is always "to worship," never "to approach for instruction," and *upa* + *sad* always "to approach for instruction," never "to

[1] *Zeitschr. d. Deutsch. Morgenl. Gesellschaft*, Bd. 50 (1896), p. 457 f.

worship"; and the reason for forming the substantive *upanishad* not from *upa* + *sad*, but from the rarer *upa* + *ni* + *sad*, was perhaps merely that the substantive *upasad* had been already adopted as the name of a well-known ceremony preliminary to the Soma sacrifice. (2) Even if mention is frequently made of worship of Brahman or the âtman, especially under a definite symbol (as *manas*, *prâṇa*, etc.), yet, strictly speaking, the âtman is not like the gods an object of worship, but an object of knowledge. Kena 1. 4 f.,—"that shouldest thou know as Brahman, not that which is there worshipped" (*na idam yad idam upâsate*); Chând. 8. 7. 1,—"the self (*âtman*) . . . that ought man to search after, that endeavour to know"; Bṛih. 2. 4. 5,—"the self, in truth, should be seen, heard, understood, and reflected upon, O Maitreyî," etc. The two passages of the Upanishads also, which Oldenberg cites in proof of worship offered to Brahman, tell in reality in the opposite direction. In Bṛih. 2. 1, Gârgya declares his worship of this or that as Brahman, until finally the king breaks off the inquiry with the words, "with all that it is not yet known" (*na etâvatâ viditam bhavati*). Then he imparts the teaching concerning the deep sleeper, and closes with the words, "his *upanishad*" (secret name, not worship) "is 'the reality of realities,'" *i.e.* the essence which is implied in all empirical existence. And if in Bṛih. 1. 4 the proposition is laid down that not the gods but the âtman alone should be worshipped, by this is to be understood merely a polemic against the worship of the gods, not a demand to "worship" the âtman as though it were only a god. This word is applicable, therefore, solely to the gods, and is used of the âtman only by zeugma,[1] and the proof of this is found

[1] If this is disputed, then, to be consistent, from passages like Bṛih. 2. 4. 5,—"the âtman in truth should be seen and heard," etc., the conclusion must be drawn that the âtman is visible and audible.

in what follows when it is said,—"He who worships another deity, and says 'He is one, and I am another,' that man is not wise."[1] Without, however, such a conception of the âtman as "He is one, and I am another," which is here interdicted, worship is altogether inconceivable, but not perhaps knowledge by immediate intuition (*anubhava*). (3) An attempt to apply the hypothesis under consideration throughout to the existing facts would demonstrate its impossibility. Thus in Taitt. 1. 3 the secret meaning (*upanishad*) of the combination of letters (*saṁhitâ*) is explained, and this being concluded various rewards are held out in prospect to him "who knows these great combinations as thus expounded" (*ya evam etâ mahâsaṁhitâ vyâkhyâtâ veda*). Here merely a knowledge of the combination of the letters is required; there is no mention of any worship in the entire paragraph. Or if we take the certainly ancient passage Kaush. 2. 1–2, where it is said of the beggar, who knows himself as the Self of all beings,—*tasya upanishad 'na yâc'ed' iti*, "his secret sign is not to beg"; it would be very difficult to say what suggestion of "worship" is found in phrases like these.

If the passages collected in my index to the Upanishads under the word Upanishad are examined, it will be at once evident that, taken together, they involve the meaning, "secret sign, secret name, secret import, secret word, secret formula, secret instruction," and that therefore to all the meanings the note of secrecy is attached. Hence we may conclude that the explanation offered by the Indians of the word *upanishad* as *rahasyam*, "secret," is correct.

[1] Bṛih. 1. 4. 10.

II. BRIEF SUMMARY OF THE HISTORY OF THE UPANISHADS

1. *The earliest Origin of the Upanishads*

The word *Upanishad* occurs with three distinct meanings as—

(1) Secret word.
(2) Secret text.
(3) Secret import.

(1) Certain mysterious words, expressions, and formulas, which are only intelligible to the initiated, are described as *Upanishad.* These contain either a secret rule for action and behaviour, as the *na yâc'et* of Kaush. 2. 1, 2, quoted above, or secret information on the nature of Brahman. When, then, the latter is described as *satyasya satyam*[1], or *tad-vanam*[2] (the final goal of aspiration), there is added, "thou hast been taught the Upanishad." Of a similar nature are secret words like *tajjalân*,[3] "in him (all beings) are born, perish, and breathe," or *neti neti.*[4] And when the worship of Brahman under such formulas is enjoined, it is not implied that *upanishad* signifies "worship," but only, as already pointed out, that meditation on Brahman under these mysterious terms must take the place of the worship of the gods.

(2) The extant texts themselves, as well as the older texts underlying them, are called Upanishads. Accordingly in the Taittirîyaka school especially a section often ends with the words,—*iti upanishad.*

(3) Very frequently it is not a word or a text, but the secret allegorical meaning of some ritual conception or practice, which is described as *upanishad*; *e.g.* in Chând. 1. 1. 10,—"for that which is executed with knowledge,

[1] Bṛih. 2. 1. 20, 2. 3. 6.
[2] Kena 31 (4. 6).
[3] Chând. 3. 14. 1.
[4] Bṛih. 2. 3. 6, and often.

with faith, with the upanishad (knowledge of the secret meaning of Udgîtha as *Om*), that is more effective."

The question suggests itself, which of these three significations is the original. We might decide for the third, and suppose that an allegorical interpretation was assigned to the ritual, and the Upanishad doctrine developed thence. This, however, apparently was not the case, and there is much to be said for the view that, as already observed above, the conceptions of the Upanishads, though they may have originated with the Brâhmans, were fostered primarily among the Kshatriyas and not within Brâhman circles, engrossed as these were with the ritual.

The Upanishads have come down to us, like the rest of the texts of the three older Vedas, through the Brâhmans. All the more striking is it, therefore, that the texts themselves frequently trace back some of their most important doctrines to kings, *i.e.* Kshatriyas. Thus, in the narrative of Chând. 5. 11-24, five learned Brâhmans request from Uddâlaka Âruṇi instruction concerning the Âtman Vais'vânara. Uddâlaka distrusts his ability to explain everything to them, and all the six therefore betake themselves to the king As'vapati Kaikeya, and receive from him the true instruction, the defectiveness of their own knowledge having first been made clear. In Bṛih. 2. 1 (and the parallel passage, Kaush. 4), the far-famed Vedic scholar Gârgya Bâlâki volunteers to expound the Brahman to King Ajâtas'atru of Kâs'î, and propounds accordingly twelve (in Kaush. 16) erroneous explanations; whereupon to him, the Brâhman, the king exhibits the Brahman as the âtman under the figure of a deep sleeper, prefacing his exposition with the remark, "that is a reversal of the rule, for a Brâhman to betake himself as a pupil to a Kshatriya in order to have the Brahman expounded to him; now I proceed to instruct you." In this narrative, preserved by two different Vedic schools, it is expressly declared that the knowledge of the Brahman as âtman, the central doctrine of the entire Vedânta, is possessed by the king; but, on the contrary, is not possessed by the Brâhman "famed as a Vedic scholar."[1] In Chând. 1. 8–9, two Brâhmans are instructed by the king Pravâhaṇa Jaivali concerning the *âkâs'a* as the ultimate substratum of all things, of which they are ignorant. And although it is said in Chând. 1. 9. 3 that this instruction had been previously imparted by Atidhanvan to Udaras'âṇḍilya, yet the names allow of the conjecture that in this case also a Brâhman received instruction from a Kshatriya. Similarly Chând. 7 contains the teaching given by Sanatkumâra, the god of war, to the Brâhman Nârada. Here the former pronounces inadequate the comprehensive Vedic learning of the Brâhman with the words: "all that you have studied is merely name."[2] Finally the leading text of the doctrine of the soul's transmigration, which is extant in three different recensions,[3] is propounded in the form of an instruction given to Âruṇi by the king Pravâhaṇa Jaivali.[4] The king here says to the Brâhman:—"Because, as you have told me, O Gautama, this doctrine has never up to the present time been in circulation among Brâhmans, therefore in all the worlds the government has remained in the hands of the warrior caste."[5]

When we consider that the passages quoted discuss such subjects as the knowledge of Brahman as âtman,[6] the knowledge of this âtman as the all-quickener,[7] and the

[1] Kaush., *l.c.*

[2] Chând. 7. 1. 3.

[3] Chând. 5. 3–10, Bṛih. 5. 2, and with considerable variations Kaush. 1.

[4] In Kaush., *l.c.*, by C'itra Gângyâyana.

[5] Chând. 5. 3. 7; in Bṛih. 6. 2. 8 the words are:—"As surely as I wish that you, like your ancestors, may remain well-disposed to us, so surely up to the present day this knowledge has never been in the possession of a Brâhman."

[6] Bṛih. 2. 1, Kaush. 4.

[7] Chând. 5. 11 f.

fate of the soul after death,[1] that is, precisely the most important points of Upanishad teaching; that not only is the king represented in them as endowed with wisdom, but is expressly contrasted with the Brâhman who is ignorant or deluded; and that these narratives are preserved to us by the Vedic S'âkhâs, and therefore by the Brâhmans themselves; we are forced to conclude, if not with absolute certainty, yet with a very high degree of probability, that as a matter of fact the doctrine of the âtman, standing as it did in such sharp contrast to all the principles of the Vedic ritual, though the original conception may have been due to Brâhmans, was taken up and cultivated primarily not in Brâhman but in Kshatriya circles, and was first adopted by the former in later times. The fact, moreover, which is especially prominent in the last quoted passages, that the Brâhmans during a long period had not attained to the possession of this knowledge, for which they nevertheless display great eagerness, is most simply explained on the supposition that this teaching with regard to the âtman was studiously withheld from them; that it was transmitted in a narrow circle among the Kshatriyas to the exclusion of the Brâhmans; that, in a word, it was *upanishad.* The allegorical method of interpreting the ritual in the light of the âtman doctrine, though it may have been already practised among the Kshatriya circles, was probably undertaken on a larger scale after the adoption of the new doctrine by the Brâhmans. It would follow that the third of the above-mentioned meanings of the word *upanishad* as "secret import" (of some ritual conception) is probably in the first instance secondary. If we ask further, which of the two other meanings, (1) secret word, (2) secret text, is the more primitive, it would seem that a transition from the second to the first is with difficulty intelligible,

[1] Chând. 5. 3 f., Bṛih. 6. 2.

but that the first passes into the second by a natural and readily comprehended change.

We may therefore assume that the doctrine of the âtman as the first principle of the universe, the gradual rise of which we have traced through the hymns of the Ṛigveda and Atharvaveda, was fostered and progressively developed by the Kshatriyas in opposition to the principles of the Brâhmanical ritual; whence the new knowledge was expressed in brief words or formulas, intelligible only to the initiated, such as *tadvanam*, *tajjalân*, *satyasya satyam*, *saṁyadvâma*, *vâmanî*, *bhâmanî*, etc. A formula of this kind was then called an *upanishad*, inasmuch as the condition of its communication and explanation was the absence of publicity. Such formulas were naturally accompanied by oral explanations, which also were kept secret, and from these were gradually developed the earliest texts that bore the name of Upanishad. The manner in which the formulas *tad vai tad*[1] or *vi-ram*[2] are discussed may serve as examples of such secret words accompanied by secret explanation.[3]

In these and similar ways the secret doctrines, *i.e.* the *vidyâs*, arose, of which mention is so frequently made in the Upanishads. Their authors or exclusive possessors were renowned in the land. Pilgrims sought them, pupils served them for many years,[4] and rich gifts were offered to them[5] in order thereby to gain the communication of the

[1] Bṛih. 5. 4.

[2] Bṛih. 5. 12.

[3] The explanations given of these secret words are not always in agreement. The definition of Brahman as *pûrṇam apravarti* is approved in Chând. 3. 12. 7, but in Bṛih. 2. 1. 5 (Kaush. 4. 8) is regarded, on the contrary, as inadmissible. Of still greater interest is the case of the Upanishad Bṛih. 16. 3, *amṛitam satyena c'hannam*, understood by others as *anṛitam satyena c'hannam*; so also Bṛih. 5. 5. 1 (*anṛitam ubhayataḥ satyena parigṛihîtam*), which again is otherwise explained in Chând. 8. 3. 5. Similarly the saying of the ancient ṛishis, *pâṅktam idam sarvam*, is differently construed in Bṛih. 1. 4. 17 and Taitt. 1. 7.

[4] Chând. 4. 10. 2.

[5] Chând. 4. 2. 1.

vidyâ. In the case of some of these *vidyâs* the name of the author is preserved. Several of them, in fact, are equipped with a formal genealogy, which recounts the original author and his successors, and usually closes with the injunction to communicate the doctrine only to a son or trusted pupil.

A suitable field, however, for the successful development of these doctrines was first opened up when they passed from the Kshatriya circles, where they had originally found a home, by ways that a few illustrations have already taught us to recognise, into the possession of the Brâhmans, whose system of scholastic traditions was firmly established. The latter eagerly adopted the âtman doctrine, although it was fundamentally opposed to the Vedic cult of the gods and the Brâhmanical system of ritual, combined it by the help of allegorical interpretation with the ritualistic tradition, and attached it to the curriculum of their schools. The Upanishads became the Vedânta.

Soon also the Brâhmans laid claim to the new teaching as their exclusive privilege. They were able to point to princes and leaders, as Janaka, Jânas'ruti, etc., who were said to have gone for instruction to Brâhmans. Authorities on the ritual like S'âṇḍilya and Yâjñavalkhya were transformed into originators and upholders of the ideas of the Upanishads, and the âtman doctrine was made to presuppose the tradition of the Veda :—" Only he who knows the Veda comprehends the great omnipresent Âtman," as it is said in a passage of the Brâhmaṇas.[1]

After the Upanishad ideas had been adopted by the S'âkhâs, and had been made a part of their Vedic system of instruction, they passed through a varied expansion and development under the hands of the Vedic teachers. To begin with they were brought into accord with the ritual

[1] Taitt. Bṛ. 3. 12. 9. 7.

tradition by interpreting the latter (in the Âraṇyakas) in the spirit of the âtman doctrine; and thus the adherents of the Ṛigveda brought it into connection with the *uktham* (hymn), those of the Sâmaveda with the *sâman*, and those of the Yajurveda with the sacrifice, especially the horse-sacrifice as being its highest form. The new doctrine, however, was further developed in a manner which altogether transcended the traditional cult, with which, indeed, it often found itself in open contradiction. In regard to this an active communication and exchange must have existed between the different schools. Definitions which by the one were highly regarded failed to meet with acceptance in another. Teachers who in the one S'âkhâ exercised supreme authority are found in another in a subordinate position (Âruṇi), or are altogether unknown (Yâjñavalkhya). Texts appear with slight variations in the different Vedic schools, whether borrowed directly or going back on either side to a common original. Other texts are met with side by side in one and the same S'âkhâ in numerous recensions, often very similar, often widely divergent from one another. This rich mental life, the details of which can scarcely be further reproduced, may not improbably have lasted for centuries; and the fundamental thought of the doctrine of the âtman have attained an ever completer development by means of the reflection of individual thinkers in familiar intercourse before a chosen circle of pupils, and probably also by public discussions at royal courts. The oldest Upanishads preserved to us are to be regarded as the final result of this mental process.

2. *The extant Upanishads*

Owing to the manner in which the Upanishads have arisen from the activity of the different Vedic schools and their intercourse one with another, we are unable to lay down any precise chronological order of succession among them. All the principal Upanishads contain earlier and later elements side by side, and therefore the age of each separate piece must be determined by itself as far as this is possible from the degree of development of the thoughts which find expression in it. Here, where we still treat of the Upanishads as a whole, we can only attempt a rough and approximate determination of the period to which in general an Upanishad belongs.

We distinguish first four successive periods of time, to which the Upanishads as a whole may be assigned.

I. THE ANCIENT PROSE UPANISHADS.—

Bṛihadâraṇyaka and Châṇdogya.
Taittirîya.
Aitareya.
Kaushîtaki.
Kena.

The last-named stands on the border-line.

These are collectively the Vedânta texts of the actually existing S'âkhâs, and in their earlier parts are usually closely interwoven with Brâhmaṇas and Âraṇyakas, of which they form the continuation, and whose ritualistic conceptions are interpreted by them in various allegorical ways. It is only the later, and as we may suppose younger texts which emancipate themselves from the ritual. The language is still almost entirely the ancient prose of the Brâhmaṇas, somewhat ponderous stilted and awkward, but not without natural charm. The order adopted above is in general chronological. The *Bṛihadâraṇyaka* and *Châṇdogya* are not only the richest in contents, but also the oldest of the extant Upanishads. As compared also with one another, the *Bṛihadâraṇyaka*, as we shall often see, shows almost without exception greater originality in the grouping of the texts. On the other hand the literary outlook of Châṇd. 7. 1. 4 (7. 2. 1, 7. 7. 1) is materially broader than that of Bṛih. 2. 4. 10 (4. 1. 2, 4. 5. 11). *Taittirîya* in its essential part is still later than *Chândogya*; cp. Chând. 6. 2 (three elements) and Taitt. 2. 1 (five elements). *Aitareya* is later than *Chândogya* (in Chând. 6. 3. 1 there are three kinds of organic beings, in Ait. 3. 3 four), and than *Taittirîya* (cp. Taitt. 2. 6, "after that he had created it he entered into it," with the more elaborate description Ait. 1. 3. 12). *Kaushîtaki*, finally, is later than all those named; for Kaush. 1 is less original than Chând. 5. 3 f., Bṛih. 6. 2, and Kaush. 3 must be later than Ait. 3. 3, Kaush. 4 than Bṛih. 2. 1. Kena stands on the border-line of this period, and by virtue of its first metrical portion already belongs to the succeeding epoch.

II. The Metrical Upanishads.—The transition is made by Kena 1–13 and the verses Bṛih. 4. 4. 8–21, undoubtedly a later addition. There follow—

Kâṭhaka
Îs'â.
S'vetâs'vatara.
Muṇḍaka.
Mahânârâyaṇa.

The last-named makes use of *Muṇḍaka*, and *Muṇḍaka* appears to use *S'vetâs'vatara*. *Îs'â* seems on the whole to be less fully developed than *S'vetâs'vatara*, and to be freer from sectarian bias; but in numerous instances it is found to be dependent on *Kâṭhaka*.[1] That *S'vetâs'vatara* is later than *Kâṭhaka* is not open to doubt; on the contrary, it is very probable, on the evidence of several passages,[2] that *Kâṭhaka* was directly employed in the composition of *S'vetâs'vatara*.

The difference between this period and the preceding is very great. The connection with the S'âkhâs appears

[1] Cp. especially Îs'â 8 with Kâṭh. 5. 13.
[2] Collected in Deussen, *Upan.*, p. 289.

sometimes doubtful, sometimes artificial, and in any case is loose. Allegories framed after the manner of the Âraṇyakas are wanting. The thought of the Upanishads is no longer apprehended as in course of development, but appears everywhere to have been taken over in its entirety. Individual verses and characteristic phrases constantly recur. The phraseology is already formed. And the language is almost throughout metrical.

III. THE LATER PROSE UPANISHADS.—

Pras'na.
Maitrâyaṇîya.
Mâṇḍûkya.

In this third period the composition returns again to prose, but a prose which is markedly different from the archaic language of the ancient Upanishads, although it does also take on, especially in the *Maitrâyaṇîya*, an archaic colouring. The style suggests that of the later Sanskrit prose; it is complex, involved, and delights in repetitions. The dependence of the thought on that of the earlier Upanishads is made manifest by numerous quotations and adaptations. That *Pras'na* is later than *Muṇḍaka* is proved by the fact that the latter is quoted in Pr. 3. 5; it is older, however, than *Maitrâyaṇîya*, for it is itself quoted in Maitr. 6. 5. The position of *Mâṇḍûkya* is difficult to determine, owing to its brevity; yet the theory concerning Om in Mâṇḍ. 3 seems to be more advanced than that of Maitr. 6. 4. The greater number of the Upanishads hitherto mentioned have found admission, sometimes with very doubtful right, to a place in the three older Vedas. Only three of them—namely, Muṇḍaka, Pras'na, and Mâṇḍûkya—appear to have belonged from the beginning to the Atharvaveda, the two first-named certainly as the original legitimate Upanishads of this fourth Veda. These two are ascribed to S'aunaka and Pippalâda, the founders of the S'âkhâs of the Atharvaveda. The later collections of Atharva Upanishads begin as a rule with the Muṇḍaka and Pras'na, and these two alone can be proved to have been known to and employed by Bâdarâyaṇa and S'ankara.

IV. The later Atharva Upanishads.—Later theological treatises retain still the form of Upanishads as a convenient method of literary composition that carries with it a degree of sanctity; while the thought concerns itself partly with the continuous development of older themes, or refrains from deviating from the beaten tracks (*Garbha*, *Prâṇâgnihotra*, *Piṇḍa*, *Âtma*, *Sarvopanishatsâra*, *Gâruḍa*), partly turns its attention to the glorification of the Yoga (*Brahmavidyâ*, *Kshurikâ*, *C'ûlikâ*, *Nâdabindu*, *Brahmabindu*, *Amṛitabindu*, *Dhyânabindu*, *Tejobindu*, *Yogas'ikhâ*, *Yogatattva*, *Haṁsa*), or of the Sannyâsa (*Brahma*, *Sannyâsa*, *Âruṇeya*, *Kaṇṭhas'ruti*, *Paramahaṁsa*, *Jâbâla*, *Âs'rama*). The difference between the two tendencies shows itself also in the fact that almost without exception the Yoga Upanishads are composed in verse, those of the Sannyâsa in prose with occasional verses inserted. A further class of Upanishads is devoted to the worship of S'iva (*Atharvas'iras*, *Atharvas'ikhâ*, *Nîlarudra*, *Kâlâgnirudra*, *Kaivalya*), or of Vishṇu (*Mahâ*, *Nârâyaṇa*, *Âtmabodha*, *Nṛisiṁhatâpanîya*, *Râmatâpanîya*, and endeavours to interpret these in the light of the âtman doctrine. They are composed for the most part in prose with an intermixture of verse. All of these Upanishads were received into the Atharvaveda, but met with no recognition from the leading theologians of the Vedânta.

3. *The Upanishads in Bâdarâyaṇa and S'ankara*

The earliest traces of a collection of Upanishads are found within the books themselves. Thus the mention in S'vet. 5. 6 of "the Upanishads that form the mystical portion of the Veda" (*veda-guhya-upanishadaḥ*), and also the passage S'vet. 6. 22, "in former times in the Vedânta was the deepest mystery revealed," seem to look back to the older Upanishads as a self-contained whole which already claimed a certain antiquity. A similar inference may be drawn from a thrice recurring verse [1] which speaks of ascetics (*yatis*) who have "grasped the meaning of the Vedânta doctrine." Still more clearly do the Upanishads appear as a complete whole when, in Maitr. 2. 3, the doctrine concerning Brahman is described as "the doctrine of all the Upanishads" (*sarva-upanishad-vidyâ*). That in so late works as the Sarva-upanishad-sâra or the Muktikâ Upanishad the Upanishads are assumed to be a whole is therefore of no further importance.

It was undoubtedly on the foundation of older and earlier works that Bâdarâyaṇa formally undertook an epitome of Upanishad doctrine in the *Brahmasûtras*, the foundation of the later Vedânta. He shows that Brahman is the first principle of the world, *samanvayât*, "from the agreement" of the Upanishad texts,[2] and proclaims the fundamental proposition "that all the texts of the Vedânta deserve credence" (*sarva-vedânta-pratyayam*).[3] Which Upanishads, however, were recognised by him as canonical cannot be ascertained from the sûtras themselves owing to their brevity, but only from S'ankara's commentary, and the decision therefore remains in many instances doubtful, since we do not know how far S'ankara followed a reliable tradition. Only in the first *adhyâya* is it possible to determine with greater certainty the Upanishad texts which Bâdarâyaṇa had in his mind, where he undertakes to establish the teaching concerning Brahman in twenty-eight *Adhikaraṇas* (sections) based on as many passages of the Upanishads.

[1] Muṇḍ. 3. 2. 6, Mahânâr. 10. 22, Kaiv. 3.
[2] 1. 1. 4. [3] 3. 3. 1.

Here, as in his entire work, the number four plays a decisive part in the arrangement of the material. Of the twenty-eight fundamental passages, twelve are taken from the Chândogya, four from the Bṛihadâraṇyaka, four from the Kâṭhaka, four from the Taittirîya and Kaushîtaki (two from each), and four from the Atharva Upanishads, namely, three from the Muṇḍaka and one from the Pras'na. The following scheme[1] shows that the order of the passages, as they are found within each of the Upanishads which he employs, is strictly observed, while in other respects the passages appear interwoven in a manner for which we seem to be able to find a reason here and there in the close connection of the subject-matter.

(1)	1. 1. 12–19.				Taitt. 2. 5.	
(2)	20–21.	Chând. 1. 6. 6.				
(3)	22.	Chând. 1. 9. 1.				
(4)	23.	Chând. 1. 11. 5.				
(5)	24–27.	Chând. 3. 13. 7.				
(6)	28–31.				Kaush. 3. 2.	
(7)	1. 2. 1–8.	Chând. 3. 14. 1.				
(8)	9–10.			Kâṭh. 2. 25.		
(9)	11–12.			Kâṭh. 3. 1.		
(10)	13–17.	Chând. 4. 15. 1.				
(11)	18–20.		Bṛih. 3. 7. 3.			
(12)	21–23.					Muṇḍ. 1. 1. 6.
(13)	24–32.	Chând. 5. 11–24.				
(14)	1. 3. 1–7.					Muṇḍ. 2. 2. 5.
(15)	8–9.	Chând. 7. 23.				
(16)	10–12.		Bṛih. 3. 8. 8.			
(17)	13.					Pras'na, 5. 5.
(18)	14–18.	Chând. 8. 1. 1.				
(19)	19–21.	Chând. 8. 12. 3.				
(20)	22–23.					Muṇḍ. 2. 2. 10.
(21)	24–25.			Kâṭh. 4. 12.		
(22)	39.			Kâṭh. 6. 1.		
(23)	40.	Chând. 8. 12. 3.				
(24)	41.	Chând. 8. 14.				
(25)	42–43.		Bṛih. 4. 3. 7.			
(26)	1. 4. 14–15.				Taitt. 2. 6.	
(27)	16–18.				Kaush. 4. 19.	
(28)	19–22.		Bṛih. 4. 5. 6.			

[1] From Deussen, *System des Vedânta*, p. 130.

The striking preference for the Chândogya suggests that an earlier work due to the school of this Upanishad was already in the hands of Bâdarâyaṇa, into which he or one of his predecessors worked sixteen extracts of importance derived from another S'âkhâ, being guided further by the principle that the original order of the extracts should be maintained. Besides the Upanishads named, Bâdarâyaṇa may with some confidence be shown to have used the S'vetâs'vatara,[1] Aitareya,[2] and perhaps Jâbâla.[3] With regard, however, to the formula of imprecation quoted in Sût. 3. 3. 25, which according to S'ankara should find a place "at the beginning of an Upanishad of the Âtharvaṇikas," and which is nowhere known to exist, I would now suggest (since throughout their works Bâdarâyaṇa and S'ankara make use only of the Muṇḍaka and Pras'na from the Atharva Upanishads, consequently recognise none but these, and since they appear to recognise the authority of the Upanishad that follows the imprecation formula), that the suspected formula may once have stood at the beginning of one of these two, perhaps of the Muṇḍaka Upanishad; somewhat after the manner in which the S'ânti formulas precede the Upanishads in some manuscripts, and in others are wanting.

To the Brahmasûtras of Bâdarâyaṇa is attached the great commentary of *S'ankara* (*circa* 800 A.D.), to whom are ascribed, besides other works, the commentaries on the *Bṛihadâraṇyaka*, *Chândogya*, *Taittirîya*, *Aitareya*, *S'vetas'vatara*, *Îs'â*, *Kena*, *Kaṭha*, *Pras'na*, *Muṇḍaka* and *Mâṇḍûkya*, which are edited in the *Bibl. Ind.*, vols. ii., iii., vii., viii. Commentaries therefore of S'ankara are missing on the *Kaushîtaki*, which was first elucidated by *S'ankarânanda* (a teacher, according to Hall, Index, p. 98. 123, of Mâdhava, who flourished 1350 A.D.), and on the *Maitrâyaṇîya*, which *Râmatîrtha* expounded.

[1] Sût. 1. 4. 8–10. [2] Sût. 3. 3. 16–18. [3] Sût. 1. 2. 32.

The commentaries, however, on the eleven Upanishads named are to be attributed in part probably not to S'ankara himself, but merely to his school, since the explanations given in the Upanishad commentaries often fail to agree with those in the commentary on the sûtras. The commentary on the *Mâṇḍûkya* which is extant under the name of S'ankara treats this and Gauḍapâda's *Kârikâ* as one, and seems to regard the whole as in no sense an Upanishad (p. 330: *vedânta-artha-sâra-saṅgraha-bhûtam idam prakaraṇa-c'atushṭayam 'om iti etad aksharam' ityâdi ârabhyate*); and with this would agree the fact that the *Mâṇḍûkya* is not quoted either in the Brahmasûtras or in S'ankara's commentary on them, while two verses from the *Kârikâ* of Gauḍapâda[1] are cited by S'ankara[2] with the words, *atra uktam vedânta-artha-sampradâyavidbhir âc'âryaiḥ.* In his commentary on the Brahmasûtras only the following fourteen Upanishads can be shown to have been quoted by S'ankara (the figures attached indicate the number of quotations),—Chândogya 809, Bṛihadâraṇyaka 565, Taittirîya 142, Muṇḍaka 129, Kâṭhaka 103, Kaushîtaki 88, S'vetas'vatara 53, Pras'na 38, Aitareya 22, Jâbâla 13, Mahânârâyaṇa 9, Îs'â 8, Paiṅgi 6, Kena 5.

Although S'ankara regards the texts of the Vedânta which he recognises as a uniform and consistent canon of truth,[3] yet he seems still to have had in his hands no

[1] 3. 15 and 1. 16. [2] P. 375. 3, 433. 1.

[3] We may compare his exposition on sûtra 3. 3. 1, p. 843:—"How then can the question arise, whether the doctrines concerning the âtman are different or not different; for we cannot suppose the aim of the Vedânta is to teach a plurality of Brahmans, like the existing plurality of phenomena, since Brahman is one and immutable. So it is not possible that concerning the immutable Brahman various doctrines should exist; for to suppose that the actual fact is one thing, and the knowledge of it another, is necessarily a mistake. And even supposing that in the different Vedânta texts various doctrines were taught concerning the immutable Brahman, only one of these could be true; the remainder on the other hand would be false, and the con-

collection of Upanishads, since he looks upon the greater number of them as still forming the concluding chapters of their respective Brâhmaṇas, to which therefore he is accustomed to refer at the commencement of the Upanishad commentary. Thus in the introduction to the commentary on the *Kena*[1] he quotes its beginning as "the beginning of the ninth adhyâya;[2] before it works have been thoroughly discussed; the acts of adoration also of the prâṇa which serves as the foundation of all works were taught; and further those also which relate to the Sâman that forms a branch of the works. Next followed the consideration of the Gâyatra-sâman, and finally the list of teachers. All the above belongs still to works," etc. On *Chândogya*, p. 2:—"The entire ritual has been rehearsed, as also the knowledge of Prâṇa-Agni, etc., as divine." On *Taittirîya*, p. 2:—"The appointed works which serve to atone for trangressions that have been committed, as also the works desirable for those who covet a definite reward, have been rehearsed in the preceding parts of the book (*pûrvasmin granthe*)." On *Bṛihadâraṇyaka*, p. 4: "The connection of this (Upanishad) with the sphere of works is as follows," etc. On *Îs'â*, p. 1:—"The mantras *îs'â vâsyam*, etc., do not apply (as we should expect) to works, but reveal the nature of the âtman who is independent of works." On *Aitareya*, p. 143:—"The works together with the knowledge relative to the lower Brahman are remitted," etc.

As may be inferred from the comments quoted, all these Upanishads appear to have been still regarded by S'ankara as the concluding portions of their respective

sequence would be loss of confidence in the Vedânta. (This, however, in Sankara's eyes would be an ἀπαγωγὴ εἰς τὸ ἀδύνατον). It is therefore inconceivable that in the individual texts of the Vedânta a difference of doctrine on the subject of Brahman should find a place."

[1] *Bibl. Ind.*, p. 28.

[2] In the recension published by Örtel it belongs to the fourth adhyâya.

Brâhmaṇas. On the other hand a similar connection with the part of a preceding work is wanting in the case of the commentaries on Kâṭhaka and S'vetâs'vatara. So also with Muṇḍaka and Pras'na, which are treated by S'ankara as one. In the introduction to Pras'na, p. 160. 2, he remarks:—"in order to examine further the subjects taught in the mantras (of the Muṇḍaka Upanishad, as it is rightly glossed), this Brâhmaṇa (the Pras'na Upanishad) is undertaken." Since, however, the Muṇḍaka and Pras'na exhibit no relationship at all, and since they are attached further to different S'âkhâs of the Atharvaveda (those of S'aunaka and Pippalâda respectively), this unity under which S'ankara treats of them is probably to be explained merely from the fact that as early as his time they were linked together as the first beginning and foundation of a collection of Atharva Upanishads. At that time probably the collection consisted only of these two, for otherwise it is hardly likely that the others would have been ignored by S'ankara so completely as was in fact the case. It is true also that the annotator *Ânandajñâna* remarks at the beginning of S'ankara's commentary on the *Mâṇḍûkya*: "Beginning with the Brahma Upanishad (he intends probably the Brahma-vidyâ Upanishad) and the Garbha Upanishad, there are extant besides many Upanishads of the Atharvaveda. Since, however, they are not employed in the S'ârîrakam (the Brahmasûtras of Bâdarâyaṇa), he (S'ankara) does not expound them." But the reason assigned is perhaps not conclusive; for which Upanishads are found in the S'ârîrakam, and which not, could only be determined by tradition or from S'ankara himself. It must therefore have been tradition or S'ankara himself that excluded other Upanishads from the Canon, whether because they were yet unknown, or because they were not yet recognised as Upanishads. And thus in fact S'ankara describes the Mâṇḍûkya, upon which nevertheless, together with Gauḍapâda's Kârikâ, he had himself commented, not as an Upanishad, but as "a literary composition containing the essence of the Vedânta (*vedânta-artha-sâra-saṅgraha-bhûtam prakaraṇam*).

4. *The most important Collections of Upanishads*

The further history of the Upanishad tradition is for a time shrouded in darkness, and only conjecturally are we able from the existing collections of Upanishads to draw some conclusions as to their origin. These collections or lists fall from the outset into two classes, in so far as they either contain the Upanishads in their entirety, or limit themselves (at least as far as the original design is concerned) to the Upanishads of the Atharvaveda. Of the former class is the Canon of the Muktikâ and the Oupnek'hat, of the latter that of Colebrooke and Nârâyaṇa.

Since the Upanishads of the three older Vedas continued to live in the tradition of the S'âkhâs, as long as these survived the secure transmission of the Upanishads concerned was assured. It was otherwise with the Atharvaveda, which was not employed at the sacrifice, and in consequence had no such firmly established tradition of the schools as the text of the three older Vedas upon which to rely for its preservation. This is shown not only by the indifference from which its Saṁhitâ has suffered, but also by the freedom with which it admitted new compositions. The latter would assuredly have been impossible as long as the tradition was under the protection of regular Vedic schools, maintaining themselves from generation to generation according to the rules of their guild. Hence is to be explained the extensive irruption of newly composed Upanishads into the Atharvaveda. As early as S'ankara we find the *Muṇḍaka* and *Pras'na* united together (*sup.* p. 32), and on these as foundation a collection of Atharva Upanishads appears to have been gradually built up, which eventually comprised 34 pieces from *Muṇḍaka* to *Nṛisiṁhatâpanîya*, and included also some whose claim to the name of Upanishads had never been previously recognised; just as in the judgement of S'ankara the Kârikâ of Gauḍapâda on the Mâṇḍûkya Upanishad, and indeed this treatise itself (*sup.* pp. 30, 33), had no claim to the position of an Upanishad. These 34 primary Upanishads of Colebrooke's list were later extended to 52 by the addition not only of a number of recent compositions, but most remarkably by the side of and among them of seven of the recognised texts of the older Vedas, viz.—35–36 *Kâṭhaka*, 37 *Kena*, 39–40 *Bṛihannârâyaṇa* (= Taitt. Âr. x.), 44 *Ânandavallî* (= Taitt. Up. 2), and 45 *Bhṛiguvallî* (= Taitt. Up. 3). In this manner the collection of 52 Upanishads first made known by Colebrooke originated, the strange combination of which we attempted to explain [1] on the hypothesis that at the time and in the region where this collection was finally put together the three older Vedas were cultivated only in the S'âkhâs of the Aitareyins, Tâṇḍins (to which the Chândogya Upanishad belongs), and Vâjasaneyins. Accordingly the Upanishads of the remaining S'âkhâs (with the exception of the *Kaushîtaki*, *S'vetâs'vatara*, and *Maitrâyaṇîya*, which were perhaps already lost or not recognised) were inserted in the existing collection of Atharva Upanishads with a view to their safe preservation.[2]

The collection of Nârâyaṇa is in exact agreement with that of Colebrooke, apart from a few variations in the

[1] Deussen, *Upan.*, p. 537.

[2] An apparently older list has been preserved in the Atharva-paris'ishṭa 2. 13 (*Berliner Handschriften*, 2. 88), which reckons only 28 Atharva Upanishads, omitting the texts of the older Vedas, but in other respects, as far as it goes, agrees with the lists of Colebrooke and Nârâyaṇa with a single exception.

order of the later treatises. The 52 Upanishads of Colebrooke are however reduced to 45, seven sectarian texts being then added to form Nos. 46–52, viz.—two *Gopâlatâpanîya, Kṛishṇa, Vâsudeva* with *Gopîc'andana, S'vetâs'vatara,* and two *Varadatâpanîya.* This inter-relation is to be explained on the theory that the number 52 had already gained a kind of canonical authority before the desire was felt to insert seven additional texts, which had now for the first time come into existence or obtained recognition. The end was attained by uniting portions that had originally belonged together, and so reducing the existing 52 numbers to 45. Thus room was found for the seven new texts within the number of the 52, thereby facilitating the recognition of the complete list as canonical.

The collection of 108 Upanishads, which the Muktikâ itself regards as later, appears to belong to an entirely different region (probably the south of India), and to a considerably more recent time. This collection includes all the treatises of Colebrooke (except the *Nîlarudra, Piṇḍa, Mahânârâyaṇa, Âs'rama*) and of Nârâyaṇa (except the *Varadatâpanîya*), although for the most part under different names and sometimes expanded by later additions to thirty or forty times their original extent. Added to these are the 11 Upanishads of the three older Vedas complete, with the exception of the Mahânârâyaṇa, and about seventy new texts found nowhere else. The circumstance that in this collection the Upanishads of the three older Vedas also find a place, and that at the very beginning of it, points to a time and region in which a living and reliable tradition of the S'âkhâs no longer existed; of which fact a further and yet stronger proof is the bold attempt, made without a shadow of justification, to assign 10 of these 108 Upanishads to the Ṛigveda, 19 to the White and 32 to the Black Yajurveda, 16 to the Sâmaveda, and 31 to the Atharvaveda, — a procedure against which the ancient Vedic schools would have strenuously protested. In other respects this collection is of great interest for the later history of the Vedânta (perhaps mainly or exclusively among the Telugu Brâhmans), and deserves closer examination now that it has been made accessible in the Devanâgarî edition of 1896. Previously there had existed only an edition in the Telugu character. It is worthy of note also that S'ankarânanda's readings often agree with those of the 108 Upanishads against those of the 52 and of Nârâyaṇa.

A position apart both from the 52 and the 108 Upanishads is occupied by that collection of 50 Upanishads which, under the name of *Oupnek'hat*, which was translated from the Sanskrit into Persian in the year 1656 at the instance of the Sultan Mohammed Dara Shakoh, and from the Persian into Latin in 1801–02 by Anquetil Duperron. The Oupnek'hat also, like the Muktikâ collection, professes to be a general collection of Upanishads. It contains under twelve divisions the Upanishads of the three older Vedas, and with them twenty-six Atharva Upanishads that are known from other sources. It further comprises eight treatises peculiar to itself, five of which have not up to the present time been proved to exist elsewhere, and of which therefore a rendering from the Persian-Latin of Anquetil is alone possible.[1] Finally, the Oupnek'hat contains four treatises from the Vâj. Saṃh. 16. 31. 32. 34, of which the first is met with in a shorter form in other collections also as the *Nîlarudra Upanishad*, while the three last have nowhere else found admission.[2] The reception of these treatises

[1] See Deussen, *Upan.*, p. 838 f.

[2] These, as belonging to the early history of the Upanishads, I have translated and discussed *sup.* I. 1 pp. 156 f., 290 f., 291 f., 335.

from the Saṁhitâ into the body of the Upanishads, as though there were danger of their otherwise falling into oblivion, makes us infer a comparatively late date for the Oupnek'hat collection itself, although as early as 1656 the Persian translators made no claim to be the original compilers, but took the collection over already complete. They seem, indeed, to have regarded it as originating in a period long past.[1] Owing to the excessive literality with which Anquetil Duperron rendered these Upanishads word by word from the Persian into Latin, while preserving the syntax of the former language,—a literality that stands in striking contrast to the freedom with which the Persian translators treated the Sanskrit text,—the Oupnek'hat is a very difficult book to read ; and an insight as keen as that of Schopenhauer was required in order to discover within this repellent husk a kernel of invaluable philosophical significance, and to turn it to account for his own system.[2]

An examination of the material placed at our disposal in the Oupnek'hat was first undertaken by A. Weber, *Ind. Stud.*, i., ii., ix., on the basis of the Sanskrit text. Meanwhile the original texts were published in the Bibliotheca Indica in part with elaborate commentaries, and again in the Ânandâs'rama series. Max Müller translated the twelve oldest Upanishads in *Sacred Books of the East*, vols. i., xv. The two longest and some of the shorter treatises have appeared in a literal German rendering by O. Böhtlingk. And my own translation of the 60 Upanishads (Leipzig, 1897) contains complete texts of this character which, upon the strength of their regular occurrence in the Indian collections and lists of the Upanishads, may lay claim to a certain

[1] See Deussen, *Upan.*, p. 535.

[2] Schopenhauer's judgement on the Oupnek'hat is quoted in Deussen, *Upan.*, p. vi.

canonicity. The prefixed Introductions and the Notes treat exhaustively of the matter and composition of the several treatises, and there is therefore no necessity to enter here further into these literary questions.

III. The Fundamental Conception of the Upanishads and its Significance

1. *The Fundamental Conception of the Upanishads*

All the thoughts of the Upanishads move around two fundamental ideas. These are (1) the Brahman, and (2) the âtman. As a rule these terms are employed synonymously. Where a difference reveals itself, Brahman appears as the older and less intelligible expression, âtman as the later and more significant; Brahman as the unknown that needs to be explained, âtman as the known through which the other unknown finds its explanation; Brahman as the first principle so far as it is comprehended in the universe, âtman so far as it is known in the inner self of man. We may take as an example the passages from S'atap. Br. 10. 6. 3, Chând. 3. 14,[1] whose sole fundamental thought consists in this, that the universe is Brahman (*sarvam khalu idam brahma*), and the Brahman the âtman within us (*esha ma' âtmâ antar hṛidaye*, etc.).[2] Another example is furnished by the story of Gârgya (Bṛih. 2. 1, Kaush. 4), who endeavours in vain to define the Brahman, until finally he is referred by the king to the âtman for its

[1] Translated in I. 1 pp. 264, 336.

[2] Böhtlingk maintains * that I had "not known (!) that *esha ma' âtmâ antar hridaye* is everywhere subject." He himself, however, involuntarily bears testimony to the correctness of my translation, when, immediately after his rendering in § 3, "this my Self in my innermost heart," in § 4 where the same phrase recurs he translates precisely as I do, "this is my Self in my innermost heart."

* *Berichte der Sächs. G. d. W.*, 1897, p. 84.

explanation. The difference between Brahman and âtman emerges most clearly where they appear side by side with one another in brief sayings. The passage Bṛih. 4. 4. 5 may serve as example:—"truly the Brahman is this Âtman" (*sa vâ' ayam âtmâ brahma*).

If for our present purpose we hold fast to this distinction of the Brahman as the cosmical principle of the universe, the âtman as the psychical, the fundamental thought of the entire Upanishad philosophy may be expressed by the simple equation:—

Brahman = Âtman.

That is to say—the Brahman, the power which presents itself to us materialised in all existing things, which creates, sustains, preserves, and receives back into itself again all worlds, this eternal infinite divine power is identical with the âtman, with that which, after stripping off everything external, we discover in ourselves as our real most essential being, our individual self, the soul. This identity of the Brahman and the âtman, of God and the soul, is the fundamental thought of the entire doctrine of the Upanishads. It is briefly expressed by the "great saying" *tat tvam asi*, "that art thou" (Chând. 6. 8. 7 f.); and *aham brahma asmi*, "I am Brahman" (Bṛih. 1. 4. 10). And in the compound word *brahma-âtma-aikyam*, "unity of the Brahman and the âtman," is described the fundamental dogma of the Vedânta system.

If we strip this thought of the various forms, figurative to the highest degree and not seldom extravagant, under which it appears in the Vedânta texts, and fix our attention upon it solely in its philosophical simplicity as the identity of God and the soul, the Brahman and the âtman, it will be found to possess a significance reaching far beyond the Upanishads, their time and country; nay, we claim for it an inestimable value for the whole race of mankind. We are unable to look into the future, we do not know what revelations and discoveries are in store for the restlessly inquiring human spirit; but one thing we may assert with confidence,—whatever new and unwonted paths the philosophy of the future may strike out, this principle will remain permanently unshaken, and from it no deviation can possibly take place. If ever a general solution is reached of the great riddle, which presents itself to the philosopher in the nature of things all the more clearly the further our knowledge extends, the key can only be found where alone the secret of nature lies open to us from within, that is to say, in our innermost self. It was here that for the first time the original thinkers of the Upanishads, to their immortal honour, found it when they recognised our âtman, our inmost individual being, as the Brahman, the inmost being of universal nature and of all her phenomena.

2. *The Conception of the Upanishads in its Relation to Philosophy*

The whole of religion and philosophy has its root in the thought that (to adopt the language of Kant) the universe is only appearance and not reality (*Ding an sich*); that is to say, the entire external universe, with its infinite ramifications in space and time, as also the involved and intricate sum of our inner perceptions, is all merely the form under which the essential reality presents itself to a consciousness such as ours, but is not the form in which it may subsist outside of our consciousness and independent of it; that, in other words, the sum-total of external and internal experience always and only tells us how things are constituted for us, and for our intellectual capacities, not how they are in themselves and apart from intelligences such as ours.

It is easy to show how this thought, which met with adequate recognition first in the philosophy of Kant, but which existed in less clearly defined form from the earliest times, is the basis and tacit presumption, more or less consciously, of all philosophy, so far at least as this name is not made to serve as a mere cloak for empirical sciences. For all philosophy, as contrasted with empirical science, is not content to learn to know objects in their circumstances and surroundings, and to investigate their causal connections; but it rather seeks beyond all these to determine their nature, inasmuch as it regards the sum-total of empirical reality, with all the explanations offered by the empirical sciences, as something which needs to be yet further explained; and this solution is found in the principle which it sets forth, and from which it seeks to infer the real nature of things and their relation. This fact, then, that philosophy has from the earliest times sought to determine a first principle of the universe, proves that it started from a more or less clear consciousness that the entire empirical reality is not the true essence of things, that, in Kant's words, it is only appearance and not the thing in itself.

There have been three occasions, as far as we know, on which philosophy has advanced to a clearer comprehension of its recurring task, and of the solution demanded: first in India in the Upanishads, again in Greece in the philosophy of Parmenides and Plato, and finally, at a more recent time, in the philosophy of Kant and Schopenhauer. In a later work we shall have to show how Greek philosophy reached its climax in the teaching of Parmenides and Plato, that this entire universe of change is, as Parmenides describes it, merely phenomenal, or in Plato's words a world of shadows; and how both philosophers endeavoured through it to grasp the essential reality, τὸ ὄν, τὸ ὄντως ὄν, that which Plato, in an expression that recalls the doctrine of the Upanishads no less than the phraseology of Kant, describes as the αὐτὸ (*âtman*) *καθ' αὑτό* (*an sich*). We shall then see further how this same thought, obscured for a time under the influence of Aristotle and throughout the Middle Ages, was taken up again in quite a different way, and shone forth more clearly than ever before in the philosophy founded by Kant, adopted and perfected by his great successor Schopenhauer. Here we have to do with the Upanishads, and the world-wide historical significance of these documents cannot, in our judgement, be more clearly indicated than by showing how the deep fundamental conception of Plato and Kant was precisely that which already formed the basis of Upanishad teaching.

The objects which lie around us on every side in infinite space, and to which by virtue of our corporeal nature we ourselves belong, are, according to Kant, not "things in themselves," but only apparitions. According to Plato, they are not the true realities, but merely shadows of them. And according to the doctrine of the Upanishads, they are not the âtman, the real "self" of the things, but mere *mâyâ*,—that is to say, a sheer deceit, illusion. It is true that the term *mâyâ* occurs for the first time in S'vet. 4. 10; and therefore some writers, whose recognition of a fact is obscured by the different language in which it is clothed, have hazarded the assertion that the conception of *mâyâ* is still unknown to the more ancient Upanishads. How in the light of this assertion they find it possible to comprehend these older Upanishads (Bṛihad. and Chând.) they themselves perhaps know. The fact is they are penetrated throughout by the conception which later was most happily expressed by the word *mâyâ*. In the very demand which they make that the âtman of man, the âtman of the universe, must be sought for,[1] it is implied that this body and this universe which reveal

[1] Bṛih. 2. 4. 5: *âtmâ vâ' are drashṭavyaḥ, s'rotavyo, mantavyo, nididhyâsitavyo*; Chând. 8. 7. 1: *so' nveshṭavyaḥ, sa vijijñâsitavyaḥ.*

themselves to us unsought are not the âtman, the self, the true reality; and that we are under a delusion if, like the demon Viroc'ana,[1] we regard them as such. All worldly objects and relationships are, as Yajñavalkhya explains in Bṛih. 2. 4. 5[a], of no value for their own sake (as "things in themselves"), but for the sake of the âtman; nay, they exist solely in the âtman, and that man is utterly and hopelessly undone who knows them "apart from the Self" (*anyatra âtmano*). This âtman, he concludes,[2] is Brâhman and warrior, is space, gods, and creatures, "this âtman is the entire universe" (*idam sarvam yad ayam âtmâ*). As when a man touches the instrument[3] he at the same time elicits the notes, so when a man has comprehended the âtman he has with it comprehended all these things:—"Verily he who has seen, heard, comprehended and known the Self, by him is this entire universe known."[4]

Immediately connected with these conceptions, and probably even with this passage from the Bṛihadâraṇyaka, is the expression in the Chândogya Up. 6. 1. 2, where that which in the former place was the climax of a development is assumed and becomes the theme advanced for discussion:—"Dost thou then ask for that instruction, by which the unheard becomes (already) heard, the uncomprehended comprehended, the unknown known?" "What then, most noble sir, is this instruction?" "Just as, my dear sir, from a lump of clay everything that consists of clay is known, the change is a matter of words alone, a mere name,[5] it is in reality only clay,—thus, my dear sir, is this instruction." Here the manifold change of the one substance is explained as mere word-play, mere name, exactly as Parmenides asserts that all

[1] Chând. 8. 8. 4.
[2] *L.c.* 2. 4. 6.
[3] Bṛih. 2. 4. 7 f.
[4] Bṛih. 2. 4. 5[b].
[5] *vâc'ârambhaṇam vikâro, nâmadheyam.*

which men regard as real is mere name.[1] Later passages employ language that is based on these conceptions, "nor is this even a plurality,"[2] and the verses preserved in Bṛih. 4. 4. 19:[3]—

In the spirit should this be perceived,
Here there is no plurality anywhere.
From death to death again he rushes blindly
Who fancies that he here sees difference.

Apt and striking also is the remark of a later Upanishad[4] that no proof of plurality can even be offered, "for no proof is possible of the existence of a duality, and only the timeless âtman admits of proof," (*i.e.* we are incapable of knowing anything outside of our own consciousness, which under all circumstances forms a unity).

It is clear from the foregoing:—(1) That the view which later was most explicitly set forth in the doctrine of *mâyâ* is so far from being strange to the oldest Upanishads that it is assumed in and with their fundamental doctrine of the sole reality of the âtman, and forms its necessary complement; and (2) that this fundamental doctrine of the Upanishads is seen to be in marvellous agreement with the philosophies of Parmenides and Plato, and of Kant and Schopenhauer. So fully indeed is this true, that all three, originating from different epochs and countries, and with modes of thought entirely independent, mutually complete, elucidate, and confirm one another. Let this then suffice for the philosophical significance of the Upanishads.

3. *The Conception of the Upanishads in its Relation to Religion*

The thought referred to, common to India, Plato, and Kant, that the entire universe is only appearance and not

[1] *τῷ πάντ' ὄνομ' ἔσται, ὅσσα βρότοι κατέθεντο πεποιθότες εἶναι ἀληθῆ.*
[2] Kaush. 3. 8. [3] cp. Kâṭh. 4. 10–11. [4] Nṛisiṁhott. 9.

reality, forms not only the special and most important theme of all philosophy, but is also the presumption and *conditio sine quâ non* of all religion. All great religious teachers therefore, whether in earlier or later times, nay even all those at the present day whose religion rests upon faith, are alike unconsciously followers of Kant. This we propose briefly to prove.

The necessary premisses of all religion are, as Kant frequently expounds:—(1) The existence of God, (2) the immortality of the soul, (3) the freedom of the will (without which no morality is possible). These three essential conditions of man's salvation—God, immortality, and freedom—are conceivable only if the universe is mere appearance and not reality (mere *mâyâ* and not the *âtman*), and they break down irretrievably should this empirical reality, wherein we live, be found to constitute the true essence of things.

(1) The existence of God will be precluded by that of space, which is infinite, and therefore admits of nothing external to itself, and nothing within save that which fills it, *i.e.* matter (the most satisfactory definition of which is "that which fills space").

(2) Immortality will be precluded by the conditions of time, in consequence of which our existence has a beginning in time by conception and birth, and an end in time by death; and this end is absolute, in so far as that beginning was absolute.

(3) Freedom, and with it the possibility of moral action, will be precluded by the universal validity of the law of causality, as shown by experience; for this requires that every effect, consequently every human action, should be the necessary result of causes which precede the action, and which therefore in the actual moment of action are no longer within our control.

The question as it concerns God, immortality, and

freedom, stands on an altogether different footing if this entire empirical reality, the occupant of space and time, and ruled by causal laws, is mere appearance and not a disposition of "things in themselves," to use Kant's words; or is mere *mâyâ* and not the *âtman*, the "self" of things, as the Upanishads teach. For in this case there is room for another, a higher order of things, which is not subject to the laws of space, time, and causality. And it is precisely this higher order of things set over-against the reality of experience, from the knowledge of which we are excluded by our intellectual constitution, which religion comprehends in faith by her teaching concerning God, immortality, and freedom. All religions therefore unconsciously depend on the fundamental dogma of the Kantian philosophy, which in a less definite form was already laid down in the Upanishads. These last therefore by virtue of their fundamental character lie naturally at the basis of every religious conception of existence.

By the side, moreover, of this their value for religion in general they have a special and very remarkable inner relation to Christianity, which we cannot state more briefly and clearly than by repeating in the present connection, where this consideration is essential, what has been before said on this subject.[1]

The Upanishads, it was pointed out, are for the Veda what the New Testament is for the Bible. And this analogy is not merely external and accidental, but is fundamental and based upon a universal law of development of the religious life which is acknowledged on both sides.

In the childhood of the human race religion enacts commands and prohibitions, and emphasizes them by promises of reward and denunciations of punishment;—it addresses itself to the self-interest, which it assumes to

[1] Deussen, *Sechzig Upanishads*, *Vorrede*.

be the centre and essence of human nature, and beyond which it does not go.

A higher grade of religious consciousness is attained with the knowledge that all actions which depend upon the motives of expectation and fear are of no value for the ultimate destiny of mankind; that the supreme function of existence does not consist in the satisfaction of self-interest, but in its voluntary suppression; and that herein first the true divine reality of ourselves, through the individual self as through an outer husk, makes itself manifest.

The primitive standpoint of righteousness by works is represented in the Bible by the Old Testament law, which corresponds in the Veda to that which the Indian theologians call the *karmakâṇḍa* (the department of works), under which name is comprised the whole literature of the Hymns and Brâhmaṇas, with the exception of portions intercalated here and there in the spirit of the Upanishads. Both the Old Testament and the *karmakâṇḍa* of the Veda proclaim a law, and hold out the prospect of reward for its observance and of punishment for its transgression. And if the Indian theory has the advantage of being able to defer retribution in part to the future, and by that means to relieve the conflict with experience that raises so many difficulties for the Old Testament doctrine of a retribution limited to this world; it is, on the other hand, the distinguishing characteristic of the Biblical law of righteousness, that it pays less regard than the Indian to ritual prescriptions, and in their place lays greater stress on a habitually blameless course of life. For the interests of human society this advantage is very great. In itself however, and as far as the moral value of an action is concerned, it makes no difference whether a man exert himself in the service of imaginary gods or in that of his fellow-men.

So long as his own well-being lies before him as the ultimate aim, either is simply a means to this selfish end, and therefore, like the end itself, from a moral point of view is to be set aside as worthless.

The recognition of this is seen in the New Testament doctrine of the worthlessness of all works, even those that are good, and in the corresponding Upanishad doctrine that altogether rejects works. Both make salvation dependent not on anything done or left undone, but on a complete transformation of the natural man as a whole. Both regard this transformation as a release from the bonds of this all-embracing empirical reality, which has its roots in egotism.

Why then do we need a release from this existence? Because it is the realm of sin, is the reply of the Bible. The Veda answers: Because it is the realm of ignorance. The former sees depravity in the volitional, the latter in the intellectual side of human nature. The Bible demands a change of the will, the Veda of the understanding. On which side does the truth lie? If man were pure will or pure intelligence, we should have to decide for one or the other alternative. But since he is a being who both wills and knows, the great change upon which the Bible and the Veda alike make salvation depend must be realised in both departments of his life. Such a change is, in the first place, according to the Biblical view the softening of a heart hardened by natural self-love, and the inclining it to deeds of righteousness, affection, and self-denial. It is however, in the second place and side by side with this, the breaking forth upon us of the light of the great intellectual truth, which the Upanishads taught before Kant, that this entire universe, with its relations in space, its consequent manifoldness and dependence upon the mind that apprehends, rests solely upon an illusion (*mâyâ*), natural indeed to us owing to the limitations of our intellect; and that there is in truth one Being alone, eternal, exalted above space and time, multiplicity and change, self-revealing in all the forms of nature, and by me who myself also am one and undivided, discovered and realised within as my very Self, as the âtman.

As surely however as, to adopt the significant teaching of Schopenhauer, the will and not the intellect is the centre of a man's nature, so surely must the pre-eminence be assigned to Christianity, in that its demand for a renewal of the will is peculiarly vital and essential. But as certainly as man is not mere will, but intellect besides, so certainly will that Christian renewal of the will make itself manifest on the other side as a renewal of knowledge, just as the Upanishads teach. "Thou shalt love thy neighbour as thyself" is the requirement of the Bible. But on what grounds is this demand to be based, since feeling is in myself alone and not in another? "Because," the Veda here adds in explanation, "thy neighbour is in truth thy very self, and what separates you from him is mere illusion." As in this case, so at every point of the system. The New Testament and the Upanishads, these two noblest products of the religious consciousness of mankind, are found when we sound their deeper meaning to be nowhere in irreconcilable contradiction, but in a manner the most attractive serve to elucidate and complete one another.

An example may show the value of the Upanishad teaching for the full development of our Christian consciousness.

Christianity teaches in spirit, even if not always in the letter, that man as such is capable only of sinful, that is selfish actions (Rom. 7^{18}), and that all good whether of purpose or achievement can only be wrought in us by God (Phil. 2^{13}). Clearly as this doctrine—for him who has eyes to see—is formulated not so much in individual expressions as rather in the entire system as such, yet it has been difficult at all times for the Church to rest satisfied with it. She has sought perpetually an opportunity of co-ordinating her own imperfect remedial measures, and of leaving open a side-door for human co-operation,—clearly because behind the sole operative power which makes God the source of all good she saw standing like a frightful apparition the grim monstrosity of predestination. And indeed this presents itself as an inevitable consequence as soon as we connect the Christian conception of the sole agency of God, as profound as it is true, with the Jewish realism adopted from the Old Testament, which sets God and man over-against one another as two mutually exclusive subsistences. In this darkness there comes to us light from the East, from India. It is true that Paul also hints at an identification of God with the ἄνθρωπος πνευματικός (1 Cor. 15^{47}), it is true that Kant endeavours to explain the marvellous phenomenon of the categorical imperative within us on the theory that the man as real ("thing in itself") lays down the law to the man as phenomenal; but how slight the significance of these timid and groping essays as compared with the profound and fundamental conception of the Vedânta, which makes its appearance everywhere in the Upanishads, that the God, the sole author of all good in us, is not as in the Old Testament a Being contrasted with and distinct from us, but rather—without impairing his absolute antagonism to the depraved self of experience (*jîva*)—our own metaphysical I, our divine self, persisting in untarnished purity through all the aberrations of human nature, eternal blessed,—in a word, our *âtman*.

This and much more we may learn from the Upanishads,—we shall learn the lesson, if we are willing to put the finishing touch to the Christian consciousness, and to make it on all sides consistent and complete.

THE SYSTEM OF THE UPANISHADS

INTRODUCTION

By a system we understand an association of thoughts, which collectively belong to and are dependent on a single centre. A system has therefore always an individual author, whether he have himself originated the thoughts brought together in the system, or have only adjusted to one another and welded into a consistent whole imperfect thoughts derived from without. In this sense a "system of the Upanishads," strictly speaking, does not exist. For these treatises are not the work of a single genius, but the total philosophical product of an entire epoch, which extends from the period of the wandering in the Ganges valley to the rise of Buddhism, or approximately from 1000 or 800 B.C. to *c.* 500 B.C., but which is prolonged in its offshoots far beyond this last limit of time. Thus we find in the Upanishads a great variety of conceptions which are developed before our eyes, and which not seldom stand to one another in irreconcilable contradiction. All these conceptions, however, gather so entirely around one common centre, and are dominated so completely by the one thought of the sole reality of the âtman, that they all present themselves as manifold variations upon one and the same theme, which is treated at one time more briefly, or again at greater length, now from the starting-point of the empirical consciousness, and now in abrupt contradiction thereto. Accordingly all individual differences are so entirely overshadowed by the one fundamental conception, that while it is true that we have before us in the Upanishads no defined system, we are able nevertheless to trace the gradual development of a system. This latter then consists in the increasingly thorough interweaving of a fundamental thought originally idealistic with the realistic requirements of the empirical consciousness, which make their influence more and more felt. That this is so will appear in the course of our exposition. These tendencies reached their climax first in post-Vedic times in the general system at once theological and philosophical, which was shaped by the hands of Bâdarâyaṇa and his commentator S'ankara, and in which full account was taken of the demands both of the idealism and the realism (by distinguishing between a higher and a lower knowledge). As the **System of the Vedânta** this became in India the universal foundation of faith and knowledge, and has remained so up to the present day, though undergoing great development on every side. It falls naturally into four main divisions, as follows :—

I. **Theology**; the doctrine of Brahman as the first principle of all things.

II. **Cosmology**; the doctrine of the evolution of this principle to form the universe.

III. **Psychology**; the doctrine of the entrance of Brahman as soul into the universe evolved from him.

IV. **Eschatology** and **Ethics**; the doctrine of the fate of the soul after death, and the manner of life which is therefore required.

The growth also of the System of the Vedânta, as it is disclosed to us in the Upanishads, may with similar propriety be discussed under these four principal heads, and the subdivisions which the nature of the subject suggests. We propose to endeavour to collect under each heading all the relevant passages of the Upanishads recognised by the later Vedânta, and where a development of thought presents itself in them we shall in many instances be furnished with a safer ground for determining the chronological position of a text as compared with earlier and later treatments of the same theme. The gain for philology therefore will consist in the provision of a more secure basis for the chronology of the Upanishad texts according to their relative age; while on the philosophical side we may hope for a deeper insight into the rise of one of the most remarkable and prolific creations of thought that the world possesses.

FIRST PART OF THE SYSTEM OF THE UPANISHADS

THEOLOGY, OR THE DOCTRINE OF BRAHMAN

I. On the Possibility of Knowing Brahman

1. *Is the Veda the Source of Knowledge of Brahman?*

Bâdarayâṇa begins the *S'ârîraka-mîmâṁsâ*, in which is contained the oldest systematic epitome of the Vedânta doctrine, with the following four sûtras:—(1) *atha ato brahma-jijñâsâ, iti*, "next what is called the search after Brahman"; (2) *janma-âdi asya yata', iti*, "(Brahman is that) from which is the birth etc. (*i.e.* birth, continuance, and end) of this (universe)"; (3) *s'âstra-yonitvâd, iti*, "an account of its originating from the (sacred) canon" (*i.e.* according to one explanation, because the sacred canon is the source of the knowledge of Brahman as already defined. To the objection that the canon has in view not knowledge but worship, it is then said); (4) *tat tu, samanvayât*, "that however on account of the agreement" (of the assertions respecting Brahman, which, if they concerned acts of worship alone, would be unnecessary, or even impossible). To establish in particular cases this agreement of all the Vedânta texts in their assertions respecting Brahman is the aim of the entire work of Bâdarâyaṇa and S'ankara. For them the whole of the Veda is of supernatural origin, breathed forth by Brahman (according to a passage to be discussed immediately), and therefore infallible. From it they construct their entire doctrine, and only in instances where the meaning of the Vedânta text is doubtful do they call in the aid of experience to give the casting vote.

The question arises, what is the teaching of the Upanishads themselves with regard to the sources from which the knowledge of Brahman is to be derived?

The very oldest Upanishad texts take for granted a rich store of literary works (transmitted of course only orally). In Bṛih. 2. 4. 10, for example, it is said:—"Just as, when a fire is laid with damp wood, clouds of smoke spread all around, so in truth from this great Being have been breathed forth the Ṛigveda, the Yajurveda, the Sâmaveda, the (hymns) of the Atharvans and the Angirases, the narratives, the histories, the sciences, the mystical doctrines (upanishads), the poems, the proverbs, the parables, and expositions,—all these have been breathed forth from him."

This passage is in many respects instructive. In the first place we infer from it that there are only three Vedas,[1] and that the hymns of the Atharvans and Angirases are not yet recognised as Veda. The first trace of such recognition is perhaps Bṛih. 5. 13, where, together with *uktham*, *yajus* and *sâman*, a fourth *kshatram* is named. This may denote the Atharvaveda, which stands in a closer relation to the warrior caste, and serves especially to ward off misfortune (*trâyate kshaṇitos*, as *kshatram* is etymologically explained). To the same purport is Bṛih. 6. 4. 13, where a son who has studied one, two, or three Vedas is distinguished from one who knows "all the Vedas," *i.e.* probably all four. The *âtharvaṇa* first appears as a fourth veda in Chând. 7. 1. 2, and under the name *atharva-veda* in Muṇḍ. 1. 1. 5; the latter name therefore is first met with in the Atharva Upanishads.

[1] So generally in the older Upanishad texts, cp. the index to my "Upanishads" under "Triple knowledge."

The above passage from Bṛih. 2. 4. 10 further enumerates a series of works the meaning of which is sometimes doubtful, but which have probably been in part incorporated in the Brâhmaṇas, in part mark the beginnings of the later epic. It is, however, especially noticeable that the "mystical doctrines" (*upanishadaḥ*) appear only in the eighth place after *itihâsaḥ*, *purâṇam*, and *vidyâ*, and are therefore under no circumstances reckoned to belong to the Veda. They had not yet become Vedânta. If therefore, finally, the later teachers of the Vedânta found on this passage their dogma that the entire Veda is breathed forth from Brahman and is therefore infallible, their conclusion would carry with it the infallibility also of the other works enumerated, and is certainly incorrect. For the passage originally asserts only that, like all other natural phenomena, the products of the mind also throughout the universe are derived from Brahman.[1] Precisely the same series of literary works, though with a few additions, is enumerated again by Yâjñavalkhya in Bṛih. 4. 1. 2, is explained as "speech" (*vâc'*), and is found to be inadequate to convey a knowledge of Brahman. At the close of this discussion therefore, Janaka, although he has "equipped his soul with that mystical doctrine," has "studied the Vedas and listened to the mystical doctrine,"[2] yet is unable to give any account of the fate of the soul after death. From this it is clear that what was then understood by *upanishad* did not of necessity include an exposition of the highest questions; exactly, indeed, as in Chând. 8. 8. 5 the erroneous teaching that the essential being of man consists in the body is characterised as *asurâṇâm upanishad.*

[1] The passage is taken up also in S'vet. 4. 18, "from him wisdom proceeded forth at the very beginning" (cp. S'vet. 6. 18, Muṇḍ. 2. 1. 4), and further in Maitr. 6. 32.

[2] *adhîtaveda* and *ukta-upanishatka*, Bṛih. 4. 2. 1.

The insufficiency of all Vedic, and in general of all existing knowledge is still more clearly laid down in Chând. 7. 1, where Nârada acknowledges to Sanatkumâra:—"I have studied, most reverend sir, the Ṛigveda, Yajurveda, Sâmaveda, the Atharvaveda as fourth, the epic and mythological poems as fifth veda, grammar, necrology, arithmetic, divination, chronology, dialectics, politics, theology, the doctrine of prayer, necromancy, the art of war, astronomy, snake-charming, and the fine arts,—these things, most reverend sir, have I studied; therefore am I, most reverend sir, learned indeed in the scripture, but not learned in the âtman. Yet I have heard from such as are like you that he who knows the âtman vanquishes sorrow. I, however, most reverend sir, am bewildered. Lead me then over, I pray, to the farther shore that lies beyond sorrow."

Another proof that the study of the Veda does not touch the most important questions is afforded by the great transmigration text, which has been preserved in a threefold form in Chând. 5. 3–10, Bṛih. 6. 2, and with considerable variations in Kaush. 1. In all three recensions S'vetaketu professes to have been taught by his father Âruṇi, but fails to answer the eschatological questions propounded by the king Pravâhaṇa (in the Kaush., C'itra), and returning in anger to his father reproaches him:—"So then, without having really done so, you have claimed to have instructed me";[1] "it was imagination, then, when you previously declared that my instruction was complete."[2]

The same thought is expressed in Chând. 6. 1, where (in a manner otherwise irreconcilable with the passages already quoted) S'vetaketu is sent from home by his father Âruṇi to study the Brahman (*i.e.* the Veda). After twelve years "he had thoroughly studied all the

[1] Chând. 5. 3. 4. [2] Bṛih. 6. 2. 3.

Vedas (*i.e.* the Saṁhitâs only of the *ṛic'*, *yajus*, and *sâman*, for from these only is he subsequently tested *infra* Chând. 6. 7. 2), and returned home full of conceit and arrogance, believing himself wise." He fails, however, to answer his father's questions on the One, the Self-existent, with whose knowledge everything is known, —"assuredly my reverend teachers did not themselves know this; for had they known it, why did they not tell it to me?" Whereupon Aruṇi imparts to him the perfect instruction.

This is the standpoint of the Taittirîya Upanishad also, when it teaches[1] that the âtman of the mind (*manomaya*, "composed of *manas*") consists of *yajus*, *ṛic'*, *sâman*, instruction (*âdes'a*, *i.e.* probably the Brâhmaṇa) and the hymns of the Atharvas and Aṅgirases; and proceeds to explain this entire âtman of the mind as a mere husk, which we must strip off in order to penetrate to the real essence of man or of nature.

The doctrine set forth in these examples finds direct expression also at an early period:—"So then, after that the Brâhman has rejected learning (*pâṇḍityam nirvidya*), he abides in childhood";[2] "He sought not after the knowledge of the books, which only gives rise to words without end";[3] "Before whom words and thought recoil, not finding him";[4] "Not by learning is the âtman attained, not by genius and much knowledge of books."[5] In Muṇḍ. 1. 1. 5 also the four Vedas are enumerated, and together with the six Vedângas are reckoned as inferior knowledge (*aparâ vidyâ*), through which the imperishable Being is not known.

This attitude of aloofness towards the Vedic knowledge is altered at first gradually and in general, as the texts of the Upanishads gain fixity, and become the

[1] Taitt. Upan. 2. 3. [2] Bṛih. 3. 5. 1. [3] Bṛih. 4. 4. 21.
[4] Taitt. 2. 4. [5] Kâṭh. 2. 23.

Vedânta.[1] Henceforth they, and the Veda with them, are regarded as sources of the highest knowledge. A first trace of this change is shown in Bṛih. 3. 9. 26, where Yâjñavalkhya inquires after the purusha of the upanishad doctrine (*aupanishada purusha*); this S'âkalya does not know, and thereupon acknowledges defeat. Further, in Chând. 3. 5. 4, where the Veda is explained to be nectar, the Upanishads, the *guhyâ' âdes'âḥ*, are the nectar of nectar. In Kena 33 the Upanishads are apparently attached to the Veda, or more precisely comprise a brief summary of the entire Vedic material of instruction under the Veda; for there the Vedas are explained to be "the sum of the parts" (*vedâḥ sarvâṅgâni*), the "secret doctrine of Brahman" (*brâhmî upanishad*, in contrast with other unrecognised Upanishads, such as the *asurâṇâm upanishad* referred to above). With the adoption of the name *Vedânta* the Upanishads are seen to be completely naturalised in the Veda. The term first occurs in S'vet. 6. 22:—"From of old was the deepest secret disclosed in the Vedânta." This transfer of the Vedânta to antiquity (*purâkalpa*) seems to show that the author looks back to the Bṛih., Chând., and other Upanishads of which he makes use from a certain distance. It might, however, be understood as a mere expression of the high value attached to them, a value that increases with the lapse of time. The Vedânta texts appear completely established in their later position as sources of the knowledge of Brahman, which is to be gained through the interpretation they offer, in the verse which occurs Muṇḍ. 3. 2. 6:[2]—*vedânta - vijñâna - sunis'c'ita - arthâḥ*, etc., "they who have correctly (*su*) penetrated the meaning of the Vedânta knowledge." With this Muṇḍ. 2. 2. 3–4 agrees, where the Upanishads, and the syllable *Om* as their most essential element, are described as the bow,

[1] *sup.* p. 21.

[2] Also Mahân. 10. 22, Kaivalya 3.

with which men shoot at Brahman as the mark. It is otherwise, however, in Muṇḍ. 1. 1. 5, where all the four Vedas are rejected. The latter passage seems therefore to be derived from an earlier period.

2. *Preparatory Means to a Knowledge of Brahman*

In later times a kind of *via salutis* was constructed in the four *âs'ramas*, or life-stages, according to which every Indian Brâhman was under obligation to devote himself first as a *brahmac'ârin* to the study of the Veda, then as *gṛihastha* to the duties of the sacrifice and other good works, next as *vânaprastha* to the practice of asceticism in the jungle, and finally towards the end of life as *parivrâjaka* (*bhikshu, sannyâsin*) to a wandering existence without possessions or home, awaiting only his soul's release and its reception into the supreme âtman.

As originally conceived we find these three *âs'ramas* in Bṛih. 4. 4. 22 :—"The Brâhmans endeavour to know him by study of the Veda (*brahmac'ârin*), by sacrifice and almsgiving (*gṛihastha*), by penance and fasting (*vânaprastha*); he who knows him becomes a *muni;* to him the pilgrims journey, when they yearn for home (*parivrâjaka*)." Here a certain value as preparatory means to a knowledge of Brahman appears to be assigned to the duties of the later *âs'ramas* (*i.e.* study of the Veda, sacrifice, asceticism).

In Chând. 2. 23. 1 it is still more clearly expressed :—"There are three branches of duty: sacrifice with study of the Veda and almsgiving is the first (*gṛihastha*); asceticism is the second (*vânaprastha*); the student (*brahmac'ârin*) who lives in the house of his teacher is the third, provided that he remains always (as *naishṭhika*) in the teacher's house. These all carry as their reward the divine worlds; he, however, who abides steadfast in Brahman wins immortality." This passage names only three *âs'ramas*, recognises their value, but contrasts with all three the "abiding steadfast in Brahman"; and this last is then subsequently developed into a fourth *âs'rama*. Another passage[1] endeavours by a series of bold etymologies to prove that sacrifice, silence, fasting, and a life in the forest (the pursuits, that is to say, of the *gṛihastha* and *vânaprastha*) are essentially *brahmac'aryam*; which term must be understood to include here not only the student-period, but in a broader sense, as the repeated reference to it shows, the entire course of life of a Brâhman regarded as the way that leads to the âtman. In all that this aim requires—that would seem to be the meaning of the passage—lies the peculiar value of the observances of the *âs'ramas*. More definitely in Kena 33, asceticism, self-restraint, and sacrifice (*tapas*, *dama*, *karman*) are described as the preliminary conditions (*pratishṭhâḥ*) of the *brâhmî upanishad*, *i.e.* of the real mystical doctrine which reveals *Brahman*. And in Kâṭh. 2. 15 all the Vedas, all the practices of *tapas* and the *brahmac'aryam*, are described as means by which the syllable *Om* (here equivalent to the knowledge of Brahman) is to be sought as the final aim. The observances of the *âs'ramas* are recognised also in Muṇḍ. 2. 1. 7, in so far as these (*tapas*, *s'raddhâ*, *satyam*, *brahmac'aryam*, *vidhi*) are here described as a creation of Brahman.

With regard to the particular âs'ramas, the study of the Veda has been already discussed above, and we propose here merely to summarise the most important teaching of the Upanishads concerning sacrifice and asceticism.

3. *The Sacrifice*

The older Upanishads were so deeply conscious of the hostile character of the entire ritualistic system of the Brâhmans that they could concede to it only a relative recognition. It is true that direct attacks are rarely found

[1] Chând. 8. 5.

in the extant texts. Antagonistic explanations, however, of the sacrificial rites are all the more frequently offered by way either of allegorical interpretation or of the substitution of other and usually psychological ideas in their place.

There is a note almost of mockery in Bṛih. 1. 4. 10 when it is said :—" He who worships another divinity (than the âtman), and says 'it is one and I am another,' is not wise, but he is like a house-dog of the gods. Therefore just as many house-dogs are useful to men, every individual man is useful to the gods. Now the theft of only one house-dog is displeasing, how much more of many? Therefore it is displeasing to them that men do not know this." The remark of Yâjñavalkhya also, in Bṛih. 3. 9. 6, sounds very contemptuous :—" What is the sacrifice ?—brute beasts !" nor is it less so in Bṛih. 3. 9. 21, where it is said that Yama (the god of the dead) has his abode in the sacrifice, but the sacrifice in the fees.

Daring remarks like these we do not find in the Chândogya, unless it be in the "Song of the Dog" in Chând. 1. 12, which seems to have been originally a satire on the greedy begging propensities of the priests, to which in later times an allegorical interpretation was given. In Chand. 1. 10–11 also the story is told, not without a malicious pleasure, how the three priests assembled at the sacrifice were put to confusion by a wandering beggar; and in Chând. 4. 1–3 Jânas'ruti, "rich in faith, open-handed, munificent" (*s'raddhâdeyo, bahudâyî, bahupâkyaḥ*), is compelled not without humiliation to seek instruction from a poor vagrant.

According to the general view, sacrifice and good works give admission only to the "way of the fathers" (*pitṛiyâna*), which after a temporary sojourn in the moon leads back to a new earthly existence. As early as Bṛih. 1. 5. 16 it is said :—" by the labour (of the sacrifice) is the world of the fathers won, by knowledge the world of the gods"; and other passages describe the way of the fathers which leads back again to earth as the fate of those "who worship in the village with the words 'Sacrifice and deeds of piety are our offering,'"[1] "who by sacrifice, almsgiving and ascetic practices gain the (heavenly) worlds,"[2] "who worship with the words 'Sacrifice and deeds of piety are our work,'"[3] "regarding sacrifice and deeds as the highest good, they know no better and are befooled."[4]

Not rarely a meaning suitable to the new doctrine is read into the existing sacrificial rites. In Bṛih. 1. 4. 6, for example, the five daily offerings (*mahâyajñâḥ*) are interpreted as a sacrifice to the âtman; and in Chând. 4. 11–14 the three sacrificial fires are explained as forms of the âtman's manifestation (*eshâ asmadvidyâ âtmavidyâ c'a*).

Yet more frequently conditions of the âtman, as embodied in the world of nature or of man, were substituted for the ceremonies of the ritual. In Bṛih. 3. 1, in place of the four priests as organs of the gods, there are found speech, eye, breath and manas as organs of the âtman. In Chând. 4. 16 the wind is explained to be the essence of the sacrifice, mind and speech the essence of the sacrificing priests. In Ait. Âr. 3. 2. 6, Bṛih. 1. 5. 23, and Kaush. 2. 5, inhalation and speech replace the *agnihotram*; and this thought is further developed on the basis of Chând. 5. 11–24 into the theory of the *prâṇâgnihotram*, a fuller discussion of which will be given below. The substitution also for the sacrifice of the man, his organs and bodily functions, is greatly favoured. For example, in Chând. 3. 16 the three life-periods take the place of the three pressings of the soma, in Chând. 3. 17 human activities of the various acts of the soma festival, and in Mahânâr. 64 the bodily organs of the implements of the sacrifice. This last thought is

[1] Chând. 5. 10. 3.
[2] Bṛih. 6. 2. 16.
[3] Pras'na 1. 9.
[4] Muṇḍ. 1. 2. 10.

carried out in extreme detail in Prâṇâgnihotra Up. 3–4. The verse Taitt. 2. 5 also belongs here, inasmuch as, correctly translated, it asserts,—"He presents knowledge as his sacrifice, knowledge as his works."

It is first in the later Upanishads that we meet with a more friendly attitude towards the sacrificial cult. In Kâṭh. 1. 17, in a style altogether excessive and opposed to the upanishad spirit, there is promised for the fulfilment of certain ceremonies and works "the overstepping of birth and death," "entrance into everlasting rest"; and in Kâṭh. 3. 2 the Nâc'iketa fire is explained as the bridge which bears the sacrificers to the supreme eternal Brahman, to the "fearless shore." Here even if we make allowance for poetical extravagance of expression, a co-operation at least with the cult for the attainment of salvation is asserted. S'vet. 2. 6–7 marks a further step in advance:—

> Where Agni from the chips of wood
> Darts forth, where Vâyu too appears,
> Where the Soma also flows freely,—
> There is the manas developed.
>
> By Savitar, at his impulse,
> Delight yourselves in the ancient prayer;
> If there you take your stand,
> The deeds of the past soil you no more.

The expression here used, "Delight yourselves in the ancient prayer" (*jusheta brahma pûrvyam*) indicates that a former practice is reintroduced and held in honour. This reaction attains its climax in the Maitrâyaṇîya Up., which explains at the very outset[1] that "the fire-laying for the ancestors" is in truth "a sacrifice to Brahman"; and in the fourth Prapâṭhaka ventures the thought that without study of the Veda, observance of caste-duties, and the following of the due brâhmanical order of life

[1] Maitr. 1. 1.

according to the âs'ramas, the deliverance of the natural âtman and its re-union with the supreme âtman are impossible. The key to the understanding of this reaction is given by the polemic against the heretics which is found in Maitr. 7. 8–10. Brâhmanism, in view of the consequences which the attitude of the earlier Upanishads had entailed in Buddhism and similar manifestations, returns to its original position.

4. *Asceticism* (*tapas*)

A feeling of admiration has always been excited when, contrary to the natural desires which all experience for life, pleasure and prosperity, there has been exhibited a self-mastery, which voluntarily submits to privations and sufferings either for the sake of the well-being of others, or independently of this external and as it were accidental aim, which indeed as far as the real worth of the respective actions is concerned is in itself without significance. An act of self-denial would seem the more pure the less it were combined with any external end, and the more it were undertaken with the sole object of subduing the selfish impulses of nature. It were as though a superhuman, supernatural power had been thereby manifested in man, which, springing from the deepest roots of his being, exalted the doer far above the world of men with its selfish interests, yea even above the world of the gods, and in another and higher order of things than ours assigned to him his place.

It is a tribute to the high metaphysical capacity of the Indian people, that the phenomenon of asceticism made its appearance among them earlier and occupied a larger place than among any other known people. (We leave out of consideration at this point the later misuse of asceticism in the interest of merely selfish aims to excite wonder or to secure profit.)

As early as the creation myths we saw how the creator of the universe prepared himself for his work by the practice of *tapas*; in which word the ancient idea of the "heat" which serves to promote the incubation of the egg of the universe blends with the ideas of the exertion, fatigue, self-renunciation, by means of which the creator is transmuted (entirely or in part) into the universe which he proposes to create. According to this conception, everything that is great in the universe is dependent on *tapas*. In a later hymn of the Ṛigveda also,[1] truth and right, and with them the entire universe, are born of *tapas*. From *s'rama* (toil) and *tapas* the first-born Skambha arose and permeated the universe,[2] in *tapas* he was rocked on the surface of the primeval waters.[3] By the *tapas* with which he discharges his duties the student of the Veda, according to another hymn,[4] satisfies his teacher, the gods, and the realms of space, ascends on high as the sun, protects both worlds, etc., in his course of life as a Brâhman. By *tapas* the ruler protects his kingdom, the gods have escaped death, the student of the Veda practised *tapas* in the primeval ocean, when he, creating the universe, stood on the water's surface. And as early even as the Ṛigveda the seven ṛishis together betake themselves to the practice of *tapas*;[5] and the souls on their entrance into heaven are apostrophised :—

> Which invincible by tapas,
> Have won their way by tapas to the light,
> That have accomplished the severest tapas—,
> To these now enter in![6]

Another hymn of the Ṛigveda[7] portrays the inspired *muni* as with long hair, in dirty yellow robes, girt only with

[1] X. 190. 1.
[2] Atharvav. X. 7. 36.
[3] Atharvav. X. 7. 38.
[4] Atharvav. XI. 5.
[5] Ṛigv. X. 109. 4.
[6] Ṛigv. X. 154. 2.
[7] Ṛigv. X. 136.

the wind he roams on the desert paths. Mortals behold only his body. But he himself, endowed with supernatural power, flies through the air, drinks with the storm-god from the bowl of both the oceans of the universe, on the track of the wind is raised aloft to the gods, transcends all forms, and as companion of the gods co-operates with them for the salvation of mankind.

By the time of the oldest Upanishad texts the ascetic life has already been elevated into a special "calling,"[1] which assumes equal rank by the side of the position of householder. Men abandon household goods and family, as Yâjñavalkhya does in Bṛih. 2. 4, and depart into the solitude of the forest in order to practise *tapas*, and by gradually increasing privations and penances to destroy in themselves the last remains of dependence on earthly existence.

It remains to inquire what attitude was adopted by the authors and defenders of the doctrines of the Upanishads in presence of this cult of an ascetic ideal.

The Chândogya Upanishad sets before us in the first place Upakosala, a student of the Veda, who grieves[2] that the teacher refuses to impart to him knowledge, and falling sick declines to take nourishment. To the invitation to eat he replies :—" Alas, in mankind there are such troops of desires. I am full of sickness, and incapable of eating." (In these words the characteristic motive of Indian, as of all asceticism, is evident.) Thereupon the three sacrificial fires take pity on him, and the instruction which they give to him begins with the words :— " Brahman is life, Brahman is joy (*kam*), Brahman is space (*kham*)." It is implied in these words that Brahman, as the principle of life, of bliss (*kam* = *ânanda*, as in Chând.

[1] *dharmaskandha*, Chând. 2. 23.
[2] *tapto brahmac'ârî*, 4. 10. 2-4.

7. 23 *sukham*), and of infinity, is not to be attained by the way of a gloomy asceticism.

In Chând. 2. 23 *tapas* is spoken of as the especial obligation of the anchorite. As such, a recognised position is accorded it by the side of the student and householder. All three "bring as their reward the divine worlds; he, however, who abides steadfast in Brahman wins immortality." This is not in contradiction with the statement of Chând. 5. 10. 1, that the way of the gods, which leads to Brahman without return, and marks still for the present time the loftiest aim, is promised to those *ye c'a ime 'raṇye 's'raddhâ tapa' iti upâsate*; for these words mean, "those who worship in the forest using the words 'faith is our asceticism.'" The reference is to the anchorite; but something else—viz. faith—is here substituted for the asceticism which is his calling.

To the same effect the Bṛihadâraṇyaka Upan. expresses itself when, reproducing this passage in an appendix,[1] it yet more definitely opens up the prospect of the way of the gods to those alone "who observe faith and truth in the forest"; but on the other hand offers only the way of the fathers in return for sacrifice, almsgiving, and asceticism. Of these last it is said[2] that through them men seek to know Brahman, *vividishanti*. More directly still Yâjñavalkhya expresses himself in Bṛih. 3. 8. 10:—"Of a truth, O Gârgî, he who does not know this imperishable one, and in this world sacrifices and distributes alms and does penance (*tapas tapyate*) for many thousands of years, wins thereby only finite (reward)." Bṛih. 5. 11 again teaches that sickness the procession to the grave and cremation are the best asceticism (*paramam tapas*). Here, then, the sufferings of life and death are rated higher than artificially induced penances.

We meet with a disposition more favourable to asceti-

[1] Bṛih. 6. 2. 15.

[2] Bṛih. 4. 4. 22.

cism as early as the Taittirîya Upanishad. The first part which is appointed for the student demands of him[1] asceticism and the study of the Veda, and quotes in this connection the views of two teachers, of whom the one requires "asceticism alone," the other only study of the Veda, "for this is asceticism." The Upanishad adopts an intermediate position by its demand for asceticism combined with the study of the Veda. In the last and latest part[2] a higher value is placed upon asceticism, where Bhṛigu is repeatedly urged by his father Varuṇa:— "By *tapas* seek to know Brahman, for *tapas* is Brahman." Following his injunction, by progressive *tapas* he rises step by step to the recognition of food, the vital breath, manas, knowledge, and finally bliss as Brahman, and with this last the highest degree attainable by *tapas* is reached. The Mahânârâyaṇa Upan., which is attributed to the Taittirîya school, is much later still; in 62. 11 it sets *nyâsa*, "renunciation," above asceticism, thereby preparing the way for the standpoint of the Sannyâsa Upanishad; of which later. Kena 33 also, as already mentioned, reckons *tapas* among the foundations (*i.e.* the presuppositions, *pratishṭhâḥ*) of Brahman; and according to S'vet. 1. 15, 16; 6. 21, the knowledge of Brahman is based upon *âtmavidyâ* (the text of the Vedânta) and *tapas*.

A step, however, far beyond all the preceding is taken by the Muṇḍaka and Pras'na in their reproduction of the above-mentioned theory of the Chând. and Bṛihad. concerning the ways of the gods and the fathers with a characteristic variation. In Muṇḍ. 1. 2. 11 the way of the gods is promised to those "who practise asceticism and faith in the forest" (*tapaḥ-s'raddhe ye hi upavasanti araṇye*); and Pras'na 1. 10 offers it to those "who have sought the âtman by asceticism, the manner of life of a Brâhman, faith and knowledge." It is remarkable that

[1] Taitt. 1. 9.

[2] Taitt. 3.

in Muṇḍ. 3. 2. 4 a spurious tapas is mentioned (*tapas aliṅgam*), *i.e.* probably one that lacks the characteristic mark of knowledge.

As was to be expected, in the Maitr. Upan. is revived the ancient Vedic standpoint in regard to *tapas*, in presence of Buddhist and other errors. It is true that asceticism alone does not suffice, for in Maitr. 1. 2 it is practised in the severest form by Bṛihadratha without procuring for him the knowledge of the âtman. As a preliminary condition, however, it is indispensable :—" without being an ascetic it is impossible either to attain the knowledge of the âtman, or to bring work to fruition." [1]

5. *Other Preliminary Conditions*

In the older Upanishads we are repeatedly met by the prohibition to communicate a doctrine or ceremony to anyone except a son or a pupil adopted by the rite of *upanayanam*. In Ait. Âr. 3. 2. 6. 9 the mystical meaning of the combinations of the letters must be "communicated to no one, who is not a pupil, who has not been a pupil for a whole year, who does not propose himself to be a teacher." [2] In Chând. 3. 11. 5 the doctrine of Brahman as the sun of the universe should "his father make known as Brahman to his eldest son alone, or to a trusted pupil, but to no one else, whoever he may be. And though he were to be offered in return for it all the kingdoms of the ocean-girdled earth, yet should he bethink himself 'the other is of greater value.'" In Bṛih. 6. 3. 12 also the ceremony of the mixed drink "must be communicated to none but a son or a pupil."

Similarly in the Upanishads we find men and gods taking the fuel in their hands, and submitting to the con-

[1] *na atapaskasya âtmajñâne 'dhigamaḥ, karmasiddhir vâ*, Maitr. 4. 3.
[2] cp. also Ait. Âr. 5. 3. 3. 4.

ditions of pupilage, just as according to Chând. 8, 11. 3 Indra himself was obliged to live with Prajâpati as a pupil for one hundred and one years in order to obtain the perfect instruction. Other examples are Kaush. 1. 1, 4. 19, Bṛih. 2. 1. 14, Pras'na 1. 1, Muṇḍ. 1. 2. 12.

Yet in the earlier period this demand is still not absolute. In Chând. 4. 9. 3 it is merely said that "the knowledge which is gained from a teacher (as opposed to supernatural instruction by beasts, fire, geese or ducks[1]) leads most certainly to the goal"; and in Chând. 5. 11. 7 the king As'vapati instructs the six Brâhmans who approach him with the fuel in their hands (in token of their wish to become pupils) *anupanîya*, "without first admitting them as his pupils." So also in Bṛih. 2. 4 Yâjñavalkhya instructs his wife Maitreyî, and in Bṛih. 4. 1–2, 3–4 the king Janaka, who yet were not strictly his pupils; and in Bṛih. 3 he imparts information on the deepest questions (as *e.g.* Bṛih. 3. 8, in the conversation with Gârgî) in the presence of a numerous circle of hearers, and only exceptionally, when he desires to explain to Ârtabhâga the mystery of the soul's transmigration, does he retire with him into privacy.[2] Ordinarily, however, a teacher is necessary to disperse the mist of empirically acquired knowledge from our eyes (*ἀχλὺν δ'αὖ τοι ἀπ' ὀφθαλμῶν ἕλον, ἣ πρὶν ἐπῆεν,*—as Schopenhauer represents the spirit of Kant saying to him in the words of Homer), and of this in particular the beautiful passage in Chând. 6. 14 treats:—"Precisely, my dear sir, as a man who has been brought blindfold from the country of Gandhâra (beyond the Indus), and then set at liberty in the desert, goes astray to the east or north or south, because he has been brought thither blindfold, and blindfold set at liberty; but after that someone has taken off the bandage, and has told him,

[1] *Tauchervogel*, "divers."

[2] Brih. 3. 2. 13.

'In this direction Gandhâra lies, go in this direction,' instructed and prudent, asking the road from village to village, he finds his way home to Gandhâra; even so the man, who in this world has met with a teacher, becomes conscious, 'To this (transitory world) shall I belong only until the time of my release, thereupon shall I go home.'" The teacher is represented as indispensable to knowledge in Kâṭh. 2. 8:—"Apart from the teacher there is no access here"; from which the incidental conclusion may be drawn, that at the time of the Kâṭh. Upan. the older Upanishads were not yet committed to writing.

The later Vedânta mentions, side by side with the external (*vâhya*) means to a knowledge of Brahman (study of the Veda, sacrifice, almsgiving, penance, fasting), as more direct (*pratyâsanna*) means the following: tranquillity of mind, self-restraint, renunciation, patience, collectedness.[1] This requirement may be traced back to Bṛih. 4. 4. 23:—"Therefore he who knows this is tranquil, self-restrained, self-denying, patient, and collected." It is true that a doubt arises whether this passage has reference to the means of acquiring the knowledge of Brahman, or rather to the fruits of that knowledge (whether *bhûtvâ* here signifies "after that he has become," or "since he is"). By the later Upanishads it is understood already, as later still by S'ankara, in the first sense, *e.g.* Kâṭh. 2. 24:—"No one who has not ceased from violence, who is restless, unsubdued, whose heart is not yet tranquil, can by searching attain unto him." The expressions here used, *avirata, as'ânta, asamâhita*, refer back unquestionably to the *s'ânto, dânta', uparatas, titikshuḥ, samâhito bhûtvâ* of the passage from the Bṛihadâraṇyaka. The same is true also of *pras'ântac'ittâya, s'amânvitâya*, declared in Muṇḍ. 1. 2. 13 to be presuppositions of instruction.

[1] Cp. also Vedântasâra 17–23.

In later Upanishads this preliminary requirement is connected with the demand already referred to for a teacher. *E.g.* S'vet. 6. 22 :—" Impart it to no one, who is not tranquil (*na apras'ântâya*), who is not a son or a pupil (*na aputrâya as'ishyâya vâ*)." Similarly, and perhaps with a reminiscence of this passage, in Maitr. 6. 29 :—" This profoundest mystery of all is to be revealed to no one, who is not a son or a pupil (*na aputrâya, na as'ishyâya*), and who has not yet become tranquil (*na as'ântâya*)."

The finding a teacher, and the five requirements of tranquillity of mind, self-restraint, renunciation, patience, collectedness, are the preliminary conditions that continually recur. With them others are occasionally mentioned; for example, in Chând. 7. 26. 2, purity of food, and as a consequence purity of nature (*sattva-s'uddhi*). The latter, like so much besides from Chând. 7, is reproduced in Muṇḍ. 3 in the verse 3. 2. 6, and thence passed over into Mahânâr. 10. 22 and Kaivalya 3–4. In Kâṭh. 6. 9 an indefinite requirement is laid down, that a man should be " prepared in heart and feeling and spirit"; and in Muṇḍ. 3. 2. 10–11 participation in the Brahmavidyâ is combined with the preliminary condition of the fulfilment of the " vow of the head" (*s'irovratam*), by which is probably to be understood, not as S'ankara *s'irasi agnidhâraṇam*, but merely the practice, which is already implied in the name Muṇḍaka, of shaving the head bare. In still later Upanishads also we occasionally meet with special limitations on this participation. Thus Nṛisiṁhap. 1. 3 prohibits the communication of the maxims of the members (not the king of the maxims[1]) to a woman or a S'ûdra, and Râmap. 84 enjoins that the diagram must not be imparted to common (illiterate, *prâkṛita*) men.

[1] *Mantrarâja, i.e.* the charm or magical song.

6. *The Standpoint of Ignorance, of Knowledge, and of superior Knowledge in relation to Brahman*

The general view that lies at the basis of the Upanishads is that Brahman, *i.e.* the âtman, is an object of knowledge. "The âtman, in truth, should be seen, heard, comprehended, reflected upon."[1] "The Self . . . that should we search for and endeavour to know."[2] To the same effect are numerous other passages. And the aim of all the Upanishad texts is to communicate this knowledge of Brahman.[3]

Very soon, however, it came to be realised that this knowledge of Brahman was essentially of a different nature from that which we call "knowledge" in ordinary life. For it would be possible, like Nârada in Chând. 7. 1. 2, to be familiar with all conceivable branches of knowledge and empirical science, and yet to find oneself in a condition of ignorance (*avidyâ*) as regards the Brahman. This thought, originally purely negative, became in course of time more and more positive in its character. It was negative in so far as no experimental knowledge led to a knowledge of Brahman; and it was positive in so far as the consciousness was aroused that the knowledge of empirical reality was an actual hindrance to the knowledge of Brahman. The conception of *avidyâ* was developed from the negative idea of mere ignorance to the positive idea of false knowledge. The experimental knowledge which reveals to us a world of plurality, where in reality only Brahman exists, and a body where in reality there is only the soul, must be a mistaken knowledge, a delusion, a *mâyâ*. This is a very noteworthy step in advance. It is the same which Parmenides and Plato took when they affirmed that the knowledge of the world of sense was mere deception, εἴδωλα;

[1] Bṛih. 2. 4. 5. [2] Chând. 8. 7. 1. [3] *brahmavidyâ, âtmavidyâ.*

which Kant took, when he showed that the entire reality of experience is only apparition and not reality ("thing in itself"). It is of the greatest interest to follow up the earliest foreshadowings of this thought in India, and to trace how the term *avidyâ* passed from the negative idea of ignorance to the positive idea of a false knowledge.

The first suggestion of this is found already in the Ṛigveda, where in X. 81. 1 it is said of the great All-father that he, when he entered into the lower world, was *prathamac'had*, "veiling his original nature."[1] Further, an obscure passage of the S'atapatha Brâhmaṇa[2] describes how Brahman, when creating the upper and the lower worlds together with their gods, "revealed" himself, how he projected himself into them by means of his two "great immensities" (*abhva*), his two "great appearances" (*yaksha*), that is to say by means of his names and forms, but how he himself "entered into the half beyond" (*parârdham agac'c'hat*).

The further development of these thoughts is found in the Upanishads. In Bṛih. 1. 6. 3 the world of names, forms, and works is defined (by means of one of those brief mystical formulæ, of which perhaps the most ancient "Upanishads" consisted, *sup.* p. 16 f.) as *amṛitam satyena c'hannam*, "the immortal (Brahman) veiled by the (empirical) reality." The explanation of the formula is added immediately :—"The Prâṇa (*i.e.* the âtman) to wit is the immortal, name and form are the reality ; by these the Prâṇa is veiled." As here (and in Taitt. 2. 6,—"as reality he becomes everything that exists ; for reality is the name given to it"), so also in Bṛih. 2. 1. 20 the word *satyam* denotes the reality of experience ; in this latter passage it is said in another "Upanishad" with an added explanation :—"Its Upanishad is 'the reality of reality,'

[1] *mukhyam, nishprapanc'am, pâramârthikam rûpam âvṛiṇvan*, Sâyaṇa.
[2] 11. 2. 3.

(*satyasya satyam*); that is to say, the vital spirits (together with the worlds, gods, and living creatures, as we may infer from that which precedes) are the reality, and he is their reality." He is—so we are to understand—in the so-called reality that part of it which is actually real. This is also the meaning of the illustrations in Bṛih. 2. 4. 7–9: the âtman is the musical instrument (drum, conch, lyre), the phenomena of the universe are its notes; just as the notes can only be seized when the instrument is seized, so the world of plurality can only be known when the âtman is known; only of him is there knowledge, all else is "not knowledge." Similarly Chând. 6. 1. 3 teaches that the "transformation" of the âtman into the manifold world of phenomena is only *vâc'ârambhaṇam*, "a matter of words," or *nâmadheyam*, "a mere name," and that "in reality" there exists only the One Being, *i.e.* the Âtman. It is only of him therefore that a real knowledge is possible. All experimental knowledge, the four Vedas and the whole series of empirical sciences, as they are enumerated in Chând. 7. 1. 2–3, are, as is there said, *nâma eva*, "mere name"; and Nârada, deeply versed as he is in them, finds himself in "darkness," from which first by the knowledge of the âtman is he guided across to the other shore.[1] Souls and the "real desires" by which they are affected for continued life after death in the world of Brahman are, as expounded in Chând. 8. 3. 1–2, by the empirical knowledge which teaches annihilation at death "veiled in unreality. They really exist, but unreality is spread over them." And "just as he who is ignorant of its hiding-place fails to find the golden treasure, though he pass and repass it continually, so all these creatures fail to find this world of Brahman though they daily enter into it; for by unreality are they turned aside."

[1] Chând. 7. 26. 2.

What is here described as empty word, mere name, darkness, unreality, *i.e.* the entire empirical knowledge of things, is further denoted by *avidyâ*, "ignorance." This term occurs perhaps for the first time in Bṛih. 4. 4. 3, 4, where it is said of the soul, when it casts off the body in death, that it "dismisses ignorance" (*avidyâm gamayitvâ*). Ignorance is henceforth the knowledge that rests on experience; true knowledge is only of Brahman. Like Plato's teaching that only the eternal is an object of ἐπιστήμη, while of the world of phenomena subject to the flux of Heraclitus only a δόξα is possible, in S'vet. 5. 1 the explanation is given:—"Ignorance is the fleeting, knowledge is the eternal,"[1] *i.e.* it is an object of knowledge. Kâṭh. 2. 1–6 contrasts ignorance and knowledge with poetic vividness; the goal of ignorance is pleasure (*preyas*), the goal of knowledge is salvation (*s'reyas*). The former says, "this is the world" (*ayam loko*); the gaze of the latter is directed on another world:—

Widely different indeed and contrasted are the things
Which men call knowledge and ignorance,
I see Nac'iketas endeavouring to gain knowledge;
The troop of pleasures has not deluded thee.

Wandering in the depth of ignorance,
Deeming themselves wise and learned,
Thus aimlessly fools tramp hither and thither,
Like blind men led by comrades blind as they.

The last verse is further amplified in Muṇḍ. 1. 2. 8–10; and both verses are quoted in Maitr. 7. 9. The subject is similarly treated in the verses Bṛih. 4. 4. 11–12, which are a later insertion (cp. Kâṭh. 1. 3):—

These worlds indeed are joyless,
Shrouded in thick darkness;
Into them after death all go
Who are unenlightened and ignorant.

---

[1] *ksharam tu avidyâ hi amṛitam tu vidyâ.*

Yet he who perceives the âtman,
And is conscious that "I am he";
What desire what love could he still have
For the body racked with pain!

The infatuation of ignorance is yet more strongly depicted in Îs'â 3:—

This universe indeed is demon-haunted,
Shrouded in thick darkness,
Therein go to death all
Who have slain their own souls.

Since the knowledge of the âtman is contrasted with the reality of experience as the realm of ignorance, it cannot be gained by mere speculation (*tarka*) concerning it, but only by a revelation communicated through the teacher.[1] According as the âtman is conceived as a divine person, this revelation is represented as an act of his grace:[2]—

Not through instruction is the âtman won,
Not through genius or much book-learning;
Only by the man whom he chooses is he comprehended:
To him the âtman reveals his essence.

Another verse,[3] which in all probability originally promised the vision of the âtman concealed in the heart to him who "by pacifying the organs of sense"[4] has become "indifferent" (*akratu*), has received a theistic colouring in S'vet. 3. 20 and Mahânâr. 10. 1, in that it represents the knowledge of the âtman (whose abode is here also still in the heart) as received "by the favour of the creator."[5] A still more pronounced theism, that has wandered far from the original conceptions of the doctrine of the âtman, is exhibited by the entire S'vetas'vatara Upanishad, and

[1] Kâṭh. 2. 7–9. [2] Kâṭh. 2. 23, repeated in Muṇḍ. 3. 2. 3.
[3] Kâṭh. 2. 20, as read by S'ankara.
[4] *dhâtu-prasâdâd*; cp. Chând. 6. 15, *âtmani sarvendriyâṇi sampratishṭhâpya.*
[5] *dhâtuḥ prasâdâd.*

especially by the prayers for spiritual enlightenment to Savitar, Rudra, and Brahman which are interwoven with it in 2. 1–5, 3. 1–6, 4. 1.

The doctrine thus far set forth, according to which Brahman or the âtman becomes known by virtue of a (metaphysical) knowledge, is transcended within the limits of the Upanishads themselves by another and undeniably more profound conception, according to which there neither is nor can be a knowledge of the âtman as the sole all-pervading essence of things. For such knowledge assumes a knowing subject and a known object, and therefore a dualism; the âtman, however, forms an absolute unity. We propose briefly to trace the development of this thought under the guidance of the texts.

The primitive source of the entire conception of the unknowableness of the âtman is to be found in the speeches of Yâjñavalkhya in the Bṛihadâraṇyaka; and the daring and abruptness with which the doctrine is here introduced, as well as the originality of the method by which it is established, seem to point to an individual as its author. In his discourse with Maitreyî Yâjñavalkhya propounds, in Bṛih. 2. 4. 12, the paradoxical assertion,—"after death there is no consciousness"; and proceeds to confirm it with the words:—"For where there is as it were a duality (in reality there is not), there one sees the other, smells, hears, addresses, comprehends, and knows the other; but where everything has become to him his own self, how should he smell, see, hear, address, understand, or know anyone at all? How should he know him, through whom he knows all this, how should he know the knower?" On careful consideration two thoughts will be found to be implied here: (1) the supreme âtman is unknowable, because he is the all-comprehending unity, whereas all knowledge presupposes a duality of subject and object; but (2) the individual âtman also ("through whom he knows all this") is unknowable, because in all knowledge he is the knowing subject ("the knower"), consequently can never be object. Essentially these two thoughts are one; for the individual âtman is the supreme âtman, and in proportion as we rise to this knowledge the illusion of the object vanishes, and the knowing subject alone remains without object; and this subject, alike in its waking hours and in dreams, fashions the objects outside of itself,—"for he is the creator."[1] The same thought is found in five other passages in the speeches of Yâjñavalkhya, and these we quote partly abridged:—"Thou canst not see the seer of seeing, thou canst not hear the hearer of hearing, thou canst not comprehend the comprehender of comprehending, thou canst not know the knower of knowing."[2] "In truth, O Gârgî, this imperishable one sees but is not seen, hears but is not heard, comprehends but is not comprehended, knows but is not known. Beside him there is no seer, beside him there is no hearer, beside him there is none that comprehends, beside him there is none that knows."[3] The same words recur almost unaltered in Bṛih. 3. 7. 23 at the close of a paragraph, and on this account the association of the thread of the universe with the inner guide appears to be less primitive. In Bṛih. 4. 3. 23–31 it is said of the deep sleeper:—"When then he does not see, yet still he is seeing, although he sees not; since for the seer there is no interruption of seeing, because he is imperishable; but there is no second beside him, no other distinct from him, for him to see." The same is then repeated of smell, taste, speech, hearing, thought, sensation, and knowledge. "For (only) where there is as it were another is the other seen, smelt, tasted, addressed, heard, conceived, felt, and known." And in Bṛih. 4. 4. 2, of the dying it is said:—"Because he has

[1] Bṛih. 4. 3. 10. [2] Bṛih. 3. 4. 2. [3] Bṛih. 3. 8. 11.

become one, therefore he sees not as they say (in reality he continues ever seeing), because he has become one, therefore he does not smell, taste, address, hear, conceive, feel, or know the other, as they say."

If we consider the originality, the close reasoning, and (as we shall see later) the agreement of the thoughts in the passages quoted with the other views of Yâjñavalkhya, we shall be led to regard as very probable the dependence of all the passages that remain to be quoted, and therefore of the entire further development of the doctrine of the unknowableness of the âtman, on the thoughts, perhaps even on the text of the Bṛihadâraṇyaka. The two passages from the Chândogya, which we have now to cite, may be regarded as early examples:—"His relations seat themselves around the dying man, and ask him, 'Do you recognise me; do you recognise me?' As long as his speech has not yet entered into the manas, his manas into the prâṇa, his prâṇa into the heat, the heat into the supreme godhead, he recognises them. But after that his speech has entered into the manas, his manas into the prâṇa, his prâṇa into the heat, the heat into the supreme godhead, then he no longer recognises them."[1] This passage, self-contained as it is, nevertheless appears in its leading ideas to be dependent already on the last-named passage of the Bṛih. 4. 4. 2, since the reverse relation is not in any case admissible. In Chând. 6. 9 and 6. 10 also the doctrine of unconsciousness on entrance into the Existent, set forth in the illustrations of the bees and the rivers, seems to be indebted to the passage first adduced from Bṛih. 2. 4. 12:—"After death there is no consciousness." And similarly the following words in Bṛih. 2. 4. 14 are echoed in Chând. 7. 24. 1:—"If a man sees no other (beside himself), hears no other, knows no other, that is the infinite (*bhûman*); if he sees, hears,

[1] Chând. 6. 15. 1–2; cp. 6. 8. 6.

knows another, that is the finite (*alpam*). The infinite is the immortal, the finite is mortal." The suddenness and disconnectedness with which this idea is introduced seems to indicate dependence on the thoughts of Yâjña-valkhya.

It is primarily due to the influence of this conception that, later on, in opposition to the general tendency of the Upanishads to seek after and to expound the knowledge of the âtman, the theory is more and more elaborated that the âtman (whose unknowableness, as we shall see subsequently, had been already so strongly emphasised by Yâjña-valkhya with his *neti neti*) is no true object of knowledge. That knowledge of the âtman, which sets it as an object over-against itself, and which therefore is still infected with duality, now appears as a lower standpoint, which must be transcended in order to attain to complete oneness with Brahman, with the âtman.

This view is set forth for the first time clearly in the magnificently elaborated description of the universe in Taitt. 2. The author of this text begins with the incorporation of the âtman in the material world and the human body, as the self dependent on nourishment. From this as mere external covering he advances, penetrating deeper and deeper into the kernel of the living being as it here presents itself, to the self of life, of mind, and finally of knowledge, *i.e.* the *vijñânamaya âtman.* This last, however, to which Brahman is an object of knowledge, is also a mere outer covering of the self composed of bliss, which realises its oneness with Brahman. At this point the question is propounded :—

> Whether any ignorant man departing reaches yonder world?
> Or whether perchance the wise departing wins the other world?

Neither the one nor the other is in effect the answer conveyed by the following words, which describe how

Brahman in creating the universe enters into it as Being, expressible, self-dependent, consciousness, reality, while it in harmony with its own nature persists as the Opposite, inexpressible, independent, unconsciousness, unreality. Bliss consists in the sense of oneness with the latter:—"For when a man finds his peace and resting-place in that invisible, unreal, inexpressible, unfathomable, then has he attained to peace.[1] If, however, a man admits therein an interval, a separation (or 'ever so small a separation' between himself as subject and the âtman as object), then his unrest continues; it is moreover the unrest of one who imagines himself wise (while making Brahman the object of knowledge)." For no language, no conception, is adequate to express Brahman:—

> Before whom words and thought recoil not finding him,
> Who knows the bliss of this Brahman,
> For him nothing excites terror any more.

If, however, Brahman cannot be reached by the way of knowledge, how can union with him be accomplished? This is the question with which the following texts are occupied. In Kena 3 a student propounds the question:—

> That to which no eye penetrates,
> Nor speech nor thought,
> Which remains unknown, and we see it not,
> How can instruction therein be given to us!

And the answer is suggested (Kena 3 and 11):—

> It is distinct from the intelligible,
> And yet it is not therefore unknown!—
> Thus have we from our forefathers
> Received in turn the instruction.
>
> Only he who knows it not knows it,
> Who knows it, he knows it not;
> Unknown is it by the wise,
> But by the ignorant known.

---

[1] *abhayam gato bhavati*, like Janaka, whom Yâjñavalkhya exhorts,—*abhayam vai Janaka prâpto 'si.* Bṛih. 4. 2. 4.

Our knowledge is addressed to the external world, but there is another way :—

> Outwards the Creator pierced the holes,
> Therefore men look outwards, not inwards ;
> The wise man right within saw the âtman,
> Fastened his gaze on himself, seeking the eternal.[1]

"Fastened his gaze on himself" is literally "turning round the eye"—*âvṛittac'akshus.*[2]

Here within us the reality of the âtman becomes an immediate certainty :[3]—

> Not by speech, not by thought,
> Not by sight is he comprehended ;
> "He is !" by this word is he comprehended,
> And in no other way.
>
> "He is !" thus may he be apprehended,
> In so far as he is the essence of both ;
> "He is !" to the man who has thus apprehended him,
> His essential nature becomes manifest.

The polemic against knowledge grows in intensity. Thus in a verse inserted later in Bṛih. 4. 4. 10 :—

> In dense darkness they move,
> Who bow the knee to ignorance ;
> In yet denser they
> Who are satisfied with knowledge.

This verse is repeated and further amplified in Îs'â 9–11 (in dependence on Kena 3) :—

> Other than that to which knowledge leadeth
> Is that to which leadeth ignorance !
> Thus have we received the teaching from our forefathers.
>
> He who recognises both wisdom and ignorance (as insufficient),
> He through both overpasses death and wins immortality.

With this is connected the demand for the suppression of the perceptions of the senses which trick us with a

[1] Kâṭh. 4. 1.
[2] cp. Jacob Böhme's "averted eye."
[3] Kâṭh. 6. 12, 13.

false knowledge. As early as Bṛih. 1. 5. 23 the injunction is given :—"Therefore must one vow only be observed; suppressing the activities of the other organs of sense, a man must inspire and exspire." Chând. 8. 15 demands that a man "reduce all his organs to inactivity in the âtman." Muṇḍaka 3. 1. 8 craves for *jñânaprasâda*, "cessation of knowledge," and in 3. 2. 7 together with works represents the *vijñânamaya âtman*[1] also as becoming one with the supreme eternal. And Maitr. 6. 19 directs that the consciousness, together with the subtle body (*liṅgam*) that sustains it, should be immersed in the unknown :—

That which abides in consciousness
Unknown, beyond conception, wrapped in mystery,
In that do thou immerse consciousness
And the liṅgam, bereft of its foundation.

All these requirements are part of the *Yoga* system, of which we shall learn to know more later as a Praxis, by which it is hoped to effect that metaphysical union with the âtman by artificial means.

II. The Search for Brahman

1. *The Âtman (Brahman) as the Unity*

As early as the times of the Ṛigveda a perception of unity had been reached, to which expression was given in hymns like Ṛigv. I. 164, X. 129. After this, however, there remained the further task of defining more closely the eternal unity which underlies all the phenomena of nature. Of such inquiry the hymn Ṛigv. X. 121 is the chief example, which, to the nine times repeated question, "Who is the god to whom we are to offer sacrifice?" in the tenth verse gives the answer: "*Prajâpati!* It is thou and no other, who holdest in thy embrace all that has

[1] Taitt. 2. 4.

come to be." We have already traced in detail[1] how this search was prosecuted through the period of the Brâhmaṇas, how Prajâpati was gradually displaced by Brahman, and how finally the most definite expression for the object of man's search was found in the conception of the âtman. Âtman is the Indian expression for that which we are accustomed to call "first principle," and is distinguished from the latter only by its defining in a clearer and more striking manner than any Western equivalent the one eternal problem of all philosophical research; for it invites us to lay hold of the individual self of man, the self of the universe, and to strip off from man and from nature everything which does not approve itself as this self, as the peculiar, most profound, and ultimate essence of things. At the same time, the less definite *Brahman* is often enough employed to express the first principle. This is the case in the passages to be discussed immediately, Bṛih. 2. 1. 1 (Kaush. 4. 1), Bṛih. 4. 1. 2–7, Chând. 5. 11. 1. Similarly S'vet. 1. 1 opens with the question,—"What is the first beginning, what is Brahman?"—and according to Pras'na 1. 1 and in the Ârsheya Upanishad, wise men come together in order to search for "Brahman."

The terms Brahman and âtman both denote, therefore, the first principle of the universe, and in this sense are ordinarily employed in the Upanishads as synonymous, and are interchanged with one another in the same text or stand side by side, as in the question proposed in Chând. 5. 11. 1:—*ko na' âtmâ, kiṁ brahma?* where S'ankara remarks that Brahman denotes the term to be defined, *vis'eshyam*, and âtman that which defines it, *vis'eshaṇam*, (which is true in general, if not precisely so here), that by *Brahman* the limitation implied in âtman is removed, and by âtman the conception of Brahman as a

[1] *Einleitung und Philosophie des Veda*, p. 132 f.

divinity to be worshipped is condemned. Both expressions however are, as this remark already shows, of indefinite connotation. The conception of Brahman is very complex, and the conception of the âtman is a negative and relative idea, which declares to us rather wherein the essence of man and of the universe is not to be sought, than affords us any positive information as to its real nature. Precisely in this its philosophical value consists. For the essence of things remains, as far as its nature is concerned, eternally unknown; and every attempt to make it an object of knowledge compels us to impose upon it definitions which are borrowed from that sphere of experimental knowledge that alone is accessible to our intelligence, and these again do not penetrate to the essential reality of things. From this realistic tendency the many false or imperfect attempts to explain Brahman and the âtman arise, which are rejected by the teachers of the Upanishads themselves, and which we have now to discuss.

2. *Bâlâki's Attempts at Explanation*

According to a narrative preserved in a twofold recension, in Bṛih. 2. 1 and Kaush. 4, the learned, famous, and proud Brâhman Bâlâki Gârgya approached the king Ajâtas'atru with the offer:—"Allow me to explain to you the Brahman." He then endeavours twelve times in succession (in Kaush. sixteen times) to define the Brahman as the soul (*purusha*) in the sun, moon, lightning, ether, wind, fire, water, etc.; and in each case the king confutes his definition by pointing to the subordinate position which the corresponding purusha occupies in the whole of nature. The Brâhman is silenced, and the king proceeds to instruct him, using the illustration of a deep sleeper. That in which his vital breaths (*prâṇâḥ*) lie dormant, and from which they issue on his waking, and with them all worlds, gods, and living creatures, is the âtman. This is the Brahman that Gârgya undertook in vain to explain. The reader's expectation of a more precise account of the relation of Brahman to the purushas of Gârgya is not fulfilled in either recension. They both are satisfied to show how on waking the prâṇas (speech, eye, ear, manas) proceed from the âtman, and as being dependent on them all worlds, gods, and living creatures.

3. *S'âkalya's Attempts at Explanation*

In a similar way, in Bṛih. 3. 9. 10–17, 26, Vidagdha S'âkalya attempts to define Brahman as forming the climax of all that the word âtman denotes (*sarvasya âtmanaḥ parâyaṇam*). After, however, having eight times in succession propounded a one-sided view that represents the earth, love, forms, ether, etc., as its basis, he is corrected by Yâjñavalkhya, who points out to him that that which he explains as the climax of all the word âtman denotes (*sarvasya âtmanaḥ parâyaṇam yam âttha*) is, on the contrary, only a subordinate purusha that rules in the bodily forms, in love, the sun, sound, etc. "He however," Yâjñavalkhya proceeds in Bṛih. 3. 9. 26, "who oversteps these purushas (is superior to them), separating them one from another and turning them back (*i.e.* inciting them to activity and recalling them), this is the purusha of the Upanishad doctrine concerning which I ask thee." S'âkalya is unable to name it, and for the error of having passed off a subordinate purusha as *sarvasya âtmanaḥ parâyaṇam* must atone by his death.[1]

[1] This is the meaning of the passage as I propose to assign the dialogue. The traditional view, which is less satisfactory, represents Yâjñavalkhya as raising the question with regard to *sarvasya âtmanaḥ parâyaṇam*, and indicating as its basis, earth, love, forms, ether, etc.; and the error of S'âkalya would then consist in his naming in answer not the âtman that Yâjñavalkhya expects in answer, but only a subordinate purusha that rules in the bodily forms, in love, the sun, sound, etc.

4. *Six Inadequate Definitions*

Precisely as in Bṛih. 2. 1 twelve defective (*ekapâd*) definitions of Brahman are criticised, in Kaush. 4 sixteen, and in Bṛih. 3. 9. 10–17 eight, so in Bṛih. 4. 1 there are six; and here Janaka approaches Yâjñavalkhya after having fortified his soul with mystic doctrines, *upanishads*, as the traveller provisions his ship or waggon.[1] These "*upanishads*" consist in six definitions of Brahman enunciated by other teachers, as speech, breath, eye, ear, manas, and heart. All these definitions may still be found in the extant texts, if not always exactly under the names assigned. For instance, for *vâg vai brahma* see Pañc'av. Br. 20. 14. 2, Chând. 7. 2. 2; for *prâṇo vai brahma*, Bṛih. 1. 5. 23, 3. 7. 1–2, Chând. 4. 3. 3, 7. 15, Taitt. 3. 3, Kaush. 2. 1, 2, 2. 13, Pras'na 2. 13; *c'akshur vai brahma*, Chând. 1. 7. 4, 4. 15. 1, 8. 7. 4, Kaush. 4. 17, 18, Bṛih. 2. 3. 5, 5. 5. 4; *s'rotram vai brahma*, Taitt. 3. 1, Kaush. 4. 14; *mano vai brahma*, Chând. 3. 18. 1, Ait. 3. 2; *hṛidayam vai brahma*, Chând. 3. 12. 4, 8. 3. 3, Bṛih. 5. 3; cp. also in general Chând. 3. 18, where *vâc'*, *prâṇa*, *c'akshuḥ*, *s'rotram* form the four feet of Brahman, and Chând. 4. 8. 3, where *prâṇa*, *c'akshuḥ*, *s'rotram*, *manas* are one of his four feet. These and all similar definitions, whether they are historical or only invented to give colour to historical tendencies, arise from the endeavour to know that which is essentially unknowable; for which purpose no resource is open but to conceive it with conscious or unconscious symbolism under the form of some one of its phenomenal appearances. The criticism to which Yâjñavalkhya subjects these six definitions of Brahman as *vâc'*, *prâṇa*, *c'akshus*, *s'rotram*, *manas*, and *hṛidayam* consists in explaining them as mere "supports" (*âyatana*), by means of which six corresponding attributes

[1] Bṛih. 4. 2. 1.

that are assumed to belong to the divine Being as *prajñâ*, *priyam*, *satyam*, *ananta*, *ânanda*, *sthiti*, manifest themselves in the space which is common to all six as basis (*pratishṭha*). If, however, we seek to ascertain further the nature of these six attributes, we are referred back again to their six manifestations in space as *vâc'*, *prâṇa*, *c'akshus*, *s'rotram*, *manas*, *hṛidayam*. And so, thrown backwards and forwards between the phenomenal forms of experience, and the empirical attributes of the divine Being which find expression in them, we learn that phenomena can only be explained by phenomena, and that it is not in this way that we can arrive at a knowledge of the nature of the Godhead. Yâjñavalkhya accordingly himself adopts another way,[1] and, starting from the question what becomes of the soul after death, first of all sketches a picture of the individual soul as it dwells in the heart encompassed and nourished by the veins, and extends its feelers, as it were, in the two eyes; then suddenly draws aside, like a veil that hides it, this entire individual soul, so that before and around and in us we see only the one omnipresent supreme soul. And thus the question concerning the future existence of the individual receives its answer in that it is deprived of all justification, and falls to the ground meaningless. Nor have we even to-day any better reply to give.

5. *Definitions of the Âtman Vais'vânara*

Owing to the ambiguity of the word the conception of the âtman, like that of Brahman, gives rise to several misunderstandings. One of these was due to the fact that beyond the cosmical meaning of the âtman as first principle of the universe there was discerned its psychical meaning, the embodiment of this principle in the self. It is thus with the five Brâhmans, who in

[1] Bṛih. 4. 2.

Chând. 5. 11 meet and propound the question :—"What is our âtman, what is Brahman?" They betake themselves with this question to Uddâlaka Âruṇi, who they know is even now engaged in studying the *Âtman Vais'vânara*, *i.e.* the âtman as the all-pervading first principle of the universe. Uddâlaka mistrusts (rightly, as his later answer proves) his ability to satisfy them, and all six proceed according to king As'vapati Kaikeya for instruction concerning the *Âtman Vais'vânara*. The king first asks the six Brâhmans in succession what it is that they "worship" as the âtman. He assumes, as this expression shows, that the Brâhmans who apply to him for instruction are still entangled in the error of regarding the âtman as an object of worship existing outside of themselves, like a new kind of divinity. This assumption is confirmed, inasmuch as the six inquirers explain the âtman in succession as the heaven, the sun, the wind, space, water, and the earth, therefore as something objective. The king rejoins :—"You all, to judge from your answers, conceive of this *Âtman Vais'vânara* as though it were something separate from yourselves, and thus you consume your food. He however who worships this *Âtman Vais'vânara* thus (placing his outstretched hand on his head from the forehead to the chin) as a span long (*prâdes'amâtram abhivimânam*), he consumes the food in all worlds, in all beings, in all selves. And of this very *Âtman Vais'vânara* (measured on the head as a span long) the bright (heaven) is the head, the all-pervading (sun) is the eye, the (wind) on its lonely path is the breath, manifold (space) is its trunk, its bodily frame, riches (water) its bladder, the earth its feet." The suggested movement of the hands, without which the passage is unintelligible, may with certainty be inferred from the original of our text in S'atap. Br. 10. 6. 1, where they are actually made. In other respects also the original passage referred to possesses several advantages, especially in its discussion not of the *Âtman Vais'vânara*, but of a symbolical interpretation of *Agni Vais'vânara*, "the all-pervading fire," as a first principle of the universe. In this light the defective answers of the six interlocutors are far more intelligible than if they inquire, in the first instance, as is the case in the secondary representation of the Chândogya, concerning the âtman as "Brahman" (first principle). The question in this form and the inquiry for the *Âtman Vais'vânara* would, strictly speaking, exclude from the very beginning such erroneous answers as were given by all six Brâhmans.

6. *Gradual Instruction of Nârada*

It is not always opponents or pupils who betray their entanglement in incorrect or defective conceptions of Brahman. We repeatedly meet with a Brâhman inquirer who, like Sanatkumâra in Chând. 7 or Bhṛigu in Taitt. 3, makes his way through a succession of inadequate conceptions in order step by step to rise to an ever purer and more refined knowledge of the Brahman or âtman. The most complete example of this kind is Chând. 7, where Sanatkumâra begins his instruction of Nârada by declaring the whole of the experimental knowledge that he has acquired to be mere name. Speech is greater than name, manas greater than speech, and in this way the inquirer, ever advancing, is led upwards from the conditioned to the conditioning, from great to greater by successive stages, in which Brahman is apprehended as *nâman, vâc', manas, saṅkalpa, c'ittam, dhyânam, vijñânam, balam, annam, âpas, tejas, âkâs'a, smara, âs'â* up to *prâṇa* (the individual soul); and from this last to *bhûman*, the absolutely "great," the "unlimited," beyond which there is nothing, that comprehends all, fills all space, and yet is identical with the self-consciousness (*ahaṅkâra*), with the soul (*âtman*) in us. The greatness of this final thought impresses us as in strange contrast to the laborious series of conceptions by which we ascend to it. It was probably intended for more patient readers than are to be found at the close of the nineteenth century, and was evidently meant, by passing from the visibly great to a still greater, to serve the purpose of exciting expectation to the highest pitch. Otherwise, in this transition from name to speech, from this to the intellectual faculties (mind, judgement, thought, intuition, knowledge), from these through the intermediary of force to the four elements (food, water, heat, space), and from these through memory and expectation to prâṇa, it is impossible, in spite of the rich poetic ornament with which these ideas are set forth, to discern a satisfactory reason for this progressive advance; and the question is perhaps justified, whether the author himself was entirely in earnest, or whether these ideas from name right up to prâṇa were not all more or less intended to serve as mere foil, in order to set in so much clearer light the absolute unconditioned and unlimited nature of the âtman, as lying above and beyond all thought. It is on other grounds remarkable that, in connection with all the members of the series that precede prâṇa, rich reward is promised to the man who "worships as Brahman" name, speech, mind, etc. The author therefore admits the possibility of "worshipping as Brahman" all these things, and in the case of many of them this may actually take place in a more or less consciously symbolic manner. For ordinary men, relying on their empirical consciousness as though on a rope, prefer to worship rather than to know. To such an end the absolute is naturally only with difficulty or not at all adapted. The use of symbols therefore for its expression is inevitable, and these in the hands of the multitude very readily become idols. The manner also is remarkable in which our author passes from *prâṇa*, the individual soul, for which the distinction of subject and object still exists, to *bhûman*, the supreme soul, for which these like all distinctions have no meaning. We seek, he says, the truth. This depends on knowledge, this again on thought, this on faith, this on self-concentration, this on productive power, this on pleasure (*sukham*, more usually *ânanda*, the so-called bliss), which exists in the unlimited, the *bhûman*. Gradually, therefore, from the sphere of the intellectual in which differences obtain, we are led upwards through an ever-increasing blending of subject and object to a region in which all distinctions are lost in the All-one.

7. *Three Different Âtmans*

The âtman is, as has often already been pointed out, an idea capable of very different interpretations. The word signifies no more than "the self," and the question then arises what we regard as our self. Three positions are here possible, according as by the âtman is understood (1) the corporeal self, the body; (2) the individual soul, free from the body, which as knowing subject is contrasted with and distinct from the object; or (3) the supreme soul, in which subject and object are no longer distinguished from one another, or which, according to the Indian conception, is the objectless knowing subject. The narrative in Chând. 8. 7–12 furnishes an illustration of these three positions. "The self (*âtman*), the sinless, free from old age, from death, and from suffering, delivered from hunger and thirst, whose wish is true, whose decree is true, that ought we to seek, that endeavour to know." Impelled by this craving, the god Indra and the demon Viroc'ana set off, and betake themselves to Prajâpati for instruction. His first lesson is as follows:—The self is that which is seen in looking into the eye of another, into a brook of water or a mirror, which is reflected again in an image complete even to hairs and nails, which decked with fair clothing appears fair, in a word, the body; "that is the self, that is the immortal, the fearless, that is Brahman." The answer satisfies both pupils, and they depart homewards; but Prajâpati looking after them says:—"So they depart, without having perceived or discovered the self." Viroc'ana and the demons rest content with this answer, and therefore all demon-like men, seeing the self in the body, deck the human frame with all kinds of finery, as though it were destined for a future life, a world beyond. Indra, on the contrary, reflecting that this self is exposed to all the sufferings and imperfections of the body, and perishes at death, feels (what everyone may feel) that no change which passes *over us* can affect *us*, and returns to Prajâpati. Prajâpati now communicates to him the second answer:—the self is that which roams about untrammelled in dreams; "that is the immortal, the fearless, that is Brahman." But even with this answer Indra cannot remain satisfied. The dream-self is not, it is true, affected by the injuries which the body experiences from objects, but yet it is virtually affected by them, seeing that it proceeds to create an objective world over-against itself. The third answer of Prajâpati now follows:—"When a man is so completely wrapped in slumber, has reached so perfect a rest, that he does not perceive any dream-image, —that is the self," thus he spake, "that is the immortal, the fearless, that is Brahman." A further objection on the part of Indra, that this amounts to entrance into a state of annihilation, Prajâpati removes by showing that the cessation of the distinction of subject and object, as this is attained in deep sleep, is rather an entrance into the fullest light, a personal identification with the supreme spirit, which as the knowing subject in us is unaffected by any change of organs or objects. The meaning of this narrative is clear. In response to the question, What is the self? three answers are possible, according as we adopt the standpoint of materialism, realism, or idealism. (1) The *material* (demoniac) answer runs,—the self is the body, and perishes with it. The theologians of the Vedânta understand even here the individual soul, and do violence to the text by transforming the man who "is seen" in the eye (mirroring himself) into one who "sees" in the eye, because otherwise Prajâpati "would have been a deceiver," since he says in fact even of this first self,—"that is the immortal," etc. Prajâpati, however, is here the representative of nature, which never speaks falsely, and yet shows itself in a certain sense double-faced, inasmuch as to the two most important questions which we can put, the question concerning freedom and the question concerning immortality, it gives to the ordinary empirical consciousness two answers, which appear to be in contradiction with one another. If we regard our actions, we see that they all necessarily proceed from their causes (character and motive) in harmony with the law of causality; and yet we bear within ourselves the invincible indestructible consciousness of freedom and responsibility for these actions. Similarly with the question of immortality. If we look without, we see our entire self entering into existence as body and perishing; and yet we are invincibly conscious within of the eternity of our being: *sentimus experimurque nos aeternos esse*, as Spinoza says. It is on this consciousness, and not on personal longings, that all proofs of the immortality of the soul depend. This consciousness it is which, clothed in empirical forms, (2) from the *realistic* standpoint exhibits the self as the individual soul, and to this the second answer of Prajâpati refers. Very beautiful is his illustration of this consciousness of a soul, free from the body and yet real and individual, by means of the dream-state, as being the only state of which we have experience, in which the soul may be observed bound by corporeal conditions but not under the limitations of individuality. This entire individual soul, however, is a false conception arising from the fact that we transfer the forms of our intellectual judgements, and especially the most general of them, the necessary existence of an object for a subject, into a region where they have no validity. From this point consciousness leads on (3) to the *idealistic* standpoint, which recognises only the one supreme soul, existing in everything, and embodied in each in its entirety. In it there is no duality, no subject and object, and consequently no consciousness in an empirical sense. Thus far it may be compared to a deep dreamless sleep. Later on we shall learn to recognise besides waking slumber and deep sleep a fourth (*turîya*) state of the soul, in which that unification, which ensues unconsciously in deep sleep, is to be realised in a consciousness which is perfect though not resting upon experience, or directed towards objects external to itself.

8. *Five different Âtmans*

As in the passage from the Chândogya discussed above three âtmans are distinguished, the corporeal individual and supreme, so a paragraph in Taitt. 2, which occupies a more advanced and developed position, assumes five âtmans (or purushas) by further division of the intermediate individual âtman into the principles of life, of will, and of knowledge. Thus are constituted the âtmans *annamaya*, *prâṇamaya*, *manomaya*, *vijñâna-maya*, and *ânandamaya*, which are manifested alike in mankind and in nature as a whole. The first four of these, like sheaths or husks (termed later *kos'as*), surround the fifth as the true kernel. Stripping off these sheaths one by one, and gradually penetrating deeper, we finally reach the inmost essential being of a man and of nature. (1) The *annamaya âtman*, "the self dependent on food," is the incarnation of the âtman in the human body and in material nature; the bodily organs are its constituent parts. (2) Within this is contained the *prâṇamaya âtman*, "the self dependent on the vital breath," the âtman as the principle of natural life. Its constituent parts are the vital breaths in man (inhalation, inter-halation, exhalation), but also in a cosmical sense the whole of space is its body, the earth its foundation. By stripping off this âtman also as a sheath we reach (3) the *manomaya âtman*, "the âtman dependent on manas" (volition), whose constituent parts are stated to be the four Vedas with the Brâhmaṇas (*âdes'a*). According to this definition we are to understand by it the principle of the will (*manas*) embodied both in men and in gods, *i.e.* of purpose directed to selfish ends. For it is this that on the human side is expressed in the Vedic sacrificial ritual. (4) Deeper still is found the *vijñânamaya âtman*, "the self dependent on knowledge," which, as the accompanying verse declares, offers knowledge in place of sacrifice and works, while recognising and worshipping the deity as a separate and independent being. This position also we must abandon like a sheath, in order finally to penetrate (5) to the *ânandamaya âtman*, "the self dependent on bliss," as the innermost kernel of man and of nature as a whole. This âtman dependent on bliss, "before whom words and thought recoil, not finding him," is no longer an object of knowledge. It is, in contrast with the reality of experience, that which lies beyond on the other side, unutterable, unfathomable, an unconsciousness, a not-reality. "For it is he who creates bliss. For when a man finds resting-place and peace in that invisible, unreal, unutterable, unfathomable one, then has he attained to peace. When, however, a man assumes therein an interval, a separation (between himself as subject and the âtman as object), then his unrest is prolonged. Moreover, it is the unrest of one who deems himself wise (while making Brahman an object of knowledge)." [1]

III. Symbolic Representations of Brahman

1. *Introduction and Classification*

By a symbol (σύμβολον) the ancient writers understood the visible sign of an invisible object or circumstance. The word itself may be derived from the piecing together (συμβάλλειν) of a broken ring or the like carried by guests, messengers, etc., as their authorisation, to the other half that has been laid by, or simply from the mutual understanding (συμβάλλειν) on which the recognition of this visible token depended. An illustration lying very near to hand for the conception of a symbol is furnished by the words which language uses. These are to be regarded collectively as the visible signs of the invisible ideas which they represent, and therefore Aristotle pertinently remarks:—τῶν δὲ ὀνομάτων ἕκαστον σύμβολόν ἐστιν: [2] and ἔστι μὲν οὖν τὰ ἐν τῇ φωνῇ τῶν ἐν τῇ ψυχῇ παθημάτων σύμβολα, καὶ τὰ γραφόμενα τῶν ἐν τῇ φωνῇ. [3] So also the Church calls its sacraments and doctrinal formulæ symbols. They are the external tokens of adhesion to its fellowship.

The Indian word for symbol, *pratîkam*, depends upon a similar conception. It denotes originally (from *prati-añc'*) the side "turned towards" us, and therefore visible, of an object in other respects invisible. In this sense the teachers of the Vedânta often speak of symbols (*pratîkâni*) of Brahman. They understand by the term definite representations of Brahman under some form perceptible by the senses, *e.g.* as name, speech, etc., [4] as *manas* and

[1] Taitt. 2. 7.

[2] De Sensu I. p. 437.

[3] De Interp. I. p. 16.

[4] Chând. 7.

âkâs'a,[1] as *âditya*,[2] as the fire of digestion,[3] or even as *om*,[4] which for the purpose of worship are regarded as Brahman, and are related to the latter as the images of the gods (*pratimâ*, *arc'â*) to the gods that they represent.[5] As early as Bâdarâyaṇa[6] the distinction is drawn between the worshippers of Brahman under such symbols and the worshippers of Brahman "endowed with attributes" (*saguṇa*). The latter possess a knowledge of Brahman, and pass accordingly by the *devayâna*, which leads to Brahman; while the worshippers of the symbol are by it hindered from discerning Brahman,[7] and hence they receive as fruit only the reward specified for each symbol.[8] In the sequel this distinction is not consistently maintained. The worship of Brahman by means of the syllable *om* leads, according to Pras'na 5. 5, by the *devayâna* to Brahman, and the worship of Brahman as prâṇa is usually assigned to that branch of knowledge which concerns itself with qualities, and only exceptionally[9] to the symbolical worships, to which, nevertheless, it belongs according to passages like Bṛih. 4. 1. 3 (*prâṇa* by the side of *vâc'*, *manas*, etc.), 2. 3. 4 (with *âkâs'a*), Chând. 3. 18. 4 (subordinated to *manas*, by the side of *vâc'*, etc.).

Nevertheless the definite conception of the symbol is wanting in the Upanishads, just as the word *pratîkam* in this sense is not there found. When, however, in the extracts discussed in the preceding chapter[10] certain concrete representations of Brahman are rejected as inadequate, though they are acknowledged to be

[1] Chând. 3. 18.
[2] Chând. 3. 19.
[3] Bṛih. 5. 9, Chând. 3. 13. 8.
[4] Chând. 1. 1.
[5] cp. S'ankara on Brahmasûtra, pp. 147. 14, 189. 8, 217. 10, 835. 9, 1059. 6; on Chândogya, pp. 9. 8, 10. 1, 21. 3.
[6] Sûtram 4. 3. 15–16, cp. 4. 1. 4.
[7] P. 1135. 7, *pratîka-pradhânatvâd upâsanasya.*
[8] *E.g.* Chând. 7. 1–14.
[9] *E.g.* on Brahmasûtra 4. 1, 5.
[10] Bṛih. 4. 1; Chând. 5. 12–17, 7. 1–14.

meritorious, as is shown by the promise of a reward, we are able, as is the case with so many doctrines of the later Vedânta, to trace in passages like those quoted the earliest rise of the conception of the symbol.

By symbol in a wider sense we understand all the representations conceived with a view to the worship of Brahman, himself incapable of representation, under some one of his phenomenal forms; and therefore especially as *prâṇa* and *vâyu*, as *âkâs'a*, *manas*, and *âditya*, as the fire of digestion and the syllable *om*. To the discussion of these symbols in the present chapter must further be added the symbolical interpretations of ritualistic conceptions, and finally the substitution for liturgical practices of others which are related to the âtman doctrine.

2. *Brahman as Prâṇa and Vâyu*

No natural phenomenon bears so ambiguous a character, none appears to be derived so immediately from the most intimate essence of things and so fully to reveal it, as the phenomenon of life, manifested in the activity of all the vital organs (*prâṇas*), but above all in the process of breathing (*prâṇa*) which determines the life itself. Hence as early as the Brâhmaṇa period the central significance of *prâṇa* (breath or life) was discussed together with its superiority to the other *prâṇas* (vital forces, as the eye, ear, speech, manas), and its identity with *Vâyu*, the god of the wind as the vital breath of the universe, was discussed. All these discussions are continued in the Upanishads, especially in the older texts, which yet are unable to apprehend the first principle of the universe otherwise than in its most obvious phenomenal forms; until the prâṇa, whether by a process of subordination or identification, retires more and more behind the âtman, and appears only as an occasional synonym for it.

That the body of all (organic) beings can be sustained

only as long as the *prâṇa* inhabits it, is taught in a passage frequently misunderstood, Chând. 1. 11. 5 :—*sarvâṇi ha vâ' imâni bhûtâni prâṇam eva abhisaṁvis'anti, prâṇam abhyujjihate.* This does not mean, as S'ankara and many with him explain it, that beings enter (at death) into *prâṇa*, and are thence born anew, but rather the contrary :—" All these creatures enter with the breath (into the body), and with the breath they again depart out." The best illustration is furnished by the metaphor Pras'na 2. 4, which contains possibly a reminiscence of our passage, and by Brahma Upanishad 1, which is dependent upon it. The illustration is employed, it is true, not of living beings, but of the individual organs in their relation to the *prâṇa*. " Just as the bees all follow the queen bee when she comes forth, and so long as she tarries all tarry, so also speech, manas, eye, and ear." The prâṇa is the fundamental and constant part of the sixteen of which man consists. In Bṛih. 1. 5. 14 this is illustrated in mythological language by the example of Prajâpati, who loses a sixteenth part each night with the waning of the moon :—" And after that at new moon he has entered with the sixteenth part into everything which has breath, thereupon is he born on the following morning (as the crescent of the new moon)." Here Prajâpati, after the loss of his fifteen changeable parts, continues to exist at the new moon with his sixteenth " unchangeable " (*dhruva*) part solely as *prâṇa* in all living beings. From a physiological point of view this thought is explained in Chând. 6. 7 ; man consists of sixteen parts, of which after a fifteen days' fast only one, the prâṇa, survives. An enumeration of these sixteen parts is undertaken in Pras'na 6. 3–4 :—" He (purusha) reflected, ' With the departure of what shall I myself depart, and with the remaining of what shall I remain ?' Accordingly he created the prâṇa " ; from which, as the passage goes on to declare, the fifteen other parts originate. Here, in harmony with the later date of the composition, the prâṇa is dependent on the purusha, *i.e.* the âtman, but is still at the same time its empirical representative. As such, as the *bhûman* brought within the circle of experience (in the distinction of subject and object), the prâṇa makes its appearance already in the beautiful description of Chând. 7. 15 :—"As the spokes are inserted into the nave of the wheel, so everything is inserted into this life (*prâṇa*). The life advances by the life (the breath), the life (breath) gives the life, it becomes the life. The life is father and mother, the life is brother and sister, the life is teacher and Brâhman. Therefore if a father or mother or brother or sister or teacher or Brâhman is used roughly, men say of you, Fie, you are a parricide, a matricide, a murderer of brother or sister, of teacher or Brâhman. Should he, however, strike even these with a spear, after the life has departed (on the funeral pyre) and they are burnt to the last hair, then it is not said, 'You are a parricide, a matricide, a murderer of brother or sister, of teacher or Brâhman'; for the life only is all this." The comparison that occurs here of the prâṇa to the nave of a wheel, in which all the spokes meet, is found again : (1) of the praṇa, in Pras'na 2. 6, in the hymn to the prâṇa here inserted, though derived from an earlier period, and which recalls not only Vâj. Saṁh. 34. 5, but also in many ways Atharvav. 11. 4; (2) of the prâṇa, which is already identified in the second place with Prajñâtman in Kaush. 3. 8 (for which is substituted, in Kaush. 4. 20, the figure of the chieftain and his people); (3) of the âtman, in Bṛih. 2. 5. 15, cp. 1. 5. 15 Muṇḍ. 2. 2. 6 Pras'na 6. 6, and interpreted in S'vet. 1. 4, in terms of Sâṅkhyan thought.

The superiority of the prâṇa to the other vital organs (eye, ear, speech, manas, etc.) is illustrated by the parable of the rivalry of the organs, which forms a favourite theme of the Upanishads. In order to test which of them is the most essential, the prâṇas (eye, ear, speech, etc.) one after another leave the body, which nevertheless still continues to exist; but when the prâṇa proposes to depart, they become conscious that none of them can exist without it. This narrative, known by the name of *prâṇasaṁvâda*, is found in Chând. 5. 1. 6–12, Bṛih. 6. 1. 7–13, Kaush. 2. 14, cp. 3. 3, Ait. Âr. 2. 1. 4, Pras′na 2. 2–4.[1] The most original form is preserved unquestionably in Chând. 5. 1. 6–12. The vital organs (only speech, eye, ear, and manas are mentioned besides prâṇa) come to Prajâpati, contending for precedence. His decision is given :—"That one amongst you, after whose departure the body finds itself in the worst condition, has the precedence among you." Thereupon in succession speech, eye, ear, and manas depart, without the body on that account ceasing to exist. "Thereupon the prâṇa proposed to go forth; but as a noble steed (if he breaks loose) tears away the foot-ropes that hold fast his feet, so he tore away with him the other vital breaths. Then they all came to him and said :—'Worthy sir, thou art he; thou hast the precedence over us, only go not forth.'" Bṛih. 6 1. 7–13 relates the story almost in the same words, but with the substitution of Brahman for Prajâpati, the addition of a sixth organ, and the further elaboration of the illustration of the steed. All these variations are in favour of the originality of the version of the Chândogya. Kaush. 3. 3 supplies only an argument which assumes the narrative in the form indicated. Kaush. 2. 14 represents all the organs as going forth together, but returning separately; on the return of the prâna the body revives. Here the motive for the united departure

[1] A further recension, according to Weber's statement, occurs in Kaush. Ar. 9. On Bṛih. 1. 5. 21, cp. also *infra*.

is wanting. Ait. Âr. 2. 1. 4 twice brings to a settlement the question which of the prâṇas is *uktham*, by the collapse of the body on the departure of the prâṇa, and again by its revival when the prâṇa returns. In this case an inferior impression is created both by the doubling of the proof of superiority, and by the application of the story to the glorification of the *uktham*. Pras'na 2. 2–4 represents the prâna indignant at the behaviour of the others preparing forthwith to depart, whereupon speech, manas, eye, and ear are carried away with it, and beg the prâṇa to remain. This is clearly an abbreviated form of the original narrative; what is new is only the substitution of the illustration of the queen bee for that of the steed. These relations are of interest, since they supply a foundation for the chronology of the corresponding texts.

Connected with this narrative of the dispute of the organs for precedence is another of the strife of the gods, *i.e.* the organs, against the demons. We limit ourselves to a comparison of the two chief recensions, Bṛih. 1. 3 and Chând. 1. 2.[1] Of these two, Bṛih. 1. 3 is unquestionably the more original. In order to vanquish the demons the gods, *i.e.* the organs, speech, smell, eye, ear, manas, and prâṇa, instruct one of their number to sing the *udgîtha*. Speech essays the task, but while singing is overcome with evil by the demons. A similar fate overtakes in succession smell, eye, ear, and manas. Finally prâṇa undertakes it, and the assailing demons are scattered before him like a clod of earth when it falls on a stone. Thereupon prâṇa leads the others away beyond the reach of evil and death, whereby speech goes to Agni, smell to Vâyu, the eye to Âditya, the ear to the heavenly regions, the manas to the moon. All these deities then, in order

[1] Other discussions of the same theme will be found in Talav. Up. Br. 1. 60, 2. 1–2, 2. 3, 2. 10–11.

to enjoy food, enter again as speech, smell, eye, ear, and manas into the prâṇa. The same idea is found in Ait. 1–2, adapted to the conception of the purusha as the primeval man. To these legends Bṛih. 1. 3. 19 attaches a glorification of the prâṇa as *Ayâsya Âṅgirasa*, as *Bṛihaspati* and *Brahmanaspati*, as *Sâman* and even as *Udgîtha*. Previously he sang the *udgîtha*, now he is the *udgîtha*. It is quite clear that we have here an amalgamation of two texts originating from different points of view. We now understand the strange version of our story in Chând. 1. 2, where the gods in their strife against the demons approach the individual organs, not for the purpose of securing that the *udgîtha* shall be sung by them, but in order to worship them as *udgîtha*. The author of this section found the story of the strife followed already (just as is the case still in the Bṛihad.) by a worship of the prâṇa as *udgîtha*. Both pieces, though radically different, and only by accident standing side by side, were blended into one whole, whereby the narrative entirely lost its original character.[1]

The last-quoted legend suggests already that the prâṇa is not merely a psychical but also a cosmical principle, that it is not only the breath of life in men, but also the universal breath of life which prevails throughout the whole of nature. This transition is very natural. Among the most diverse peoples, from the purusha of the hymn Ṛigv. X. 90 to the giant Ymir of the Edda, we meet with the tendency to regard mankind as a microcosm, and *vice versâ* the universe as a *makranthropos*. This thought depends, in the first instance, upon the fact that that which is manifested in nature as a whole, with all its phenomena, finds its most definite and complete expression in man. But in detail also the human organism enters into manifold relations

[1] See further, Deussen, *Upan.*, p. 66 ff.

with the external world. By means of its various organs and functions it extends itself, as it were, over-against the surrounding phenomena of nature, and accommodates itself to them. The organs of nutrition correspond to the constitution of food, the breathing organs to the atmosphere; the structure of the feet corresponds to the earth, upon which they will have to move; and in the curvature of the head the vaulting of the heaven seems to be reproduced.[1]

It is perhaps due to considerations of this nature that as early as the hymn of the purusha,[2] describing the transformation of the primeval man into the universe, his head becomes the heaven, his navel the atmosphere, his feet the earth, his eye the sun, his manas the moon, his mouth Indra and Agni (fire), his ears the heavenly regions, and his prâṇa the wind. In general, precisely as we were led to recognise in prâṇa the central organ of life, as explained above, so that which corresponds to it in the universe, the wind, must become the vital principle of nature, whether we regard it merely as the prâṇa that pervades the whole universe, as in the hymns elsewhere quoted,[3] or contrast *vâyu* and *prâṇa* as cosmical and psychical analogies, as is the case in the following passages.

In Bṛih. 1. 5. 21–23 the narrative of the rivalry of the organs appears in a new form, in so far as side by side with the psychical organs, speech, eye, ear, and prâṇa, their cosmical equivalents also, fire, sun, moon, and vâyu, come forward in mutual rivalry. Since these last cannot be said to depart from the body, this feature of the narrative is necessarily omitted, and there is substituted for it in the case of the psychical organs exhaustion, in the case of the cosmical a temporary entrance into repose.

[1] cp. Plat. Tim. 44 D. [2] Ṛigv. X. 90. 13–14.
[3] Atharvav. 11. 4 and Pras'na 2. 5–13; cp. Deussen, *Upan.*, p. 562.

Only prâṇa and vâyu do not become exhausted; accordingly the others take refuge in them, and at the close it is said that the sun rises and sets in the (cosmical) prâṇa. A similar conception lies at the foundation of the magnifying of the wind in Bṛih. 3. 3. 2:—"The wind therefore is the particular (*uyashti*), and the universal (*samashṭi*)." In another version of the same narrative, Bṛih. 3. 7, the wind (cosmical and psychical) is celebrated as the thread of the universe (*sûtram*) which holds together all beings:—"By the wind as thread, O Gautama, this world and the other world and all creatures are bound together. For this very reason, O Gautama, it is said of a dead man, 'his limbs have been relaxed'; for by the wind as thread, O Gautama, were they bound together."[1] Just as the prâṇa binds things together from without, so, as is explained in the following words of Bṛih. 3. 7. 3–23, the *Antaryâmin* (inner guide), *i.e.* the *âtman*, rules them from within. The connecting together prâṇa and antaryâmin is part of the attempt, thus early made, to advance from the symbolical method to that of abstract conception, of which more will later be said.

Since it has been already shown in Ait. Br. 8. 28 in the *brahmaṇaḥ parimaraḥ*, the "dying (of the foes) around the magic spell (uttered by the king)," how the natural phenomena, lightning, rain, sun, moon, and fire, become extinct in the wind and emerge from it again, Kaush. 2. 12–13 proceeds to teach the *daivaḥ parimaraḥ*, the "dying of the gods around (the prâṇa)." The cosmical divinities (fire, sun, moon, lightning), and the corresponding psychical divinities (speech, eye, ear, manas) do not die, when their brahman (here, their phenomenal form) vanishes; their brightness only they deliver over to other gods, while they themselves with their prâṇa enter, the cosmical into vâyu, the psychical into prâṇa, which in

[1] Bṛih. 3. 7. 2.

essence are one :—" All these divinities therefore enter into the prâṇa, and die in the prâṇa ; they are not, however, lost when they enter in, but arise again from him." Here *vâyu-prâṇa* appears as the true first principle of the universe, while the " brahman " is to be interpreted as only its manifestation in natural phenomena, and therefore is apparently subordinated to the prâṇa.

The entrance of all the gods of nature into vâyu, and of all the gods of the senses into the prâṇa which is identical with it, is also the theme of a discussion which is frequently met with, but occurs in its best and probably most original form in S'atap. Br. X. 3. 3. 5–8. There inquiry is made for " the fire, which is this universe," and the answer is given,—" In truth, the prâṇa (breath, life) is this fire. For when a man sleeps, his speech enters into the prâṇa, the eye enters into the prâṇa, the manas enters into the prâṇa, the ear enters into the prâṇa ; and when he awakes, from the prâṇa are they reborn. Thus far in relation to the self. Next in relation to the gods. In truth, Agni is that which this speech is here, yonder Âditya is this eye, yonder moon this manas, and the heavenly regions this ear. But yonder vâyu (wind), which purifies there as it blows, is this prâṇa (breath). When now the fire (agni) is extinguished, it is blown out in the wind ; therefore we say, it has been blown out, for it is blown out in the wind. And when the sun (âditya) sets, it enters into the wind ; and similarly the moon and the heavenly regions are dependent on the wind ; and from the wind they are reborn. He therefore who departs from this world knowing this enters with his speech into the fire, with his eye into the sun, with his manas into the moon, with his ear into the heavenly regions, with his prâṇa into vâyu ; for from them he has arisen, and from these divinities, whom he ever loves, united to them he finds rest." This speculation was later on associated with the legend of S'aunaka and Abhipratârin, who during a meal were importuned by a *brahmac'ârin*, who proposed to them a riddle on this subject. In this form, which is apparently no longer preserved, the narrative became again the groundwork of Talav. Up. Br. 3. 1–2, where the text is further elaborated and expounded, and also of Chând. 4. 2–3, which seems to be more faithful to the original form. The whole discussion, however, together with the legend, is comprised within a second legend, while (quite incongruously) both the discussion and the story of the beggar student are put into the mouth of Raikva as he gives instruction to Jânas'ruti.[1]

Conceptions such as those referred to account for the fact that in the Upanishads we frequently meet with the explanation that Brahman, whose nature it is sought to ascertain, is the prâṇa, the breath of life that pervades both the universe and the human body. This is the case in the definition of Bṛih. 4. 1. 3, judged by Yâjñavalkhya to be inadequate, *prâṇo vai brahma*; or Bṛih. 5. 13, where *uktham*, *yajus*, *sâman*, and *kshatram* (*i.e.* probably the four Vedas, as the sum of all that was originally denoted by *brahman*) are explained as the prâṇa. We shall meet later on with other passages of this character, in which the prâṇa is recognised as a first principle, but immediately set aside, as for instance Chând. 4. 10. 5, *prâṇo brahma, kam brahma, kham brahma*; and we propose to cite here two more passages only, Kaush. 2. 1 and 2. 2, in which a beginning seems to be made towards such a superseding of prâṇa. Both passages, the one on the authority of the Kaushîtaki, the other on that of the Paiṅgya, explain the prâṇa as brahman. Both draw thence the inference that he who knows himself as the prâṇa that fills all things does not need to beg for food

[1] cp. Deussen, *Upan.*, pp. 117–120.

(*na yâc'et* is his "upanishad"), since he enjoys nourishment in all beings. According to the first passage, speech, eye, ear, and manas are the servants of prâṇa; according to the second, they encompass it, speech around the eye, this again around the ear, this around the manas, and this around the prâṇa. But of the last also it is said, He is set around (*ârundhate*). Around what is not stated. But in this may be found the first intimation of the great truth formulated in Taitt. 2. 2, that the *prâṇamaya âtman* also is not the kernel, but only the innermost sheath.

3. *Other Symbols of Brahman*

The two most important types besides the prâṇa under which Brahman is to be worshipped appear to be *manas* and *âkâs'a*. The principal relevant passage is Chândogya 3. 18:—"The manas is to be worshipped as Brahman; thus far in relation to the self. Next in relation to the godhead; the âkâs'a (ether, space) is (to be worshipped) as Brahman. Thereby both are taught, that in relation to the self, and this in relation to the godhead." It is further expounded how Brahman as manas has as his four feet the cosmical organs, speech, breath, eye, ear, and similarly as âkâs'a the cosmical gods, fire, wind, sun, and the heavenly regions. A passing attempt to elevate the manas (the will) into a universal principle has been elsewhere cited.[1] Unfortunately the attempt is not carried any further, but the manas is allowed to remain a mere symbol of Brahman. Besides our passage, Chând. 7. 3 may be quoted, where the manas occurs as the third of the symbols there enumerated, beyond which there is a still higher; and Bṛih. 4. 1. 6, where the upanishad *mano vai brahma* is attributed to Satyakâma (inconsistently with

[1] *Einleitung und Philosophie des Veda*, p. 206; for an estimate of this conception we refer to the discussion there.

the instruction given to him in Chând. 4. 9. 3), and is regarded as inadequate. By the side of the manas the passage quoted above names the âkâs'a (ether, space; strictly speaking, space conceived as a material element) as a symbol of Brahman (for an alternative and parallel explanation of it as Brahman can only be intended to be understood symbolically), no doubt on account of the omnipresence of space; just as a passage often quoted by S'ankara but not yet identified says of Brahman that he is *âkâs'avat sarvagatac' c'a nityaḥ* "omnipresent like space, eternal," and Newton designated space the *sensorium* of God, while Kant a century later showed the god, whose *sensorium* space is, to be the intellect (*manas*) in our inner self. In older texts of the Upanishads, *âkâs'a* (space) is frequently explained to be Brahman, without any clear consciousness that this representation is merely symbolical. Chând. 1. 9. 1:—"It is the âkâs'a, out of which all these creatures proceed, and into which they are again received, the âkâs'a is older than they all, the âkâs'a is the ultimate end." Bâdarâyaṇa is right in asserting[1] that by the âkâs'a here Brahman is to be understood, "because his characteristics" are found. So also in Bṛih. 5. 1. 1, in an appendix containing much that is old:—"Om! the firmament is Brahman, the primeval, air-filled firmament." And again probably in Chând. 3. 12. 7–9:—"This so-called Brahman is the same as yonder space without man; and yonder space without man is the same as this space within man; and this space within man is the same as this space within the heart. That is the perfect, the immutable." It was soon, however, felt that the representation of Brahman as âkâs'a could only be tolerated in a symbolical sense. Gârgya, in Bṛih. 2. 1. 5,[2] explains the spirit in space as Brahman, and the answer is given (obviously directed

[1] Sûtr. 1. 1. 22, *âkâs'as tal-lingât.*

[2] cp. Kaush. 4. 8.

against the passage from Chând. 3. 12. 9 just cited), that it is only "the full, the immutable." In Chând. 4. 10. 5 *kham* (space) is playfully identified with *kam* (= *ânanda*, bliss). In Chând. 3. 18. 1, âkâs'a is, as we saw, only in a symbolical sense together with manas admitted as Brahman as an object of worship. Thus in Chând. 7. 12 the âkâs'a appears as a mere symbol, beyond which there is a greater; and in Chând. 8. 1. 1, characteristically diverging from the above quoted passage Chând. 3. 12. 7–9, it is no longer a question of regarding space in the universe as Brahman, or space in the heart, but that which is within this space (*tasmin yad antar*). We are unable therefore to agree with Bâdarâyaṇa when, in the student's benediction Chând. 8. 14, he proposes to understand Brahman by the âkâs'a. The meaning rather is, perhaps intentionally, directed against such an interpretation :—The âkâs'a is that (only) which holds asunder name and form; that which is in these two (*te yad antarâ*), that is Brahman, that is the immortal, that is the âtman. That is to say, Brahman has been expanded into names and forms, according to Chând. 6. 3. 3. The most decided polemic however against a confusion of âkâs'a and Brahman is in Bṛih. 3. 7. 12 :—"He who, dwelling in the âkâs'a, is distinct from âkâs'a, whom the âkâs'a knows not, whose body the âkâs'a is, who rules the âkas'a from within, he is thy soul, the inner guide, the immortal."[1]

As early as the period preceding the Upanishads we were able to discern a series of attempts to regard the first principle of the universe as inherent in the sun, but at the same time by means of metaphorical interpretations to advance beyond this conception as being merely symbolical. These attempts were continued in the Upanishads. In Kaush. 2. 7 a ceremony is taught, which by means of a worship of the rising mid-day and setting sun delivers from all sin

[1] cp. also Bṛih. 3. 8. 11, 4. 4. 17, 20.

committed by day or by night. Chând. 3. 19. 1 enjoins in addition the worship of the sun as Brahman; and that this representation is merely symbolic appears from what follows, where the sun is regarded not as the original creative principle, but, falling back upon representations discussed elsewhere,[1] as the first-born of creation. With the attempts to which reference is there made to interpret these views of Brahman as the sun, and to see in the natural light a symbol merely of the spiritual light, is to be classed especially the paragraph Chând. 3. 1–11, which undertakes on a larger scale to depict Brahman as the sun of the universe, and the natural sun as the phenomenal form of this Brahman. It may be regarded as a further endeavour to penetrate beyond the symbol to the substance when, in a series of passages, it is no longer the sun, but the *purusha* (man, spirit) in the sun, and the corresponding *purusha* in the eye that is described as Brahman. In Chând. 1. 6–7 it is said in an adaptation of the Udgîtha (which the Udgâtar had to sing); as the Udgîtha is lord over *ṛic'* and *sâman*, so over the cosmical gods is lord "the golden man (*purusha*), who is seen within the sun with golden beard and golden hair, altogether of gold to the finger-tips"; and over the psychical gods "the man who is seen within the eye." The former is lord over the worlds which lie beyond the sun, and over the desires of the gods; the latter over the worlds which lie on this side of the eye (therefore within man), and over the desires of men. According to Mahânâr. 13, the ṛic', sâman, and yajus (and therefore the Brahman embodied in the Veda) are compared to the orb of the sun, its flame, and the purusha in this flame,—"as this triple knowledge does he gleam, who as golden purusha is therein in the sun"; while the identity of this purusha with that in men has been already asserted in Taitt. 2. 8:[2]—"He who dwells

[1] *Allgemeine Geschichte*, I, 1. pp. 253, 251. [2] cp. also Taitt. 3. 10.

here in men and that one yonder in the sun are the same." This thought is further developed in Bṛih. 5. 5, where among other things it is said:—"Yonder man who is in the orb of the sun, and this man who is in the right eye, these two depend on one another. The former depends by its rays on the latter, and this by the breath of life on the former. This one, when he determines to go forth, gazes at that orb of the sun pure (from rays); those rays do not interfere with him." Accordingly in Bṛih. 5. 15[1] the dying man entreats the sun:—"Disperse thy rays, concentrate thy splendour; yea, I see thee, thou lovely form; and he there, that man there, I am he himself." A similar conception underlies the explanation of themselves given in Chând. 4. 11–13 by the three sacrificial fires in their instruction of Upakosala as the man in the sun, the moon, and the lightning; whereupon the teacher in a subsequent correction remarks:—"They have told you only its environment, but I will tell you its real nature . . . the man who is seen in the eye, he is the âtman—thus he spake,—he is the immortal, the fearless, he is Brahman." Sun, moon, and lightning are, as he further shows, only the uppermost stations of the way of the gods, by which "the man who is not as a man" (*purusho 'mânavaḥ*) guides the soul to eternal union with Brahman. These views are apparently criticised in Kaush. 4,[2] when Gârgya among his sixteen definitions of Brahman proposes the man in the sun, the moon, the lightning, and the right eye, and is therefore turned away by Ajâtas'atru.

Prâṇa, *manas*, *âkâs'a*, and *âditya* are the most important symbols under which the worship of Brahman is enjoined. Theoretically, indeed, all the objects of worship recognised and enumerated in Chând. 7. 1–15, viz.—*nâman*, *vâc'*, *manas*, *saṅkalpa*, *c'ittam*, *dhyânam*, *vijñâ-*

[1] cp. also Îs'â 16. [2] cp. Bṛih. 2. 1.

nam, balam, annam, âpas, tejas, âkâs'a, smara, âs'â, prâṇa are to be regarded as such; and the modes of representation of Brahman as *vâc', prâṇa, c'akshus, s'rotram, manas, hṛidayam,* which in Bṛih. 4. 1 are treated as imperfect and yet are not rejected, stand in a similar position, and so also *annam, prâṇa, c'akshus, s'rotram, manas* in Taitt. 3. 1. The warmth of the body and the buzzing in the ear do duty also as symbols of Brahman on the ground of Chând. 3. 13. 7–8, where it is said of the light which is above the heaven and at the same time within men, *i.e.* of Brahman:—"His sight is that here in the body when he is touched a warmth is felt; his hearing is that when the ears are kept closed there is heard, as it were, a humming like a crackling as of a roaring fire. This ought we to worship as his sight and his hearing." Just as the section from which this passage is taken stands in a peculiar, still unexplained relation to the doctrine of the *âtman vais'vânara* and the *prâṇâgnihotram* connected with it,[1] so the parallel doctrine of the *agni vais'vânara*[2] is attached to a cognate expression in Bṛih. 5. 9, which traces back the buzzing in the ear and the fire of digestion to the *vais'vânara* fire in men (just as in Chând. 3. 13. 7–8 the humming in the ear and the bodily warmth is traced to the Brahman fire in men). Both amount essentially to the same thing, since, according to the doctrine of the *prâṇâgnihotra* (which will have to be further considered later on), digestion is a consumption of the sacrificial food by the fire of prâṇa; and this we have already learnt to recognise as a symbol of Brahman.

Among the symbols by which the suprasensible Brahman is represented to sentient perception is finally to be reckoned the sacred syllable *om,* which of all the symbols came to be the most important and fruitful. It was closely connected with the *yoga* practice, one of the

[1] Chând. 5. 11–24. [2] S'atap. Br. 10. 6. 1.

most peculiar phenomena of Indian religious life, which later on will claim consecutive treatment.

4. *Attempts to interpret the Symbolical Representations of Brahman*

It is a weighty saying, that we must not put new wine into old wine-skins. But this requirement (like so many other of the requirements of Jesus) is on too lofty a plane, too unpractical, takes too little account of human relations and weaknesses, to be capable of more than approximate fulfilment. For it lies in the nature of things, that advance in the religious sphere can never be simple and absolute, but rather that by the side of the newer and better that which is old and dead must ever be still preserved, because it is regarded as something sacred. We shall see later how entirely Christianity was compelled to put its new wine into the old skins. Philosophy pursues a somewhat more untrammelled course. External liberty, however, is still not internal; and even in the course of development of the newer philosophy from Cartesius to Kant and onwards (to the greatest of all the battles for freedom that mankind has ever waged), we are only too often reminded of Goethe's grasshopper "that ever flits, and flitting leaps, and still in the grass sings its old song."

It was exactly the same in India. Those symbolical representations of Brahman as prâṇa, âkâs'a, etc. were too deeply rooted in the consciousness for it to be possible to throw them overboard without further trouble. There followed a series of attempts to preserve the symbols, while combining with them a truer conception of Brahman. The section Kaush. 3–4 is especially typical of this method of procedure. The important fact, taught principally by Yâjñavalkhya, and perhaps first grasped by him, that Brahman, the âtman, must be sought above all in the knowing subject, *i.e.* in the consciousness (*prajñâ*), had found a place alike in the schools of the Sâmaveda,[1] and in those of the Ṛigveda; although the latter, to judge from Ait. Âr. 2. 1–2, adhered especially closely to the symbolic representation of Brahman as prâṇa. While, however, amongst the Aitareyins the new knowledge of Brahman as *prajñâ* (consciousness) is attached immediately to this representation,[2] the Kaush. Up. endeavours to effect a reconciliation of the two by means of the equation, prâṇa = prajñâ. Kaush. 3 shows in a better way how the objects of sense are dependent on the organs of sense, and the latter in turn on the consciousness (*prajñâ*, *prajñâtman*). But like a false note there runs through the whole the assertion put forward again and again:—"What however the prâṇa is, that is the prajñâ, and what the prajñâ is, that is the prâṇa." The sole reason advanced for this bold identification is,—"for both dwell united in the body, and unitedly depart out of it."[3] A similar attempt to identify the *prâṇa* and the *âkâs'a*, and both with *ânanda*, "bliss," which forms the essence of Brahman, is found in Chând. 4. 10. 5:—"Brahman is life (*prâṇa*), Brahman is joy (*kam* = *ânanda*), Brahman is the expanse (*kham* = *âkâs'a*); to which the fires that impart this instruction add in explanation:—"In truth, the expanse, that is the joy, and the joy, that is the expanse"; and they expound to him how that Brahman is life and the broad expanse. A still more comprehensive blending of symbols with reality is undertaken by the very complex paragraph, Bṛih. 2. 3. Here "two forms" of Brahman are distinguished, the material (mortal, abiding, existing), and the immaterial (immortal, departing, other-worldly). (1) The material Brahman is physical nature and the human body; the sun and the eye are its

[1] Chând. 8. 12. 4, Kena 1–8.
[2] Ait. Up. 3 = Ait. Âr. 2. 6.
[3] Kaush. 3. 4.

essence. (2) The immaterial Brahman is vâyu and âkâs'a, prâṇa and the void in man; the purusha in the sun and the eye is its essence. Thus far therefore we are dealing with the symbolical. But this is abruptly transcended when the purusha is further identified by means of the famous formula of Yâjñavalkhya *neti neti* and the upanishad *satyasya satyam* borrowed from Bṛih. 2. 1. 20 with the unknowable super-essential Brahman. A similar blending virtually takes place in Bṛih. 3. 7, when vâyu-prâṇa as the world-thread (*sûtram*) and the âtman as the inner guide (*antaryâmin*) are discussed in the same context, and are therefore probably identified. The prayer of the student also in Taitt. 1. 1[1] is remarkable, because a perfectly clear consciousness of the symbolical representation of Brahman by vâyu is therein expressed:—"Reverence to Brahman! Reverence to thee, Vâyu! for thou art the visible Brahman, thee will I recognise as the visible Brahman." In later texts prâṇa has become occasionally a synonym for âtman, as in Kâṭh. 6. 2; or is made dependent on the latter, as in Pras'na 3. 3, where the prâṇa (perhaps following Ṛigv. X. 121. 2, Kâṭh. 3. 1, and anticipating the "reflection" between souls and objects in the Sânkhya philosophy) is described as the copy or shadow (c'hâyâ) of the âtman. It was reserved for the reactionary spirit of the Maitr. Up. 6. 1–8 to rehabilitate prâṇa and âditya, and to enlarge upon their identity as well as the manner of their worship in tedious speculations.

5. *Appendix: Interpretations of and Substitutes for Ritual Practices*

The partial interpretation in the oldest parts of the Upanishads of certain ritual conceptions and practices which are deeply rooted in consciousness in the light of the doctrine of Brahman, and the partial substitution for

[1] cp. also I. 12.

them of new ceremonies more in harmony with the spirit of the new doctrine, is related to the symbolical view of Brahman. We propose briefly to indicate the leading characteristics on both sides.

That India more than any other country is the land of symbols is owing to the nature of Indian thought, which applied itself to the most abstruse problems before it was even remotely in a position to treat them intelligently. As early as the period of the Brâhmaṇas the separate acts of the ritual were frequently regarded as symbols, whose allegorical meaning embraced a wider range. But the Âraṇyakas were the peculiar arena of these allegorical expositions. In harmony with their prevailing purpose, to offer to the Vânaprastha an equivalent for the sacrificial observances, for the most part no longer practicable, they indulge in mystical interpretations of these, which are then followed up in the oldest Upanishads. In the latter we often see the fundamental conception of the âtman doctrine appearing in symbolical guise, and we should be disposed to trace in allegorical speculations of this nature the earliest origin of the Upanishad doctrine. That it is not so, that the doctrine of the âtman as the sole reality has not been developed originally from ritualistic conceptions, but was adapted to them first in later times, we have inferred above (p. 17 ff.) from the tradition surviving still in numerous instances in the Upanishads, that it was kings, *i.e.* Kshatriyas, from whom the Brâhmans first received the most important elements of the âtman doctrine. This they then appropriated in their own way, combining it in allegorical fashion with the entirely heterogeneous methods of the ritual. This view finds an unexpected but all the more valuable confirmation in the manner in which the different schools of the Veda arrived at the conception of the âtman, or the prâṇa as its precursor. It is evidenced, that is to say, by the fact that each Veda starts from the ritual service peculiar to it, the adherents of the Ṛigveda from the *uktham*, those of the Sâmaveda from the *udgîtha*, and the schools of the white Yajurveda from the *as'vamedha*, in order by a symbolical interpretation to arrive at the conception of the prâṇa or âtman. It is however inconceivable that the âtman doctrine should have originated on so different yet parallel lines of development, while the facts are completely explained on the supposition that the doctrine of the prâṇa-âtman was taken over from another source, and harmonised by each school to the best of its ability with the ruling ideas of its ritual. This we propose to illustrate by a few examples.

The chief function of the priests of the Ṛigveda is the recitation of the *s'astram* (hymn of praise), which was chosen for the purpose on each occasion from the hymns of the Ṛigveda. The *uktham* however is "the most beautiful, most famous, most potent among the s'astras."[1] This is identified by the Aitareyins under several allegorical forms with the prâṇa;[2] while the Kaushîtakins identify the *uktham* with Brahman (materialised in ṛic', yajus, sâman).[3] As the priests of the Ṛigveda regarded the *uktham* as the climax of their service, so those of the Sâmaveda looked upon the chanting of the *udgîtha*, which was similarly identified with the syllable *om*, the *prâṇa*, the sun, or the *purusha* in the sun and the eye; while in Chând. 2 the complete *sâman*, whose climax is formed by the chanting of the *udgîtha*, is compared with various cosmical and psychical conditions. The early portions of the Upanishad-Brâhmaṇa, which, including the Kena Upan., belongs to the Talavakâra school of the Sâmaveda, is concerned with allegories of an entirely similar character. For the priests of the Yajurveda who are entrusted with the carrying out of the sacred rites a similar part is taken

[1] Kaush. 2. 6. [2] Ait. Âr. 2. 1–3. [3] Kaush. 2. 6.

by the act of sacrifice itself, and here again also it is the highest of all the sacrificial observances, viz. the horse-sacrifice (*âs'vamedha*), with which Bṛih. 1. 1–2 begins, in order to recognise in the steed the universe, into which Prajâpati is transformed with the object of again offering himself in sacrifice. In Taitt. Saṁh. 7. 5. 25 also this allegorical interpretation of the horse of the sacrifice as the universe is found, and in Taitt. Up. 1. 5 in a different way the interdict of the sacrificial animal is broken through, in that a fourth sacred word of the sacrifice *mahas*, which must denote Brahman, is added to the three *bhûr bhuvaḥ svar*, which are interpreted as earth, atmosphere and heaven. The remaining schools of the Yajurveda appear to have started in their allegorising from another aspect of the cult, from the disposal of the sacred fire-altars, as may be inferred from Kâṭh. 1 and Maitr. 1. 1.[1] Throughout, however, we see how the ritual representations are, according to the Vedic schools themselves, only different means whereby expression may be given under an allegorical garb to thoughts common to all.

Of other allegorical interpretations we will cite further only that of the *Gâyatrî*, the first in order of Vedic metres, consisting of three feet (⏑–⏑–⏑–⏑–, thrice repeated), to which an imaginary fourth was afterwards added. In this quadrupedal form the Gâyatrî is a symbol of Brahman, who is likewise four-footed. Later on we shall have to consider this four-footed character of Brahman, and its connection with the four states of the soul, waking, dreaming, deep sleep, and *turîya*. In their manner of treatment of the symbolical Gâyatrî the two chief texts adopt entirely different methods. According to Chând. 3. 12, the text of the Veda and all created things, the earth, the body, the heart, and the vital organs, these six form the one sixfold foot of the Gâyatrî, and the three remaining feet[2]

[1] cp. Maitr. 6. 33.

[2] With reference to Ṛigv. X. 90, 3.

are immortal in heaven, and are symbolised by space, the physical body and heart; in Bṛih. 5. 14, on the contrary, three feet of the Gâyatrî appear under a material form as the worlds, the vedas, and the vital breaths, while only the fourth (*turîya*) is transcendent, and finds expression symbolically in the sun, the eye, truth, power, and life.

In this way on the rise of the new teaching an attempt was made to preserve the traditional heirlooms of the ritual, while transforming them into symbols of the âtman doctrine. Soon however men went further, and endeavoured to supersede the most important of the traditional observances by other ceremonies adapted to the teaching concerning the âtman. In Bṛih. 3. 1, for example, for the four priests (hotar, adhvaryu, udgâtar, brâhman) the four cosmical and the corresponding psychical phenomenal forms of the âtman are substituted (as fire and speech, sun and eye, wind and breath, moon and manas), and instead of the usual rewards there was introduced union with the âtman as realised in the universe. Similarly in Chând. 4. 16. 2, instead of the brâhman his manas is introduced, and instead of the hotar, adhvaryu, and udgâtar, the vâc' embodied in them.

A further attempt to transcend the sacrificial ritual is found in the conception of the man himself and his life as an act of service. Thus in Chând. 3. 16 the three periods of human life appear in place of the three bruisings of the Soma, and in a different way in Chând. 3. 17 the functions of hungering, eating, begetting, etc., replace the chief acts of the Soma sacrifice. In detail this thought is carried out by assigning the different organs and functions to the requirements and acts of the sacrifice,[1] and elsewhere with still greater elaboration.[2]

Finally, in many of the instances enumerated it remains doubtful whether it is intended merely to inter-

[1] Mahân. 64.

[2] Prâṇâgnih. Upan. 3–4.

pret allegorically the still existing sacrificial cult, or to set it aside and replace it by physical and psychical conditions. The latter is distinctly the case with the last and most important phenomenon that we have to notice, where the *agnihotram* is replaced by the *prâṇa-agnihotram.*

The *agnihotram*, consisting in a twice repeated libation of boiled milk, which was poured into the fire every morning at sunrise and at sunset every evening, and thus was offered to the gods, and with them to all beings, had to be maintained throughout his life (*yâvaj-jîvam*) by the man who had once entered into the estate of a householder. After the prâṇa, indwelling in us all, had been introduced in place of the gods, the attempt was made to replace the *agnihotram* or fire-sacrifice by a *prâṇa-agnihotram*, a sacrifice offered in the fire of prâṇa. The continual inspiration and exspiration necessary for the maintenance of life (*prâṇa*) might be regarded as such. A first trace of this idea may be found in the words of Bṛih. 1. 5. 23 :—"Therefore if a man would observe a vow, he should inhale and exhale and wish, 'May not evil or death seize me.'"[1] This "inner agnihotram"[2] occurs with a more developed character and a clearer repudiation of the agnihotram cult in Kaush. Up. 2. 5 :—"These two sacrifices (of inspiration and speech, *i.e.* exspiration[3]) are endless and immortal; for whether awake or asleep they are continually being offered. The other sacrifices, on the contrary, are limited, for they consist of works. Therefore the wise men of old (who in the Upanishads are cited quite commonly as authority when novel ideas are introduced) did not offer the agnihotram." Like the breathing here, so the nutrition of the body also might be conceived as a sacrifice offered in the fire of diges-

[1] cp. also Ait. Âr. 3. 2. 6. 8.

[2] *ântaram agnihotram* ; cp. also Kaush. Âr. 10.

[3] cp. Pras'na 4. 4 : "The two libations of the exspiration and inspiration."

tion (identified in Bṛih. 5. 9 with the *agni vais'vânara*), and be substituted for the traditional agnihotram. Here also is found the first trace of the thought in Bṛih. 1. 5. 2:—"For all food which he (who knows this) consumes, that he presents (to the âtman and through it) to the gods." An amplified description of this new kind of agnihotram appears first in Chând. 5. 19–24. There is no further need of a specially prepared milk offering, "whatever food is nearest to hand, that is suitable for sacrifice."[1] Sacrifice is offered also in the *âhavanîya* fire of the mouth, since the five libations, of which this sacrifice presented to the prâṇa consists, *viz.*—the inspiration, inter-spiration, exspiration, the all- and up-breathing, and with them the corresponding five organs of sense, are for the benefit of the five nature gods and the five world spheres.[2] In a neighbouring passage the rinsing of the mouth customary before and after eating is conceived as a swathing of the prâṇa with water.[3] Both acts, the nourishing and the swathing of the prâṇa (with obvious reference to Chând. 5. 24), are connected together, and provided with corresponding rules in Maitr. 6. 9. According to this passage also, the customary agnihotram seems to be superseded by the prâṇâgnihotram (*âtman eva yajati*), while in the appendix Maitr. 6. 34 both are preserved side by side in that the *agnihotram* restored to its rightful position is conceived as the "openly made" *prâṇâgnihotram.* A final step in this development is indicated in the Prâṇâgn. Up. 1–2, which, presupposing apparently all the passages just quoted, declares the customary agnihotram to be superfluous, and for the prâṇâgnihotram prescribes a minutely elaborated ritual.

[1] Chând. 5. 19. 1.
[2] cp. the more detailed discussion in Deussen, *Upan.*, p. 146 f.
[3] Chând. 5. 2. 2; cp. Bṛih. 6. 1. 14.

IV. The Essential Brahman

1. *Introduction*

In the later Vedânta, by a combination of his three essential attributes, Brahman is described as *sac'c'idânanda, i.e.* as " being (*sat*) mind (*c'it*) and bliss (*ânanda*). This name does not occur in any except the latest of the Upanishads, and has not yet been found in Bâdarâyaṇa or S'ankara. We are able however, with a measure of probability, to trace in the Upanishads the steps that led up to it, inasmuch as the more reflection on Brahman was emancipated from symbolic representations, the more it was concentrated on these three ideas, just as occasionally also a combination of them was attempted. Thus at the close of his great discussion with the nine interlocutors, Yâjñavalkhya declares, turning to them all:[1] " Brahman is bliss and knowledge " (*vijñânam ânandam brahma*); and in the following section,[2] where he reduces six symbolical methods of representation to their true value, *satyam*, *prajñâ* and *ânanda* also appear side by side with three other attributes of the divine being. Taitt. 2. 1 approximates yet closer to the character of the formula that was customary later, when it is said in a poetical passage that forms the climax of the development of thought:—

> He who knows Brahman
> As truth, knowledge, infinite (*satyam jñânam anantam*),
> Hidden in the cavity (of the heart) and in farthest space,
> He obtains every wish
> In communion with Brahman, the omniscient.

Since here, at the opening of the Ânandavallî, a reference to Brahman as *ânanda* (bliss) would be entirely in place, while there was no special occasion to describe

[1] Bṛih. 3. 9. 28.

[2] Bṛih. 4. 1.

the Brahman as *anantam* (infinite) just at this point where stress was to be laid especially on his indwelling in the heart, the suggestion has been made[1] that *anantam* might not improbably be an ancient error, ratified after a time by tradition, for *ânandam,* which arose from the fact that the three predicates were taken for nominative, a position very rarely occupied by *ânandam.* If this is accepted we should have here the earliest occurrence of the formula so celebrated in later times. It must be admitted however that the force of our argument is weakened by the consideration that it is apparently a quotation that lies before us, and that this as such may not so confidently be brought into harmony with the following words. It is also difficult to understand how, assuming the universality of the reading *anantam,* a tradition of *ânandam* (in *sac'c'idânanda*) could have maintained itself by its side. A combination of the four predicates mentioned is found in the somewhat late Upanishad Sarvopanishatsâra, No. 21, where Brahman is defined as "true, knowledge, infinite, bliss."[2] An explanation of these four conceptions is added, and then it is said:—"That of which these four realities (being, knowledge, infinite, bliss) are a characteristic, and which subsists without change in space, time, and causality (*des'a-kâla-nimitteshu*), is called the supreme âtman or the supreme Brahman, indicated by the word 'that' (in *tat tvam asi*)." Thus we see the origin of the formula *sac'-c'id-ânanda,* which appears as such first (apart from Taitt. 2. 1) in Nrisiṁhottaratâp. 4. 6. 7 and Râmapûrvatâp. 92, Râmottaratâp. 2. 4. 5, and is subsequently employed times without number. Let us also use it as a framework in

[1] See Deussen, *Upan.*, p. 225.

[2] *satyam jñânam anantam ânandam brahma*; for which Codex क, with a more definite reference to Taitt. 2. 1 and Bṛih. 3. 9. 28, reads,—*satyam jñânam anantam brahma, vijñânam ânandam brahma.*

order to summarise the most important conceptions of the Upanishads under the headings,—Brahman as *sat*, as *c'it*, and as *ânanda*. In the present chapter we have yet to discuss the contradictory nature of Brahman and his unknowableness.

2. *Brahman as Being and not-Being* (*sat* and *asat*), *as Reality and not-Reality* (*satyam* and *asatyam*)

As early as Ṛigveda X. 129. 1, with a degree of philosophical insight remarkable when the date is considered, it is said of the primeval condition of things, the primeval substance, therefore of Brahman in the later sense, that at that time there was *na asad, na u sad*, "neither not-being nor yet being." Not the former, for a not-being neither is nor has been; not the latter, because empirical reality, and with it the abstract idea of "being" derived from it, must be denied of the primeval substance. Since however metaphysics has to borrow all its ideas and expressions from the reality of experience, to which the circle of our conceptions is limited, and to remodel them solely in conformity with its needs, it is natural that in process of time we should find the first principle of things defined now as the (not-empirical) being, now as the (empirical) not-being. The latter occurred already in the two myths of the creation:[1]—"This universe in truth in the beginning was not-being; for they say, What was this not-being?"[2] and "This universe in truth in the beginning was nothing at all. There was no heaven, no earth, no atmosphere. This being that was solely not-being conceived a wish, May I be,"[3] etc. Similarly, in some passages of the Upanishads:—"This universe was in the beginning not-being; this (not-being) was being. It arose; thereupon an egg was

[1] See *Allgemeine Geschichte*, I. 1, pp. 199, 202.
[2] S'atap. Br. 6. 1. 1. 1.
[3] Taitt. Br. 2. 2. 9. 1.

developed," etc.[1] And in Taitt. 2. 7, where the verse is quoted :—

Not-being was this in the beginning ;
From it being arose.
Self-fashioned indeed out of itself,
Therefore is it named "well-fashioned."

The preceding words show clearly how this is to be understood, for there at the beginning the verse is quoted, "He is not as it were not-being, who knows Brahman as not-being," and it is then further explained how Brahman creates the universe, and as the (empirical) not-being, the unreal, is contrasted with it as the being, the real. "After he had created it, he entered into it ; after he had entered into it, he was :—

The being and the beyond (*sat* and *tyat*),
Expressible and inexpressible,
Founded and foundationless,
Consciousness and unconsciousness,
Reality and unreality.

As reality he became everything that existed ; for this men call reality (*tat satyam iti âc'akshate*)." A similar distinction is drawn as early as Bṛih. 2. 3. 1,—"In truth, there are two forms of Brahman, that is to say :—

The formed and the unformed,
The mortal and the immortal,
The abiding and the fleeting,
The being and the beyond (*sat* and *tyam*)."

This passage, in spite of the air of a compilation which the chapter of which it forms the opening wears, gives an impression of greater age, and perhaps the passage from the Taittirîya is connected with it, and develops the thought further by more clearly contrasting Brahman as the beyond, inexpressible, foundationless, unconscious, unreal with the universe as the being, expressible, founded, conscious, real. At the same time this decides the question, which may well

[1] Chând. 3. 19. 1.

have agitated men's minds at that time, whether the universe originated from the being or the not-being; at which question the (probably older) passage Chând. 6. 2. 1 glances:—"Being only, my good sir, this was in the beginning, one only and without a second. Some indeed say that this was not-being in the beginning, one only and without a second; from this not-being being was born. But how, my good sir, could this be so? How could being be born from not-being? Being therefore rather, my good sir, this was in the beginning, one only and without a second." In harmony with the position thus taken up in the following exposition of Chând. 6, Brahman is usually named *sat* "being" or *satyam* "reality."

The word *satyam* (reality) also is used precisely as *sat* with a twofold meaning. While it denotes Brahman in the section Chând. 6 just referred to (so especially in the well-known formulas,—*tat satyam*, *sa âtmâ*, *tat tvam asi*), and is found with this meaning in Bṛih. 5. 4, in the same Upanishad Bṛih. 2. 1. 20 [1] *satyam* is on the contrary the reality of experience, and Brahman is contrasted with it as *satyasya satyam*, that which alone in this reality is truly real:—"Its secret name (*upanishad*) is 'the reality of reality'; that is to say, the vital breaths (*prâṇâḥ*) are the reality, and it is their reality." The same words recur in Bṛih. 2. 3. 6; that they are here borrowed is evident from the fact that reference to the empirical reality as "the vital breaths" (*prâṇâḥ*) was justified by the preceding words in Bṛih. 2. 1. 20 only, and not in Bṛih. 2. 3. 6. In Bṛih. 1. 6. 3 also, as in these passages, *satyam* denotes the real in an empirical sense:—"It is the immortal, veiled by the reality (*amṛitam satyena c'hannam*); the prâṇa, that is to say, is the immortal, name and form are the reality; by these that prâṇa is veiled." The words *amṛitam satyena c'hannam* appear to be one of

[1] =2. 3. 6.

those ancient mystical formulæ, accompanied by their explanation, which we have already conjecturally assigned as the oldest form of the Upanishads. Since the opposite of *satya* (true) is usually *anṛita* (untrue), it is perhaps conceivable that the formula in another recension took the form *anṛitam satyena c'hannam.* This would explain the curious play upon the word *satyam* which is carried out in Bṛih. 5. 5. 1 :—" This *satyam* consists of three syllables. The first syllable is *sa*, the second *ti*, the third *yam*. The first and the last syllables are the truth (*satyam*), in the middle is the untruth (*anṛitam*); this untruth is enclosed on both sides by the truth (*anṛitam ubhayataḥ satyena parigṛihîtam*); by this means it becomes an actual being" (by Brahman the universe acquires its reality). The three syllables are differently explained in Chând. 8. 3. 5, *sa* as the immortal, *ti* as the mortal, and *yam* as the point of meeting (*yam, yac'c'hati*) of both; and again differently in Kaush. 1. 6 the syllable *-tyam* in the word *satyam* has reference to the gods and the vital breaths (external and internal nature), and the syllable *sat-* to the "being" distinct from the gods and the vital breaths, and exalted above them.

For the later Upanishads the question whether Brahman is (not-empirical) being or (empirical) not-being has no further significance. These, like all other pairs of opposites, are transcended by Brahman. He is "neither being nor not-being";[1] "higher than that which is and that which is not";[2] he comprehends in himself empirical reality, the realm of ignorance, and eternal reality, the kingdom of knowledge :—

> Two there are that in the eternal infinite supreme Brahman
> Lie hidden, knowledge and ignorance;
> Ignorance is fleeting, knowledge eternal.
> Yet he who as lord ordains them is that other.[3]

---

[1] S'vet. 4. 18. [2] Muṇḍ. 2. 2. 1. [3] S'vet. 5. 1.

3. *Brahman as Consciousness, Thought* (*c'it*)

The conception of the *âtman* implies that the first principle of things must above all be sought in man's inner self. The inner nature of a man however is not accessible in the same way as his exterior. While the external appearance as body with all its organs and functions is exposed to view, and both the outer form and the inner play of bones and joints, of sinews, muscles and nerves, lie open to investigation on all sides, the knowledge of our inner nature is very limited and one-sided. We have no immediate perception of the body from within in the totality of its organs and their functions, like our view of it from without. Rather is our inner nature like a great house with many floors, passages and chambers, of which only a part is illuminated by a light burning in an upper storey, while all the rest remains in darkness, but is none the less real and existing. On first entering such a house, the mistake might easily arise of imagining the light the centre of the house, and that the accommodation of the latter extended only as far as the rays of the light reached, and all else since it was invisible might be regarded as altogether non-existent. It is due to this cause that the philosophising spirit of mankind in India, Greece, and modern times has with remarkable unanimity fallen into an error, which we can most briefly describe by the word *intellectualism*, and which consists in the belief that the innermost essence of man and of the universe, call it Brahman, first principle or deity, can bear any similarity or analogy or identity with that which we meet with here "behind man's pale forehead," as consciousness, thought or spirit. Yet whatever judgement may be passed on the value of this conception, in any case the entire development of philosophy from Plato and Aristotle to the present with few exceptions has been dominated by the thought that the nature of the soul, and in connection therewith the nature of god, is to be conceived as something related or analogous to human thought, as reason, spirit or intelligence. And as in Western philosophy the origin of this thought may be traced as far back as Xenophanes (οὖλος ὁρᾷ, οὖλος δὲ νοεῖ, οὖλος δέ τ' ἀκούει), and Parmenides (τωὐτὸν δ' ἐστὶ νοεῖν τε καὶ οὕνεκέν ἐστι νόημα), so in India the leading advocacy if not the earliest origination of the very same idea is attached to the name of Yâjñavalkhya. All his views put forward in the Bṛihadâraṇyaka Upanishad centre in the conviction that Brahman, the âtman, is the knowing subject within us; and on this very account, as we shall see later on, is unknowable.

Thus in Bṛih. 3. 4 he is invited by Ushasta to explain "the immanent, not transcendent Brahman, that as soul is within all." For answer he refers to the soul, which by inspiration and exspiration, by the intermediate and the up-breathing, manifests itself in experience as the vital principle. To the objection that this is only to point to the fact, not to give an explanation of it, he rejoins:—"Thou canst not see the seer of seeing, thou canst not hear the hearer of hearing, thou canst not comprehend the comprehender of comprehension, thou canst not know the knower of knowledge; he is thy soul, that is within all." And to confirm the assertion that the knowing subject here characterised by him constitutes not only the essence of the soul but, in and with that, the essence of the godhead, he adds, "Whatever is distinct from that is liable to suffering."

He concludes therefore his description in Bṛih. 3. 8. 11 of the almighty being who sustains and pervades space, and with it the entire universe, with the words:—"In truth, O Gârgî, this imperishable one sees but is not seen, hears but is not heard, comprehends but is not comprehended, knows but is not known. Beside him there is none that sees, beside him there is none that hears, beside him there is none that comprehends, beside him there is none that knows. In truth, O Gârgî, in this imperishable one is space inwoven and interwoven." (It cleaves, according to Kant, to the knowing subject.)

In the instruction given to Maitreyî, in Bṛih. 2. 4. 11, Yâjñavalkhya compares the âtman to the ocean. As this is the meeting-place of all waters, so the âtman as eye is the meeting-place of all forms, as ear of all sounds, as nose of all smells, etc. For the correctness of our view of this passage let Bṛih. 1. 4. 7 in the first instance bear testimony:—"as breathing he is named breath, as speaking speech, as seeing eye, as hearing ear, as understanding mind; all these are but names for his operations." So also Chând. 8. 12. 4:—"When the eye is directed on space, he is the spirit in the eye, the eye (itself) serves (only) for seeing; and if a man desires to smell, it is the âtman, the nose serves only for smelling; and if a man desires to speak, it is the âtman, the voice serves only for speaking; and if a man desires to hear, it is the âtman, the ear serves only for hearing; and if a man desires to understand, it is the âtman, the mind is his divine eye. With this divine eye, the mind, he perceives these joys and delights therein." If we consider that this thought is here somewhat abruptly joined on to that which precedes, and in general occupies an isolated position in the circle of the ideas of the Chândogya, while with Yâjñavalkhya it forms the central point of all his reasoning, it becomes probable that borrowing has taken place on the side of the Chândogya. The same may be true of the entire exposition of Kaush. 3, which traces out in detail the dependence of the objects of sense on the organs of sense, and of the latter again on the *prajñâtman*, the "self-consciousness" (repeatedly explained as identical with the âtman); whereupon it is said in close accord with the above passages:—"Into him as eye all forms are gathered, by the eye he reaches all forms; into him as ear all sounds are gathered, by the ear he reaches all sounds," etc.

The most complete exposition by Yâjñavalkhya of his theory of the âtman as the knowing subject persisting without change through the states of waking, dreaming, deep sleep, death, migration and final deliverance of the soul is found in the incomparable section Bṛih. 4. 3–4. Here the king Janaka first proposes the question,—"What serves man for light?" Yâjñavalkhya returns an evasive answer,—the sun serves him for light. When, however, the sun has set?—The moon. And when this also has set?—The fire. And when this also is extinguished?—The voice. And when this also is silenced?—"Then is he himself (*âtman*) his own light." "What do you mean by self?" "It is the spirit behind the organs of sense which is essential knowledge, and shines within in the heart." The further description is given how this spirit, while remaining the same, roves through this world in waking and dreaming, through the world of Brahman in deep sleep and death; how in waking it surveys the good and evil of this world without being moved thereby, "for nothing cleaves to this spirit" (the knowing subject stands opposed to everything that is objective); how in dreaming it builds up a world for itself, "for it is the creator"; how finally, in deep dreamless sleep, wrapped round by the self that consists of knowledge, the *prâjña âtman*, *i.e.* the absolute knowing subject, it has no consciousness of objects, and yet is not unconscious;—"when then he sees not, yet is he seeing, although he sees not; since for the seer there is no interruption of seeing because he is imperishable; but there is no second beside him, no other distinct from him for him to see."[1] Compare the cognate passage Bṛih. 2. 1. 17–20, according to which on falling asleep all the *prâṇas* (eye, ear, etc.) enter into the âtman, and on waking all the vital spirits, worlds, gods and living beings spring forth from him again like sparks from the fire. The above passage Bṛih. 4. 4. 1 f. further describes how at death all the vital powers gather around the knowing subject, in order with him to go forth to a new incarnation,—"because he has become one, therefore he does not see, as they say" (in reality he continues ever seeing); and how finally after deliverance has been attained the body is cast off like the skin of a snake, "but the bodiless, the immortal, the life is pure Brahman and pure light" (*i.e.* the knowing subject). "In truth," it is said in conclusion, "this great unbegotten self is of the vital organs that which consists of knowledge." This identity of Brahman with the knowing subject, which forms the ruling conception in the thought of Yâjñavalkhya, is most clearly expressed in a (certainly later) modification of the illustration of the lump of salt (preserved in its original form in Bṛih. 2. 4. 12):—"It is like a lump of salt, that has no (distinguishable) inner or outer, but consists through and through entirely of savour; so in truth this âtman has no (distinguishable) inner or outer, but consists through and through entirely of knowledge."[2]

How deep Yâjñavalkhya's conception of Brahman as the knowing subject has penetrated we see from the fact that it dominates the entire succeeding development of ideas, as we propose briefly to show.

In the first place, we must here recall to mind the description of Brahman as "the light of lights."[3] This expression is nothing more than an epitome of the thought expounded above, that the âtman is itself its own light,

[1] Bṛih. 4. 3. 23.

[2] Bṛih. 4. 5. 13.

[3] *jyotishâm jyotis*, Bṛih. 4. 4. 66; taken over thence in Muṇḍ. 2. 2. 9, Bhag. Gîtâ 13. 17.

when sun, moon and fire cease to shine. Thus too is to be explained the splendid verse that occurs thrice in different schools :[1]—

> There no sun shines, no moon, nor glimmering star,
> Nor yonder lightning, the fire of earth is quenched ;
> From him, who alone shines, all else borrows its brightness,
> The whole world bursts into splendour at his shining.

The original position of this verse is in the Kâṭhaka Upanishad, though this treatise otherwise frequently betrays its dependence on Bṛih. 4. 3–4.[2] Of Chând. 8. 12. 4 we have already spoken above. When further it is said, in the well-known passages Chând. 8. 3. 4 and 8. 12. 3,[3] that the soul in deep sleep is raised from out of this body, enters into the purest light (*param jyotis*) and thereby assumes its proper form, the peculiar designation of Brahman as *param jyotis* may well recall Yâjñavalkhya's conception of the âtman, which as the knowing subject is its own light.

Associated with this thought, and like it of great antiquity in India, is the conception of the divine world as an eternal kingdom of light, in contrast to the darkness of this earth.[4] This conception is combined further on with the philosophical thought that the âtman as the knowing subject is its own light, to form the frequently recurring idea of the eternal day of Brahman. This is the case perhaps as early as Chând. 3. 11, where the description is given how the sun after the close of the thirty-one world-periods will "no longer rise or set, but remain stationary in mid-heaven"; how moreover for the wise this condition is already attained now, so that for them there is perpetual day (*sakṛid-divâ ha eva asmai bhavati*).

[1] Kâṭh. 5. 15, S'vet. 6. 14, Muṇḍ. 2. 2. 10.
[2] cp. Kâṭh. 4. 3–5, 5. 8.
[3] cp. Maitr. 2. 2, Brahma Up. 1.
[4] cp. the proverbial sayings quoted in Bṛih. 1. 3. 28, Chând. 3. 17. 6.

More is found in Chând. 8. 4. 2, where Brahman is compared to a bridge :—" Therefore, in truth, even the night, if it crosses this bridge, is changed into day, for this world of Brahman " (which is in the heart) " is perpetual light (*sakṛid vibhâta*)." The following passages are dependent upon this :—" the darkness gives place, now there is no longer day nor night";[1] "when the darkness (of ignorance) is pierced through, then is reached that which is not affected with darkness; and he who has thus pierced through that which is so affected, he has beheld like a glittering circle of sparks Brahman bright as the sun, endowed with all might, beyond the reach of darkness, that shines in yonder sun as in the moon, the fire and the lightning";[2] meditation on *om* leads in the highest degree " to the eternal day of Brahman, whence is the source of lights ";[3] "for him (the sannyâsin) there is neither day nor night; therefore it was said also by the ṛishi,[4] 'for it is a perpetual day';[5] in yoga the spirit becomes " wholly the light of knowledge alone, the eternal, sleepless and dreamless, without name and form, altogether resplendent,[6] omniscient,—to him worship is of no more account ";[7] " the eternal, free from slumber and dreams, is then his own light;[8] for ever light[9] is this being, this essential being in himself."[10]

That the âtman is the knowing subject within us, and cannot therefore be an object of worship, is enforced also in the opening verses of the Kena Upanishad. Here in connection with a verse preserved in two very different forms in Bṛih. 4. 4. 18 and Kena 2, which demands that the eye shall be acknowledged solely as eye, the ear solely as ear,[11] etc., and that accordingly they shall be regarded

[1] S'vet. 4. 18. [2] Maitr. 6. 24. [3] Nâdabindu 17.
[4] Chând. 3. 11. 3. [5] Kaṇṭhas'ruti 2. [6] Chând. 8. 4. 1.
[7] Gauḍapâda (on the Mâṇḍûkya) 3. 35.
[8] cp. Bṛih. 4. 3. 14, Kâṭh. 5. 15. [9] Chând. 8. 4. 1.
[10] Gauḍapâda, *ib.*, 4. 81. [11] Bṛih. 4. 4. 18.

as mere instruments,[1] the thought is further developed that speech, thought, eye, ear and the organ of smell do not aid in perceiving Brahman, but themselves first, as objects, are perceived by Brahman as the subject.[2]

The conviction that the âtman is the knowing subject has finally found an entrance also into the schools of the Ṛigveda, although these are wont more usually to exalt the âtman as *prâṇa* or *purusha* (in the sense of Ṛigveda X. 90). With this is immediately connected, in Ait. 3, the doctrine that the âtman is not that with which we see, hear, smell, speak or taste (the organs of sense), but is solely and alone consciousness (*prajñâ*) :—" Everything that this heart and mind are, reflection, meditation, deliberation, invention, intelligence, insight, resolve, purpose, desire, suffering, recollection, idea, force, life, love, will,—all these are names of consciousness." All gods, all elemental forces, all beings, " all this is guided by consciousness, grounded in consciousness ; by consciousness this universe is governed, consciousness is its foundation, consciousness is Brahman."

The second of the schools of the Ṛigveda, Kaush. 3 and 4, proceeds on somewhat different lines. Here the traditional view of Brahman as *prâṇa* is combined with the new recognition of Brahman as *prajñâtman* (the self of consciousness) by means of the assertion which accompanies an admirable proof of the dependence of all the objects and organs of sense on consciousness, and which is constantly repeated :—" what the prâṇa is, that is the prajñâ, and what the prajñâ is, that is the prâṇa." This identification of conceptions so heterogeneous seems to show that the doctrine of Brahman as the knowing subject (*prajñâ*) among the Kaushîtakins, and probably also among the Aitareyins, is borrowed, and presumably is adopted from the circle of thought of Yâjñavalkhya.

[1] Kena 2 ; cp. in illustration Chând. 8. 12. 4, Kaush. 3. 8.
[2] Kena 2–8.

In the later philosophy this doctrine has shaped itself into the broader conception of Brahman or the âtman as the "spectator" (*sâkshin*). This occurs first in S'vet. 6. 11 (*sâkshin*) and Pras'na 6. 5 (*paridrashṭar*), perhaps in connection with Bṛih. 4. 3. 32 (*salila*).[1]

4. *Brahman as Bliss* (*ânanda*)

It is essential to the deeper religious consciousness to regard the earthly life not as an end in itself, but merely as a road by which we must travel to our true destination. The three great religions of mankind therefore, Brâhmanism, Buddhism, and Christianity, and not less the philosophy of Schopenhauer, which represents Christianity in its purest form, agree in teaching that the highest aim of our endeavour is deliverance from the present existence. This view assumes that this earthly existence is a condition from which we need deliverance, and is to that extent a conception of it which has been briefly and well described as pessimism,—although recently the sensational philosophy has laid its hands upon this word, and has practised so childish a play upon it that we shrink from using it any longer. The pessimistic view of life is only so far justified as it is a presumption of the doctrine of deliverance, so far therefore as it belongs, for example, to the real and original Christianity : ὁ κόσμος ὅλος ἐν τῷ πονηρῷ κεῖται.[2] In this sense pessimism is also the latent underlying view of the Upanishad teaching. And the later systems of Buddhism and the Sâṅkhya philosophy which are founded upon it, as well as some of the more recent Upanishads, take pleasure in dwelling upon this theme, as will subsequently be shown; for men lend a willing ear to the story of their own sufferings. In

[1] Further references are given in the Index to the Upanishads under the word "spectator."

[2] 1 Jo. 5^{19}.

contrast to these the older Upanishads are content in a discreet and, as it were, modest style to recall occasionally the nature of existence, full of suffering and exciting longings for deliverance. Nor is this ever done in a better or more fitting manner than in the difficult words that suggest a wide experience,—*ato 'nyad ârtam*, "what is distinct from him, that is full of suffering."[1] Contrasted with all that is distinct from him and therefore involved in suffering, Brahman is described in one of the passages where this formula occurs as that which "oversteps hunger and thirst, pain and illusion, old age and death,"[2] or according to other passages as "the self (*âtman*), the sinless, free from old age, free from death and free from suffering, without hunger and without thirst."[3] "His name is 'exalted,' for he is exalted above all evil,"[4] etc. All these frequently recurring descriptions are summed up in the designation of Brahman as *ânanda*, "bliss."

The view that the gods, in contrast to the suffering world of men, enjoy an untroubled felicity, is probably common to all peoples. But in the Upanishads bliss appears not as an attribute or a state of Brahman, but as his peculiar essence. Brahman is not *ânandin*, possessing bliss, but *ânanda*, bliss itself. This identification of *Brahman* and *ânanda* is effected through the medium of the view that, on the one hand, the deep, dreamless sleep, by destroying the existing contrast of subject and object, is a temporary union with Brahman; while on the other hand, since all suffering is then abolished, the same state is described as a bliss admitting of no enhancement.[5]

[1] Bṛih. 3. 4. 2, 3. 5. 1, 3. 7. 23.
[2] Bṛih. 3. 5. 1.
[3] Chând. 8. 1. 5, 8. 7. 1.
[4] Chând. 1. 6. 7.
[5] cp. Plato, *Apol.* 40*d*, where Socrates speaks of a night ἐν ᾗ οὕτω κατέδαρθεν ὥστε μηδ' ὄναρ ἰδεῖν, and is of opinion that even the King of Persia has not many days or nights which are comparable with this in happiness; cp. Shakespeare also, *Hamlet*, III. i.,— "and by a sleep to say we end The heartache and the thousand natural shocks That flesh is heir to,—'tis a consummation Devoutly to be wish'd."

We propose now to show how the conception of Brahman as bliss is originally based on these ideas. Here too the Bṛihadâraṇyaka takes the leading place.

"When however he is overcome by deep sleep, when he is conscious of nothing, then the veins called *hitâḥ* ("beneficent") are active, seventy-two thousand of which ramify from the heart outwards in the pericardium; into these he glides, and reposes in the pericardium; and like a youth or a great king or a great Brâhman enjoying an excess of bliss (*atighnîm ânandasya*) reposes, so he also then reposes."[1] This passage[2] appears to be traceable back to the detailed description of deep sleep in Bṛih. 4. 3. 19–33, which, although it does not yet define the number of veins, in its exaltation of bliss in 4. 3. 33 gives the key to the *atighnîm ânandasya*, and in general (apart from interpolations) makes an impression of greater originality. Here, after a description of deep sleep as the state "in which he, fallen asleep, experiences no further desire, and sees no dream image," and after mention of the veins, the transition is described from the dream consciousness to the consciousness of deep sleep,—from the consciousness of being this or that to the consciousness of being all (*aham eva idam sarvo 'smi*), whereby subject and object become one; it is then said:—"That is his real form, in which he is exalted above desire, and is free from evil and fear. For just as one who dallies (the original meaning of *ânanda*) with a beloved wife has no consciousness of outer or inner, so the spirit also, dallying with the self whose essence is knowledge (*prâjñena âtmanâ*, *i.e.* with Brahman) has no consciousness of inner and outer. That is his real form, wherein desire is quenched, and he is himself his own desire, separate from desire and from distress. Then the father is no longer father, the mother no longer mother, the worlds no longer worlds, the gods no longer

[1] Bṛih. 2. 1. 19.

[2] Like its parallel, Kaush. 4. 19.

gods, the vedas no longer vedas," etc., all contrasts have disappeared, "then is he unaffected by good or evil, then has he subdued all the griefs of his heart." This state is then further described as one of pure knowledge, of existence as subject without object (cf. the νόησις νοήσεως), and it is then added,—"This is his supreme goal, this is his supreme happiness, this is his supreme world, this is his supreme bliss; by a small portion only of this bliss all other creatures live." In explanation of this sentence (which for that reason is probably original here, and borrowed from this place in Taitt. 2. 8, where the thought is further developed) the proof is finally offered by means of a progressive advance through six (in Taitt. 2. 8, ten) grades, how the highest human bliss is only a billionth part (in Taitt. 2. 8, a hundred trillionth) of bliss in the world of Brahman,—"and this is the supreme bliss, this is the world of Brahman" (which is in the heart).

In this passage of the Bṛihadâraṇyaka we evidently have before us the origin of the doctrine of Brahman as bliss. The entire passage treats of deep sleep, and describes it on the one hand as union with Brahman, on the other as a state of supreme unsurpassable bliss, until in the concluding words,—"this is the supreme bliss, this is the Brahman world,"—the identification of Brahman and bliss is complete. That by "the Brahman world" is to be understood not the world of Brahman, but Brahman as the world (not *brahmaṇo lokaḥ*, but *brahma eva lokaḥ*) is already justly remarked by the commentator, p. 815. 5. and 915. 7. Accordingly the entire doctrine of Brahman as bliss appears to rest upon this passage, in which we are able to observe its birth,[1] and the consideration of the remaining passages that contain this doctrine makes it appear quite possible that they are all derived from our

[1] The description of all the gods as *ânanda-âtmânaḥ*, given as early as S'atap. Br. X. 3. 5. 13, is an entirely different thing.

passage, Bṛih. 4. 3. 19–33. We have already discussed Bṛih. 2. 1. 19 (and Kaush. 4. 19). The word *ânanda* does not occur in the Chând. Up.; but when it is said in Chând. 4. 10. 5:—"Brahman is life (*prâṇa*), Brahman is joy (*kam*), Brahman is space (*kham*)," *kham* stands here for *âkâs'a* and *kam* for *ânanda*; and the formal setting side by side of the three ideas, *prâṇa*, *ânanda*, *âkâ's'a* gives the impression of a later attempt at harmonisation. Chând. 7. 23 also, where pleasure (*sukham*, here = *ânanda*) is identified with Bhûman (*yo vai bhûmâ tat sukham*) by the following description which is given of *bhûman* as the knowing subject without object suggests the conjecture of a dependence again on the circle of thought of Yâjñavalkhya. The Kaushîtaki Upanishad celebrates Brahman, as noticed above, as the *prâṇa* identical with the *prajñâ*, and accordingly employs the word *ânanda* only in its original meaning of "sexual desire.' It is all the more surprising that in Kaush. 3. 8, after it has just been said that we ought not to seek for *ânanda* but for the *ânandasya vijñâtar*, there is immediately added:—"This prâṇa however is the prajñâtman, is bliss (*ânanda*), never ageing, and immortal." Here the borrowing of the word *ânanda* from another circle of thought is quite unmistakable.

The chief passage treating of Brahman as bliss is the Ânandavallî, Taitt. 2.[1] Where the *annamaya*, *prâṇamaya*, *manomaya* and *vijñânamaya âtman* are in turn stripped off as mere husks in order to penetrate to the *ânandamaya âtman* as kernel. Of this âtman consisting of bliss it is then said:—"Love is his head, joy his right side, joyousness his left side, bliss his trunk, Brahman his under part, his base." Brahman, that is here described as the base of the self consisting of bliss, is originally non-existent (*i.e.* only metaphysically existing), and fashions

[1] Taitt. 3 is only an imitation.

himself out of himself, as is further said, therefore is he named well-fashioned. "What this well-fashioned one is, in truth, that is the essence; for when a man receives this essence, then is he full of bliss; for who could breathe, who live, if that bliss were not in the *âkâs'a* (the void, from which the universe originated). For it is he who creates bliss. For when a man finds his peace, his resting-place, in that invisible, unreal, inexpressible, unfathomable one, then has he attained to peace." Further, a warning is given against pushing the craving for knowledge too far, and against continuing to distinguish in the self consisting of bliss a subject and object, whereby again a man would fall under the dominion of fear. Then Taitt. 2. 8 follows with the heading,—"This is the treatise on bliss (*ânandasya mîmâṅsâ*)." Here we find the very same ascription of power to bliss which is already known from Bṛih. 4. 3. 33; in the latter passage it stands naturally as explanatory of the preceding sentence, while in Taitt. 2. 8 it is introduced under an especial title, and without such connection with the preceding. This circumstance, as well as the increase of endowment from six limbs to ten with several details, makes it probable that the two texts do not spring from a common source, but that Taitt. 2. 8 depends directly on Bṛih. 4. 3. 33. If this is accepted, then Taitt. 2 might prove to be directed polemically against Bṛih. 4. 3–4. For the expression *vijñânamaya âtman* (*purusha*) denotes, in Bṛih. 4. 3. 7, 4. 4. 22,[1] the knowing subject apart from object, and therefore the supreme; while in Taitt. 2. 5 this *vijñânamaya* is conceived as subject contrasted with object, and contrary to Bṛih. 4. 3 is brought down to a mere preliminary grade of the *ânandamaya*.

All later passages depend partly on Bṛih. 4. 3,[2] partly on Taitt. 2, as for example Mahânâr. 63. 16, Maitr. 6. 13,

[1] cp. 2. 1. 16. [2] cp. Muṇḍ. 2. 2. 7, Mâṇḍ. 5 with Gauḍ. 1. 3–4.

6. 23, 6. 27, 7. 3, Tejobindu 8 (*ânandam nandana-atîtam*), Sarvop. 9–13, etc. The earliest description of the *annamaya*, etc. as "sheaths" (*kos'as*) is found perhaps in the verse Maitr. 6. 27. Several of the later passages add the conception of the *ânandamaya* as the innermost kernel (corresponding to the original intention); others, in the poetical description of it in Taitt. 2. 5, still discern a multiplicity (*priyam*, *moda*, *pramoda*, *ânanda*), and conceive it therefore as a fifth sheath, in which *brahman*, designated in Taitt. 2. 5 the "foundation," holds its place as kernel; a view which gave rise in the later Vedânta to an important discussion.

5. *Negative Character and Unknowablenesss of the essential Brahman*

We have seen how the descriptions of Brahman as being, thought and bliss (*sac'-c'id-ânanda*), which are common in the later Vedânta, are founded on the ancient Upanishads, and how their statements concerning Brahman may be comprehended under these three ideas. But no definite conclusion is by this means reached on these lines as to the nature of Brahman. For the being, which Brahman is, is not to be understood as such being as is known to us by experience, but is rather, as we saw, in an empirical sense a not-being. The descriptions of Brahman as the knowing subject within us are usually accompanied by the assertion that this knowing subject, the "knower of knowing," remains himself always unknowable, the intention being merely to deny thereby of Brahman all objective existence. The bliss also, which is described as the essence of Brahman, is not such a bliss as we know or experience, but is only such as holds sway in deep dreamless sleep, when the distinction of subject and object and therefore consciousness has ceased. Accordingly all three definitions of Brahman as being, thought or bliss are in essence only negative. Being is the negation of all empirical being, thought the negation of all objective being, bliss the negation of all being that arises in the mutual relation of knowing subject and known object; and therefore as the final result and main dogma of the Upanishad teaching the conclusion is reached, as far as his peculiar and essential being is concerned, Brahman is absolutely unknowable.

This unknowableness of Brahman, the âtman, is already most emphatically declared by the ancient Upanishads. Yâjñavalkhya sums up his speculations concerning the âtman no less than four times[1] in the celebrated formula:—"He however, the âtman, is not so, not so (*neti, neti*). He is incomprehensible, for he is not comprehended; indestructible, for he is not destroyed; unaffected, for nothing affects him; he is not fettered, he is not disturbed, he suffers no harm." "In truth, this great unbegotten self does not grow old or decay, and is immortal, fearless, is Brahman."[2] "That it is, O Gârgî, which the wise call the imperishable (*aksharam*); it is neither thick nor thin, neither short nor long, neither red (like fire) nor fluid (like water), neither shadowy nor dark, neither wind nor ether (space), not adhesive (like gum), without taste or smell, without eye or ear, without speech, without understanding, without vital force and without breath, without mouth or size, without inner or outer; never consuming anything, nor consumed by any."[3]

It is upon these passages that the amplifications of the later Upanishads depend. Thus in Kâṭh. 2. 18, where it is said of the "seer" (*vipas'c'it, i.e.* the knowing subject):—

> The seer is not born and does not die,
> He does not originate from any, nor become any,
> The Ancient One, from everlasting abides everlastingly,[4]
> Nor is he slain, for it is the body that is slain.

---

[1] Bṛih. 4. 2. 4, 4. 4. 22, 4. 5. 15, 3. 9. 26,—a fifth occurrence, Bṛih. 2. 3. 6, is borrowed.

[2] Bṛih. 4. 4. 25.

[3] Bṛih. 3. 8. 8.

[4] Bṛih. 4. 4. 18.

Similarly in Muṇḍ. 1. 1. 5 :—"The higher (knowledge) however is that by which that imperishable one[1] is known ; that which

Invisible, incomprehensible, without genealogy, colourless,
Without eye or ear, without hands or feet,
Eternal, pervading all and over all, scarce knowable,
That unchangeable one
Whom the wise regard as being's womb."

Further :—

"That which remains inaudible, intangible, invisible,
Which can neither be tasted nor smelt, imperishable,
That abides eternal, without beginning or end, greater than the greatest,
He who knows that has escaped from the jaws of death."[2]

And :—

"He stretches himself around, without frame or sinews,
Pure, unsullied, invulnerable, free from evil,
Gazing forth, by himself alone, all-embracing,
For each after its kind has he for all time determined the goal."[3]

The passage Chând. 8. 1. 5[4]—"that is the âtman, the sinless, free from old age, free from death and suffering, without hunger or thirst," seems to depend on Bṛih. 3. 5, —"that (âtman), who oversteps hunger and thirst, pain and illusion, old age and death." In Chând. 6. 8–16, on the other hand, the various phenomena of nature that engage attention are traced back to their unknowable source, of which it is said in the celebrated refrain nine times repeated :—"What that subtle being (*i.e.* that unknowable, *aṇiman*) is by which this universe subsists, that is the real, that is the soul, that art thou (*tat tvam asi*), O S'vetaketu?"

The unknowableness of Brahman, which in the above passages led to a denial to him of all empirical predicates, is expressed in poetic style also by ascribing to Brahman

[1] *aksharam*, cp. Bṛih. 3. 8. 8.
[2] Kâṭh. 3. 15.
[3] Îs'â 8.
[4] =8. 7. 1.

the most contradictory and irreconcilable attributes, as shown in the following two passages :—

"He stays, yet wanders far from hence,
He reposes, yet strays everywhere around,
The movement hither and thither of the god,
Who could understand besides me?"[1]

"One,—motionless and yet swift as thought,—
Departing, not even by gods to be overtaken;
Standing still he yet overtakes all runners,—
In him the god of the wind interwove the primeval waters.

Resting is he and yet restless,
Afar is he and yet so near!
He is within all,
And yet yonder outside of all."[2]

Here the opposite predicates of nearness and distance, of repose and movement, are ascribed to Brahman in such a manner that they mutually cancel one another, and serve only to illustrate the impossibility of conceiving Brahman by means of empirical definitions.

The impossibility of knowing Brahman is however most clearly expressed in the formula of Yâjñavalkhya already quoted,—*neti, neti* (*na iti, na iti*), "it is not so, it is not so." As to its original meaning there is some doubt. According to Hillebrandt,[3] *na* is not the negative, but an affirmative particle signifying "in truth," "it is." Or the formula might be rendered '*na iti na*' *iti*, Brahman "is not not," is the negation of negation, "a denial of a denial," the "*nihtesniht, daz ê was denne niht*," as M. Eckhart expresses it.[4] These ideas however are opposed not only to the consistency with which in the four passages in which this formula originally appears[5] it is applied to the elucidation of a series of negative predicates,[6] but also

[1] Kâṭh. 2. 21.
[2] Îs'â 4–5.
[3] In a review of my translation of the Upanishads, *Deutsche Literaturz.*, 1897, p. 1929.
[4] ed. Pfeiffer, pp. 322, 539.
[5] Bṛih. 4. 2. 4, 4. 4. 22, 4. 5. 15, 3. 9. 26.
[6] *agṛihyo na hi gṛihyate*, etc.

to all the Indian explanations of the formula with which we are acquainted. Such an explanation is already offered in Brih. 2. 3. 6 :—*na hi etasmâd—iti neti—anyat param asti*, "for there is no other (definition) beyond this, that it is not so"; or (less appropriately), "for there no other beside this (Brahman), therefore it is said, it is not so." According to this explanation *na iti* stands for *na evam*, as Bâdarâyaṇa already explains :[1]—*prakṛita-etâvattvam hi pratishedhati*, "for it (the passage) denies the aforesaid[2] being-so-and-so," and S'ankara (while giving the two explanations quoted above) confirms this sûtra. Similarly at an earlier period :—

> The saying, "it is not so, not so,"
> Rejecting all that can be expressed in word;
> As the assertion of unknowableness proves,
> Can only be referred to Him.[3]

We have already learnt from the philosophy of Kant that the entire empirical order of things is subject to the laws of space, time and causality,[4] and that the self-existent, or in Indian language Brahman, in contrast with the empirical system of the universe, is not like it in space but is spaceless, not in time but timeless, not subject to but independent of the law of causality. This proposition could not express an eternal truth valid alike for all ages and peoples without having been anticipated by all the metaphysicians of the past, and therefore also in the Upanishads. We propose to investigate this point here, merely prefacing the remark that those ancient times were frequently unable to formulate the idea of a spaceless, timeless, causeless existence in its abstract simplicity, but only to conceive its representation in experience. On this assumption spacelessness is regarded as a disengage-

[1] Sûtram 3. 2. 22. [2] Bṛih. 2. 3. 6.

[3] Gauḍapâda, Mâṇḍûkyakârikâ 3. 26.

[4] *des'a-kâla-nimitta*, as it is already expressed in a later Upanishad, and quite a dozen times by S'ankara.

ment of Brahman from the laws of space, which assigns limits to everything and appoints it a definite place and no other, while Brahman is described as omnipresent, all-pervading, unlimited, infinitely great and infinitely small. Similarly the timelessness of Brahman appears as freedom from the limitations of time, as an eternity without beginning or end, or again as instantaneous duration occupying no time (as lightning). And finally, Brahman's independence of causality is exhibited as freedom from all the laws of becoming, the universal rule of which is causality, as causelessness, absolute self-existence, and unchanging endurance.

(1) *Brahman as spaceless.* In Bṛih. 3. 8. 7 it is said :—" That which is above the heaven, O Gârgî, and that which is beneath the earth, and that which is between them, the heaven and the earth, that which men call the past, present and future, that is woven within and throughout in space." " But wherein then is space woven within and throughout ?" The answer is given in a magnificent description of Brahman as the imperishable (*aksharam*), and in conclusion it is said :—" In truth, in this imperishable one is space woven within and throughout, O Gârgî." " This Brahman is independent of earlier and later, of inner and outer ; this âtman is Brahman, the all-perceiving."[1] " The front (eastern) regions of the heaven are his front organs, the right (southern) regions of the heaven are his right organs, the hinder (western) regions of the heaven are his hinder organs, the left (northern) regions of the heaven are his left organs, the upper regions of the heaven are his upper organs, the lower regions of the heaven are his lower organs, all the regions of the heaven are all his organs."[2] " It however (the unlimited, the *bhûman*) is beneath and above, in the west and the east, in the south and the north ; it is this whole universe.—Next for the self-consciousness : I

[1] Or all-prevading, *sarvânubhû*, Bṛih. 2. 5. 19.

[2] Bṛih. 4. 2. 4.

(*aham*) am beneath and above, in the west and in the east, in the south and in the north; I am this whole universe.—Next for the soul (*âtman*): The soul is beneath and above, in the west and in the east, in the south and in the north; the soul is this whole universe."[1] Cp. the passage Maitr. 6. 17:—"Brahman in truth was this universe at the beginning, the one, the infinite; infinite towards the east, infinite towards the south, infinite in the west, infinite in the north, and above and beneath, infinite on all sides. For him there is no eastern, or any region of the heaven at all, no athwart, no beneath or above." In Chând. 3. 14. 3 also:—"This is my soul (*âtman*) in my heart, smaller than a grain of rice or barley or a mustard-seed, than a grain or the kernel of a grain of millet; this is my soul in my heart, greater than the earth, greater than the air, greater than the heaven, greater than these worlds." Passages like these are in the mind of the writer when in a frequently recurring verse[2] Brahman is named "the smallest of the small and the greatest of the great"; and when the epithets "omnipresent"[3] and "all-prevading"[4] are applied to him. The description also of him as "indivisible"[5] implies independence of space, since all that is in space is divisible. Since further all that is in space as being divisible involves a plurality, to deny all plurality of Brahman[6] amounts to a rejection of the predicates of space as in Kâṭh. 4. 10–11:—

> That which is here is also there,
> That which is there is also here;
> From death to new death he rushes
> Who fancies that he here sees difference!

---

[1] Chând. 7. 25. [2] Kâṭh. 2. 20, S'vet. 3. 20, Mahân. 10. 1.

[3] *sarvaga*, S'vet. 6. 17, Muṇḍ. 3. 2. 5; *sarvagata*, S'vet. 3. 11. 21, Muṇḍ. 1. 1. 6.

[4] *vibhu*, Kâṭh. 2. 22, 4. 4; *vyâpaka*, Kâṭh. 6. 8.

[5] *nishkala*, S'vet. 6. 19, Muṇḍ. 2. 2. 9; *akala*, S'vet. 6. 5, Pras'na 6. 5, Maitr. 6. 15.

[6] As in Kaush. 3. 8 (*no etan nânâ*), Bṛih. 4. 4. 19.

In the spirit should this be noted,
Here there is no plurality at all;
From death to new death he strides,
Who fancies that he here sees difference!

(2) *Brahman is timeless.* Even more definitely than of space, the predicate of time is denied of Brahman. This is already the case in some of the passages quoted. Further in the descriptions of him as "independent of past and future";[1] "Lord of the past and future";[2] "exalted above the three times";[3] at whose feet time rolls along, as it is said in the splendid description of Bṛih. 4. 4. 16–17:—

At whose feet rolling on
In years and days time passes by,
Whom as the light of lights the gods
Adore, as immortality.

On whom the fivefold host of living beings,
Together with space[4] depend,
Him know I as my soul,
Immortal the immortal.

More profound still is the thought of Maitr. 6. 15:—"In truth, there are two forms of Brahman, time and not-time. That is to say, that which existed before the sun is not-time, and that which began to be with the sun is time, is the divisible." Perhaps this beginning of time at a definite moment is to be understood here only in a figurative sense, as in Plato.[5] Just as Brahman's independence of space is figuratively represented not only under the figure of infinite vastness, but also at the same time of infinite littleness,[6] so his independence of time appears on the one hand as infinite duration,[7] on the other

1 Kâṭh. 2. 14.
2 Bṛih. 4. 4. 15, Kâṭh. 4. 5. 12. 13.
3 S'vet. 6. 5.
4 Bṛih. 3. 8.
5 Tim. 37 D *seq.*
6 Smaller than a grain of rice, etc., Chând. 3. 14. 3; smallest of the small, Kâṭh. 2. 20; of the size of a needle's point or the ten-thousandth part of the tip of a hair, S'vet. 5. 8–9.
7 *anâdi*, *anantam*, Kâṭh. 3. 15, S'vet. 5. 13; *sanâtana*, Kâṭh. 5. 6, Kaivalya 8, etc.

as an infinitely small moment, as it is symbolically represented in consciousness by the instantaneous duration of the lightning, or of the flash of thought. This is so as early as Vâj. Saṁh. 32. 2. The principal passage is Kena 29–30 :—"Concerning it this explanation is given. That which in the lightning makes it lighten, and men cry 'ah' and shut their eyes,—this, that men cry 'ah' (is its explanation) in relation to the godhead. Now in relation to the self. When something enters as it were into the soul, so that thereby a man is reminded of something in an instant, this idea (is its explanation)." Further descriptions of Brahman as lightning are found in Bṛih. 2. 3. 6, 5. 7. 1, Mahân. 1. 8. Taken together, their aim is to lay stress upon his instantaneousness in time, that is in figurative language his timelessness.

(3) *Brahman is independent of causality.* Causality is nothing else than the universal rule according to which all changes in the world proceed. Where there is no change there is no causality. It amounts therefore to an assertion of Brahman's independence of causality when, as early as the most ancient Upanishad texts, although they are not yet able to grasp the conception of causality in the abstract, all change is denied of Brahman. This is the case when, in Bṛih. 3. 8, Brahman is celebrated as "the imperishable" (*aksharam*). Only of this is knowledge possible, as Plato also teaches, while of all that is subject to the flux of becoming there is merely δόξα, to use Plato's word, or ignorance, as it is said in S'vet. 5. 1.[1] The absolute changelessness (*i.e.* independence of causality) of Brahman is very definitely expressed in passages like Bṛih. 4. 4. 20 :—

As unity we must regard him,
Imperishable, unchanging,
Eternal, not becoming, not ageing
Exalted above space, the great self.

[1] *ksharam tu avidyâ hi, amṛitam tu vidyâ.*

That no becoming touches the essential reality of things is taught by Chând. 6. 1. 3 :—"Change (*vikâra*) is a mere matter of words, nothing but a name." And in Kâṭh. 2. 14 Brahman is sought for as one that is—

> Independent of good and evil,
> Independent of becoming and not-becoming,
> Independent of past and future,
> That thou seest to be such, declare.

And of the "seer" (*i.e.* Brahman as the knowing subject) it is said in Kâṭh. 2. 18 :—

> The seer is not born, and does not die,
> Springs not from any, nor becomes any;
> From everlasting he abides for ever the ancient one,
> He does not perish, for it is the body that perishes.

An emphatic repudiation of becoming is contained in a passage that has been misunderstood by both Indian and European commentators, Îs'â 12–14 :—

> Into dense darkness he enters
> Who has conceived becoming to be naught,
> Into yet denser he
> Who has conceived becoming to be aught.
>
> Different is it from coming into being,
> Different also from not coming into being;
> Thus have we from the ancient seers
> Received the doctrine.
>
> He who knows (as non-existent)
> Both becoming and not-becoming,
> He passes through both
> Beyond death, and has immortality.

That by *sambhûti* and *asambhûti* here must be understood the coming into being and passing away (in place of the opposition of contraries is put that of contradictories) is confirmed by Gauḍapâda also :—

> By combating the *sambhûti* [1]
> A coming into being is repelled;
> "Who could bring him forth?"
> This saying [2] shows him to be causeless.[3]

---

[1] Îs'â 12. [2] Bṛih. 3. 9. 28. [2] Mâṇḍûkyâ-Kârikâ 3. 25.

The same thought is elsewhere developed in detail,[1] that the relations of cause and effect (*kâraṇam* and *kâryam*), source and result (*hetu* and *phalam*), perceived and perceiving, are unthinkable of the self-existent (Brahman).

The result of all the investigations of the present chapter is to show that in his essential nature Brahman is and remains completely unknowable. Neither as the (metaphysical) being (*sat*), nor as the knowing subject within us (*c'it*), nor as the bliss (*ânanda*) that holds sway in deep sleep when the opposition of subject and object is destroyed, is Brahman accessible to knowledge. No characterisation of him therefore is possible otherwise than by the denial to him of all empirical attributes, definitions and relations,—*neti, neti*, "it is not so, it is not so." Especially is he independent, as we have shown, of all limitations of space, time and cause, which rule all that is objectively presented, and therefore the entire empirical universe.

This conclusion is already implied in the first sentence with which Indian philosophy begins in the Ṛigveda,—in the thought, namely, of the essential unity of things. For this unity excludes all plurality, and therefore all proximity in space, all succession in time, all interdependence as cause and effect, and all opposition as subject and object.

In another connection[2] passages have been already discussed which assert the absolute unknowableness of Brahman. Here we append to them merely a beautiful story which S'ankara[3] reports as *s'ruti*, and which therefore he derived possibly from a lost or still unrecognised Upanishad.

When Bâhva was questioned by Vâshkali, he expounded the nature of Brahman to him by maintaining silence, as the story relates. "And he said, 'Teach me, most reverent

[1] Mâṇḍûkya-Kârikâ 4. 11–31.
[2] *Supra*, p. 79 ff.
[3] On Brahmasûtra, 3. 2. 17.

sir, the nature of Brahman.' The other however remained silent. But when the question was put for the second or third time he answered, 'I teach you indeed, but you do not understand; this âtman is silence.'"

V. Brahman and the Universe

1. *Sole Reality of Brahman*

Brahman is the âtman, "the self," is that in men and in all the objects of the universe which remains over when we abstract from them everything in them that is not-self, alien or different. There is however in the whole universe, alike in heaven and on earth, nothing besides the âtman:—"There is no second outside of him, no other distinct from him."[1] "There is here no plurality at all,"[2] and consequently there can be no question of anything existing outside of the âtman, of a universe in the proper sense of the term. With the knowledge of the âtman therefore everything is known:—"In truth, he who has seen, heard, comprehended and known the âtman, by him is this entire universe known,"[3] just as with the sounding of the drum, the conch-horn or the lyre, all the notes, as it were, of these instruments are already coincidently sounded.[4] The doctrine of the âtman is that very instruction, which was asked for in Chând. 6. 1. 2:—"by which (even) the unheard becomes (already) heard, the uncomprehended comprehended, the unknown known"; the âtman is "that with the knowledge of which this entire universe becomes known."[5] As from a lump of clay all that consists of clay is known, from an ingot of copper all that consists of copper, from a pair of nail-scissors all

[1] Bṛih. 4. 3. 23–30.
[2] *na iha nânâ asti kiñc'ana*, Bṛih. 4. 4. 19, Kâṭh. 4. 10–11.
[3] Bṛih. 2. 4. 5. [4] Bṛih. 2. 4. 7–9. [5] Muṇḍ. 1. 1. 3.

that consists of iron,—"the change is a mere matter of words, nothing but a name,"—so with the knowledge of the âtman all is known.[1] The distinguishing essence of the fire, the sun, the moon and the lightning has vanished, the change is a mere matter of words, nothing but a name.[2] This was recognised by the ancient seers when they said:—"No longer now can anyone bring before us anything which we have not (already) heard, understood and known."[3] Therefore for him who knows the âtman the unknown is only "as it were" (*iva*) unknown;[4] there is only "as it were" a duality,[5] "as it were" another,[6] "as it were" a plurality,[7] and it happens only "as it were" that the âtman imagines an object or is moved towards it.[8] Strictly speaking, such an "as it were" or *iva* should be supplied to every page and every line in which the Upanishads are concerned with something other than the âtman. It is however very easily understood that this is not always done. And just as Parmenides and Plato, without thereby involving themselves in self-contradiction, regard the very universe, whose reality they deny, from that standpoint of experience which is natural to us all as though it were real; so we are not to discover a contradiction when the teachers of the Upanishads occasionally regard and treat the universe as real from the standpoint of realism, of *avidyâ*, where indeed we all begin and on which all practical living is based, so long as in the background of consciousness the conviction remains unmoved of the sole reality of the âtman, and thence determines, even if only tacitly, all the thoughts. Probably however a contradiction was introduced when and in proportion as the realistic view implanted in us all by the nature of our

[1] Chând. 6. 1. 3–5. [2] Chând. 6. 4. 1–4. [3] Chând. 6. 4. 5.
[4] Chând. 6. 4. 7. [5] *dvaitam iva*, Bṛih. 2. 4. 14. [6] Bṛih. 4. 3. 31.
[7] *nânâ iva*, Bṛih. 4. 4. 19, Kâṭh. 4. 10, 11.
[8] *dhyâyati iva, lelâyati iva*, Bṛih. 4. 3. 7.

intellect so completely gained the upper hand that the fundamental conception of the Vedânta of the sole reality of the âtman became obscured by it. Wherever this occurs in the Upanishads the original standpoint of the Vedânta is abandoned, and another standpoint prevails, that of the later Sâṅkhya system, whose primary origin we shall have to look for in that realistic tendency of the mental constitution of man which can never be entirely suppressed, and whose origin and gradual accession of strength within the sphere of the Upanishad doctrine itself we shall have to consider and trace out in a later connection.

For the moment however we turn aside from this, and hold fast to the pure and original Upanishad doctrine, that it is the standpoint of *avidyâ* which we take up when we proceed now to consider Brahman in his relations to the universe, (1) as the cosmical principle, (2) as the psychical principle, and (3) as a personal god (*îs′vara*).

2. *Brahman as the Cosmical Principle*

The relation of the first principle of things to created nature, or to use popular language, of God to the universe, is a problem which can never be completely solved, for a solution is excluded by the constitution of our intellectual powers. In proportion as we attempt to understand that relation—that is, to conceive it under the categories of our intellect, space, time and causality—we fall into an erroneous, or to put it more mildly into a figurative representation of the facts; and in proportion as we endeavour to rise above a mere figurative representation we are compelled to relinquish a real understanding. Four stages may be distinguished in the comprehension of that problem, which we may describe, at first in general and with reservation of their special application to India, as realism, theism, pantheism and idealism.

(1) *Realism.*—Matter exists independently of God, and from eternity. God is degraded to a mere world-fashioner (δημιουργός), or, so far as creative power is transferred to matter itself, is altogether set aside, as in the Sâṅkhya.

(2) *Theism.*—God creates the universe out of nothing, and the latter then has a real existence independently of God. This is the standpoint of the Old Testament. As soon as the attempt is seriously made to grasp the relation of God to the universe, in proportion as this takes place God becomes more and more entangled in the universe, until He is completely merged in it and disappears. Theism degenerates into pantheism, which is its necessary consequence. The later philosophy furnishes an example. After Descartes had attempted to formulate in logical terms the theism of the Middle Ages which was based on the Old Testament, we see how, under the hands of his successors Geulincx and Malebranche, God is more and more absorbed into the universe until finally He becomes completely identified with it. The same thing occurs in the pantheism of Spinoza. It is remarkable that this decisive refutation of that Biblical view of the universe which originated from Judaism and was adopted in the Middle Ages was effected by a Jew.

(3) *Pantheism.*—God creates the universe by transforming himself into the universe. The latter confessedly has become God. Since it is real and also infinite, there is no room for God independently of the universe, but only within it. The terms God and universe become synonymous, and the idea of God is only retained in order not to break with tradition.

(4) *Idealism.*—God alone and nothing besides him is real. The universe as regards its extension in space and bodily consistence is in truth not real; it is mere illusion, as used to be said, mere appearance, as we say

to-day. This appearance is not God as in pantheism, but the reflection of God, and is an aberration from the divine essence. Not as though God were to be sought on the other side of the universe, for he is not at all in space; nor as though he were before or after, for he is not at all in time; nor as though he were the cause of the universe, for the law of causality has no application here. Rather, to the extent to which the universe is regarded as real, God is without reality. That he is real, nay the sole reality, we perceive only so far as we succeed in shaking ourselves free theoretically and practically from this entire world of appearance.

All these stages are represented in the teaching of the Upanishads, and thus it presents a very varied colouring of idealistic, pantheistic or theistic shades without becoming contradictory in the proper sense of the term. For the fundamental thought, that is held fast at least as a principle at all stages, even at the lowest which maintains the independent existence of matter, is the conviction of the sole reality of the âtman; only that side by side with and in spite of this conviction more or less far-reaching concessions were made to the empirical consciousness of the reality of the universe, that could never be entirely cast off; and thus the universe disowned by the fundamental idealistic view of the sole reality of the âtman was yet again partially rehabilitated. This was effected either by regarding it pantheistically as an apparition of the only real âtman, or theistically as created by and out of the âtman, but yet contrasted with it as separate, or realistically as *prakṛiti* occupying from the very beginning an independent position by the side of the *purusha*, although in a certain sense dependent on the latter. Of the theistic conception, and the realistic that paved the way for the Sâṅkhya, both of which make their appearance only occasionally, we shall have to speak in a later connection. Here we propose in the first instance to enter upon the fundamental idealistic view, in order to show how by accommodation to the empirical consciousness, which regards the universe as real, it passes over into the pantheistic doctrine, which is the prevailing one in the Upanishads.

Strongly idealistic, and at the same time expressing most clearly the peculiar spirit of the Upanishad teaching, are the passages which declare that with the knowledge of the âtman all is known,[1] and which accordingly deny a universe of plurality.[2] But with this thought a height was reached on which a prolonged stay was impracticable. Passages therefore of this kind are comparatively rare. The universe was still something existing; it lay there before their eyes. It was necessary to endeavour to find a way back to it. This was accomplished without abandoning the fundamental idealistic principle, by conceding the reality of the manifold universe, but at the same time maintaining that this manifold universe is in reality Brahman.[3] Idealism therefore entered into alliance with the realistic view natural to us, and became thereby pantheism. This was the case already in the definition of Brahman as *satyasya satyam*, "the reality of reality."[4] The universe is reality (*satyam*), but the real in it is Brahman alone. The same is true when in Chând. 6. 1 f. the rise of the manifold universe from the sole existing one is traced in a realistic manner, accompanied by the repeated assurance that all these changes are "dependent on words, a mere name." With

[1] Bṛih. 2. 4. 5, Chând. 6. 1. 2, Muṇḍ. 1. 1. 3.
[2] *na iha nânâ asti kiñc'ana*, Bṛih. 4. 4. 19, Kâṭh. 4. 10–11.
[3] *sarvam khalu idam brahma*, Chând. 3. 14. 1.
[4] Bṛih. 2. 1. 20.

this are connected the numerous passages which celebrate Brahman as the active principle through the entire universe:—"He is all-effecting, all-wishing, all-smelling, all-tasting, embracing all, silent, untroubled."[1] "The âtman is beneath and above, in the west and in the east, in the south and in the north; the âtman is this entire universe."[2] The sun rises from him, and sets again in him.[3] All the regions of the sky are his organs,[4] the four quarters of the universe (east, west, south, north), the four divisions of the universe (earth, air, sky, ocean), the four lights of the universe (fire, sun, moon, lightning), and the four vital breaths (breath, eye, ear, manas), are his sixteen parts.[5]

Fire is his head, his eyes sun and moon,
His ears the regions of the sky,
The revealed Veda is his voice,
The wind his breath, the universe his heart, from his feet is the earth,
He is the inmost self in all things.[6]

In what manner however is the relation of Brahman to this his evolution as the manifold universe to be conceived? We should say:—As identity, in this following the later Vedânta, which appeals to the word used to express attachment.[7] But this word is a mere makeshift; there is still always a broad distinction between the one Brahman and the multiplicity of his appearances, nor were ancient thinkers or indeed any thinkers before Kant able to rise to the conception that the entire unfolding in space and time was a merely subjective phenomenon. Here a further concession must be made to the empirical consciousness, tied down as it is to space,

[1] Chând. 3. 14. 2. [2] Chând. 7. 25. 2; imitated in Muṇḍ. 2. 2. 11.
[3] Bṛih. 1. 5. 23, Kâṭh. 4. 9, and similarly as early as Atharvav. X. 8. 16.
[4] Bṛih. 4. 2. 4. [5] Chând. 4. 4–9. [6] Muṇḍ. 2. 1. 4.
[7] Chând. 6. 1. 3; Sûtra 2. 1. 14, *tad-ananyatvam, ârambhaṇa-s'abda-âdibhyaḥ.*

time and causality. Brahman was regarded as the cause antecedent in time, and the universe as the effect proceeding from it; the inner dependence of the universe on Brahman and its essential identity with him was represented as a creation of the universe by and out of Brahman. We find ourselves at a point where we apprehend the creation theories of the Upanishads, unintelligible as they are from the standpoint of its idealism, from an unconscious accommodation to the forms of our intellectual capacity. The further elaboration of the doctrine of the creation of the universe will occupy us in the chapter on the Cosmology. Here only a few passages need be quoted, which set before us the essential identity of the created universe with the creator. "Just as the spider by means of its threads goes forth from itself (*tantunâ uc'c'aret*), as from the fire the tiny sparks fly out, so from this âtman all the spirits of life spring forth, all worlds, all gods, all living beings."[1] The illustrations of the spider and the fire are further elaborated in Muṇḍ. 1. 1. 7 and 2. 1. 1:—

> As a spider ejects and retracts (the threads),
> As the plants shoot forth on the earth,
> As the hairs on the head and body of the living man,
> So from the imperishable all that is here.
>
> As the sparks from the well-kindled fire,
> In nature akin to it, spring forth in their thousands;
> So, my dear sir, from the imperishable
> Living beings of many kinds go forth,
> And again return into him.

That the material substance of things also is derived solely from Brahman is taught in connection with the illustration of the spider in S'vet. 6. 10, where Brahman is described as the god "who spiderlike by threads which proceed from him as material (*pradhânam*) concealed

[1] Bṛih. 2. 1. 20.

his real nature." The last words mean that Brahman, by not (in a theistic sense) bringing objects forth from himself, but (in a pantheistic sense) changing himself into the objects, "has concealed his real nature" (*svabhâvato . . . svam âvṛiṇot*). In this sense it is said as early as Ṛigveda X. 81. 1 that Vis'vakarman by his entrance into the lower world was "concealing his original state" (*prathamac'had*). Similarly Bṛih. 1. 4. 7 declares that the âtman has "entered" into this universe "up to the finger-tips, as a knife is hidden in its sheath, or the all-sustaining fire in the fire-preserving (wood). Therefore is he not seen; for he is divided; as breathing he is named breath, as speaking speech, as seeing eye," etc. According to Bṛih. 1. 6. 3, the âtman is *amṛitam satyena c'hannam*, "the immortal, concealed by (empirical) reality"; and in Bṛih. 2. 4. 12 it is said:—"It is with him as with a lump of salt, which thrown into the water is lost in the water, so that it is not possible to take it out again; whence however we may always draw, it is salt throughout." The same thought is developed, perhaps on the basis of this passage in the narrative of Chând. 6. 13. That objection was taken to such a method of representation is shown by the parallel passage Bṛih. 4. 5. 13, where the words quoted above from Bṛih. 2. 4. 12 are altered as follows:—"It is with him as with a lump of salt, which has no (distinguishable) inner or outer, but throughout consists entirely of taste," etc. In a similar way efforts are made in other passages to show that Brahman by his transformation into the universe has forfeited nothing of the perfection of his own nature. As early as Ṛigveda X. 90. 3 it is said that all beings are only a fourth of the purusha, while the three other fourths remain immortal in heaven. The same teaching is found in Chând. 3. 12. 6, the verse from the Ṛigveda being repeated, and similarly in the concluding verse Maitr. 7. 11; while according to Bṛih. 5. 14, one foot of Brahman (under the figure of the Gâyatrî) consists of the three worlds, the second of the triple knowledge of the Veda, the third of the three vital breaths, while the fourth exalted above the dust of earth shines as the sun. Still more clearly is it taught already in S'atap. Br. 11. 2. 3 that Brahman, after having created the three worlds with that which lies above and beyond them, himself entered "into that half beyond." The infinite nature of Brahman is also taught in harmony with Atharvav. X. 8. 29 by the verse Bṛih. 5. 1 :—

> Though a man journey from the perfect to the perfect.
> Yet that which is perfect yet remains over and above all.

The same theme is elaborated in greater detail in the beautiful verses of Kâṭh. 5. 9–11 :—

> The light, as one, penetrates into space,
> And yet adapts itself to every form ;
> So the inmost self of all beings dwells
> Enwrapped in every form, and yet remains outside.
>
> The air, as one, penetrates into space,
> And yet adapts itself to every form ;
> So the inmost self of all beings dwells
> Enwrapped in every form, and yet remains outside.
>
> The sun, the eye of the whole universe,
> Remains pure from the defects of eyes external to it ;
> So the inmost self of all beings remains
> Pure from the sufferings of the external worlds.

3. *Brahman as the Psychical Principle*

Brahman is the âtman. The first principle of all things is not, as might be imagined, in part only, but undivided, completely and as a whole present in that which I with true insight find within me as my own self, my ego, my soul. Of the value of this thought which governs all the speculations of the Upanishads we have formed an estimate in the Introduction.[1] Here we propose to select from the large number of passages which give expression to it only so many as are necessary in order to show that this thought also, precisely as that of Brahman as first principle of the universe, is in its original purpose idealistic, that is, denies the multiplicity of the universe around us; but that it receives a gradually increasing realistic colouring in proportion as we endeavour to conceive it under the forms of our knowledge, adapted as these are to realism.

Yâjñavalkhya begins his instruction of Maitreyî in Bṛih. 2. 4 with the words:—"In truth, not for the husband's sake is the husband dear, but for the sake of the self (the soul, *âtman*) is the husband dear." Similarly all the objects of the world,—wife, sons and possessions, the estate of a Brâhman or a warrior, worlds, gods, living beings and the entire universe are dear to us not in themselves or for their own sake, but only for the sake of our own self. How this is to be understood is shown by the conclusion which immediately follows, and which is inferred from it:—"The self, in truth, should be seen, heard, comprehended and reflected on, O Maitreyî; in truth, he who has seen, heard, comprehended and known the self, by him this entire universe is known." This implies that all reality is and remains limited to our own self, and that we know love and possess all things in the universe only so far as they subsist in our consciousness, as they are grasped and entertained by our knowing self; there is no universe outside of the âtman, our self, our soul. This is the standpoint of complete idealism, which denies the reality of the manifold universe, as it is further expounded by passages like Bṛih. 2. 1. 16 and 20, where it is taught that all worlds, gods and living creatures spring from the spirit consisting of knowledge (*vijñânamaya purusha*) like sparks from the fire; or, as in Bṛih. 3. 4 and 3. 5, where

[1] *Sup.* p. 39 f.

inquiry is made for the "Brahman that is within all as soul," and the answer is given :—"It is thy soul, that is within all," which as the knowing subject remains unknowable [1] and with the consciousness of which the whole universe, all children, possessions and wisdom vanish into the nothingness which they really are.[2] In the latter passage an inclination is already revealed towards the realism which is natural to us all, inasmuch as the existence of the external world is not denied; the objects are there, but as far as their essential nature is concerned they are nothing but the âtman alone. Similarly in the important and well-known passage Chând. 6. 8–16, where a series of mysterious phenomena and relations of nature and life are traced back to their unknowable original source, and of this it is then said in a nine-times repreated refrain :—"What that subtle being (that unknowable, *aṇiman*) is, of which this whole universe is composed, that is the real, that is the soul, that art thou, O S'vetaketu!"

This doctrine of the sole reality of the âtman, the soul in us, is in opposition to our innate and invincible conviction of the reality of the external world that surrounds us, and this opposition is intentionally brought into relief in a large number of passages, which with great boldness of metaphysical insight identify the soul in us as the inconceivably small with nature without us as the inconceivably great. "He is all-effecting, all-wishing, all-smelling, all-tasting, embracing all, silent, untroubled;—this is my soul in my heart, smaller than a grain of rice or barley, or a mustard seed, than a grain or the kernel of a grain of millet; this is my soul in my heart, greater than the earth, greater than the atmosphere, greater than the heaven, greater than these worlds."[3] "In truth, great as is this world-space, so great is this space within the heart; in it are contained both the heaven and the earth;

[1] Bṛih. 3. 4. [2] Bṛih. 3. 5. [3] Chând. 3. 14. 2.

both fire and wind, both sun and moon, both lightning and stars, and whatever is possessed or not possessed in this life, all that is therein contained."[1] "Now however the light which shines there beyond the heaven behind all things, behind each, in the highest worlds, the highest of all, that is assuredly this light which is here within in men."[2] The soul, as these passages teach, embraces the universe; it is moreover as it were all-pervading, the *antaryâmin*, the "inner guide" in everything:—"He who dwelling in the earth is distinct from the earth, whom the earth knows not, whose body the earth is, who rules the earth from within, he is thy soul, the inner guide, the immortal."[3] This speculation is then further extended to several cosmical and psychical relations, and it is said in conclusion:—"He sees but is not seen, hears but is not heard, comprehends but is not comprehended, knows but is not known. There is no seer beside him, no hearer beside him, no comprehender beside him, no knower beside him. He is thy soul, the inner guide, the immortal. All that is distinct from him is liable to suffering." According to this, the *antaryâmin*, *i.e.* the power that dwells and rules in everything, is in its essence consciousness; for, as is stated in Ait. 3. 3, all gods, all substances and all organic beings, "all this is guided by consciousness, based upon consciousness; by consciousness the universe is guided, consciousness is its foundation, consciousness is Brahman."

Although according to this and many other passages the first principle of the universe dwells within us as consciousness or the knowing subject, yet its seat is not in the head but in the heart. "In truth, this great unborn self is that among the vital organs which consists of knowledge (*vijñânamaya*). Here within the heart is a cavity, therein he resides who is the lord of the universe,

[1] Chând. 8. 1. 3. [2] Chând. 3. 13. 7. [3] Bṛih. 3. 7. 3.

the governor of the universe, the chief of the universe; he is not exalted by good works, he is not degraded by evil works; he is the lord of the universe, he is the governor of living beings, he is the protector of living beings; he is the bridge which holds asunder these worlds, and prevents them from clashing together."[1] Kaush. 3. 8 may perhaps be derived from this passage:—"He is the protector of the universe, he is the governor of the universe, he is the lord of the worlds; and this is my soul, that ought men to know." Similarly numerous passages in the later Upanishads celebrate Brahman as "implanted in the cavity of the heart."[2] The identity of the âtman in us with the âtman of the universe is expressed by the *tat tvam asi* of Chând. 6. 8–16, and also by the *etad vai tad*, "in truth this is that," of Bṛih. 5. 4, which is probably an imitation of the other. The same formula is found twelve times in Kâṭh. 4. 3–6. 1 in a prose passage appended to the verses. The highest bliss, according to Kâṭh. 5. 14, consists in the consciousness of this thought. We quote in this connection only Kâṭh. 4. 12–13:—

> An inch in height, here in the body
> The purusha dwells,
> Lord of the past and the future;
> He who knows him frets no more,—
> In truth, this is that.
>
> Like flame without smoke, an inch in height
> The purusha is in size,
> Lord of the past and the future;
> It is he to-day and also to-morrow,—
> In truth, this is that.

As here the purusha is compared to a smokeless flame, so in imitation of this passage, in S'vet. 6. 19, it is

[1] Bṛih. 4. 4. 22; an indirect reference to Bṛih. 3. 8. 9.

[2] *nihito guhâyâm*, first in Taitt. 2. 1; then Kâṭh. 1. 14, 2. 20, 3. 1, 4. 6–7; Muṇḍ. 2. 1. 10, 3. 1. 7, etc.

likened to a fire whose fuel is consumed;[1] while in S'vet. 5. 9 the contrast between the âtman within us and the âtman in the universe is pushed to an extreme:—[2]

> Split a hundred times the tip of a hair,
> And take a hundredth part thereof;
> That I judge to be the size of the soul,
> Yet it goes to immortality.

The description of the âtman as a smokeless flame in the heart has been developed in the Yoga Upanishads into the picture of the tongue of flame in the heart, the earliest occurrence of which is perhaps Mahân. 11. 6–12.[3]

We saw above how the doctrine of Brahman as the cosmical principle was represented in accommodation to the empirical mode of thought as a creation of the universe in time by Brahman as its first cause. The same spirit of accommodation lies at the basis of the form assumed by the doctrine of Brahman as the psychical principle, viz., that Brahman after having created the universe enters into it as the individual soul. "This universe was at that time not unfolded; but it unfolded itself in name and form. . . . into it that (âtman) entered up to the finger-tips. . . . this therefore which here (within us) is the âtman is the trace (to be pursued) of the universe; for in it the entire universe is known," etc.[4] The last words prove that the entrance of the soul, as described, into the universe which it has created is merely a metaphor designed to render intelligible the assumed identity of the soul with the first principle of the universe. It then however more and more stiffens into an actual realism, as the following passages show. "Into citadels he entered as a bird, into citadels as a citizen."[5] "So

[1] Similarly Maitr. 6. 34, Brahmavidyâ 9, Nṛisiṁhott. 2.
[2] Surpassed however in Dhyânab. 6.
[3] cp. Brahmavidyâ 10, Yogas'ikhâ 6, Yogatattva 9–11, Maitr. 6. 30.
[4] Bṛih. 1. 4. 7.
[5] Bṛih. 2. 5. 18.

into these three divinities (the three elements) that divinity entered with this living self, and separated out from one another names and forms."[1] "After he had practised self-mortification he created this entire universe, whatever exists; after he had created it, he entered into it."[2] The same conception, even more realistically depicted, is found as early as Ait. 1. 11, 12:—"And he considered,—In what way shall I enter into it? . . . so he split the crown of the head, and entered through this gate." The later the realism is, the more pronounced it becomes. Maitr. 2. 6 may serve as an example: Prajâpati created numerous creatures, "these he saw standing unconscious and lifeless like a stone, motionless like the trunk of a tree; therefore he had no joy; and he resolved,—I will enter into them, in order to awaken consciousness within them; accordingly he made himself a wind, and determined to enter into them," etc.

We see therefore the original idealism by reason of a progressive accommodation to the demands of our intellectual capacity harden into a realism, which in no respects falls behind the Semitic.[3]

4. *Brahman as a personal God* (*îs'vara*)

The attempt to clothe the fundamental idealistic conception which refuses to recognise a universe independent of the âtman, and which lies at the foundation of the thought of the Upanishads, in intelligible, *i.e.* realistic forms, led at first, as we saw, to a pantheism which concedes to the empirical consciousness the reality of the universe, and at the same time asserts the sole existence of the âtman by declaring that this entire universe is nothing else than the âtman. This assertion was essentially dogmatic, and amounted to this, that the universe as a phenomenal form of the âtman took up a

[1] Chând. 6. 3. 3 [2] Taitt. 2. 6. [3] Gen. 2^7.

position over-against the âtman itself as a second; although the endeavour was strenuously made to reconcile this contradiction by the reiterated assurance that the universe is identical with the âtman, the infinitely great without us with the infinitely great within. A further step in the same direction that tended towards realism is implied when the âtman as first principle is contrasted not only with the universe, whose outward form it has put on, but also with the âtman within us with which it is originally identical. Thus is brought into existence the theism which is found in some of the later Upanishads. It has not arisen from the ancient Vedic polytheism, but first makes its appearance long after this has been superseded by the âtman doctrine; the âtman is not a "god," *deva*, in the ancient Vedic sense, but he is the "lord," *îs'vara*. The difference of the two modes of representation will become clear if we first gather together the most important data with regard to the position of the ancient Vedic gods in the Upanishads.

The existence of the ancient Vedic gods Indra, Agni, Varuṇa, etc. is as little denied by the Upanishads as that of the Greek by Xenophanes. But as by the latter all the other gods equally with men are subordinated to the one god (εἷς θεὸς ἔν τε θεοῖσι καὶ ἀνθρώποισι μέγιστος), so in the Upanishads all the ancient Vedic gods are created by the âtman and dependent on him. From the âtman proceed, like the sparks from the fire, all worlds, all living beings, and no less all gods;[1] on him all the gods depend;[2] by him they were created as the guardians of the universe;[3] "therefore when the people say of each separate god, 'Sacrifice to this, sacrifice to that,' (it should be known that) this created universe proceeds from him alone; he therefore is all the gods. This (creation) here is an overplus of creation of Brahman. Because he created the

[1] Bṛih. 2. 1. 20. [2] Kâṭh. 4. 9. [3] Ait. 1. 1. 3.

gods higher (than he himself is), and because he as mortal created the immortals, therefore is it called the overplus of creation" (*atisṛishṭi*).[1] It is further related[2] how the âtman created the divine Kshatriyas (Indra, Varuṇa, Soma, etc.), Vais'yas (the Vasus, Rudras, Âdityas, etc.), and S'ûdras (Pûshan). According to Bṛih. 1. 3. 12–16, it is the organs of the prâṇa, viz. speech, smell, eye, ear, manas, which are by him led beyond the reach of death, and now continue to exist as the gods Agni, Vâyu, Âditya, the heavenly regions and the moon. The number of the gods was in Vedic times usually given as thirty-three. The vague and arbitrary character of this reckoning Yajñavalkhya, in Bṛih. 3. 9. 1, brings home in the following way :—Why thirty-three? why not three hundred and three? or three thousand and three? or both together (3306)? and if we say thirty-three, it might just as well be reduced to six, or three, or two, or one and a half, or one, which is the prâṇa. All these numbers, 3306, 33, 6, 3, 2, 1½, as the manifold forces, parts and organs of nature, come back finally to a unity,—"the prâṇa, thus he said, this men call Brahman, the yonder (*tyad*)." The dependence of all these nature-gods on Brahman is described in the myth of Kena 14–28 :—Agni is unable to burn a blade of grass, Vâyu is unable to blow away a wisp of straw, apart from the will of Brahman, which is effective in all the gods. Brahman dwells, according to Bṛih. 3. 7, as the inner guide (*antaryâmin*) in all parts of the universe, and no less in all the corresponding gods. All the gods pursue their tasks, according to a verse preserved in Taitt. 2. 8 and Kâṭh. 6. 3, "from fear" of Brahman; and according to Kaush. 1. 5, even Indra and Prajâpati, the door-keepers of the heavenly world, are not able to prevent the entrance of the soul of him who knows Brahman, or to turn it back. And just as the power of the gods is

[1] Bṛih. 1. 4. 6.

[2] Bṛih. 1. 4. 11–13.

dependent on Brahman, so their knowledge also is imperfect; they are not in possession from the very beginning of the knowledge of Brahman.[1] Accordingly in Chând. 8. 7 f. they depute Indra to obtain from Prajâpati the knowledge of the âtman, and for the first time, after they have obtained it, they worship him in the world of Brahman as the self; thereupon they possess all worlds and all desires.[2] In this respect the gods have no advantage over men:—"Whoever of the gods perceived this ('I am Brahman') he became Brahman; and similarly of the ṛishis, and similarly of men. . . . And to-day also, he who knows this 'I am Brahman' becomes this universe; and even the gods have no power to prevent his so becoming; for he is the soul (*âtman*) of it."[3]

These passages make clear the part which the gods play in the texts of the oldest Upanishads. It is quite a different matter however, not to be confused with the other, when individual gods appear occasionally as symbolical representatives of the âtman, as for example Indra in Bṛih. 1. 5. 12, Ait. 1. 3. 14, Kaush. 2. 6, 3. 1, Varuṇa in Taitt. 3. 1, or Prajâpati in Chând. 8. 7 f.

The monotheism which meets us in some later Upanishads has not been developed from this ancient Vedic polytheism, which still has its echoes in the Upanishads, but from entirely different premisses. The proof of this is furnished already by the external fact that the personal god of the Upanishads, usually and apart from exceptions,[4] is called not *deva* (god), but *îs'*, *îs'a*, *îs'âna*, *îs'vara* (the lord), and in later times commonly *parames'vara* (the supreme lord). As these names already show, we must look for the origin of the theism of the Upanishads in such

[1] cp. Bṛih. 1. 4. 10, 4. 3. 33, 5. 2. 1, Taitt. 2. 8, Kaush. 4. 20, Kâṭh. 1. 21.
[2] Chând. 8. 12. 6.
[3] Bṛih. 1. 4. 10.
[4] Such as Kâṭh. 2. 12. 21, S'vet. 1. 8, and frequently.

texts as celebrate the âtman as the "inner guide" (*antaryâmin*) in all the parts and forces of nature and of mankind,[1] and which represent all effects in the universe as the result of his command (*pras'âsanam*), as in Bṛih. 3. 8. 9:—"At the bidding of this imperishable one, O Gârgî, sun and moon are held asunder," etc. Here it is the "imperishable" (*aksharam*, neuter) that is spoken of, which for the moment is poetically personified. This is not yet theism, but only the first step towards it. Similarly in Bṛih. 4. 4. 22:—"Here within the heart is a cavity, therein he dwells, the lord of the universe, the governor of the universe, the chief of the universe; he is not exalted by good works, he is not degraded by evil works; he is the lord of the universe, he is the governor of living beings, he is the protector of living beings; he is the bridge that holds asunder these worlds, and prevents them from clashing together." The same is the case with the temporary personification of Brahman as the refuge of love, the lord of love, the lord of brightness;[2] and in the injunction of Îs'â. 1 also, "to sink in god" the universe (*îs'â vâsyam idam sarvam*) there is still no theism, for the god who is here referred to is, as the following verses show,[3] the âtman within us. The doctrine of a personal god, and with it predestination, appears to be taught also in Kaush. 3. 8:—"He is not exalted by good works nor degraded by evil works, but it is he who inspires to do good works the man whom he will lead on high out of these worlds, and it is he who inspires to do evil works the man whom he will lead downwards. He is the guardian of the universe, he is the ruler of the universe, he is the lord of the worlds,—and he is my soul (*âtman*), that ought man to know." As the last sentence shows, it is still man's own self again that determines him to good or evil, and accordingly there is still no theism. The latter first

[1] Bṛih. 3. 7. 3–23. [2] Chând. 4. 15. 2–4. [3] vv. 6, 7.

certainly appears, where the âtman is contrasted not only with the universe, but also with the self within us. This seems evidently to be the case first in the Kâṭhaka Upanishad, where in 3. 1 the supreme and the individual self are distinguished as light and shadow; and according to 2. 23 the knowledge of the âtman depends upon a kind of free grace :—

> Only by the man whom he chooses is he comprehended,
> To him the âtman reveals his essence.

Whether Kâṭh. 2. 20 also is to be understood in a theistic sense depends upon whether we read *dhâtu-prasâdâd* "by the repose of the elements," or *dhâtuḥ prasâdâd* "by the grace of the creator" (having regard to the majesty of the âtman). On the recurrence of the verse in S'vet. 3. 20 and Mahân. 1.10 it is in any case to be interpreted in a theistic sense.[1]

We come next to the S'vetâs'vatara Upanishad, the leading example of the theistic teaching of the Upanishads, in which God and the soul, though their original identity is not denied, are yet clearly distinguished from one another. Thus in S'vet. 4. 6, 7 it is said :—[2]

> Two bright-feathered bosom friends
> Flit around one and the same tree;
> One of them tastes the sweet berries
> The other, without eating, merely gazes down.
>
> On such a tree the spirit, depressed,
> In its weakness mourns, a prey to illusion,
> Yet when it gazes worshipping on the might
> And majesty of the other, then its grief departs.

These verses are repeated in the Muṇḍ Up. 3. 1. 1, 2, but since elsewhere this Upanishad breathes a pantheistic spirit, they are probably borrowed here from the theistic S'vetâs'vatara. But in the latter also traces of the

[1] cp. also S'vet. 6. 18, *âtma-buddhi-prasâdam.*
[2] Interpreting the verse Ṛigv. I. 164. 20.

idealism that regards everything besides the âtman as unreal, and of the pantheism that identifies the universe with the âtman, both of which were taken over from the earlier Upanishads, continue to exist side by side with the theism; thereby making its representations often contradictory and philosophically unintelligible. This is the case when in 4. 10 the universe is declared to be *mâyâ* (illusion) caused by the supreme god; although with the reality of the universe the reality of god also in lost, and only the âtman within us survives as real. Or when in S'vet. 1. 6 the distinction of soul and god (the swan and the drover) is explained to be illusory, and at the same time the removal of this illusion appears as a grace of the supreme god, who is thereby first contrasted with the soul as another. Hence it follows that the S'vetâs'vatara is a work brimful of contradictions. It is like a *codex bis palimpsestus.* Beneath the characters of theism are discerned, half obliterated, those of pantheism, and under the latter again those of idealism. Just as in the later Vedânta, so already in S'vet. 5. 5, 6. 4, 6. 11, 6, 12 the task of bringing works to maturity and apportioning their fruit to the souls is indicated as the chief function of *îs'vara*; although to the Upanishad also this entire conception of the *îs'vara*, as later in the Vedânta, proves to be merely exoteric, and is not to be derived with certainty from 3. 7.

The theism of the S'vetâs'vatara is adopted and further developed by the later Upanishads, which endeavour to establish a connection with the popular religions by attaching the âtman of the Upanishad doctrine to the cult of S'iva (the beginning of which we may observe in the S'vet. Up.) or of Vishṇu. But even in them the original idealism, which dissolves universe and god in the âtman, reveals itself. This is the case in Nṛisiṁhottara-tâpanîya Up. 1, where the "fourth" and highest state of the soul, the *turîya*, is distinguished from its three states of waking, dreaming and deep sleep, and is represented as the abyss of the eternal unity, in which all distinctions of being and knowing vanish, the entire expanse of the universe is obliterated, "and even *îs'vara* (the personal god) is swallowed up by the *turîya* (the fourth), by the *turîya*."

SECOND PART OF THE SYSTEM OF THE UPANISHADS

COSMOLOGY, OR THE DOCTRINE OF THE UNIVERSE

VI. Brahman as Creator of the Universe

1. *Introduction to the Cosmology*

The sûtras of Bâdarâyaṇa define Brahman as that *janma-âdi asya yata' iti*, "whence is the origin, etc. (*i.e.* the origin continuance and end) of this (universe)." This definition goes back in the first instance to Taitt. 3. 1:—"That in truth out of which these creatures arise, whereby they having arisen live, and into which they at death return again, that seek thou to know, that is Brahman." It is to be noted however that in this passage of the Upanishad there is no mention as in the sûtra of an origin continuance and end of the universe as a whole, but only of the individual beings. The case would be different with a still older passage, Chând. 3. 14. 1, if we could follow S'ankara:—"Assuredly this universe is Brahman; it should be worshipped in silence as *Tajjalân*." The word *Tajjalân* is a mysterious name of the universe as identified with Brahman that occurs only here, and it is explained as follows by S'ankara on Chând. 3. 14. 1:—"From this (*tad*) Brahman by development into fire, water, earth, etc. the universe has arisen (*jan*); therefore it is called *taj-ja*. So on the reverse path to that by which it has arisen it disappears (*lî*) into the very same Brahman, *i.e.* it is absorbed into his essence; therefore is it called *tal-la.* And in the same way finally it is Brahman in whom the universe at the time of its origin breathes (*an*), lives and moves; therefore is it called *tad-anam.* Therefore in the three periods (past, present and future) it is not distinct from the essential Brahman, since there is nothing which lies outside of and beyond these."[1] When Böhtlingk[2] declares this explanation of S'ankara to be ungrammatical, on the ground that *upâsîta* must have an object, and accordingly proposes to find the secret name in *jalân* alone, he is met by the entirely analogous case of Kena 31, *tadd ha tad-vanam nâma, tad-vanam ity upâsîta-vyam*; in other respects no alteration would be introduced. According to S'ankara's view therefore we should have before us already in the name *tajjalân* (= *tad-ja-la-an*) a summarising of the three attributes of Brahman as creator preserver and destroyer of the universe. Whether this is correct, whether in so ancient an Upanishad it is possible to assume already the doctrine of the destruction of the universe, and whether we ought not rather here also to think of a simple destruction of individual beings, will later on become a subject of investigation. Meanwhile we propose to arrange our presentation of the cosmology according to these three attributes of Brahman, and accordingly to treat in order of Brahman as creator preserver and destroyer of the universe. When moreover S'ankara asserts in the passage quoted, and in many others, that the whole doctrine of the creation is not to be understood in a literal sense, but should be employed merely to teach the essential identity of the universe and Brahman, this also needs a fuller investigation and discussion of the question how far a creation of the universe is possible from the standpoint of the âtman doctrine.

[1] cp. the consistent explanation which S'ankara gives on Brahmasûtra 1. 2. 1, for which see p. 87 of my translation.

[2] *Berichte der Sächs. Ges. d. W.*, 1896, p. 159 f.; 1897, p. 83.

2. *The Creation of the Universe and the Doctrine of the Âtman*

We have above in the first part of our work learnt to recognise a series of descriptions of the creation of the universe from the Hymns and Brâhmaṇas, and to point out as a feature common to many of them that (1) the original principle, (2) creates matter out of itself, and then (3) as first-born enters it. We propose in the first place briefly to survey here the chief passages that set forth this doctrine.

Ṛigv. X. 129:—In the beginning there is only 'that one' (*tad ekam*). It exists as a dark undulation, shut in by a shell (*apraketam salilam*), out of which by tapas that one was first born as *Kâma* or *Manas* (that is to say, according to the conception of vers. 4).

Ṛigv. X. 121:—Prajâpati begets the primeval waters, and issues forth from them as golden germ (*hiraṇya-garbha*).

Ṛigv. X. 81, 82:—Vis'vakarman fashions the worlds sunk in the primeval slime, *i.e.* in the primeval waters, and then issues forth from these waters as the primeval germ that conceals all the gods.

Ṛigv. X. 72:—Brahmaṇaspati fashions the *aditi* (*salilam, uttânapad, sad*), and himself issues forth from it as Daksha.

Ṛigv. X. 125:—It is Vâc' that at the beginning actuated the father of the universe, and then was again born in the waters of the sea, in order to distribute herself over living beings.

Ṛigv. X. 90:—From Purusha (as *Âdipurusha*, Sây.) is born Virâj, and from the latter again Purusha (as *Nârâyaṇa*, the "son of Purusha," or "son of the waters," *i.e. Hiraṇyagarbha*).

S'atap. Br. 6. 1. 1:—Purusha Prajâpati creates the waters, enters into them as an egg in order to be born from them, and issues forth from them as Brahman.

Atharvav. 11. 4:—Prâṇa begets the universe, and issues forth from it as first-born (as *apâm garbha*, v. 26).

Atharvav. 10. 7. 7, 8:—Skambha, in whom Prajâpati sustained and nourished the whole universe, entered into the universe with a part of himself.

Taitt. Âr. 1. 23:—Prajâpati, building up the worlds, entered as first-born of the creation with his own self into his own self.

Vâj. Saṁh. 34. 1–6:—The mind (*manas*) includes all things in itself, and dwells in men as immortal light.

The motive of the conception that dominates all these passages may be described to be the recognition of the first principle of the universe as embodied in nature as a whole, but especially and most of all in the soul (the universal and the individual soul). Hence the idea arose that the primeval being created the universe, and then as the first born of the creation entered into it. This traditional view we shall find appearing frequently even in the Upanishads.

In what way however is this possible, since the entire doctrine of the creation of the universe and of the entrance of the creator into the universe that he has created is in contradiction to the âtman doctrine of the Upanishads, strictly interpreted?

The assertion is frequently made by the Upanishads, as we saw,—and this is involved in the very conception of the âtman,—that the âtman is the sole reality, that there can be nothing beside it, and therefore with the knowledge of the âtman all is known. From this point of view no creation of the universe by the âtman can be taught, for there is no universe outside of the âtman. But the loftiness of this metaphysical conception forbade its maintenance in the presence of the empirical consciousness which teaches the existence of a real universe. It was necessary to concede the reality of the universe, and to reconcile with this the idealistic dogma of the sole reality of the âtman by asserting that the universe exists, but is in truth nothing but the âtman. Even from this standpoint, which declares the identity of the âtman and the universe, no doctrine of the creation of the universe was possible. It was only by making a further concession to the empirical consciousness, and maintaining no more than an actual identity of the âtman and the universe, never carried out in detail, but framed on a causal relation between the âtman as first cause and the universe as its effect,—it was only then possible and necessary to formulate a theory to explain how the universe as effect had proceeded from or been created by the âtman. This step involved a further inevitable consequence. According to the creation doctrine the universe had come forth from the âtman as another distinct from it. It was necessary to secure its return into the âtman if the original fundamental doctrine of the sole reality of the âtman were not to be absolutely rejected. This motive gave rise to the doctrine that the âtman as soul (universal and individual soul) had entered into the universe that it had created, as we find the doctrine set forth in the Upanishads. It was then possible for the authors of the Upanishads side by side with their fundamental idealistic view to maintain in a modified and more developed form the traditional doctrine of the Ṛigveda, according to which the first principle creates the material universe and then as first-born enters into it. When therefore the professors of the Vedânta, Bâdarâyaṇa,[1]

[1] Sûtra 2. 1. 14.

Gauḍapâda,[1] and S'ankara,[2] maintain that the sacred writings teach a creation of the universe only by way of concession to man's faculty of understanding, their assertion is not to be entirely rejected. It needs to be modified only in the one point that this is not a conscious but an unconscious concession made to the empirical view that demands a real universe held together by causal connections of space and time; and with this limitation even the Upanishads, in spite of their âtman doctrine that denies the existence of the universe, teach its creation by the âtman and the latter's entrance into it, as the following passages show:—

Bṛih. 1. 4. 7:—"The universe before us was once not unfolded; it was then unfolded in name and form; . . . that âtman has entered into it up to the finger-tips, as a knife is hidden in a sheath, the all-sustaining (fire) in the fire-preserving (wood)."

Chând. 6. 2, 3:—"Alone existing, my dear sir, was this in the beginning, one only without a second. . . . It proposed:—I will become many, will propagate myself; thereupon it created the heat." From heat water proceeds, from water food (*i.e.* the earth). "That divinity proposed:—I will now enter into these three divinities (heat water and food) with this living self (the individual soul), and unfold thence name and form."

Taitt. 2. 6:—"He (the âtman) desired:—I will become many, will propagate myself. Accordingly he practised self-mortification. After having practised self-mortification he created the entire universe, whatever exists. After having created it, he entered into it."

Ait. 1. 1:—"In the beginning this universe was the âtman alone; there was nothing else there to strike the

[1] Mâṇḍûkya-kârikâ 1. 18, 3. 15.

[2] On Brahmasûtra 4. 3. 14, and frequently.

eye. He deliberated :—I will create worlds ; accordingly he created these worlds, the ocean, atmosphere, death, the waters." Further in 1. 3. 11 :—" He deliberated :—How can this (human frame) exist apart from me ? And he deliberated :—In what way shall I enter into it ? . . . . accordingly he split open the crown of the head, and entered by this door."

As far as the relative age of the passages quoted is concerned, the order that I have chosen may be expected to prove the order also of history. Bṛih. 1. 4. 7 is the least developed. Chând. 6. 2, 3 describes the process of creation in detail, but recognises only three elements. Taitt. 2. 1 represents the five elements as proceeding from the âtman. Ait. 3. 3 cites the five elements, and describes them for the first time with the later technical term *pañc'a mahâbhûtâni* ; the finished picture moreover in Ait. 1. 3. 11 of the âtman's entering into man by the seam of the skull makes this passage appear as the latest among those quoted.

3. *The Creation of Inorganic Nature*

In the whole of nature no distinction is so sharply drawn as that between the inorganic and the organic ; and this distinction dominates the Indian view of nature also, in so far as they both, the inorganic no less than the organic, are derived from the âtman, but in quite a different sense. All organic bodies, and therefore all plants, animals, men and gods, are wandering souls, are therefore in essence the âtman itself, as it, for reasons which have still to be considered, entered into this manifold universe as wandering individual soul. Inorganic bodies, on the contrary,[1] *i.e.* the five elements, ether, wind,

[1] Named *mahâbhûtâni* on account of their bulk by Ait. 3. 3, Maitr. 3. 2, Prâṇagnihotrop. 4.

fire, water, earth, though they are ruled by Brahman,[1] and remain under the protection of individual deities,[2] yet are not wandering souls, as are all plants, animals, men, and gods, but are only the stage erected by Brahman on which the souls have to play their part. Before we consider the origin of the elements from Brahman, and in the immediately following section of the entrance of Brahman into them as the soul, a few words of introduction are necessary on the creation myths of the Upanishads.

It was shown above (pp. 183–186) how it became possible for the teachers of the Upanishads, in spite of the doctrine of sole existence which they defended, and which denied the existence of the universe outside of the âtman, by an unconscious approximation to the empirical view to adopt the traditional scheme of the creation myths. Thus in Chând. 4. 17. 1–3, and in a briefer form Chând. 2. 23, a creation myth is reproduced, in part verbally, which we have already come to know from Ait. Br. 5. 32 and S'atap. Br. 11. 5. 8.[3] A creation myth is attached to the conception of the egg of the universe, whose earliest origin we have found in the "vital force that was enclosed in the shell,"[4] and in the "golden germ";[5] and the progressive development of the same idea met us already in S'atap. 6. 1. 1 and 11. 1. 6. This myth is preserved in Chând. 3. 19:—"This universe was in the beginning not-being; this (not-being) was being. It arose. Then an egg was evolved. It lay there a whole year long. Thereafter it split open; the two halves of the shell were, the one of silver, the other of gold; the silver half is this earth, the golden is yonder heaven," etc. (On these predecessors the representation in Manu 1. 9–13 depends.)

The conception of the egg of the universe appears in

[1] Bṛih. 3. 7. 3–14.

[2] Bṛih. 2. 1. 5–8, 2. 5. 1–10.

[3] Deussen, *Allgemeine Einleitung u. Philosophie des Veda*, pp. 183, 189.

[4] Ṛigv. X. 129. 3.

[5] *hiraṇyagarbha*, Ṛigv. X. 121. 1.

a more characteristic context together with that of the premundane purusha [1] in the creation myth at the beginning of the Aitareya Upanishad that belongs to the Ṛigveda :—"In the beginning the âtman alone was this universe; there was nothing else at all to meet the eye. He deliberated:—I will create worlds." Accordingly after he had created the earth and the atmosphere, the waters above and below, he drew forth the purusha from the waters, and gave him shape. Brooding over these waters they opened "like an egg," the mouth, nose, eyes, etc. of which are then developed, and from them the eight psychical organs, and from these in turn Agni, Vâyu, Âditya, etc. as the eight guardians of the universe, who finally take up their abode in men as speech, breath, sight, etc. Although however the human frame is thus animated by the organs of sense that spring from the purusha, it can only exist after the creator through the fissure of the skull (*vidṛiti*) has entered into it as individual soul. The tendency of this myth is clear. The purusha, that in Ṛigv. X. 90 had been the first principle, becomes here a power dependent on the âtman; and similarly only the organs of man's soul are ascribed to the purusha, but the soul itself to the âtman.

The most original and significant creation myth of the Upanishads is the representation of the evolution of the universe from the âtman in Bṛih. 1. 4. Here the traditional form of the creation myth appears only as a veil lightly thrown over the whole. The aim is not to relate a consistent history of the creation, but rather in a series of loosely connected creation pictures to teach the absolute dependence of all existing beings on the âtman. Accordingly the perpetual return of created things into the âtman is used to show how the division of

[1] Ṛigv. X. 90.

the universe into male and female, and then into the different species of animals by the flight of the female before the male, how the evolution of name and form, and the entrance of the âtman into them, together with the creation of the castes of the gods and afterwards of men, etc., how all this signifies only the self-evolution of the âtman to become the manifold universe, and the essential identity of all its phenomena with the âtman. Through the consciousness "I am Brahman" (*aham brahma asmi*)[1] the âtman becomes the universe, "and to this day whoever knows this 'I am brahman' he becomes this universe; nor have even the gods power to prevent his so becoming. For he is its soul (*âtman*)." Thus the traditional doctrine of the creation is preserved only as an external form. It serves merely to exhibit the sole reality of the âtman under the different phenomena of the universe.

From this lofty standpoint we see the Upanishads ever turning back to the realism natural to us, in order to teach in detail a creation of the universe, and of the elements of which it consists.

Like the Greek philosophers, Philolaus, Plato and Aristotle, most of the Indian thinkers distinguish five elements, — ether, wind, fire, water and earth. A dependence however of the Greek idea on the Indian, or the Indian on the Greek, is not to be thought of for this reason, if for no other, that the order of the elements is different, inasmuch as the Greeks place fire between ether and air, the Indians air between ether and fire. Further also because on both sides independently of one another the simple observation of nature led to the thought of the five compound states of matter, viz. the solid, fluid, gaseous, permanently elastic and the imponderable, as the five component parts of the material universe, to which correspond, as we shall see, the five

[1] Bṛih. 1. 4. 10.

specific energies of the organs of sense. The result is that both in the Greek and in the Indian philosophy we see the doctrine of the fivefold character of the elements gradually formed out of simpler conceptions.

The oldest element with the Indians is water. As early as Ṛigv. X. 129. 3 the first principle appeared as a "dark undulation" (*apraketam salilam*). In Ṛigv. X. 121. 9 Prajâpati begets "the great sparkling waters." These again appear in Ṛigv. X. 82. 1 as the primeval slime in which in the beginning heaven and earth were plunged; and in Ṛigv. X. 72. 4–6 as the "wave-surge," that is identical with *Aditi*, etc. In the Upanishads also the conception of the primeval waters still survives. "The waters are the body of that prâṇa!"[1] "This earth, the air, the heavens, the mountains, gods and men, domestic animals and birds, vegetables and trees, wild creatures down to worms, flies and ants, are nothing but this water under solid conditions, they are all nothing but this water under solid conditions."[2] In Kaush. 1. 7 also Brahman speaks to the soul that knows itself to be identical with him:—"The primeval waters in truth are my universe (as *hiraṇyagarbha*), and it is thine." In Kâṭh. 4. 6 again it is said of the purusha that he existed before the primeval waters; and the latter are to be understood in the following verse[3] by "*Aditi* the sustainer of the god that springs forth together with them to life." It also "dwells in the cavity of the heart" (in which according to Chând. 8. 1. 3 heaven and earth are confined), that is the primeval waters also are a product of the âtman dwelling in the heart. Therein, according to Îs'â 4, *Mâtaris'van*, (*i.e.* probably the prâṇa) has already interwoven the primeval waters; according to Mahânâr. 1. 4 he has sown by water the

[1] Bṛih. 1. 5. 13.
[2] Chând. 7. 10. 1.
[3] cp. Ṛigv. X. 72. 5, *supra*.

germ of life on the earth. The cosmogony also of Ait. 1. 1 is to be explained on the same principle. It seems to be especially closely connected with Ṛigv. X. 82. 1. There it is said that in the beginning the worlds were plunged in the *ghṛitam* of the primeval waters, and that the creator, having first fastened the extreme ends (which could only stand fast out of the waters), spread out heaven and earth between them. This gives the key to Ait. 1. 1, where it is said:—"He deliberated:—I will create worlds, the ocean, the realms of light, death, the waters (*ambho, marîc'îr, maram, âpas*). That is the ocean, beyond the heaven; the heaven is its floor. The atmosphere is the realms of light. Death is the earth. The waters are whatever is beneath it." After this description we have the waters as the two ends of the universe, above and below, and between them the clear atmosphere (hence called *marîc'îr*), and the dark earth (hence dead), *i.e.* the *sûrtam* and the *asûrtam rajas* of Ṛigv. X. 82. 4. By a reference to this passage the otherwise isolated description of the construction of the parts of the universe in Ait. 1. 1 seems to find a complete explanation. The same Upanishad further on [1] enumerates the five elements as usually given by later writers.

A further step is taken in Bṛih. 1. 2. 2, where we find the one element of the primeval waters replaced by three. Here also Prajâpati forms the water by his song of praise. From its churning the earth arises, fire from the labour and heat involved in the movement.

The leading authority for the number three of the elements is Chând. 6. 2. Here the waters are no longer the starting-point, but take their place between the subtler fire and the grosser earth. The tendency to choose for common subjects mystical terms intelligible only to the initiate (which in the Brahmasûtras is carried to an

[1] Ait. 3. 3.

absurd extreme) is exhibited in the description side by side with water whose name is retained of fire as *tejas* (heat), of earth as *annam* (food). The evolution of these three elements from one another and ultimately from the self-existent, *i.e.* Brahman, is systematically described and established:—"He proposed:—I will be many, will propagate myself. Accordingly he created heat (*tejas*). This heat proposed:—I will become many, will propagate myself. Accordingly it created the waters (*âpas*). Therefore when a man feels the heat of pain or perspires, water (*i.e.* tears, sweat) is produced from the heat. These waters proposed:—We will become many, will propagate ourselves. Accordingly they created food (*annam*). Therefore when it rains, abundant food is produced, for from the waters is produced food for man's eating." Then after the account of the entrance of the self-existent as individual soul (*jîva âtman*) into the three deities that he has created, *i.e.* into the elements, there follows next the order of development from one another, how the self-existent "made threefold" the elements that he had created, and alloyed each of them with constituent parts of the other three. Thus for example it is shown of fire, sun, moon and lightning, that the red in them consists of heat, the white of water, the black of food. According to this the substances recurring in nature are not pure elementary substances, but compounds of which, as Bâdarâyaṇa says,[1] *vais'eshyât tu tadvâdas tadvâdaḥ*; which admits of a literal rendering, *denominatio fit a potiori.* In this theory of the threefold division of the primitive elements lies the earliest germ of the later distinction of pure substances (*tanmâtra*) and gross elements (*sthûlabhûtâni*). This distinction is first drawn in Pras'na 4. 8, where there are distinguished—"The earth and the earth-substance (*pṛithivî c'a pṛithivîmâtrâ*

[1] Sûtra 2. 4. 22.

c'a), the water and the water-substance, heat and the heat-substance, the wind and the wind-substance, the ether and the ether-substance." The expressions here used, *pṛithivîmâtrâ*, *apomâtrâ*, *tejomâtrâ*, *vâyumâtrâ*, *âkâs'amâtrâ*, were later comprehended under the term *tanmâtra*, "subsisting from this alone," which is found first in Maitr. 3. 2, and later on in Prâṇâgnihotrop. 4, Mahop. 1. (A derivation from *tanu-mâtra*, as might perhaps be maintained, is not to be thought of, after what has been said.) In the verse Manu 1. 27 (which is disconnected from the context) the tanmâtras are referred to as *aṇvyo mâtrâḥ*, and in the Sâṅkhya philosophy they play an important part, as will later be shown. Bâdarâyaṇa does not name them, and S'ankara[1] mentions them as technical terms of the Sâṅkhya only to reject them, although in his doctrine of the subtle body a kindred conception finds a place. The three elements having been increased to five, each was then conceived as fivefold instead of threefold, in such a way, according to the Vedântasâra, that half of each of the fivefold elements was pure, and the other half was made up of the remaining four elements; so that *e.g.* natural water consists of a half water together with an eighth of earth, fire, air and ether. The theory however propounded in Vedântasâra 128 in connection with this triple or fivefold distribution, according to which the earth can be smelt, tasted, seen, felt and heard, water be tasted, seen, felt and heard, fire be seen, felt and heard, the wind felt and heard, and the ether merely heard, must not be regarded as suggesting it. For this theory implies not the compounded but the uncompounded elements, which as they proceed forth from one another preserve the attributes of the elements from which they have proceeded (the wind can be heard as well as felt, because it has proceeded from the audible ether). On the contrary,

[1] In his commentary on 2. 2. 10, 14.

the theory is opposed to the triple or fivefold distribution, since for example the fivefold ether, for the very reason that the four other elements are intermingled in it, can no longer be merely audible, but must be capable also of being felt, seen, tasted and smelt. Beyond however the observation that in all of them there are traces of all,[1] we were able to indicate, as suggesting the triple or fivefold distribution, only the fact that the human organism, although it takes up nothing but simple substances as food, yet assimilates from them all three elements, food water and heat, which according to the description attached to the threefold distribution of the elements in Chând. 6. 5 are requisite for its growth.

A great advance on the passage discussed,[2] which represents only three elements, viz.—fire water and earth, as proceeding forth from Brahman, is found in the later insertion of ether (or space, *âkâs'a*) and wind (*vâyu*), which in earlier times, as we saw, had themselves been regarded as symbolical representations of Brahman, as the two subtlest elements between Brahman and fire. By this means the number of five elements was obtained, and this with few exceptions was assumed by all the later philosophers of India. The earliest passage that represents the five elements as proceeding forth according to the scheme laid down in Chând. 6. 2, the first from Brahman and each in succession from its immediate predecessor, is Taitt. 2. 1 (enumerations like Bṛih. 4. 4. 5 do not enter into consideration), a passage which has acquired a fundamental meaning in Indian philosophy:—"From this âtman, in truth, has the ether (space) arisen, from the ether the wind, from the wind the fire, from the fire the water, from the water the earth." This number of five elements corresponds, as we shall see later, to the

[1] cp. *πᾶν ἐν παντὶ μεμῖχθαι*, Anaxagoras in *Ar. Phys.* 1. 4. 187, *b* 1.
[2] Chând. 6. 2 f

number of five organs of knowledge (hearing, touch, sight, taste, smell) which has suggested if not the primary enunciation, yet the definite arrangement of the five elements. Each element has its assigned quality (sound, resistance, colour, flavour, odour), and besides this, as already remarked above, the qualities of those elements out of which each has proceeded. Later passages of the Upanishads, in which the five elements are partly enumerated, partly referred to, are Ait. 3. 3 (still unarranged); S'vet. 2. 12, 6. 2 (cp. also Kâṭh. 3. 15); Pras'na 6. 4, Maitr. 3. 2, 6. 4, Âtma 2, Piṇḍa 2, Prâṇâgnihotra 4.

4. *Organic Nature*

The essential identity of the universe with Brahman is thus represented as a creation of the universe by Brahman with a view to suit man's intellectual capacity, which is adjusted to relations of cause. According to the meaning of the Indian word for creation, *sṛishṭi*, this is to be thought of as a discharge, a setting free or emission, an emergence therefore of the universe from Brahman; although this is really in contradiction with the fundamental dogma of the sole reality of Brahman. The doctrine therefore of the creation of the universe, if this last were not to be contrasted with Brahman as a second and foreign, demanded for its completion the idea that Brahman himself having created the universe entered into it as soul. "Into it (the universe) that one (the âtman) has entered up to the finger-tips."[1] "Thereupon that deity (Brahman) entered into these three deities (the elements) with this living self (*jîva âtman*, the individual soul), and separated out thence name and form."[2] "After he had created it, he entered into it."[3] "Thereupon he cleft asunder here the crown of the head, and entered through this gate."[4] Brahman creates the

[1] Bṛih. 1. 4. 7. [2] Chând. 6. 3. 3. [3] Taitt. 2. 6. [4] Ait. 1. 3. 12.

organisms as citadels (*puras*), and then enters into them as citizen (*purusha, i.e.* as the soul), cp. Bṛih. 2. 5. 18 :—

> As citadels he created the bipeds,
> As citadels the quadrupeds also ;
> Into the citadels he entered as a bird,
> Into the citadels as citizen.

All living creatures, and therefore all plants, animals, men and gods, are abodes of this character, into which Brahman has entered as individual soul.

> From him the gods in their many forms have sprung,
> The blessed ones also ; from him, men, cattle and birds,
> Inspiration and exspiration, rice and barley,

as it is expressed in Muṇḍ. 2. 1. 7, echoing Ṛigv. X. 90. 8 and Atharvav. XI. 4. 13. Accordingly all living creatures are Brahman :—" This (consciousness, *i.e.* the âtman) is Brahman, this is Indra, this is Prajâpati, this is all the gods ; it is the five elements, earth, wind, ether, water, lights ; it is the tiny living creatures, and whatever is similar to them ; it is the seed of one and another kind ; it is that which is born of an egg or the mother's womb, of sweat or from a shoot ; it is horses, cattle, men, elephants,—all that lives, all that walks or flies, all that is motionless." [1] By the " motionless " (*sthâvaram*) the plant world is to be understood. On the entire passage S'ankara remarks :— " Thus in the individual bodily forms from Brahman down to a blade of grass (*brahmâdi-stambaparyanteshu*, an expression frequently employed later) Brahman assumes this or that name and form." A division of organic beings into three classes, " born from the egg, born alive, and born from the germ," is found as early as Chând. 6. 3. 1, to which the foregoing (later) passage adds as a fourth class, " born from sweat " (insects and the like). In each of these phenomenal forms the entire Brahman dwells.

[1] Ait. 3. 3.

Brahman is called *Sâman*, "because he is equivalent (*sama*) to the ant, the gnat, the elephant, these three world-regions, to this entire universe."[1] Chând. 6. 11. 1 furnishes an example of the animation of plants in the case of the tree which exists "penetrated through and through by the living self (*jîva âtman*, the individual souls), exuberant and joyful." That the migration of soul extends to the plant world also is taught by Kâṭh. 5. 7 :—

> The one enters into the maternal womb,
> Incorporating himself in bodily form,
> Into a plant another moves,
> Each according to his works or knowledge.

According to the above the migration of souls extends to the world of the gods :—"As a sculptor takes the material from a statue, and chisels therefrom another newer fairer form, so this soul also, after it has shaken off the body and rid itself of ignorance (temporarily), creates for itself another newer fairer form, whether of the fathers or the Gandharvas or the gods or Prajâpati or Brahmân or other beings."[2] The coming forth of the creatures from Brahman, after their entrance into him (in deep sleep and in death), like the nectar of the flowers into the honey or the rivers into the ocean, takes place unconsciously :—"Therefore in truth none of all these creatures when they come forth again from the self-existent one know that they come forth again from the self-existent one; that whether they were tiger here or lion or wolf or boar or worm or bird or gadfly or gnat, whatever they may have been, thereto are they again fashioned."[3] Cp. the similar and perhaps borrowed enumeration in Kaush. 1. 2 —"Whether in this world he be worm or fly or fish or bird or lion or boar or stinging insect or tiger or man, whatever he was formerly, in this or that place is he reborn, each according to his works or according to his knowledge."

[1] Bṛih. 1. 3. 22. [2] Bṛih. 4. 4. 4. [3] Chând. 6. 10. 2.

A mythical description of the origin of human and animal kinds is given in Bṛih. 1. 4. 3–4. The âtman is originally neither male nor female, but (as in the myth of Aristophanes in Plato *Symp.* 189 C *seq.*) an undistinguished union of the two, which is cleft asunder, and in the act of begetting attains to a fresh unity. Thereupon the female flees, and hides herself successively in the different species of animals, the cow, horse, ass, goat, sheep, down to the ant; the âtman however pursues her through all the forms, and thus begets individual creatures of each kind. We might be tempted to read a deeper meaning into this myth. The male principle would be the will which desires to manifest itself, the female the essence of the forms (the Platonic idea) which although derived from the will is yet distinct from it and flees from it, until the creative will gains the mastery, in order in it to give expression to all its own being. In any case the myth asserts that all animal and human forms are essentially similar, and are alike incarnations of the âtman.

In what follows[1] is described how the âtman creates above and beyond himself the various classes of gods:—"Because he created the gods to be higher (than he himself is), and because he being mortal created the immortal, therefore is he called the overplus of creation (*atisṛishṭi*)." This much at least is implied, that the âtman incorporated in man contains in himself the principle of all higher worlds and beings.

5. *The Soul of the Universe* (*Hiraṇyagarbha, Brahmân*)

The soul of the universe is related to the body of the universe as the individual soul to its body. This as denoted by Brahmân (masc.), distinguished from Brahman (neut.) the first principle, or even by *Hiraṇyagarbha*, which

[1] Bṛih. 1. 4. 6, 11–15.

according to Ṛigv. X. 121. 1 came forth as the first-born of creation from the primeval waters which were created by the first principle. Because it is the first principle itself which appears in its creation as first-born, therefore the latter also is denoted by Brahmân with change of gender and accent, as though it were Brahman personified. In the texts of the older Upanishads this conception is but little developed. In Bṛih. 4. 4. 4, as quoted above, Brahmân (unquestionably to be taken as masc.) also appears together with Prajâpati and the other gods as an example of a soul subject to transmigration. In Ait. 3. 3 Brahmân is named at the head of the living beings, in whom the âtman manifests himself.[1] In Kaush. 1 again, where this Brahmân conceived as a person receives the souls as they arrive in the other world, his identity with *Hiraṇyagarbha* is indicated by the closing words :—"The primeval waters, in truth, are my universe, and they are thine."[2] Otherwise in older texts the personal Brahmân[3] is mentioned only as the bearer of the divine revelation[4] who communicates it to mankind. So in Chând. 3. 11. 4, 8. 15, Muṇḍ. 1. 1. 1–2, and frequently in later Upanishads.

This conception of the first-born of creation as the original source of all wisdom is carried further first in the S'vetâs'vatara Upanishad (which in general inclines towards a personification of the divine), and here it is described as the *Brahmân*, *Hiraṇyagarbha* the "golden germ," or even in one passage[5] with a poetic and metaphorical use of the

[1] In this passage also it is natural to read *esha brahmâ* instead of *esha brahma*, as it is printed by an oversight in Ait. Âr. 2. 6. 1. 5, p. 299. 3 ; cp. also the words of Sâyaṇa that immediately follow :—*anena pul-liṅgena brahmas'abdena* '*Hiraṇyagarbhaḥ samavartata agre*' *ity-âdi-s'âstra-prasiddhaḥ prathamaḥ s'arîrî vivakshitaḥ.*

[2] Kaush. 1. 7.

[3] Or occasionally in his place *Parameshṭhin* or *Prajâpati*, *e.g.* Bṛih. 2. 6. 3, 4. 6. 3, 6. 5. 4.

[4] As Vena before him, cp. *Allgemeine Einleitung*, p. 252 f.

[5] 5. 2.

word as the "red wizard," *kapila ṛishi*,[1] an expression that has led many into the mistaken belief that here, in a Vedic Upanishad, Kapila the founder of the Sâṅkhya system was named as the first-born of creation! Had the author of our Upanishad, so strongly opposed to all dualism and atheism, known him (which we do not believe), he would have assuredly characterised him with altogether different epithets. The opinion that Kapila is here named is only possible so long as the passage is isolated and treated without regard to the connection of the Upanishad as a whole, which in four other passages gives expression to the very same thought that occurs here. It celebrates Rudra (S'iva), in whom it sees the primeval being, as the original source of all wisdom:—"from him wisdom emanated at the very beginning";[2] "he is called the primal purusha, the great one";[3] it is he "who created the god Brahmân in the beginning, and who communicates to him the Vedas also";[4] "who formerly begat Hiraṇyagarbha";[5] "who himself saw Hiraṇyagarbha arise";[6] and with reference to the last passage it is then said:—"He who in spirit went pregnant with that first-begotten red wizard (*kapilam ṛishim*),[7] and saw him born."[8] The word *tam* pointing back, and the expression *jâyamânam c'a pas'yet*, compared with *pas'yata jâyamânam* 4. 12, assuredly place the reference to the latter passage, and consequently to Hiraṇyagarbha, beyond doubt.

Of later Upanishads mention must be made that according to Nârâyaṇa 1 Brahmân originates from *Nârâyaṇa*, and that according to Atharvas'iras 6 the egg of the universe originates from *Rudra*, according to Mahâ 3 from *Nârâyaṇa*, and Brahmân from this in turn. He is also indicated as the source of knowledge in Piṇḍa 1,

[1] *i.e.* red like gold. [2] S'vet. 4. 18; cp. Bṛih. 2. 4. 10.
[3] *agryaḥ purusho mahân*, 3. 19; cp. *mahân âtmâ*, Kâṭh. 3. 10, 6. 7.
[4] 6. 18. [5] 3. 4. [6] 4. 12. [7] Mentioned in 3. 4 and 4. 12. [8] 5. 2.

Gâruḍa 3, and (under the name *Hiraṇyagarbha*) Mahâ 4. In contrast with the self-conscious *jîva* (the individual soul) Hiraṇyagarbha is described in Nṛisiṁhott. 9 as "self-conscious of all" (*sarvâhammânin*).

To the series of primeval beings, primeval waters, and first-born (*Brahmân, Hiraṇyagarbha*) there corresponds the description of *purusha*, *avyaktam*, and *mahân âtmâ* given after abandoning the mythological form in Kâṭh. 3. 10–11, 6. 7–8, as the three earliest principles. Here, in contrast with the individual âtman, the *mahân âtmâ* (the great self, corresponding to the *mahân purusha* of S′vet. 3. 19), is the soul of the universe, *i.e.* the "self-conscious of all" Hiraṇyagarbha. *Buddhi* is still subordinated to the *mahân âtmâ* in Kâṭh. 3. 10. A combination of the two leads later on to the cosmical intellect (*mahân, buddhi*) of the Sâṅkhya philosophy. On other lines the νοῦς of the Neo-platonists that emanates from ἕν, just as the "pure knowing subject" (the eternal eye of the universe) of the philosophy of Schopenhauer, corresponds to the cosmical intellect as sustainer of the universe (*Hiraṇyagarbha, Mahân*). For the metaphysical comprehension of the universe this idea is indispensable. We know (and the Indians knew also as early as Bṛih. 2. 4. 5) that the entire objective universe is possible only in so far as it is sustained by a knowing subject. This subject as sustainer of the objective universe is manifested in all individual subjects, but is by no means identical with them. For the individual subjects pass away,[1] but the objective universe continues to exist without them; there exists therefore the eternal knowing subject also (*Hiraṇyagarbha*) by whom it is sustained. Space and time are derived from this subject. It is itself accordingly not in space and does not belong to time, and therefore from an empirical point of view it is in general non-existent; it has no empirical, only a metaphysical reality.

[1] "After death there is no consciousness," Bṛih. 2. 4. 12; cp. 3. 2. 12.

VII. Brahman as Preserver and Ruler

1. *Brahman as Preserver of the Universe*

Since in reality the âtman alone exists, and the universe, so far as it has a general existence, is essentially only the âtman, it follows that the things of this universe, so far as we may concede to them a reality at all, can only hold it in fee from the âtman. They are related to the latter as the sparks to the fire whence they leap forth, and with which they are essentially identical in nature :—" As the tiny sparks leap forth from the fire, so from this âtman all vital spirits spring forth, all worlds, all gods, all living creatures."[1] This illustration is expanded in greater detail in Muṇḍ. 2. 1. 1 :—

> As from the well-kindled fire the sparks,
> Essentially akin to it, leap forth a thousandfold,
> So, my dear sir, from the imperishable
> The varied living creatures come forth,
> And return into it again.

All the things of the universe are, as this passage asserts, " essentially akin to it,"[2] are the âtman himself, and it is he alone who lies outspread before our eyes as the entire universe : —

> Fire is his head, sun and moon his eyes,
> His ears the regions of the sky,
> His voice is the revelation of the Veda,
> Wind is his breath, the world his heart, from his feet arises the earth,
> He is the inner self in all creatures.[3]

How the one âtman is expanded into the manifold universe remains a mystery, and can only be explained by illustrations. Thus in Chând. 6. 12 the teacher causes a fruit of the Nyagrodha tree (whose shoots grow downwards

[1] Bṛih. 2. 1. 20 ; cp. Kaush. 4. 20.

[2] *sarûpa*, or *svarûpa*, "having its form."

[3] Muṇḍ. 2. 1. 4.

and strike new roots in the earth, so that a whole grove springs up from one tree), to be brought and opened, and after the student has found in it only a quite small kernel, and within this nothing at all, the teacher addresses him: —"The subtle essence, which you do not observe, my dear sir, from this subtle essence in truth this great Nyagrodha tree has sprung up. Be confident, my dear sir, whatever this subtle essence is, of which this universe is a subsistence (a 'having this as its essence,' *aitadâtmyam*), that is the real, that is the soul, that art thou, O S'vetaketu."

The expansion of the unity into plurality is elucidated also by the frequently misunderstood comparison of Kâṭh. 6. 1:—

> With its root on high, its shoots downwards,
> Stands that eternal fig-tree.

All who here take *mûla* in *ûrdhvamûla* as plural, and render "die Wurzeln," "the roots," "les racines," etc., have failed to grasp the meaning of the comparison, which consists precisely in showing how from the one Brahman as root the multiplicity of the phenomena of the universe arises. The universe therefore is likened to an as'vattha tree, in the case of which, like our own linden, from the one root the rich variety of its branches and shoots springs. The difference is that in the as'vattha which represents the universe the one root Brahman is above, and the many shoots of its manifestations are here below on the earth. It is altogether misleading to think here of the Nyagrodha tree (*ficus indica*), which sends its shoots into the earth where they strike new roots. The as'vattha (*ficus religiosa*) is entirely distinct from it in growth and foliage. It is interesting to see that the passage of the Kâṭhaka discussed is to all appearance already referred to in S'vet. 3. 9.[1] When it is said in this passage:—"rooted

[1] As also Mahânâr. 10. 20.

in heaven like a tree the One stands,"[1] the explanation is found in the passage Kâṭh. 6. 1, and only there.

From the universal diffusion of the âtman its omnipresence in the phenomenal forms of the universe results, as is described in Kâṭh. 5. 2, where use is made of the verse Ṛigv. IV. 40. 5 :[2]—

> In the ether he is the swan of the sun, in the air Vasu,
> The priest at the altar, the guest on the threshold,
> He dwells in man and at a distance, in law, in space,
> He as supreme Right springs forth from the waters, from cattle, right, and the hills.

With a reference to the verse Vâj. Saṁh. 32. 4, the divine omnipresence is depicted in S'vet. 2. 16–17 :—

> He is god in all the regions of the universe,
> Born of older time and in the body of a mother;
> He was born, and will be born,
> Is present in men, and omnipresent.
>
> The god, who is in the fire and in the water,
> Who has entered into the entire universe,
> Who dwells in vegetables and in trees,
> To this god be honour, be honour!

It is a consequence of the omnipresence of the âtman that all creatures share in the bliss which is his essence (*sup.* p. 140 ff.) :—"From a small portion only of this bliss other creatures have their life";[3] "for who could breathe, who live, if that bliss were not in the âkâs'a; for it is he who creates bliss."[4] Therefore longing for the âtman is innate in all beings, and equally for him who knows himself as the âtman :—"His (Brahman's) name is 'longing for him' (*tadvanam*), as 'longing for him' ought he to be worshipped. He who knows himself as such, for him assuredly all beings long."[5]

[1] cp. also the tree of the universe in S'vet. 6. 6.
[2] = Mahânâr. 10. 6, cp. the further references there.
[3] Bṛih. 4. 3. 32.
[4] Taitt. 2. 7.
[5] Kena, 31; cp. the saying of Aristotle, κινεῖ δὲ ὡς ἐρώμενον.

Every effect in the universe is wrought by the âtman:—"It is he who causes the man whom he will lead on high from these worlds to do good works, and it is he who causes the man whom he will lead downwards to do evil works."[1] Even the gods do their work only by virtue of the power which he confers on them; no blade of grass can be consumed by Agni, or swept away by Vâyu, apart from the will of Brahman.[2]

The most beautiful picture of the omnipotence of the imperishable one, *i.e.* the âtman, is found, partly dependent on the hymn to Prajâpati in Ṛigv. X. 121, in Yâjñavalkhya's discourse with Gârgî, Bṛih. 3. 8. 9:—

"At the bidding of this imperishable one, O Gârgî, sun and moon are kept asunder; at the bidding of this imperishable one, O Gârgî, heaven and earth are kept asunder; at the bidding of this imperishable one, O Gârgî, the minutes and the hours are kept asunder, the days and nights, the fortnights, the months, the seasons and the years; at the bidding of this imperishable one, O Gârgî, the streams run from the snow-mountains, some to the east and others to the west, whithersoever each goes; at the bidding of this imperishable one, O Gârgî, men praise the bountiful givers, the gods desire the sacrificer, the fathers the offerings to the dead."

This passage, in which all dispositions in space and time, as well as every effect in nature and every desire of men, gods, and manes are ascribed to the âtman, has been often imitated. The comparison of the âtman in Bṛih. 4. 4. 22[3] to a *setu*, a word that denotes not only the (connecting) "bridge," but also the (separating) "dike," depends probably upon its first part which speaks of the power of the âtman to keep asunder:—"he is the Lord of the universe, he is the ruler of living beings, he is the protector of living beings; he is the bridge which (the

[1] Kaush. 3. 8. [2] Kena, 17–23. [3] Quoted in Maitr. 77.

dike which) keeps asunder these worlds, to prevent their clashing together." The last words recur in Châṇd. 8. 4. 1:—"The âtman, he is the bridge (the dike) that keeps asunder these worlds to prevent their clashing together." When however it is further said:—"This bridge neither day nor night cross, nor old age, nor death, nor suffering," etc., we have, with a sudden change of the point of view, in place of the dike that separates the relative parts of the universe, a bridge that connects the present with the future world. And this circumstance affords probably a reliable proof of the important conclusion that the similarly sounding words are derived from Bṛih. 4. 4. 22, and their original meaning being lost were reproduced in Châṇd. 8. 4. 1. The conception thus modified of the bridge of immortality is then further taken over, apparently from Châṇd. 8. 4. 1, by S'vet. 6. 19 and Muṇḍ. 2. 2. 5. The entire preceding paragraph in Muṇḍ. 2. 1 is in reality an interweaving of the passage quoted [1] with Ṛigv. X. 90 and other additions.[2]

2. *Brahman as Ruler of the Universe*

When it is said in the words quoted from Bṛih. 4. 4. 22, and also in Kaush. 3. 8 (probably in imitation of this passage):—"He is the protector of the universe, he is the ruler of the universe," two things are implied: (1) that the âtman as protector of the universe maintains things in their condition. This point has been already discussed,—and (2) that he as ruler of the universe guides the creatures in their action. For this latter statement the principal chapter to be considered, together with several that have been already quoted, is Bṛih. 3. 7, which treats of the âtman as the *antaryâmin*, *i.e.* the "inner guide." Yâjñavalkhya begins his instruction on this subject in Bṛih. 3. 7. 3 with the words:—"He who dwelling on the earth is distinct from the earth, whom

[1] Bṛih. 3. 8.

[2] See Deussen, *Upan.*, p. 550 f.

the earth knows not, whose body the earth is, who rules the earth from within, he is thy soul, the inner guide, the immortal." What is here asserted of the earth is then further affirmed, with continual repetition of the same formula, of eleven other natural phenomena (water, fire, atmosphere, wind, sky, sun, heavenly regions, moon and stars, ether, darkness and light), then of all living creatures, and finally of the eight organs (breath, speech, eye, ear, manas, skin, intellect, seed); all these natural phenomena, living creatures, and organs are thus the body of the âtman, but are distinct (*antara*) from him, do not know him, and yet are ruled by him from within. The passage also is frequently used in the sequel. This is especially the case in Mâṇḍûkya 6, and in its reproduction in Nrisiṁhap. 4. 1, Nrisiṁhott. 1, Râmott. 3; also Brahmop. 1 and Bâshkala. A (worthless) definition of the Antaryâmin is given in Sarvopanishatsâra No. 19:—"When the âtman as the cause of the natural constitution of compounds endowed with the supreme (consciousness) etc., appears in all bodies, like the string threaded through the store of pearls, he is then called the inner guide" (*antaryâmin*). In the Vedântasâra § 43 the *antaryâmin* is identified with *Îs'vara*. A similar place is held by it in the system of Râmânuja.

To the *antaryâmin* of Bṛih. 3. 7 there corresponds in the "honey-doctrine" of Bṛih. 2. 5 the "mighty immortal spirit" (*tejomaya amṛitamaya purusha*), who dwells in all cosmical and psychical phenomenal forms, and therefore renders possible their mutual influence. Here also the valuable fundamental thought is presented in a form which for us has little attraction, in that the same stereotyped formula is repeated fourteen times in succession, a different idea being employed each time:—"This earth," so the section begins, "is the honey of all living creatures, is the honey of all living creatures; but that which on the earth that mighty immortal spirit is, and that which in relation to the self that corporeal mighty immortal spirit is, it is even that which is the soul (*âtman*) here. This is the immortal, this is Brahman, this the universe." The same which is here affirmed of earth and body is then further affirmed, with invariable repetition of the same formula, of water and seed, fire and speech, wind and breath, sun and eye, etc. The eye is nourished (exists) by the sun, and the sun by the eye (it would not be there if no eye beheld it), and this mutual dependence is only possible because in both the same mighty immortal spirit, *i.e.* the âtman, dwells.[1]

By the side of these leading passages it will be sufficient merely to make brief mention of the twelve or sixteen purushas put forward as Brahman by Bâlâki Gârgya in Bṛih. 2. 1, Kaush. 4, with which Ajâtas'atru contrasts the âtman as he "who is the creator of all those spirits, whose work this universe is."[2] Just as the eight purushas regarded as the âtman by Vidagdha S'âkalya in Bṛih. 3. 9. 10–18, 26 (corporeality, desire, the sun, hearing, the shadow, the mirror, water, the son), with which Yâjñavalkhya contrasts the "spirit of the Upanishad doctrine" (*aupanishada purusha*), "who impelling asunder these spirits, and driving them back, steps over and beyond them," *i.e.* who spurs them on to their work, recalls them from it, and is pre-eminent over them.[3]

3. *Freedom and Constraint of the Will*

In connection with the doctrine of Brahman as ruler of the universe, we propose briefly to consider the question of the freedom and constraint of the human will. Since the entire universe, so far as in general it has any exist-

[1] In the introduction to our translation of this paragraph (*Upan.*, p. 420) we have already called attention to the similar teaching of Kant of the "affinity of phenomenal forms," which is possible only through the "synthetic unity of apperception," *i.e.* through the knowing subject.

[2] Kaush. 4. 19. [3] Bṛih. 3. 9. 26.

ence, is only the self-manifestation of the âtman, there can be as little question in the Upanishads as with Spinoza of a freedom of the will within the range of nature. Such a freedom would assume a different character of the âtman. The standpoint of the Upanishads therefore is a rigid determinism :[1]—" Man is altogether fashioned out of desire (*kâma*); according to his desire is his discernment (*kratu*); according to his discernment he does his work (*karma*)."[2] "At the bidding of this imperishable one, O Gârgî, men praise the bountiful givers, the gods desire the sacrificer, the fathers the offerings to the dead."[3] They all, men, gods and fathers, cannot act otherwise than is in harmony with their nature. "For just as men here below pursue the aim after which each aspires, as though it were done at command, whether it be a kingdom or an estate, and live only for that (so in their aspiration for heavenly reward they are the slaves of their desires)."[4]

The words that immediately follow stand in sharp contrast to this statement. Just as Kant, after having in the most decisive manner affirmed the empirical constraint of the will by the eclipse of the sun which may be calculated beforehand, forthwith asserts in the very same line "that man is free,"[5] so it is said further on in the passage quoted :—"Therefore he who departs from this world without having known the soul or those true desires, his part in all worlds is a life of constraint; but he who departs from this world after having known the soul and those true desires, his part in all worlds is a life of freedom."[6] The meaning of this contrast is evident; as sharers in the continuity of nature we are, like it, subject to necessity; but we are free from it as

[1] Bṛih. 4. 4. 5.
[2] Compare the similar remark in S'atap. Br. X. 6. 3, and Chând. 3. 14. 1.
[3] Bṛih. 3. 8. 9.
[4] Chând. 8. 1. 5.
[5] *Krit. d. prakt. Vernunft*, p. 120, Kehrb.
[6] Chând. 8. 1. 6; cp. the similar statements in Chând. 7. 25. 2, 8. 5. 4.

soon as, by virtue of the knowledge of our identity with the âtman, we are set free from this continuity of nature. That the âtman is exempt from the constraint of causality we have already seen (p. 154 ff.). Each of us is this eternally free âtman. We do not first become the âtman, but we are it already, though unconscious of the fact. Accordingly we are already free in reality, in spite of the absolute necessity of our acts, but we do not know it. "Just as he who does not know the hiding-place of a treasure of gold does not find it, although he may pass over it again and again, so none of these creatures find the world of Brahman, although they daily enter into it (in deep sleep); for they are constrained by unreality."[1] "Those therefore who find this world of Brahman by Brahmac'âryam (a life spent as a Brahman student in study and self-mortification), of such is this world of Brahman, and such have part in all worlds in a life of freedom."[2] The constraint of the will, absolute as it is, yet belongs entirely to the great illusion of the empirical reality, and vanishes with it. The phenomenal form is under constraint, but that which makes its appearance in it, the âtman, is free. The real consistency of the two points of view is expressed in the words:—"It is he who causes the man whom he will lead on high out of these worlds to do good works, and it is he who causes the man whom he will lead downwards to do evil works."[3] How this thought assumes the form of a doctrine of predestination, in proportion as the âtman is conceived as a personal god, has been already shown (p. 172 ff.). But the entire doctrine of predestination, like the theïsm on which it depends, is in the Upanishads only an attempt to express in empirical forms what is essentially foreign to them. The eternally free âtman, who determines our doing and abstaining, is not another, contrasted with us, but our own self. Therefore

[1] Chând. 8. 3. 2. [2] Chând. 8. 4. 3. [3] Kaush. 3. 8.

it is said of the âtman :—"He fetters himself by himself (*nibadhnâti âtmanâ âtmânam*), like a bird by its nest."[1] And in Pras'na 3. 3 the answer to the question, how the âtman enters into this body is given :—"he enters into this body *manokṛitena*," which if we follow S'ankara would here mean "by the action of his will," although grammar requires a different conception (as *mano-'kṛitena*, "unconsciously)," an objection which (in spite of Ṛigv. I. 187. 7) it is difficult to pass by with a *sandhir ârshaḥ* (as Anandajñâna says).

4. *Brahman as Providence*

While the control of the universe may be ascribed to an impersonal principle (acting as *antaryâmin*, "inner guide"), Providence implies a personal God. In harmony with this in the ancient Upanishads we see a belief in Providence, like theism, make its appearance only here and there as a poetical form of representation. It is only in the later Upanishads that with the personification of the âtman belief in a divine providence also acquires a firmer consistency. The conception of Ait. 1. 2 is mythical throughout, describing how the deities, (*i.e.* the organs of sense and the corresponding nature gods), produced by the âtman from the purusha, plunge into the ocean, suffer hunger and thirst, and then receive from the âtman mankind allotted to them as a domicile, in which they may enjoy food, which they are then however compelled to share with the demoniac powers of hunger and thirst. The "well-being" also (*i.e.* probably "adaptability") which in Taitt. 2. 7 is declared to be the essence of the universe, and (by means of a play on the words *sukṛita* and *svakṛita*) is deduced from the fact that the universe is only a self-manifestation of the Brahman who is essentially bliss, can only be regarded as the first

[1] Maitr. 3. 2.

germ of a belief in a providence that guides to ends. Such a providence appears more clearly as early as Kâṭh. 5. 13:—

> He who as the eternal creates the temporal,
> Himself pure bliss, as spirit creates the spirits, as one the many,
> He who, the wise, sees them dwell in himself,
> He alone and no other has eternal peace.

The concession which the first half of this verse makes to theism is retracted in the second half, and it is characteristic that in the reproduction of this verse in S'vet. 6. 13 the second half is altered in a theistic sense:—

> He who by examination (*sâṅkhyam*) and devotion (*yoga*)
> Knows this primeval one as god, is freed from all fetters.[1]

A significant advance in the direction of theism and belief in providence is found in the thought which is repeated from Kâṭh. 5. 13 in Îs'â 8, where it is said (word for word):—"The wise, thoughtful, all-comprehending, self-existent one has assigned ends *yâthâtathyato* for all time." The word *yâthâtathyato*, interpolated later as the metre shows, gives evidence of a further advance upon the original verse; "in proportion to the quality," *i.e.* according to (*yathâ*) the works of the individual soul, so (*tathâ*) has the wise thoughtful one (*kavir manîshî*) determined beforehand the ends (the fruit of actions, the doing and suffering of each soul). This is already, unless we have read too much into the verse, the part which *îs'vara* plays in the later Vedânta. The works of the soul are the seed-corn, which in close correspondence with its quality is made to grow by god as the rain; just as by the seed the plant, so by the works of the earlier existence the future life is determined both as regards its doing and its suffering. A clear distinction between these two is not

[1] According to some, the author here, as a foundation for his theism appeals to the atheistic Sâṅkhya system!

to be found even in the later Vedânta. In general this later Vedânta standpoint is anticipated by the S'vetâs'vatara Upanishad, which in harmony with its theistic colouring depicts the âtman as "the overseer of actions,"[1] "the only free one, who multiplies the one seed of many who are by nature free from actions,"[2] who apportions to each his qualities,[3] who executes justice, restrains the evil, allots good fortune,[4] "who, himself colourless, but endowed abundantly with powers, assigns the numerous colours to appointed ends,"[5] who brings to maturity the actions of the soul:—

When every birth comes to maturity with his being,
Whatever is to ripen, he makes it all to grow;
He as one, guides here all and each,
Apportioning to each his peculiar gifts.[6]

It is moreover characteristic of this Upanishad (which we compared above to a *codex palimpsestus*), that the ancient Upanishad thought ever and anon makes itself apparent through this elaborate theistic doctrine of recompense; by virtue of which it is God Himself who fetters Himself as soul to continually new forms corresponding to the actions that have been committed:—

As soul he chooses many forms both gross
And subtle, corresponding to his virtue;
And that which bound him by the power of his work and of himself
To this, binds him also to another.[7]

We see therefore the thinkers of the Upanishads, after they have wandered in obedience to the empirical determination of their intellect, into realistic modes of representation, constantly returning to the original idealism.

[1] S'vet. 6. 11.
[2] S'vet. 6. 12; in reality the soul is actionless like the âtman, which it is.
[3] S'vet. 6. 4.
[4] S'vet. 6. 6.
[5] S'vet. 4. 1.
[6] S'vet. 5. 5.
[7] S'vet. 5. 12.

5. *Cosmography of the Upanishads*

The views that are found in the Upanishads with regard to the universe and its parts are scanty in detail, and possess little consistency.

As concerns, to begin with, the geographical horizon, it is seen to be essentially limited by the ranges of the Himâlaya and Vindhya on the north and south,[1] and by the river basins and mouths of the Indus and Ganges on the west and east. Day is born in the ocean towards the east, night in the ocean towards the west.[2] "These streams, my dear sir, flow in the east towards the morning, and in the west towards the evening; from ocean to ocean they flow (uniting together), they become open sea."[3] What lies beyond these limits appears to be unknown. Only in a quite late Upanishad that is founded upon the Râmâyaṇa is mention made of Laṅkâ in (*sic*) Ceylon[4] and similar names. But even the country of the Indus appears as almost unknown. Noble steeds are brought thence,[5] perhaps salt also;[6] the people of Gandhâra (west of the Indus, and south of Peshawar) appear in Chând. 6. 14 as distant; the Brahman students penetrate in their wanderings as far as the *Madras* (on the Hyphasis).[7] Just as Yâjñavalkhya appears as the greatest personality in the Upanishads, so Janaka appears as the centre of the intellectual life of the court that surrounds him; he is king of Videha (north-east of Patna), where in Bṛih. 3. 1. 1 the Brâhmans also of the Kurus and Pañc'âlas (who dwell farther west, between the Ganges and the Jumna) gather together to the great

[1] Kaush. 2. 13.
[2] Bṛih. 1. 1. 2.
[3] Chând. 6. 10. 1; whether we are to think here with S'ankara *in loc.* of a return of the water of the sea into the rivers by means of clouds and rain is in view of the wording of the text very questionable; cp. Chând. 2. 4. 1.
[4] Râmapûrvat. 43. 45.
[5] Bṛih. 6. 1. 13.
[6] Bṛih. 2. 4. 12, 4. 5. 13; cp. Maitr. 6. 35.
[7] Bṛih. 3. 3. 1, 3. 7. 1.

argumentative contest described in Bṛih. 3. 1–9. Together with these, reference is made to the courts of Ajâtas'atru, king of Kâs'i (around Benares),[1] and of Jîvala, king of the Pañc'âlas.[2] The Kekayas, on the upper course of the Hydraotes, as repositories of the knowledge stored up in the Upanishads, seem to belong to the far north-west; whose king As'vapati imparts instruction on the Vais'vânara to the six Brâhmans who approach him.[3] Apart from these, in the enumeration in Kaush. 4. 1 of the peoples who have sought the renowned Vedic scholar Gârgya Bâlâki, are named probably all the tribes who took an active part in the intellectual life of the period. They are these:—the Us'înaras, Satvans, and Matsyas, west of the Jumna; the Kurus and Pañc'âlas between the Jumna and Ganges; the Kâs'îs east of the latter, and still farther east the Videhas. No common name for the Âryan races or their country is found in the ancient Upanishads. In Nâdabindu 12 for the first time *Bhâratam varsham* occurs as a name of Âryan India. The "five races of five"[4] appear to denote merely the indefinite multitude[5] of all the races of mankind.

The earth is surrounded by water.[6] According to a late text, it has oceans, mountains, and seven islands or continents.[7] The conception of heaven and earth as the two halves of the egg of the universe recurs.[8] A similar view appears to lie at the basis of the cosmography described in Bṛih. 3. 3. Here the same concentric arrangement holds in the universe as in the different layers in an egg, viz.—(1) in the middle the (inhabited)

[1] Bṛih. 2. 1, Kaush. 4.

[2] Chând. 5. 3–10, Bṛih. 6. 2; for whom in Kaush. 1 C'itra Gângyâyana is introduced.

[3] S'atap. Br. 10. 6. 1, Chând. 5. 11–24.

[4] *pañc'a pañc'ajanâḥ*, Bṛih. 4. 4. 17; cp. the remark there.

[5] cp. *pañc'anadam*, *Allgemeine Einleitung*, p. 73.

[6] Chând. 3. 11. 6.

[7] Nṛisiṁhap. 1. 2, 5. 2.

[8] Chând. 3. 19.

world, (2) around this the earth, (3) around this again the sea. The world is in breadth 32 days' journey of the chariot of the sun, the earth 64, the sea 128; according to which measurement the diameter of the egg of the universe would amount to 416 courses of the sun. "There," *i.e.* where heaven and earth as the two layers of the egg of the universe meet one another, "is a space as broad as the edge of a razor or the wing of a fly" (between the two layers), through which access is obtained to the place where the offerers of the horse-sacrifice are, *i.e.* probably to the "back of heaven" (*nâkasya pṛishṭham*) mentioned in other passages as being "free from suffering,"[1] where according to Taitt. Âr. 10. 1. 52 union with Brahman is obtained,[2] but according to Vâj. Saṁh. 15. 50 recompense for good works, and the latter according to Muṇḍ. 1. 2. 10[3] is transitory. A second scheme of cosmography, though put forward by Yâjñavalkhya in Bṛih. 3. 6 in the same context, is irreconcilable with that mentioned in Bṛih. 3. 3. According to this theory the universe inwoven with the water is besides "inwoven and interwoven" with ten other layers, *i.e.* is overlaid by them, or, perhaps more correctly, is altogether surrounded by them. These ten layers (the worlds of the wind, the atmosphere, the Gandharvas, the sun, moon, stars, the gods, Indra, Prajâpati and Brahman) recall the degrees of bliss of Bṛih. 4. 3. 33 and Taitt. 2. 8, as well as the stations of the way of the gods.[4] The difference is that in these, as we shall see later, measurements of time and space are co-ordinated together, exactly as in Chând. 2. 10. 5 similar terms are added together without consideration.[5]

The prevailing view in the Upanishads is the

[1] *nâkam=na akam*, Chând. 2. 10. 5.
[2] *brahma salokatâ*; cp. also Mahânâr. 1. 1, 10. 21, 63. 5.
[3] cp. Kâṭh. 3. 1.
[4] Chând. 4. 15. 5, 5. 10. 1–2, Bṛih. 6. 2. 15, and especially Kaush. 1. 3.
[5] cp. also Bṛih. 1. 1.

traditional one, according to which there are three world-regions, earth, air and heaven, to which Agni, Vâyu and Âditya correspond as rulers.[1] The fragment of a verse also which is inserted in Chând. 8. 5. 3 is to be interpreted in this sense (that this is so is shown by Atharvav. 5. 4. 3 also):—*tṛitîyasyâm ito divi.* The reference is not here, as often elsewhere, to three heavens, but the words mean, —"In the heaven, which is (reckoned) the third from here." According to Ait. 1. 1. 2 the primeval waters extend above and below the three regions (earth, air and heaven). Bṛih. 3. 8. 4 teaches that all three are inwoven in the âkâs'a, as the latter in Brahman. Very often earth, air and heaven are denoted by the three mystic syllables of the sacrifice (*vyâhṛitis*) *bhûr*, *bhuvaḥ*, *svar*. In Taitt. 1. 5 a fourth *mahas* is added to them, denoting probably Brahman. Later, three higher worlds, *janas*, *tapas*, and *satyam*, were imposed above these four, and so the number seven was obtained, the first mention of which as far as our knowledge goes is in Muṇḍ. 1. 2. 3, and the first enumeration of them in Taitt. Âr. 10. 27–28. Later lists are given in Nâdabindu 3–4, Nṛisiṁhap. 5. 6. In course of time a distinction was drawn between *bhûr*, *bhuvaḥ*, *svar*, *mahas*, *jana(s)*, *tapas*, and *satyam* as the seven upper worlds, and *atala*, *pâtâla*, *vitala*, *sutala*, *rasâtala*, *mahâtala*, *talâtala*[2] as the seven lower. Even this number was exceeded, and in Atharvas'iras 6 nine heavens, nine atmospheres, and nine earths are reckoned.

The number also of the heavenly regions is differently given. In Chând. 4. 5. 2 four are enumerated (east, west, south and north; five in Bṛih. 3. 9. 20–24; six in Bṛih. 4. 2. 4, Chând. 7. 25; eight (four poles, and four intermediate between the poles) in Maitr. 6. 2, Râmap. 71–72, 87, 89.

[1] Chând. 1. 3. 7, 2. 21. 1, 3. 15. 5, Bṛih. 1. 2. 3, 1. 5. 4, 3. 9. 8, Pras'na 5. 7, etc.

[2] Âruṇeya Up. 1; cp. Vedântasâra § 129.

Astronomical conceptions are only slightly developed in the Upanishads. Sun and moon enter principally into consideration, in so far as they form stations for the soul on its journey to the other world, a subject that will later demand treatment. If the texts of Chând. 4. 15. 5, 5. 10. 2 are to be followed, the sun is nearer to us than the moon. The red white and black aspects of the sun depend, according to Chând. 3. 1 f., on the juices of the different Vedas dissolved in it. According to Chând. 6. 4. 2–3, sun and moon also, like everything else in the universe, consist of the three elements; the red in them of fire, the white of water, the black of earth. The sun moves in winter and summer alternately for six months to the south and six to the north.[1] It is disc-shaped (*maṇḍalam*).[2] The purusha of the sun dwells therein, who is usually hidden by the rays,[3] but by these same rays is brought into connection with the purusha in the eye,[4] or with the veins of the heart.[5] The moon is (as in Ṛigv. X. 85. 5) the soma cup of the gods, which is alternately drained by them and again filled;[6] on the other hand, the waxing and waning of the moon depend on the arrival of the dead therein and their return.[7] The two conceptions are combined in Bṛih. 6. 2. 16. According to Bṛih. 1. 5. 14, the moon is Prajâpati as prâṇa, whose fifteen parts alternately disappear and are again restored. At an eclipse the moon is held in the jaws of *Râhu.*[8] All night long the moon holds on her course among the other constellations (*nakshatram*), on which she depends like the Sâman on the Ṛic'.[9] The same 27 constellations are traversed, according to Maitr. 6. 14, by the sun on his yearly journey, and therefore on each of the twelve

[1] Chând. 4. 15. 5, 5. 10. 1–3, Bṛih. 6. 2. 15–16.

[2] Bṛih. 2. 3. 3, 5. 5. 2–3, Mahânâr. 13.

[3] Bṛih. 5. 5. 2, 5. 15, Îs'â 16.

[4] Bṛih. 5. 5. 2.

[5] Chând. 8. 6. 2.

[6] Chând. 5. 10. 4.

[7] Kaush. 1. 2, 2. 8; differently in 2. 9.

[8] Chând. 8. 13. 1.

[9] Chând. 1. 6. 4.

months $\frac{27}{12}$ *aksha tras*, *i.e.* nine quarters (*navâṁs'akam*) of them are covered. The planets (*grahâḥ*) are first mentioned in Maitr. 6. 16. In a very late text[1] their number is given as nine, and therefore together with sun and moon *Râhu* and *Ketu* also (the head and tail of the dragon) are reckoned with them. S'ukra, Venus,[2] and S'ani, Saturn are especially mentioned with Râhu and Ketu.[3] Of movements affecting the cosmos there are mentioned in Maitr. 1. 4:—"the drying up of great seas, shattering of mountains, oscillations of the pole-star (*dhruva*), straining of the ropes of the wind (which bind the constellations to the pole-star), sinkings of the earth, and overthrow of the gods from their place."

As curiosities of natural science we will cite further that the rain has its origin from the sun,[4] while heat occasions storm and rain,[5] just as indeed in men warmth draws forth sweat and heat tears of pain;[6] also that according to Maitr. 6. 27 "a piece of iron buried in the earth enters forthwith into the substance of the earth." The anatomical and physiological views of the Upanishads will later on be discussed.[7]

VIII. Brahman as Destroyer of the Universe

1. *The Kalpa Theory of the later Vedânta*

Before we trace in the Upanishads the development of the doctrine of Brahman as destroyer of the universe, it is worth while to glance at the theory of the later Vedânta, which is the result of this development. According to the Vedânta system, the actions of each life-history find their precisely equivalent recompense in the

[1] Râmottarat. 5. [2] Maitr. 7. 3. [3] Maitr. 7. 6.
[4] Mahânâr. 63. 16, Maitr. 6. 37; cp. Manu 3. 76. [5] Chând. 7. 11. 1.
[6] Chând. 6. 2. 3. [7] Chap. XII. 6.

next succeeding life. Each life both in doing and in suffering is only the fruit of the actions of a preceding birth. Hence it follows that each existence always presupposes an earlier, that consequently no existence can be the first, and that the migration (*saṁsâra*) of souls is maintained from all eternity. The absence of a beginning of the saṁsâra (*saṁsârasya anâditvam*) is therefore a necessary consequence of the Vedânta teaching; and this is not only assumed by Gauḍapâda[1] and defended by S'ankara, but occurs also already in the sûtras of Bâdarâyaṇa,[2] and is actually found in some of the later Upanishads.[3] This absence of a beginning to the circuit of the souls' migration is in contradiction to the numerous creation theories of the Upanishads, which collectively teach a creation of the universe at one time, as is at once proved by the constantly recurring expression, "At the beginning."[4] In order to assert the absence of a beginning of the saṁsâra as demanded by their system, and yet to uphold the Upanishad doctrine of a creation, the theologians of the Vedânta conceive the creation of the universe as an event recurring periodically from all eternity. The universe created by Brahman persists through an entire world-period (*kalpa*), after which it returns into Brahman, only to issue again from him; since at each dissolution of the universe there are works of the soul that still survive, and these demand for their expiation a renewed existence and therefore a re-creation of the universe:—

> All living beings, O Kaunteya,
> Return back into my nature
> At the end of the world; at the world's beginning
> I re-create them anew.[5]

---

[1] Mâṇḍûkya-kârikâ 4. 30. [2] 2. 1. 35.

[3] *e.g.* Sarvop. 23; cp. the drastic description of Yogatattva 3–5.

[4] *agre*, Ait. 1. 1. 1, Chând. 3. 19. 1, 6. 2. 1, Bṛih. 1. 2. 1, 1. 4. 1, 10, 17, 5. 5. 1, Taitt. 2. 7. 1, Maitr. 2. 6, 5. 2.

[5] Bhag. Gîtâ 9. 7, cp. 8. 17–19.

For proof S'ankara relies, as perhaps Bâdarâyaṇa before him,[1] on the verse in Ṛigv. X. 190. 3 :—

Sûryâ-c'andramasau dhâtâ yathâpûrvam akalpayat,

in which according to the context *yathâpûrvam* signifies only "one after the other," not as S'ankara maintains,[2] "as before." The other passage also, on which his theory rests :—"I will enter into these three divinities with this living self,"[3] does not prove, as he believes, that the "living self" existed already before the creation. This entire conception of a periodically recurring creation and destruction of the universe is still entirely foreign to the older Upanishads. In order to trace its origin we shall have to distinguish, (1) the return of individuals into Brahman, (2) that of the universe.

2. *Return of Individuals into Brahman*

The first starting-point of the conception of Brahman as destroyer of the universe is formed probably by the fact of death, which presents itself as the result of experience, and engages attention at all times, and therefore also as early as that ancient period. After men had become accustomed to see in Brahman the power which as *prâṇa* brings forth and sustains life, it was an easy step to restore it to the same power "when it wearies of bearing the burden," and to see in Brahman as *prâṇa* "the cause of death and of life."[4] Therefore as early as S'atap. Brâh. 11. 3. 3. 1 we find it said :—"Brahman handed over the creatures to death"; and in S'atap. Brâh. 13. 7. 1. 1 again :—"He sacrificed himself in all beings, and all beings in himself." This thought is further expanded by the Upanishads. In Bṛih. 1. 2. 1 "death and hunger" (*mṛityur, as'anâyâ*) figure as creators of the universe :—"all that he created he resolved to devour ;

[1] 2. 1. 36.
[2] p. 495. 7.
[3] Chând. 6. 3. 2.
[4] Taitt. Âr. 3. 14. 1–2, Atharvav. 11. 4. 11.

because he devours (*ad*) everything, therefore is he the *Aditi* (the infinite)." And in Bṛih. 1. 5. 3 Prajâpati creates the all-embracing principles, manas, speech and prâṇa, as food for himself. In the words of Kâṭh. 2. 25 :—

He consumes both the Brâhman and the warrior,
As though they were bread soaked in the sauce of death,

a poetical echo of passages of this kind seems to be before us. In Chând. 1. 9. 1 it is said of the âkâs'a (ether, space, as the symbol of Brahman) :—"It is the âkâs'a whence all these creatures proceed, and into which they again descend." And in Taitt. 3. 1 a distinctive mark of Brahman is given :—"That in truth out of which these beings arise, by which they when they have arisen live, into which they at death again enter, that seek to know, that is Brahman." In all these passages the reference is solely to the descent of individual beings into Brahman, not to that of the universe. So also in Muṇḍ. 1. 1. 7, where Brahman is compared to the spider, which sends forth the threads and draws them in again ; and in Muṇḍ. 2. 1. 1, where living beings in their numerous kinds issue forth from the imperishable and enter into him again. In the same sense it is said of the âtman in Mâṇḍ. 1. 6 :—"He is the cradle of the universe, for he is the creation and the end of living beings" ; and in Nârây. 1 of Nârâyaṇa :—"All gods, all ṛishis, all metres, and all creatures originate solely from "Nârâyaṇa, and are lost in Nârâyaṇa." We may compare also the beautiful verses of C'ûlikâ 17–18 :—

In him in whom this universe is interwoven,
Whatever moves or is motionless,
In Brahman everything is lost,
Like bubbles in the ocean.

In him in whom the living creatures of the universe
Emptying themselves become invisible,
They disappear and come to light again
As bubbles rise to the surface.

To these passages also the doctrine of the disappearance of the universe in Brahman appears to be still unfamiliar. And therefore we must hesitate to find it with S'ankara in the mystical name *Tajjalân*,[1] discussed above;[2] since this idea is still foreign to all the rest of the Upanishads, and the conception of Brahman as the cause of the rise, continuance and disappearance of individual beings is sufficient to explain the term. Still less can we refer the words of Vâj. Saṁh. 32. 8,

tásmin idam saṁ- c'a vi- c'a eti sarvam,

to a dissolution and re-creation of the universe. Judging from the entire context, they signify only that the vein is "the centre and circumference of the universe."[3] The case stands otherwise with the repetition of these words in S'vet. 4. 11.[4] Here from their relation to the other passages of the S'vet. Up. they gain a new significance, which we now proceed to discuss.

3. *Return of the Universe as a Whole into Brahman*

Among the new and fruitful thoughts in which the S'vet. Up. is so rich is to be counted that also of the periodical dissolution and re-creation of the universe by Brahman. "He (Rudra as a personification of Brahman) dwells in the creatures, and burning with fury at the end of time he as lord dashes to pieces all created things";[5] he regulates all the aims of the creatures, "until finally the whole is lost in him, who is the beginning."[6] And we must understand similarly the words of Vâj. Saṁh. 32. 8 quoted above, when they recur in this connection;[7] it is god, "in whom the universe

[1] Chând. 3. 14. 1. [2] p. 180 f.

[3] cp. the translation, *Allgemeine Einleitung u. Philosophie des Veda*, p. 294.

[4] And in Mahânâr. 1. 2, which is dependent upon it.

[5] S'vet. 3. 2. [6] S'vet. 4. 1. [7] S'vet. 4. 11.

is lost and reappears" (*yasmin idam saṁ- c'a vi- c'a eti sarvam*). This process however of the creation and dissolution of the universe is not unique, but is continually being repeated. In S'vet. 5. 3 "the god, who many times spreads forth one net after another in space and again draws it in," is compared to a spider.[1] The reason also for this periodically recurring re-creation of things is indicated in S'vet. 6. 3–4, where it is said, following upon a description of the work of creation :—

> That which he created he then takes back again,
> Becoming one with the being of being;
> In order then . . .
> To begin afresh the work rich in the guṇas,
> Apportioning to each their attributes.

That it is only the soul's actions which prompt the creator to "apportion to each all their attributes (*sarvân bhâvân viniyojayet*) is asserted by the immediately succeeding words :—

> Where they are not there action comes to nought,
> Thither he departs actionless, in reality another;

i.e. where the *bhâvas* which constitute the empirical nature are destroyed by knowledge, actions come to nought, and a re-creation no longer takes place.

The following passages from later Upanishads that treat of Brahman as destroyer of the universe are noteworthy :—

"It is he who, when the universe is dissolved, alone remains on the watch; and it is he who then (again) from the depths of space wakens to life the pure spirits." [2]

"When Rudra lies in the coils of the snake, then created things are absorbed into him. When he draws breath, the darkness arises, from the darkness water," etc.; [3] cp.

[1] As in Muṇḍ. 1. 1. 7; cp. S'vet. 3. 1, 6. 10.
[2] Maitr. 6. 17.
[3] Atharvaс'iras 6.

the preceding passage :—" He who consuming all the forces of life, while consuming them, as the eternal one gathers together and again evolves them," etc.[1] This passage may however also be understood of sleeping and waking.

The fire that destroys the universe (*saṁvartako 'gniḥ*) is mentioned in Atharvas'ikhâ 1, and in the two reproductions of this passage, Nṛisiṁhap. 2. 1 and Nṛisiṁhott. 3. We close with the beautiful verse Kaivalya 19, where he who knows himself as the âtman speaks :—

> In me the universe had its origin,
> In me alone the whole subsists,
> In me it is lost,—this Brahman,
> The timeless, it is I myself!

4. *On the Origin of the Doctrine of the Dissolution of the Universe in Brahman*

Brahman is the womb whence all living beings proceed, and it was very natural to assume that they return at death into Brahman whence they have come forth; for as Anaximander already says :—" that from which existing things originate, into it they necessarily also disappear." Accordingly we see formulated, as was shown above, in the texts of the oldest Upanishads and even earlier, the doctrine of Brahman as destroyer of individual creatures. Thence has been developed first in later times, from the S'vetâs'vatara Upanishad and onward, the doctrine of the periodical destruction of the universe by Brahman, precisely as the teaching of Heracleitus that all things come forth from fire (ὁδὸς κάτω), and return into it (ὁδὸς ἄνω), signified originally a twofold process linked together everywhere in the universe in the rise and disappearance of individual creatures, which was then however generalised, whether by Heracleitus himself or by his successors the Stoics, into a periodically recurring dis-

[1] Atharvac'iras 4.

solution of the universe in fire (ἐκπύρωσις) and reconstruction out of it (διακόσμησις). Of the causes which in Greek philosophy may have led to this generalisation we learn nothing more precisely. In India to a great extent it gave support to the doctrine of recompense, inasmuch as the latter, as already shown, was only capable of being reconciled with the doctrine of a creation, if for the single creation taught in the ancient Upanishads there was substituted an eternally recurring process, a re-creation of the universe occurring after each dissolution, and determined by the actions of the souls. On its very first appearance the doctrine of the dissolution of the universe is connected with that of recompense, as is shown by the passages quoted above,[1] and especially S'vet. 6. 4 (" where they are not, there work comes to nought"). Whether however the original motive for the doctrine of the dissolution and periodical reconstruction of the universe lay in the wish to maintain, after the manner of the later Vedânta, the traditional doctrine of creation side by side with the later doctrine of recompense; or only in the natural attempt to generalise the dissolution of objects, which experience showed to be the case, into a universal dissolution, just as the entire doctrine of a creation of the universe originally rested on a generalisation of the observed origin of individuals,—to decide this is perhaps not possible in presence of the partial and ambiguous expressions of the S'vet. Upanishad.

IX. The Unreality of the Universe

1. *The Doctrine of Mâyâ as the Basis of all Philosophy*

When Kant in his inquiry into the capability of the human intellect drew the conclusion that the entire

[1] p. 224 f.

universe, as we know it, is only appearance and not reality, he said nothing absolutely new, but only in more intelligible demonstrated form uttered a truth which in less intelligible shape had been in existence long before him; which indeed as intuitive half-unconscious knowledge had from the very beginning formed the basis of all philosophy. For if the objects of the universe were not, as Kant asserted, mere phenomena, but exactly as they appear to our consciousness in space and time had a real existence apart from that consciousness and in themselves, then an empirical discussion and inquiry into nature would lead to final and sufficient conclusions respecting the essence of things. In opposition to this empirical method of treatment philosophy from the very beginning has endeavoured to find the essential nature, or as it is usually expressed, the first principle of the universe. This search moreover always assumes the consciousness, even if still quite undefined, that this first principle, this essence of things, is not given already in the objects themselves, as they present themselves to our eyes in space and time; that, in other words, the entire aggregate of experience, external and internal, always shows us merely how things appear to us, not how they are in themselves. And the more definitely conscious the several schools of philosophy are of their proper function as opposed to the empirical science, the more clearly does this knowledge come to the front. This is the case in Greek philosophy, when Parmenides asserts the empirical reality to be mere show, or Plato to be mere shadows[1] of the true reality; and in Indian philosophy, when the Upanishads teach that this universe is not the âtman, the proper "self" of things, but a mere *mâyâ*, a deception, an illusion, and that the empirical knowledge of it yields no *vidyâ*, no true knowledge, but remains entangled in *avidyâ* in

[1] Rep. vii. i.

ignorance. Since the expression *mâyâ* in this sense can be pointed out only comparatively late, not earlier, that is to say, than S'vet. 4. 10, the theory has been propounded that we ought to recognise in this doctrine a secondary speculation only developed in course of time from the theory of the universe adopted in the Upanishads. We propose now to show that this is not the case, but rather that the older the texts of the Upanishads are, the more uncompromisingly and expressly do they maintain this illusory character of the world of experience; but that this peculiar and apparently far-fetched idea is seldom expressed in absolute simplicity, and usually appears under forms which are completely explained as an adoption of the empirical modes of knowledge which are natural to us all, and refuse to be shaken off.

2. *The Doctrine of Mâyâ in the Upanishads*

There are in the literature of the Upanishads some texts which, judged by all external and internal criteria, claim a higher antiquity than others; as for example the chapters of the Bṛihadâraṇyaka Upanishad, where Yâjñavalkhya's views of the universe are developed.[1] We shall see how in these chapters more distinctly than in any other place the doctrine of the sole reality of the âtman and the unreality of a manifold universe outside of the âtman is enunciated. First however we propose to show how, as early as the ancient Vedic philosophy that preceded the Upanishads, the seed was sown which by Yâjñavalkhya, whoever he may have been, was developed into the great fundamental thought of the Upanishads, which occupies the attention of all succeeding ages.

We saw[2] how as early as the later hymns of the Ṛigveda the thought was introduced, which here as always marks the first step in philosophy, the thought

[1] Bṛih. 2. 4, and 3. 1–4. 5.

[2] *Allgemeine Einleitung u. Philosophie d. Veda*, pp. 103–127.

of the unity of existence. It involves, if only in germ and half unconsciously, the knowledge that all plurality—consequently all proximity in space, all succession in time, all interdependence of cause and effect, all contrast of subject and object—has no reality in the highest sense. When it is said in Ṛigv. I. 164. 46:—*ekam sad viprâ bahudhâ vadanti*, "the poets give many names to that which is only one," it is implied therein that plurality depends solely upon words ("a mere matter of words," as it is said later),[1] and that unity alone is real. In the attempt also to define more closely this unity, as we have traced it through the period of the Hymns and the Brâhmaṇas, the thought more or less clearly finds expression that it is not plurality that is real, but only unity;—"the one, besides which there was no other";[2] "the one, inserted into the everlasting nave, in which all living beings are fixed."[3] When also it is said:—"This entire universe is the purusha alone, both that which was and that which endures for the future,"[4] it is implied that in the entire universe, in all past and future, the one and only purusha is the sole real. The common people however do not know this; they regard as the real not the stem, but "that which he is not, the branches that conceal him";[5] for that "in which gods and men are fixed like spokes in the nave," the "flower of the water" (*i.e.* Brahman as Hiraṇyagarbha), "is concealed by illusion."[6] This idealism, which denies the existence of the manifold universe, gained strength and complete definition by the introduction and ever firmer grasp of the conception of the

[1] Chând. 6. 1. 3.
[2] Ṛigv. X. 129. 2.
[3] Ṛigv. X. 82. 6.
[4] Ṛigv. X. 90. 2.
[5] *asac'-c'hâkhâm pratishṭhantîm*, Atharvav. X. 7. 21; cp. also Dhyânab. 10.
[6] *mâyâ*, Atharvav. X. 8. 34; on passages like these, and the verse Ṛigv. VI. 47. 18, interpreted in a similar sense as early as Bṛih. 2. 5. 19,—*indro mâyâbhiḥ pururûpa' îyate*,—the later introduction of the term *mâyâ* into philosophy in S'vet. 4. 10 may depend.

âtman or self. This conception, as has often been pointed out, is essentially negative, and to that end claims to strip off from an object all that can be stripped from it, which therefore does not belong to the inalienable substance of its self, and is accordingly not-self. So long as only the âtman of an individual was taken into consideration, this not-self might perhaps be the self of another individual, and consequently real; so soon however as the conception of the âtman of the universe, the "great omnipresent âtman,"[1] which is "greater than heaven space and earth,"[2] was attained, that which as not-self was excluded from the âtman was by that very fact excluded from the sum of being, and therefore from reality. This cosmical âtman moreover, which admits no reality outside of itself, was at the same time present, small as a grain of rice," etc.,[3] whole and undivided in a man's own self; and this identity of the cosmical and the psychical principle was always visibly preserved by the word âtman :—the self in us is the pathfinder of the great omnipresent Âtman.[4] It is precisely this thought that is the starting-point of the teaching of the Upanishads, as it recurs almost word for word in the first instance in one of the oldest texts, Bṛih. 1. 4. 7 (which rests on the authority of Yâjñavalkhya, Bṛih. 1. 4. 3):—"this therefore is the trace of the universe, which is the âtman here (in us), for in it man recognises the entire universe, . . . therefore is this dearer than a son, dearer than a kingdom, dearer than all else; for it is closer than all, for it is this soul (*âtman*)."

A further amplification of this thought, which as already said goes back probably to the authority of Yâjñavalkhya, is found in the discourses of Yâjñavalkhya with his wife Maitreyî, the high antiquity of which is testified both on internal grounds and by the double

[1] Taitt. Brâh. 3. 12. 9. 7.
[2] S'atap. Brâh. X. 6. 3.
[3] S'atap. Brâh. X. 6. 3.
[4] Taitt. Brâh. 3. 12. 9. 7.

recension of it, in two collections which antedate our Upanishad, and were first united with it at a later period.[1] Yâjñavalkhya begins his instruction with the sentence:—"In truth, not for the husband's sake is the husband dear, but for the self's sake is the husband dear." The same is then asserted, with constant repetition of this formula, of wife, sons, kingdom, Brâhman and warrior castes, world-regions, gods, living creatures, and the universe; they are all dear, not on their own account, but for the sake of the self. By the self is to be understood here, as the conclusion of the paragraph shows,[2] the consciousness, the knowing subject within us. And the thought is that all objects and relations of the universe exist for us, and are known and loved by us only in so far as they enter into our consciousness, which comprehends in itself all the objects of the universe, and has nothing outside of itself. Therefore it is said further:—"The self in truth we should comprehend, should reflect upon, O Maitreyî. He who has seen, heard, comprehended and known the self, by him this entire universe is known." As the notes of a drum, a conch-shell, or a lute have no existence in themselves, and can only be received when the instrument that produces them is struck, so all objects and relations of the universe are known by him who knows the âtman.[3] In the âtman as the knowing subject space with all its contents is interwoven;[4] all the heavenly regions are its organs;[5] the universe of names forms and works, "although it is threefold is one, that is the âtman"; he is the immortal, which is concealed by the (empirical) reality,[6] he is the reality of reality;[7] from him spring forth, as sparks from

[1] Bṛih. 2. 4 and 4. 5; cp. Deussen, *Upan.*, pp. 376–378.

[2] Bṛih. 2. 4. 14.

[3] Bṛih. 2. 4. 7–9.

[4] Bṛih. 3. 8. 11, 4. 4. 17.

[5] Bṛih. 4. 2. 4.

[6] *amṛitam satyena c'hannam*, Bṛih. 1. 6. 3.

[7] *satyasya satyam*, *i.e.* that of the reality which is truly real.

the fire, all the vital spirits, all worlds, all gods, all living creatures;[1] in him they all are fixed, like spokes in the nave of a wheel;[2] "he oversteps in sleep this universe, and the forms of death";[3] only "as it were" he plans and moves;[4] only "as it were" is there a duality;[5] only "as it were" does another exist;[6] he stands as spectator alone and without a second;[7] there is in no wise a plurality:[8]—

> In thought should it be heeded,
> Here is no plurality anywhere;
> By death is he bound fast to death
> Who here contemplates plurality.

The passages quoted belong almost entirely to the oldest Upanishad literature that we possess, and thus we meet, not for the first time in the later stream of this literature but equally at its beginning, a distinct entirely self-consistent idealism, connected with the name of Yâjñavalkhya, and according to which the âtman, *i.e.* the knowing subject, is the sustainer of the universe and the sole reality; so that with the knowledge of the âtman all is known. This thought which first makes its appearance in the discourses of Yâjñavalkhya in the Bṛihadâraṇyaka is never again surrendered, and dominates, it is true with certain empirical modifications of which it will be necessary subsequently to treat, the entire development of the doctrine of the Upanishads up to its conclusion with Bâdarâyaṇa and S'ankara. In the Upanishads we find it appearing in different forms. Thus upon it depends the question, which stands at the commencement of the Muṇḍ. 1. 3:—"What is that, most worthy sir, with the knowledge of which this entire

[1] Bṛih. 2. 1. 20.
[2] Bṛih. 2. 5. 15.
[3] *mṛityo rûpâṇi*, Bṛih. 4. 3. 7.
[4] Bṛih. 4. 3. 7.
[5] Bṛih. 2. 4. 14.
[6] Bṛih. 4. 3. 31.
[7] Bṛih. 4. 3. 32.
[8] Bṛih. 4. 4. 19.

universe becomes known." The same question moreover, going back to Bṛih. 2. 4. 5 (and 1. 4. 7), forms also the starting-point of a text so old as C'hând. 6. 1. 2 :—"Have you then sought for the instruction according to which (even) the unheard becomes (already) heard, the uncomprehended comprehended, the unknown known?" The expressions *s'rutam*, *matam*, *vijñâtam* recurring here already in the same form suggest a dependence of this passage on Bṛih. 2. 4. 5. In another way also we seem to be able to render this dependence very probable. We have already above found the Châandogya Upanishad reproducing word for word the passage in Bṛih. 3. 8. 9 touching the âtman as holding apart the phenomenal forms of the universe, as it was condensed in the description of the âtman as "the bridge that holds apart from one another,"[1] and betraying its dependence on the first passage by the fact that it no longer correctly interprets the meaning of the repeated words, since immediately after it represents the bridge separating the phenomenal forms of the universe as a bridge uniting the present world with the next. The case is exactly similar when the assertion of Bṛih. 2. 4. 5 that with the knowledge of the âtman all is known reappears in Chând. 6. 1. 2 in the request for the instruction by which even that which is still unheard, uncomprehended, unknown becomes already heard, comprehended, known. For the true answer to this request clearly consists in the fact that, as Bṛih. 2. 4. 5 and Muṇḍ. 1. 1. 3 agree in stating, with the knowledge of the âtman all is known. The author however of Chând. 6. 1 f. does not give this answer, but develops instead of it his theory of the three primitive elements, heat water and food, with the knowledge of which everything in the universe is known,

[1] Bṛih. 4. 4. 22 :—*esha setur vidharaṇa' eshâm lokânâm asambhedâya*; cp. *sa setur vidhṛitir eshâm lokânâm asambhedâya*, Chând. 8. 4. 2.

because it is only a compound of these;[1] and further, in the three similes of the (white) clay, the (red) copper, and the (black) iron,[2] this tracing back of the white red and black element in things to water heat and food is already foreshadowed. The author therefore has failed to understand the meaning of the request for that with the knowledge of which all is known (*i.e.* for the one âtman); or rather, has intentionally altered it, and that in a sense which, while he sees the unchangeable not only in the "one without a second," but in his triple classification also into heat, water and food, abandons the monism of the doctrine of the Upanishads and arrives at a triad of invariable essences combined in unity, thereby laying the earliest foundation for the Sâṅkhya doctrine of *prakṛiti* and the three *guṇas* combined in it. Otherwise and apart from this resolution of the unity into a triad, he holds fast to the fundamental proposition of Yâjñavalkhya, asserting that all change is "a mere matter of words, a simple name," and that in truth there are only heat, water and food,[3] although these last also, according to his own theory,[4] are merely transformations of the "one without a second." Therefore as a matter of inference in any case the qualification "depending on words and a mere name" would seem to underlie his judgement. All this shows that here the fundamental monistic position of Yâjñavalkhya has been taken over from tradition, but its bearing is no longer perfectly understood.

We meet further on with the same fundamental principle of the sole reality of the âtman (the knowing subject) and the unreality of all else, when it is said in Taitt. 2. 6 of the empirical reality :—"for this men call reality"; and when in Ait. 3. 3 it is explained that all the phenomena of the universe are "guided by conscious-

[1] Chând. 6. 4. [2] Very different from the similes of Bṛih. 2. 4. 7 f.
[3] Chând. 6. 4. [4] Chând. 6. 2.

ness, founded in consciousness"; and when in Kaush. 3. 8 the proposition "this also is still a plurality" is interpreted to mean that as the spokes in the nave so "the elements of being are fixed in the elements of consciousness, and the elements of consciousness in the prâṇa," seeing that it is the self of consciousness and bliss, undecaying and immortal.

In later Upanishads we have to note that the emphatic denial of plurality in the verse quoted from Bṛih. 4. 4. 19 is repeated and amplified in the verses Kâṭh. 4. 10–11; and that finally, in S'vet. 4. 10, the advance of the realistic spirit of the Sâṅkhya is opposed by the assertion that the whole of *prakṛiti* is mere *mâyâ.* Faithful to the fundamental principle of Yâjñavalkhya, the Îs'â Upanishad in its opening words requires us "to sink the universe in God," and adds to the denial of plurality in verses 12–14 the denial of change. Muṇḍ. 1. 1. 3 makes inquiry, as has been shown, for the âtman as that with the knowledge of which all is known. Mâṇḍûkya 7 describes the âtman as "effacing the entire expanse of the universe, tranquil, blissful, free from duality." And even the late Maitr. Up. 6. 24 explains the proposition that all plurality is mere appearance by the brilliant comparison of the âtman with an *alâtac'akram,* a spark which, made to revolve, appears as a fiery circle. An expansion of this illustration is given by Gauḍapâda in the Mâṇḍûkya Kârikâ 4. 47–52; and this entire work is in general an eloquent exposition of the thought of the sole reality of the âtman, which is traced back to the oldest Upanishad texts, and is thenceforward uninterruptedly maintained.

3. *The Doctrine of Mâyâ as it is presented under Empirical Forms*

The philosophy of Yâjñavalkhya, as it meets us in the Bṛihad. Up., can be comprised in the sentence :—The âtman is the knowing subject in us. Hence it follows immediately:—(1) That the âtman, as the knowing subject, is itself always unknowable; (2) that there is not and never can be for us reality outside of the âtman (a universe outside of our consciousness). Both consequences are recognised and clearly stated by Yâjñavalkhya; they mark the climax of the philosophical conceptions of the Upanishads, the first for theology, the second for cosmology; and together they seem to bar any further progress in philosophical thought. The inquiring mind of man could not however rest here; in spite of the unknowableness of the âtman, it proceeded to treat the âtman (*i.e.* God) as an object of knowledge; and in spite of the unreality of the universe outside of the âtman it proceeded to concern itself with the universe as though it were real. This gives rise in theology to numerous methods of representing the âtman by the help of metaphor, and these, though they are based upon an inadmissible drawing of the âtman down into the sphere of human knowledge, play around the accepted fundamental dogma of the unknowableness of the âtman, and are resolved again into it. And the result of this very application of the categories of empirical knowledge beyond their rightful limits is that in the cosmology the traditional pantheistic, cosmogonistic and theistic ideas re-assert themselves even subsequent to the knowledge of the sole reality of the âtman; while they endeavour in various ways to bring a firm conviction of the reality of the external universe, such as is derived from the empirical capacity of the intellect, into harmony with this fundamental doctrine of the sole reality of the âtman. The fundamental doctrine is thus clothed in the empirical forms of knowledge which are innate within us and assert their right; while the metaphysical dogma is gradually more and more superseded by empirical intellectual methods. In this way is originated a series of conceptions which, following up what has already been said, we propose here at the close briefly to survey; they remodel the original idealism into the theories of pantheism, cosmogonism, theism, atheism and deism.

(1) *Idealism.*—The âtman is the sole reality; with the knowledge of it all is known; there is no plurality and no change. Nature which presents the appearance of plurality and change is a mere illusion (*mâyâ*).

(2) *Pantheism.*—The fundamental idealistic view, whose originality and high antiquity is certified by the texts of Yâjñavalkhya, unites with the conviction of the reality of the external universe, founded on the empirical view, to form the doctrine which occupies the largest place in the Upanishads. The universe is real, and yet the âtman is the sole reality, for the âtman is the entire universe. We may describe this theory as pantheistic, although in its origin it is very different from modern pantheism. The pantheism of the later philosophy has been developed as an inevitable consequence from the theism of the Middle Ages; the pantheism of the Upanishads is founded on the attempt to assert the doctrine of the sole reality of the âtman over-against the obtrusive reality of the manifold universe. The Upanishads find a peculiar pleasure in identifying the âtman as the infinitely small within us with the âtman as the infinitely great outside of us.

(3) *Cosmogonism.*—The identity of the âtman and the universe could never be more than a mere assertion. In order to make it intelligible, a further step was necessary which transformed empirical methods of regarding things into metaphysical by substituting for an identity, perpetually asserted but never comprehensible, the relation of causality that experience had made familiar, and by conceiving the âtman as cause, which produced the universe from itself as effect. It then became possible to return to the old cosmogonies, and to revive them on the basis

of the originally antagonistic Upanishad doctrine. After creating the universe the âtman enters into it as soul. By this definition the doctrine that the âtman, *i.e.* the self, the soul in us, is identical with the first principle of all things, is brought into harmony with the doctrine of a creation of the universe out of the âtman.

(4) *Theism.*—The doctrine that the âtman created the universe, and then as soul entered into it, is not yet theism. This step is first taken when a distinction is drawn between the âtman as creator of the universe and the âtman entering into the creation, *i.e.* between the supreme and the individual soul. They are opposed, at first insensibly, as light and shadow,[1] then with ever-increasing clearness, until the complete theism of the S'vetâs'vatara Upanishad is attained. It is characteristic of this work that, side by side with its proper theism, all the preliminary steps are retained.

(5) *Atheism.*—By this separation of God and the soul the existence of God himself was brought into question. The soul was contrasted with him, existed therefore independently and apart from him. The sole function remaining for God was to fashion forth material nature as the arena of recompense for the actions committed by the independent souls. It was only necessary to transfer the powers needful for this purpose to matter itself, and God as creator of the universe would be superfluous. Henceforward there exist only souls (*purusha*), burdened with their actions and receiving recompense from birth to birth, and the primitive matter (*prakṛiti*), which evolves from itself perpetually anew the stage for this recompense. This is the transition from the Vedânta doctrine of the Upanishads to the Sâṅkhya system, the origin of which from the Upanishad teaching will be more closely considered in the next chapter.

(6) *Deism.*—When from considerations of practical

[1] Kâṭh. 3. 1.

convenience there is attached to the atheistic Sâṅkhya teaching, in a purely external manner and without affecting the essential principles of the system, the doctrine of a personal god, there is produced the Yoga system, which will be discussed later, and which is rather deistic than theistic. It is distinguished from the deism of later times by the fact that the latter had endeavoured to find a safe method of eliminating from the natural order of things God who had been retained only nominally as cause of the universe; while the Yoga was concerned to restore the conception of God already eliminated in the Sâṅkhya to a system which had been devised without it. The two methods lead to the same result. The system stands by itself; and the conception of God is preserved side by side with it, but exerts no further influence on its teaching.

X. The Origin of the Sâṅkhya System

1. *Brief Survey of the Doctrine of the Sâṅkhya*

The rise of the Sâṅkhya system, the authorship of which is attributed to the entirely mythical *Kapila*, is one of the most difficult and obscure problems in the region of Indian philosophy. Our previous investigations will enable us to face this question from the right standpoint. It will be shown that the Sâṅkhya in all its component parts has grown out of the Vedânta of the Upanishads, and is nothing more than an extreme carrying out of the realistic tendency, whose appearance and gradually increasing influence we have already traced within the limits of Upanishad teaching itself, in the pantheistic cosmogonistic and theistic changes of the fundamental idealistic view. We premise a brief summary of the leading points of the later Sâṅkhya teaching, since this is essential for the understanding of what follows.

The fundamental conception and ultimate assumption of the system is the dualism of *prakṛiti* (nature) and *purusha* (spirit). There exist together with and in one another from eternity two entirely distinct essences, but no attempt even is made to derive them from a higher unity or to trace them back to it.

(1) The *purusha*, already existing from the first as a plurality, the knowing subject, as it is disengaged from and contrasted with all that is objective.

(2) The *prakṛiti* (*pradhânam*), comprising everything that is not purusha or subject, everything therefore which in any way has merely an objective existence, whether it is still undeveloped (*avyaktam*, natura naturans), or already developed (*vyaktam*, natura naturata).

Purusha and *prakṛiti*, subject and object, are closely connected together from eternity, or rather appear to be so, and the sufferings of existence are dependent on this apparent connection, the removal of which the Sâṅkhya system sets before itself as its proper aim.

This object is attained as soon as the *purusha* recognises its entire distinctness (*viveka*) from the *prakṛiti*. This separateness has existed in fact from the beginning, but unknown to itself; when once this knowledge has been gained, none of the sufferings of the universe are any longer its sufferings. But they are also no longer those of prakṛiti, since all the latter's sufferings, as soon as it ceases to be "reflected" in the purusha, or "enlightened" by him, are no longer experienced and consequently are no longer sufferings. Deliverance is found in the dissolution of this bond between purusha and prakṛiti, which has an only apparent existence from eternity. For the purusha this consists merely in its ceasing to illuminate the sufferings of prakṛiti; for prakṛiti, on the other hand, in that its sufferings are no longer illuminated, consequently are no longer experienced, and therefore cease to be sufferings. Deliverance is therefore an event which does not concern the purusha (to it nothing happens), but the prakṛiti; whence is derived the assertion, strange at first sight, that "not the purusha, but the prakṛiti only is fettered, is a wanderer, and delivered."[1]

This process of deliverance is to be conceived as individual. There are a multitude of purushas existing from the beginning. Some of these attain to knowledge, others do not; the prakṛiti which is attached to the one gains deliverance, but not that which is bound to the other. The inference is that for prakṛiti also the process of deliverance is not cosmical but psychical and individual. The plurality of purushas involves a plurality if not of the prakṛiti, yet of that element in it which enters into activity. Behind the prakṛiti again, individualised as the *liṅgam*, stands the universal cosmical prakṛiti, of which no further mention is made. In any case, the entire process, which we have now to describe, is to be conceived as repeated for each individual purusha, and therefore as psychical and individual.

The prakṛiti, in order to bring about in the purusha the recognition of its distinctness, and therewith its own release, unfolds itself repeatedly before the eye of the purusha. Since the purusha is individual, the self-unfolding of the prakṛiti, which ceases in the case of the purushas that have been delivered, but is perpetually renewed in the case of the imprisoned ones until they gain deliverance, must be conceived as individual. It consists in the evolution of the *Mahân* (the *Buddhi*, "the great," "the consciousness") from the prakṛiti, of the *Ahaṅkâra* (the "I-maker") from the *Mahân*, and from the *Ahaṅkâra* on the one hand *manas* and the ten *indriyas* (the organs of knowledge and of action), and on the other hand the five *tanmâtras* (subtle elements), and

[1] Sâṅkhya-kârikâ 62.

from these finally the five *bhûtas* (elements). The following scheme may serve to mark the relation :—

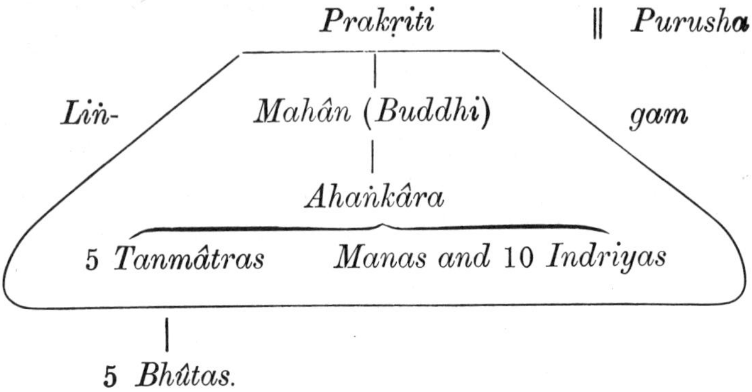

The eighteen first products of prakṛiti, viz.—*mahân*, *ahaṅkâra*, *manas*, *indriyas*, and *tanmâtras*, form the subtle body, which surrounds the soul, and accompanies it on all its wanderings. It is termed *liṅgam*, because it is the "mark" by which the different purushas are distinguished; for in themselves these collectively are mere knowing subjects and nothing more, and would consequently be completely identical and indistinguishable, if they had not their proper *liṅgas* (empirical characteristics), differing from one another. All liṅgas of course originate from the one prakṛiti; but the latter consists of the three *guṇas* (best translated "factors"; cp. *guṇayati*, "to multiply") *sattvam* (the light, clear, intellectual), *rajas* (the active, strenuous, emotional), and *tamas* (the dark, gloomy, inert); and the different qualities of the liṅgas depend upon the different combination of the three guṇas. The proportion of the three guṇas in the liṅgam appears to vary, and to this cause are due the fifty *bhâvas* or states of the liṅgam.

Every life-history is a new self-unfolding of the prakṛiti before the purusha concerned by means of the liṅgam. From the tanmâtras contained in the liṅgam arise (afresh, as we must suppose, at each self-unfolding, each life-history) the *bhûtas* or gross elements (ether, wind, fire, water, earth). The consequence is (1) that each purusha, as it has its own liṅgam, possesses also its own gross world of matter, arising out of it; and (2) that for the purusha which has gained deliverance, since there is no further unfolding of the liṅgam, no gross world of matter any longer exists. So that the Sâṅkhya system also is essentially idealistic, strenuous opponents as its interpreters are of the idealism of the Buddhists.

Certainly behind the individual unfoldings of prakṛiti by *mahân*, *ahaṅkâra*, *manas*, etc., there must exist a corresponding general unfolding of a cosmical *mahân*, *ahaṅkâra*, *manas*, etc. Yet this thought occurs quite incidentally, plays no part, and seems like a forced concession to realism. It is impossible in fact to see what purpose it would serve, since each liṅgam evolves from itself afresh in each life-history the five gross elements, and therefore the external world of matter.

The original purpose of the system appears to have been different. The entrance of the *ahaṅkâra* or "I-maker" into the order of development points to this, and is only intelligible if it is in it that the transition lies from an evolution that is universal and cosmical to one that is psychical. The *prakṛiti* common to all is undoubtedly cosmical, and the *buddhi* also seems to be cosmical, as its name *mahân*, "the great," indicates, as the intelligence that issues from the unconscious and sustains the phenomenal universe;[1] a psychical offshoot of it however as individual *buddhi* is introduced into the liṅgam. The essential element of the liṅgam is therefore the *ahaṅkâra*, as the principle of individualisation, from which are derived on the one hand the individual intelligence (*manas* and the *indriyas*), on the other hand the *tanmâtras*, and from

[1] The *Hiraṇyagarbha* of the Vedânta.

the latter the gross elements, renewed for each individual. When finally the interpreters justify the series *buddhi, ahaṅkâra, manas* by pointing out that the *manas* frames the ideas, the *ahaṅkâra* appropriates them to itself individually, and the *buddhi* stamps them as resolves (*adhyavasâya*), a dependence of the *buddhi* on *ahaṅkâra* and *manas* would be inferred ; which again would lead us to expect precisely the reverse genealogical succession.

The more closely this system is investigated the more unsatisfactory and incomprehensible from a philosophical point of view will it be found to be. The whole becomes intelligible for the first time when we regard it as the final resultant and the blending together of a series of very heterogeneous ideas, which have been handed down from earlier times, and the origin of which we propose now to point out in detail.

2. *Origin of Dualism*

As there can be, to use popular language, only one God and no more, so it is involved in the nature of a philosophical principle to be a unity, from which the variety of the phenomenal universe is derived. It follows that monism is the natural standpoint of philosophy, and wherever dualism has appeared in its history it has always been the consequence of antecedent stress and difficulty, and as it were a symptom of the wane of the philosophising spirit; just as the dualism of Empedokles, Anaxagoras and Democritus was occasioned by the apparently irreconcilable opposition of the doctrines of Heracleitus and Parmenides, and the dualism of Descartes had its ultimate source in the unnatural separation of the abstract and the concrete representations (*cogitatio* and *extensio*), which began with Plato and Aristotle. In a similar way the dualism of the Sâṅkhya doctrine also cannot be regarded as a primitive view of nature ; for how should two principles like purusha and prakṛiti, distinct from first to last, be accidentally lighted upon in infinite space and infinite time, and further be so marvellously suited to one another that they could unite to evolve a universe? The result attained is rather to be conceived as the consequence of a natural disintegration of the doctrine of the Upanishads, as we propose now to show.

The thought of the Upanishads in its pantheistic form asserted, as above shown, that Brahman created the universe and then as soul entered into it.[1] The individual soul is in no respect different from Brahman, but is very Brahman complete and entire. Individuality as much as the plurality of souls is mere appearance. This appearance however is transformed into reality as the method of empirical knowledge gains acceptance. Pantheism becomes theism, according to which the individual soul makes its appearance over-against the supreme soul with a reality of its own, and the result is the plurality of individual souls,—the first dogma which divides the Sâṅkhya from the Vedânta, and consequently the first *reductio ad absurdum* of this theory of the universe. For the soul remains as before, in accordance with Yâjñavalkhya's teaching, the knowing subject. A plurality of knowing subjects! What philosophical mind can admit this thought? The knowing subject is in me (*aham brahma asmi*) and nowhere else, for everything beside me is object, and for this very reason not subject.

A further consequence of theism is atheism. The division of the âtman into supreme and individual souls must lead to the destruction of the one branch, the supreme soul, since it had derived its vital force solely from the âtman existing in me, which indeed alone exists. After its separation from the latter it could only with difficulty be maintained at all. No more was necessary than to transfer the creative faculties (the *guṇas*, viz.—*sattvam*,

[1] *tat sṛishṭvâ tad eva anuprâvis'at*, Taitt. 2. 6.

rajas and *tamas*) to matter itself, and God became superfluous. The S'vet. Up. protests in vain against the irruption of the realistic tendency, in vain asserts that it is the divine power that lies hidden in its own guṇas,[1] that the threads of the web of the *pradhânas* proceed only from God,[2] that indeed the entire prakṛiti is only an illusion wrought by God.[3] When the existence of God was no longer certified by my âtman, the attestation of him in general ceased to be sufficiently strong to prevent his being abandoned by the unscrupulous realism of the Sâṅkhya; and in this way from the ancient trinity (god, universe, and soul), which was in reality a unity,[4] the dualism of *prakṛiti* and *purusha* originated. Nothing further could then be determined as to their origin, or how they came to be so suited to one another as to be able to combine for a common end, as the strong man blind and the lame man with sight.[5]

3. *Origin of the Evolutionary Series*

As early as the cosmogony of the Ṛigveda there usually appears at the head of the development of the universe a triad of principles, in so far as (1) the primal being evolves from out of himself, (2) primitive matter, and himself takes form in the latter as (3) the first-born of creation.[6] This series of the three first principles, which becomes more and more typical, is the ultimate basis of the three highest principles of the Sâṅkhya,—(1) *purusha* (2) *prakṛiti*, and (3) *mahân* (*buddhi*); except that the purusha, in consequence of its division into supreme and individual souls, and the consequent inevitable destruction of the first (the primal being), continues to exist only in

[1] S'vet. 1. 3.
[2] *S'vet.* 6. 10.
[3] S'vet. 4. 10, *mâyâm tu prakṛitim vidyâd, mâyinam tu mahes'varam.*
[4] S'vet. 1. 7. 12, etc.
[5] Sâṅkhya-kârikâ 21.
[6] *Hiraṇyagarbha*, *Brahmân*; *sup.* p. 182 f.

its derivatives, the individual souls. And these last as such are no longer a first principle, but, as was shown in the previous section, appear in co-ordination contrasted with the prakṛiti. An early foreshadowing of this view may be found already in Bṛih. 1. 4. 6, when it is said:—"This only, food and eater, is this entire universe." These words are at any rate interpreted of prakṛiti and purusha in the oldest exposition of the Sâṅkhya philosophy known to us [1] in a chapter which by the direct contrast it sets up between purusha and prakṛiti opposes itself not only to the teaching of the Upanishads, even where a tendency towards the Sâṅkhya is already observable, but also to the remaining parts of the same Upanishad.[2] This origin of the three highest principles of the Sâṅkhya explains also the phenomenon which was formerly unintelligible, that the intellectual element, after having been assigned to the purusha (the knowing subject), and therefore apparently dismissed, re-appears on the objective side as *buddhi* or *mahân*, *i.e.* "the great." This term appears (as far as we know) in all the passages where the gender can be determined to be masculine,[3] and is found as early as the Upanishads. So perhaps in the verse quotation Kaush. 1. 7 in the form *ṛishir brahmamayo mahân*; as the *mahân âtmâ* of Kâṭh. 3. 10, 13 and 6. 7; as the *agryaḥ purusho mahân* of S'vet. 3. 19, understanding the expression to mean "the first arisen great purusha," and therefore identifying it with the *hiraṇyagarbha* of 3. 4, 4. 12, the *ṛishiḥ kapilaḥ agre prasûtaḥ* of 5. 2, the *jñaḥ sarvagaḥ* of 6. 17, and the *Brahmân* of 6. 18, to whom the primal being delivered the Vedas, and from whom ancient wisdom has issued forth in 4. 18. It is, as a comparison of these passages proves, *Hiraṇyagarbha*,

[1] Maitr. 6. 10. [2] *e.g.* 5. 2 and 6. 11–13.

[3] It occurs mostly in compounds as *mahad-âdi*, *mahat-tattvam*, "the essence of the great."

first-born in Ṛigv. X. 121 from the primeval waters, the intelligent principle of the universe, the mind as sustainer of the phenomenal universe, which divested of mythological form comes forth in the Sâṅkhya as the *mahân*, the cosmical *buddhi*, from the prakṛiti. From this in turn the *ahaṅkâra* as the individual principle is evolved, on which again depend the individual organs of knowledge (*manas* and *indriyas*), and their objects (*tanmâtras*, *bhûtas*). By its entrance into the liṅgam (the psychical organism) the mahân or buddhi acquires a psychical significance as the organ of judgement by the side of its original cosmical meaning.

At the basis of the entire formation of this series appears to be the thought that evolution from the primeval being adopts the same order as the return into it, only in a reverse direction. Now the Upanishads teach a threefold return into Brahman,—(1) in sleep, (2) in death, and (3) in yoga; and in the description of this threefold entrance into Brahman all the principles gradually come to light which in the evolutionary scheme of the Sâṅkhya are united into one. We will establish this in a few leading passages.

(1) In the deep sleep, which is an entrance into Brahman, according to Chând. 4. 3. 3, speech, eye, ear and manas enter into the prâṇa; and according to Pras'na 4, in dream-sleep the indriyas enter into manas, and both in deep sleep into the tejas. In the words that follow[1] the entrance of the five bhûtas and the five tanmâtras into the âtman is described, together with the five organs of knowledge and the five of action, and also manas, buddhi, ahaṅkâra, c'ittam, tejas, prâṇa, and the functions that belong to them. It is not expressly stated that the order of entrance corresponds to the series given from last to first, but on the analogy of other passages it is quite admissible.

[1] Pras'na 4. 7 ff.

(2) At death, according to Chând. 6. 8. 6,[1] speech enters into manas, manas into prâṇa, prâṇa into tejas, tejas into the supreme godhead. Just as here by speech all the indriyas are apparently intended, so by tejas we seem to be obliged to understand all the three primeval elements (*tejas, âpas, annam*, of which indeed, according to Chând. 6. 5. 4, speech, prâṇa and manas consist), which, as we shall see later, have been developed into prakṛiti with its three guṇas.

(3) In yoga, according to Kâṭh. 3. 10–13,[2] the senses and their objects are absorbed into manas, the latter into buddhi (=*jñânâ' âtmâ = sattvam*), this again into *mahân âtmâ*, and this finally into *avyaktam* (=*s'ânta' âtmâ*), by which means the purusha is isolated from them all, and its deliverance is effected. We should thus obtain for the return into the first principle at death yoga and deep sleep respectively the following succession:[3]—

At Death (Chând. 6. 8. 6).	In Yoga (Kâṭh. 3. 10–13, 6. 7–11).	In Deep Sleep (Prâs'na 4. 7).
parâ devatâ	*purusha*	*âtman*
tejas (*âpas, annam*)	*avyaktam* (*s'ânta' âtman*)	{ *prâṇa* *tejas*
prâṇa	{ *mahân âtmâ* *buddhi*	{ *c'ittam* *ahaṅkâra* *buddhi*
manas	*manas*	*manas*
vâc' (etc.)	*arthâḥ* and *indriyâṇi*	*tanmâtra, bhûta, indriya*

With these steps of the involution into the primeval essence (that are found at death, in deep sleep, and in yoga) should be compared the steps of the evolution of things from the primeval essence, as they appear first in Muṇḍ. 1. 1. 8–9, 2. 1. 2–3 (not yet perfectly distinct, a

[1] cp. 6. 15. 2.
[2] Kâṭh. 6. 7–11 is in essential agreement.
[3] The order in Pras'na 4 is doubtful.

few points remaining doubtful) and in a more intelligible form in the later Sâṅkhya :[1]—

Muṇḍ. 1. 1. 8–9.	Muṇḍ. 2. 1. 2–3.	The Later Sâṅkhya.
yaḥ sarvajñaḥ, sarvavid	*purusha*	} *prakṛiti* ‖ *purusha*
annam (=*avyâkṛitam*, S'aṅk.)	*aksharam*	
prâṇa (=*Hiraṇyagarbha*, S'aṅk.)	*prâṇa*	{ *mahân* *ahaṅkâra*
manas	*manas*, and organs of sense	*tanmâtra* *manas* and *indriyas*
satyam, lokâḥ, karmâṇi	the elements	*bhûtas*

A comparison of these tables renders it very probable that the true motive for the order of evolution in the Sâṅkhya doctrine is, together with the triad of first principles adopted from the Ṛigveda (primal being, primitive matter, Hiraṇyagarbha, which become purusha, prakṛiti and mahân), the succession of entrance into Brahman in deep sleep, death and yoga, which is taught in the Upanishads. And thus it becomes intelligible that when the later followers of the Sâṅkhya endeavour to justify their order by the psychological process in learning, they can do it only in an artificial way that from a philosophical point of view is unsatisfactory.

4. *Origin of the Doctrine of the Guṇas*

The most characteristic feature of the Sâṅkhya system is the doctrine of the three *guṇas*, which depends upon the thought that the three forces that are active in the psychical organism, viz.—*sattvam*, *rajas* and *tamas* (which approaches the modern distinction of sensibility, irritability and reproduction) are also present in prakṛiti, and constitute its entire substance.[2] Novel as this doctrine

[1] First perhaps in Maitr. 6. 10.

[2] The prakṛiti is in essence nothing but potentiality (therefore *avyaktam*), *i.e.* the aggregate of the three factors (*guṇa*, formed after *dviguṇa*, *triguṇa*, etc.,

appears on its first introduction in the S'vetâs'vatara Upanishad,[1] it yet depends upon older premisses. We begin accordingly with the verse S'vet. 4. 5 :[2]—

> The one she-goat, red and white and blackish,
> Casts many young, which are fashioned like to her;
> The one ram leaps on her in the ardour of love,
> The other ram abandons her, his companion.

That this verse expresses the fundamental thought of the Sâṅkhya doctrine is not open to question. The manifold relations of the many purushas to the one prakṛiti cannot be more effectively illustrated than by the manifold relations of the many rams to the one she-goat. Under these circumstances the reference of the description of the she-goat as "red, white and black" (*lohita-s'ukla-kṛishṇa*, according to the reading of S'aṅkara) to the three guṇas of which prakṛiti consists is inevitable. At the same time however these three expressions, both by the names themselves and by their order, which according to the Sâṅkhya doctrine ought to be different, point back to Chând. 6. 4, where everything in the universe is shown to consist of the three elements (which have proceeded from the one existing being), heat, water and food. There is present in all things (fire, sun, moon and lightning are given as examples) the red (*lohita*) heat, the white (*s'ukla*) water, and the black (*kṛishṇa*) food. The recurrence of these expressions in the same order in S'vet. 4. 5 proves that they are beyond question correctly referred by Bâdarâyaṇa and S'aṅkara[3] to Chând. 6. 4. We must

cp. *guṇayati*, to multiply), which are involved in all existing things; and all psychical organisms (*liṅga*) together with material nature (*bhûta*), which is merely their foil, are derived from the various combinations of these (*anyonya-abhibhava-âs'raya-janana-mithuna*). Everything that is is therefore a product of *sattvam* (joy, φιλία), *rajas* (pain, νεῖκος), and *tamas* (indifference, apathy).

[1] 1. 3, 4. 5, 5. 7, 6. 3–4, 6. 11, 6. 16.

[2] =Mahânâr. 10. 5.

[3] Sûtra 1. 4. 8–10.

nevertheless agree with the opponent whom S'aṅkara introduces in referring the verse with the following words to the Sâṅkhya doctrine :—" In this verse by the words 'red and white and black' are to be understood *rajas*, *sattvam* and *tamas*. The red is *rajas* (emotion), because it naturally makes red (puts into agitation, *rañjayati*); the white is *sattvam* (essentiality, good), because it naturally makes bright; the black is *tamas* (darkness), because it naturally darkens. It is the equilibrium of these guṇas, which is described here according to the quality of the parts of which it consists as 'red and white and black.' And because this is primitive it is called *ajâ* (the she-goat, and also 'the unborn'), while the followers of the Sâṅkhya say of it,—'primeval nature creates, but is not created.'[1] . . . That primitive substance therefore brings forth many young endowed with the three guṇas; and of it is it said that the one unborn (or ram, *ajâ*), *i.e.* the one purusha, 'cherishes' (leaps upon) 'her in the ardour of love,' in inclination, attachment; while he in consequence of ignorance regards her as his own self, and accordingly from inability to distinguish looks upon himself as the vehicle of lust, indifference and blindness (which compose the essence of *sattvam*, *rajas* and *tamas*), and therefore remains ensnared in the migration of souls; while on the contrary another 'unborn,' *i.e.* a purusha, who has gained the knowledge of difference and is no longer attached to it ('it,' that is to say, the primeval substance), 'abandons' her, 'the companion,' whose enjoyment has come to an end; he therefore abandons her, that is to say, he is delivered from her."

In this controversy both sides are right. The Vedântist, inasmuch as the verse unquestionably refers back to Chând. 6. 4; and the Sâṅkhyist, inasmuch as the

[1] Sâṅkhya-kârikâ 3.

three constituent elements, which according to Chând. 6. 2 proceed from the 'one without a second,' and of a mixture of which everything in the universe consists, have been psychologically transformed into the three guṇas. These three likewise are the primal elements, only that each of these primal elements has become the vehicle and expression of one of the three fundamental psychical forces which rule in our inner being. Since the word *guṇa* (factor) would apply equally well to the primal elements and the primal forces (there is implied in it nothing more than that everything which originates from the primeval substance is "threefold," *triguṇam*); and since in all the passages of the S'vet. Up., in which it occurs for the first time,[1] it may very well be understood still as fundamental element in the sense of Chând. 6. 2, and the related verse S'vet. 4. 5, nothing prevents us from assuming that that transformation of the three primal elements into three primal forces,—or rather, the conception of each of the three primal elements as vehicle of a definite primal force,—has been first developed later on in direct connection with the above verse.[2] The process was completed with and by the introduction of the names *sattvam*, *rajas* and *tamas*, which in the sense here in question are not authenticated earlier than Maitr. 3. 5, 5. 2, etc.[3]

5. *Origin of the Doctrine of Emancipation*

Both Vedânta and Sâṅkhya proclaim as their fundamental view the proposition :—Deliverance is gained by knowledge. This proposition is in harmony throughout with the assumptions of the Vedânta teaching, but not with those of the Sâṅkhya.

According to the doctrine of the Upanishads, the âtman

[1] 1. 3, 4. 5, 5. 7, 6. 3–4, 6. 11, 6. 16.

[2] S'vet. 4. 5.

[3] On Atharvav. X. 8. 43, cp. *Allgemeine Einleitung*, p. 324.

alone is real. The manifold universe is an illusion. This illusion is penetrated by the awakening of knowledge, and it is in this that deliverance consists. Here all is perfectly consistent.

It is otherwise in the Sâṅkhya. Here matter is as truly real as the soul, and therefore cannot be recognised by the latter as an illusion, as in the Vedânta. The illusion, which has to be penetrated, is concerned in this case solely with the union between prakṛiti and purusha. This thought however cannot be sustained from a philosophical point of view. For a union either really subsists, or it does not. If it is real no advance of knowledge can lead to a dissolution of the union, but at the most to a clear consciousness of it, whereby however it is still far from being dissolved. The keen sword of knowledge can cleave the mist of an illusion, but cannot sever an actually existing union. If, on the other hand, the union between the two realities purusha and prakṛiti is not real, it has no existence at all. It is then not true that purusha "enlightens" prakṛiti, not true that prakṛiti "is reflected" in purusha; and this illumination or reflection may not be employed to explain the phenomenon of suffering, for it does not itself exist.

The pessimism also by which the Sâṅkhya system is dominated testifies to the derivative character of its theory of emancipation. Even the ancient Upanishads occasionally refer to the painful nature of existence,[1] and according to them too with the illusion of empirical existence the possibility of the suffering involved in it disappears.[2] This however is still only an indirect result, and the chief stress is laid on the deliverance from natural *avidyâ* by the knowledge of the âtman. It is otherwise in the further course of development. The pessimistic view

[1] *ato 'nyad ârtam*, Bṛih. 3. 4. 2, 3. 5. 1, 3. 7. 23.

[2] *tarati s'okam âtmavid*, Chând. 7. 1. 3.

comes increasingly to the front. It occupies a greater space already in Kâṭh. 1, a still greater in the speech of Bṛihadratha in Maitr. 1. The climax of this pessimistic movement is reached in the Sâṅkhya system, which regards philosophy as a whole as no more than a search for means to avert the threefold suffering.[1] Such a standpoint, where it makes its appearance in philosophy, is everywhere a symptom of exhaustion. Philosophy is originally based on a pure desire for knowledge, and knows no other aim than the search for truth. Only when this desire is weakened does philosophy become a mere means to an end, a *remedium* for the suffering of existence. This was the case in Greece in the schools that succeeded Aristotle; it was so also in India in the Sâṅkhya system and in Buddhism.

[1] Sâṅkhya-kârikâ 1.

THIRD PART OF THE SYSTEM OF THE UPANISHADS

PSYCHOLOGY, OR THE DOCTRINE OF THE SOUL

XI. THE SUPREME AND THE INDIVIDUAL SOULS

1. *The Theory of the later Vedânta*

THE Vedânta of S'ankara and his school makes a distinction between the supreme soul (*paramâtman*) and a multitude of individual souls (*jîva âtman, s'ârîra âtman*). The former is omniscient, omnipotent, omnipresent; the latter are limited in wisdom, power and capacity of movement. The former is neither active nor passive, and is therefore free from the very beginning; the latter are active and receptive, and are therefore entangled in the eternal round of saṁsâra, and stand in need of deliverance. Yet the individual âtmans are not properly distinct from the supreme âtman. Each of them is in full and complete measure the supreme âtman himself, as he manifests himself, though his real nature is concealed by the *upâdhis* (*manas*, *indriyas*, etc.). These *upâdhis* are unable to change his real nature, as little as the purity of the rock crystal is destroyed by the red colour with which it is externally smeared. Rather is it solely *avidyâ*, ignorance, which imposes the upâdhis on the supreme âtman, and thus comes to regard him as an individual âtman. Accordingly the entire individual soul as such has no reality, and yet the system cannot avoid treating it as a reality, and discussing in detail its organs and attributes, its wandering and final deliverance. This internal contradiction inherent in the system, as well as the designation of two different and yet not different entities by the one word âtman, points to the conclusion that the whole theory of a twofold soul, supreme and individual, is of secondary origin. We have now to trace its rise in the Upanishads.

2. *Originally only one Soul*

The texts of the oldest Upanishads do not recognise two souls, but only one. "It is thy soul, which is within all."[1] He who while dwelling in the earth, the water, the fire, in space, wind, heaven, sun, etc., is distinct from them, whose body they are, who rules them all from within, "he is thy soul, the inner guide, the immortal. He sees but is not seen, hears but is not heard, comprehends but is not comprehended, knows but is not known; there is none beside him that sees or hears or comprehends or knows."[2] This âtman who alone exists is the knowing subject in us, and as such sustains the whole universe of conceptions, in which is everything and beyond which nothing, and with the knowledge of the âtman therefore all is known.[3] This is the point of view of pure idealism, which denies the existence of a manifold universe, and of everything outside the knowing subject. It becomes pantheism, when it concedes a relative existence to the universe, but identifies this entire universe with the âtman, the knowing subject. Such an identification however, often as it is repeated, is always very obscure, and in order to bring it within the range of empirical comprehension a return is effected to the old cosmogony, and it is taught that the âtman created

[1] Bṛih. 3. 4. 1, 3. 5. 1. [2] Bṛih. 3. 7. 3–23. [3] Bṛih. 2 4. 5.

the universe and then entered into it as soul:—*anena jîvena âtmanâ anupraviśya.*[1] Here for the first time we meet with the word *jîva âtman,* which later denotes "the individual soul" as contrasted with the supreme. But no such contrast yet exists here. It is the âtman himself who alone exists and creates the universe, who as *jîva âtman* enters into the universe that he has created. Neither from the point of view of pure idealism, nor in its empirical varieties of pantheism and cosmogonism, does any opposition exist between the supreme and individual souls. The contrast between them is first seen at the moment in which the âtman who creates the universe and then enters into his creation becomes a duality, the parts of which are set over-against one another. We have described this further accommodation to the empirical consciousness as theism, since here the original unity of the âtman is divided into God and the soul.

3. *The Individual Souls by the side of the Supreme*

All the Upanishads, even the oldest, when they discuss the conditions of bondage in the *saṁsâra* and of deliverance therefrom, distinguish between the imprisoned soul and that which has been delivered, between the soul entering on deliverance and that to which it enters in; and thus often enough a poetical personification of the two conditions is arrived at, as of the souls imprisoned in saṁsâra, and of the divine emancipated souls. An example is furnished by Chând. 3. 14. 4:—"To him shall I departing hence enter in"; or Kaush. 1, where a description is given how the souls that reach the other world appear before the throne of Brahmân (masc.), and are questioned by him with regard to their knowledge. The answer however that is rendered:[2]— "The self of every being art thou, and what thou art, that am I," proves that these

[1] Chând. 6. 3. 2. [2] Kaush. 1. 6.

poetical contrasts remain throughout dominated by the consciousness of the unity of the âtman. A real distinction between the individual and the supreme soul is first found in those texts in which the latter becomes concrete in the idea of a personal god over-against the souls, whose "grace" then is the condition of deliverance. This first occurs, as we saw before, in the Kâṭhaka Upanishad, and in harmony with this we meet the first real distinction of supreme and individual souls in Kâṭh. 3. 1 :—

Two, quaffers of the recompense for their deeds,
Yonder in the other world, entered into the pit;
Light and shadow are they called by him who knows Brahman.

The unity of the two souls here distinguished is expressed in the fact that the "quaffing of the recompense" which is true only of the individual souls is ascribed to both, and also that the supreme soul is designated as the light, to which the individual soul clings as mere unsubstantial shadow.[1] On this passage Pras'na 3. 3 probably depends :—"From the âtman this prâṇa originates; as the shadow on a man, so it projects itself on the other." In the words that immediately follow[2] we meet also for the first time with the description of the individual soul as the *bhoktar*, the "enjoyer," that through the whole course of life has to enjoy, *i.e.* to expiate the fruit of the works of the preceding life. This enjoyer, the individual soul, results from the union of the âtman (the supreme soul) with the organs, manas and the indriyas.[3] The description of the individual soul as *bhoktar* recurs in S'vet. 1. 8, 9, 12; 5. 7. The borrowing from Kâṭh. 3. 4 is, to judge from the entire relation of the two works, quite beyond doubt. Precisely the same contrast between individual and supreme souls is stated with remarkable heightening of the

[1] cp. Kâṭh. 6. 5. [2] Kâṭh. 3. 4. [3] Kâṭh. 3. 4.

effect in S'vet. 4. 6–7,[1] adapting the verse Ṛigv. I. 164. 20 :[2]—

> Two fair-plumaged close friends
> Surround one and the same tree ;
> One of them tastes the sweet berries,
> The other, without eating, only gazes downwards.[3]
>
> To such a tree the spirit sunk down
> In its impotence mourns, a prey to delusion,
> Yet when it worships and beholds of the other
> The omnipotence and majesty, then its grief departs.

The entire adhyâya, S'vet. 5, serves as a further exposition of this contrast. Here, to begin with, vv. 2–6 depict the supreme soul, how at the beginning it gave birth to Hiraṇyagarbha (*kapila ṛishi*) as first-born, how it ever expands and contracts the web of the broad universe, how as Îs'vara exacting recompense it makes to grow and brings to maturity the fruit of all works. Then follows in vv. 7–12 the description of the "other" (the expression links itself with the verses 4, 7 already quoted), i.e. the individual soul :—

7. The doer of works of inevitable result, abundant in fruit,
Yea and the enjoyer of that which he does,
He wanders as lord of life, in every form,
Wrought of the three guṇas, on triple path, even according to his work.

8. An inch in height, shining like the sun,
Endowed with thought and self-consciousness,
By virtue of his buddhi, his âtman,
The other appears, small as a needle's point.

9. Split a hundred times the tip of a hair,
And take therefrom a hundredth part,
That deem I the size of the soul,
And yet it wins immortality.

---

[1] Muṇḍ. 3. 1. 1–2 also is probably dependent on it.

[2] On the original meaning, cp. *Allgemeine Einleitung*, pp. 112, 113.

[3] Ṛigv. I. 164. 20.

10. He is neither male nor female,
And yet is he not neuter;
Even according to the body which he chooses,
He resides in this or in that.

11. Through the delusion of thought, touch, sight,
He moves as soul, in harmony with his work,
By the eating, drinking, begetting, which he himself effects,
Changing here and there into various forms.

12. As soul he selects many gross forms,
Many subtle also, corresponding to his virtue;
And that which fetters him by force of his deeds and self
To these, fetters him also to others.

The individual soul is here contrasted with the supreme soul as being endowed with *saṅkalpa* (the activity of the *manas*), *ahaṅkâra* and *buddhi*, enjoying the fruit of its action; and is described in a descending scale as "an inch in height," "small as a needle's point," small as the ten-thousandth part of the tip of a hair,—"and it," so it is further said, "wins immortality"; *i.e.* after getting rid of the delusion of empirical reality, we recognise this infinitely small individual soul as identical with the infinitely great supreme soul. The clear distinction and yet repeatedly asserted identity of the two is already the standpoint of the later Vedânta, as it has been characterised above at the beginning of this Chapter.

4. *Reason for the Assumption of Bodily Form*

If however the individual soul is a mere apparition as compared with the supreme soul, how comes the eternally free and blessed supreme soul to assume this apparitional form, and as individual soul, having strayed from its true being to become fettered, to wander and to suffer? This question first arises in the latest Upanishads, and the answers to it are very indefinite and unsatisfactory.

In Pras'na 3. 1 the question is proposed:—"Whence

does this prâṇa (the individual soul) originate, and how does it enter into this body? and the answer runs:—From the âtman (the supreme soul) this prâṇa originates; as the shadow on a man, so he projects himself on it; and he enters into this body *manokṛitena*." This term S'aṅkara explains as *manaḥ-saṅkalpa-ic'c'hâ-âdi nishpanna-karmanimittena*, "because of his works which have originated from the will, desire, etc. of the manas"; thus actions and imprisonment in the saṁsâra as their inevitable consequence would be the result of the free will of the soul. It must be admitted that this explanation is disputable on grammatical grounds, since *manokṛitena* can only be resolved as *mano-(a)kṛitena*, and would mean,—Without assent of its will, contrary to its will the soul is involved in the saṁsâra.

The answer which is given to the same question in Maitr. 3. 2, falling back upon the terminology current later in the Sâṅkhya, shows a deeper insight. After establishing the distinction between the immortal (supreme) âtman and the natural (individual), it goes on to say here:—"Assuredly his immortal âtman continues to exist (uncontaminated) like the drops of water on the lotus flower (which only apparently assume its colouring); but yet this âtman is overcome by the guṇas of prakṛiti. Being thus overcome then it falls into an illusion, and because of this illusion it fails to recognise the august and holy creator subsisting in itself; but torn asunder and defiled by the stream of guṇas it becomes without support, weak, broken down, sensual, disordered, and a prey to delusion fancies 'This is I,' 'This is mine,' and fetters itself by its own action, as a bird by its nest."

Finally the verse may be quoted which forms the conclusion of the Maitr. Up. 7. 11:—

To taste of reality and illusion
The great Self becomes twofold.

According to this the individual soul would be dependent on the desire of the supreme soul to experience the illusion of a life in the world as well as eternal reality.

In ancient times therefore the same difficulties were encountered which meet us when we search for causal relations in a sphere which by its very nature is beyond the reach of the entire rule of causality.

XII. The Organs of the Soul

1. *Later View*

Here also it is worth while to begin with the teaching of the later Vedânta in order then to trace in the sphere of the Upanishads the development which led up to it.

In agreement with the views of modern physiology, S'aṅkara distinguishes (1) *manas* and *indriyas* (the organs of relation), and (2) the five *prâṇas* (the organs of nutrition), with which are associated as accompanying *upâdhis* of the soul (3) *sûkshmam s'arîram*, the subtle body, and (4) a factor that changes from one birth to another, *karma*, the actions of each several existence.

(1) To the brain as the central organ, and its two dependents the sensible and the motor nerves, corresponds the relation of *manas* (mind and conscious will) to the five *jñâna—indriyas*, or organs of knowledge (these are, following the order of the five elements to which they correspond,—hearing, touch, sight, taste and smell), and the five *karma-indriyas*, or organs of action (speech, hands, feet, and the organs of generation and secretion). The jñâna-indriyas convey the impressions of the senses to the manas, which manufactures them into ideas (*saṅkalpa*). On this side therefore it corresponds to our mind. These ideas are then formed into resolves (*saṅkalpa*) by the manas in its function as " conscious

will," and are carried into execution by the five karma-indriyas. The assigning a common organ (*manas*) for mind and conscious will, and a common function (*saṅkalpa*) for ideas and resolves corresponds to the physiological fact, according to which the brain both shapes the impressions of the sensible nerves into ideas, and also carries into execution these ideas, so far as they become resolves of the will, by means of the motor nerves. Manas in S'aṅkara's view is the sole internal organ. Buddhi, ahaṅkâra and c'ittam, which are treated as separate organs by the Sâṅkhya and Yoga, are with him merely functions of manas.[1]

(2) Breathing, circulation of the blood, and nourishment equally with the quickening of the body are the functions of the prâṇa, which penetrates the whole body in its varieties as *prâṇa*, *apâna*, *vyâna*, *udâna* and *samâna*. According to S'aṅkara, the *prâṇa* causes exspiration (*uc'c'hvâsa*), the *apâna* inspiration (*nis'vâsa*).[2] The *vyâna* sustains life when the breath is arrested. The *samâna* is concerned with digestion. The *udâna* effects the departure of the soul from the body at death. According to other teachers,[3] the *prâṇa* serves for breathing, the *apâna* for evacuation, the *vyâna* for quickening, the *udâna* for the departure of the soul, the *samâna* for the assimilation of food.

(3) A third companion of the soul in its wanderings is the "subtle body" (*sûkshmam s'arîram*), *i.e.* "the subtle parts of the elements which form the seed of the body" (*deha-vîjâni-bhûta-sûkshmâṇi*). While the gross body is dissolved at death, the subtle body departs with the

[1] Sûtram 2. 4. 6, 2. 3. 22.

[2] cp. S'aṅkara on Chând. 1. 3. 3:—*yad vai purushaḥ prâṇiti, mukha-nâsikâbhyâm vâyum vahir niḥsârayati, sa prâṇa-âkhyo vâyor vṛitti-vis'esho; yad apâniti, apas'vasiti, tâbhyâm eva antar âkarshati vâyum, so 'pâno, 'pâna-âkhyâ vṛittiḥ* (otherwise on Chând. 3. 13. 3, Pras'na 3. 5).

[3] *e.g.* Vedântasâra 94–98.

organs. It is related to the gross body as the seed to the plant, or as the functions of seeing, hearing, etc., which depart with the soul, to the physical eye and ear.

(4) Besides this substratum of the elements (*bhûta-âs'raya*), out of which the body is built up in the following birth, the soul lastly is further attended by the ethical substratum (*karma-âs'raya*), which determines the character of the new body and life. This ethical substratum is formed by the actions committed in the course of each several life, and is therefore different for each soul and for each life course. Without these factors the souls with their organs would be indistinguishable from one another.

2. *The Âtman and the Organs*

"In the beginning the âtman alone in the form of a man was this universe. He gazed around; he saw nothing there but himself. Thereupon he cried out at the beginning:—'It is I.' Thence originated the name I. Therefore to-day, when anyone is summoned, he answers first 'It is I'; and then only he names the other name which he bears."[1] According to this passage, the first consciousness, and therefore the starting-point and vehicle of all certainty is self-consciousness,[2] and that for the supreme as well as for the individual soul, for the two are one. Only later, when this original idealism had been obscured by the advancing realism, and a distinction had been set up between supreme and individual soul, does *ahaṅkâra* appear among the functions or organs of the latter,[3] as though the âtman the creator of the universe were something other than the self in me; a proposition which to the Indians as well as to Descartes serves already

[1] Bṛih. 1. 4. 1.

[2] In Chând. 7. 25. 1 termed *ahaṅkâra*.

[3] For the first time in S'vet. 5. 8 and Pras'na 4. 8; so later on in Maitr. 2. 5, 3. 2, 6. 5, Prâṇâgnihotra 4, Mahâ 1, and in the Sâṅkhya.

as the alpha and omega of all knowledge of the truth. "The self is the basis (*âs'raya*) for the validity of proof, and therefore is constituted also before the validity of proof. And because it is thus formed it is impossible to call it in question. For we may call a thing in question which comes up (*âgantuka*) to us (from without), but not our own essential being. For if a man calls it in question, yet is it his own essential being."[1] This thought is found expressed in the Upanishads, besides the passage above quoted from Bṛih. 1. 4. 1, in S'vet. 1. 2 also, in so far as it is there said :—

> There are time, nature, necessity, chance,
> Primitive matter, spirit,—is the union of these
> As primal basis conceivable? Not so. For it is one Self.

All the first principles proposed by other schools, time, nature, necessity, etc., are to be abandoned, *âtmabhâvât*, because the self, the âtman, is to be assumed as the first principle of things, since it is the necessary presupposition of them all.

This âtman which in each one of us, as before the beginning of things is conceived as the I, as the passage from the Bṛih. sets forth further from the empirical standpoint, created the universe of names and forms, and then as soul entered into it :—" right to the tips of the fingers " he fills the body, and is hidden in it like the knife in the sheath or the fire in the fuel. "Therefore he is not seen, for he is divided; as breathing he is called breath, as speaking speech, as seeing eye, as hearing ear, as understanding mind; all these are only names for his effects."[2] As eye he is the centre (*ekâyanam*) of all forms, as ear the centre of all sounds, etc.[3] "When the eye directs itself into space, it is the spirit in the eye, the eye (itself) serves (only) for seeing; and if a man desires to smell, that is the

[1] S'aṅkara on Brahmasûtra 2. 3. 7.
[2] Bṛih. 1. 4. 7.
[3] Bṛih. 2. 4. 11.

âtman, the nose serves only for odours,"[1] etc. The eye is nothing but eye, the ear nothing but ear, of that he who knows Brahman is aware,[2] and abandons the hearing of hearing, the thought of thinking, the speaking of speech, etc., in order to grasp that by which speech, breath, eye, ear and manas are harnessed and dismissed to their occupations.[3] This essential identity of the organs with the âtman, when regarded empirically, appears as a creation of them from it :—" from it originates breath, the mind, and all the senses."[4] According to Chând. 6. 5, manas, prâṇa and speech are the most subtle product of the elements, food, water and heat, created by the âtman. To the organs of the individual âtman there correspond in the universe the forces of nature (nature gods) as organs of the cosmical âtman. Following up the ideas, which we learnt to know from the hymn of the purusha,[5] Ait. 1. 1–2 represents the gods Agni, Vâyu, Âditya, Dis′, etc. as originating from the mouth, nose, eyes, ears, etc. of the primeval man, and these then enter into the individual man as speech, smell, sight, hearing. According to the Bṛih. Up., on the contrary, which in general prefers to start from the individual,[6] the individual organs, speech, smell, eye, ear, manas, which are born at first as children of Prajâpati, are filled with evil by the demons, and then by the prâṇa are led beyond the reach of evil and death, to enjoy a continued existence as fire, wind, sun, the heavenly regions and the moon.[7] The later theory[8] of the protectorate which the nature gods exercise over the psychical organs depends upon conceptions of this kind. It makes its appearance first in Bṛih. 4. 4. 1, where a

[1] Chând. 8. 12. 4.
[2] Bṛih. 4. 4. 18.
[3] Kena 1–2 ; cp. the paraphrase of this passage in Maitr. 6. 31.
[4] Muṇḍ. 2. 1. 3.
[5] Ṛigv. X. 90. 13–14 ; cp. *Allgemeine Einleitung*, p. 157.
[6] cp. especially Bṛih. 1. 4. 6 *ad fin.*
[7] Bṛih. 1. 3. 11–16 ; cp. Chând. 1. 2.
[8] *e.g.* Pras′na 3. 8.

description is given how at death the material eye is set free,[1] and the spirit that dwells in the eye returns outwards to the sun,[2] while the psychical organ of the faculty of sight gathers with the rest of the organs in the heart around the soul, in order to journey forth in its company.

The names and number of the organs are still uncertain in the older texts. In Chând. 3. 1. 3 and Bṛih. 6. 4. 5 f. the word *indriyam* has still the meaning of "force"; it is first employed by Kaush. 2. 15, Kâṭh. 3. 4 as a name for the organs, as the physical forces in man. In the older texts the organs collectively are called the *prâṇas*, the "vital breaths," by virtue of a *denominatio a potiori*, from the organ of breathing (*prâṇa*), as being the most important and that upon which the life is dependent. "Therefore they are not called voices, eyes, ears, minds, but vital breaths (*prâṇâḥ*), for the breath (*prâṇa*) is all of them."[3] As regards the number also of the organs, no agreement exists. It is frequently mentioned that man, like Prajâpati in his character as the moon,[4] consists of sixteen parts. This is the case in the narrative of Chând. 6. 7.[5] How little what was intended by the sixteen parts was understood is shown by S'atap. Br. X. 4. 1. 17, where the sixteen syllables of the words *loman, tvac', asṛij, medas, mâṁsam, snâvan, asthi, majjâ* (hair, skin, blood, sap, flesh, sinew, bones, marrow) do duty as such. In Pras'na 6 the sixteen parts are enumerated as (1) *prâṇa*, (2) *s'raddhâ*, faith, (3–7) the five elements, (8) *indriyam*, the organs of sense considered as one, (9) *manas*, (10) *annam*, food, (11) *vîryam*, strength, (12) *tapas*, (13) *mantrâḥ*, (14) *karman*, (15) *lokâḥ*, (16) *nâman*. The same are to be understood in S'vet. 5. 14, according to the commentary. It is perhaps on this sixteenfold enumeration of the parts

[1] Bṛih. 4. 3. 36.
[2] cp. the amplifications in Bṛih. 3. 2. 13.
[3] Chând. 5. 1. 15.
[4] Bṛih. 1. 5. 14.
[5] cp. Muṇḍ. 3. 2. 7, Pras'na 6.

of a man that the later summary of the organs as the ten indriyas with manas and the five prâṇas depends. By the "seven prâṇas" of Muṇḍ. 2. 18 should be understood, as in S'atap. Br. VI. 4. 2. 5 and elsewhere, the seven openings in the head; these with the two lower are described in S'vet. 3. 18 and later[1] as the nine gates of the city of the body. Adding the navel and Brahmarandhram[2] the number becomes eleven.[3] An older verse[4] describes the head as a drinking bowl with the opening at the side, on whose edges (the seven openings in the head) seven ṛishis (the seven organs of sense) dwell, who are identical with the seven guardians of the universe. A modification of this verse[5] names speech as the eighth, and therefore by the seventh ṛishi (after ears, eyes, nostrils) *vâc'* must again be understood as the organ of taste, and to this the explanation that follows[6] refers.

The seven so-called openings of the head have undoubtedly been the starting-point for the original enumeration of the organs of sense, as is clear from the fact that in the texts of the older Upanishads only speech, breath (smell), eye, ear and manas as a fifth are usually named as organs of sense (*prâṇas*).[7] Where the number is fewer, special reasons are generally present, as in Bṛih. 3. 1. 3–6, where the number four is found, or Chând. 3. 13. 5, 5. 23. 2, where the surprising omissions are perhaps to be explained by the fact that smell was supposed to be already included in the five prâṇas.[8] Where more than five organs are named the additions are usually appended to, or even made to precede the original speech, breath, eye, ear, manas. Thus in Bṛih. 2. 5. 1–7 (*s'arîram*, *retas*), 3. 2.

[1] *e.g.* Yogas'ikhâ 4, Yogatattvam 13, Bhag. G. 5. 13.

[2] Ait. 1. 3. 12.

[3] Kâṭh. 5. 1.

[4] Atharvav. X. 8. 9.

[5] Bṛih. 2. 2. 3.

[6] Bṛih. 2. 2. 4.

[7] This is the case in Bṛih. 1. 3. 2–6, 1. 4. 7, 2. 2. 3, Chând. 1. 2. 2–6, 2. 7. 1, 2. 11. 1, 3. 18. 1–6, 8. 12. 4–5, Kena 1. 4–8.

[8] cp. Taitt. 1. 7.

13, 3. 7. 16–23 (*tvac′*, *vijñânam*, *retas*), 4. 1. 2–7 (*hṛidayam*).[1] Bṛih. 3. 2. 2–9 is peculiar, where eight organs of sense are enumerated as the eight *grahas* or seizers (organ of smell, speech, tongue, eye, ear, manas, hands, skin), to which their objects correspond as *atigrahas* or over-seizers (smell, name, taste, form, sound, desire, action, touch). The assigning here of the names *prâṇa* and *apâna* severally to the organ of smell and to smell itself will be discussed later on. The name *graha* (seizer) for the organs of sense, according to S′aṅkara[2] would signify that by them the soul is fettered to objects (*badhyate kshetrajño 'nena graha-sañjñakena bandhanena iti*). In this may be found a confirmation of our conjecture[3] that the later conception of the "bands of the heart"[4] is derived from this passage or the view contained in it, that *graha* and *atigraha* tie the knots, which are unloosed on deliverance. The name *indriyas* for the organs of sense first meets us in the Upanishads in the rite of Kaush. 2. 15. The later enumeration of ten together with manas is followed with one exception. In the summary at the close they are again described by the old name of *prâṇas*. The oldest passage which cites the ten later *indriyas* complete, with the addition of *manas* and *hṛidayam*, is Bṛih. 2. 4. 11.[5] With *manas* but without *hṛidayam* in the later total of eleven they appear first in Pras′na 4. 2, in evident contrast with the five prâṇas; while in the continuation of the passage[6] there are enumerated the five elements, five tanmâtras, ten indriyas with their objects, together with manas, buddhi, ahaṅkâra, c′ittam, tejas and prâṇa. This passage is at one and the same time the pre-

[1] cp. Ait. 1. 1. 4, Kaush. 3. 5.

[2] On Brahmasûtra 2. 4. 6.

[3] See Deussen, *Upan.*, p. 430.

[4] First in Chând. 7. 26. 2, then Kâṭh. 6. 15, Muṇḍ. 2. 2. 8, 3. 2. 9, and as "bands of ignorance" in Muṇḍ. 2. 1. 10.

[5] =4. 5. 12.

[6] Pras′na 4. 8.

cursor of the Vedânta's sixteenfold enumeration of the psychical organs, and of the Sâṅkhya's twenty-five principles.

3. *Manas and the Ten Indriyas*

The earliest passage in which, as in the later Vedânta, the indriyas are specified as neither more nor less than ten, subordinated to the manas as the central organ, and with it placed in contrast with the five prâṇas as the forces of unconscious life that are active even in sleep, is Pras'na 4. 2. As the rays of light are gathered into the sun at sunset "so also (on falling asleep) all this becomes one in the manas as supreme deity; therefore it comes to pass that then nothing is heard by a man, nothing seen, nothing smelt, nothing tasted, and nothing felt, nothing spoken, nothing comprehended, nothing begotten, nothing evacuated, no motion hither and thither, but as it is said he is asleep. Then the fires of prâṇa awaken (*prâṇa, apâna, vyâna, samâna, udâna*, which are then further explained) in this city (of the body)." This conception of *manas* as the central organ of the faculties of knowledge and action, of the powers of perception and conscious determination, and therefore of that which we call "mind" and "conscious will," was at first gradually elaborated. Originally *manas* had a more general meaning, and in its indefinite character corresponded nearly to our "disposition," "feeling," "heart," "spirit." As such manas represents not infrequently the spiritual principle in general, and becomes sometimes a name for the first principle of things, Brahman or the âtman.[1] Even in the Upanishads, epithets of Brahman like *manomaya*, "consisting of manas," are occasionally found,[2] and manas is one of the

[1] cp. the tendency pointed out, *Allgemeine Einleitung*, pp. 205, 206, to conceive Prajâpati as manas, and especially the beautiful hymn Vâj. Saṁh. 34. 1–6 (translated *ib.*, p. 335), which as *S'ivasaṅkalpa* was included by the Oupnek'hat even in the Upanishads.

[2] Chând. 3. 14. 2, Bṛih. 5. 6. 1, Taitt. 1. 6. 1, Muṇḍ. 2. 2. 7.

symbols under which Brahman is worshipped.[1] In Ait. 3. 2 also manas appears still among the functions or modifications of Brahman described as "consciousness" (*prajñânam*) :—"what this heart and manas is, reflection, imagination, meditation, invention, mind, insight, resolve, purpose, desire, emotion, recollection, conception, force, life, love, will,—all these are names of consciousness." Nay, even in the section Kaush. 3, where generally manas appears in its later signification as an organ side by side with speech, sight, hearing,[2] and as such is subordinated to "consciousness" (*prajñâ* = *prâṇa* = *brahman* ; cp. 3. 8 :— "we should not seek for manas, but to know the thinker), even here in 3. 7, in contradiction to the ordinary usage, manas is again employed in the old way as a synonym for "consciousness" :—"For speech bereft of prajñâ (consciousness) cannot bring any name whatever to consciousness, for it is said, 'My manas (mind) was elsewhere (*anyatra me mano 'bhût*), therefore have I not become conscious of that name." Precisely the same is then further said of the remaining organs, breath, eye, ear, tongue, etc., until the series reaches manas, where the formula is dropped, in order to conceal the contradiction in the double use of the word. In its second narrower meaning as the psychical organ of conception and will manas stands originally on a line with the organs of sense, as is shown by the description of the organs of sense (*prâṇas*) quoted above, and frequently repeated as speech, breath, eye, ear and manas. All five are subordinated to the âtman :—"As breathing he is called breath, as speaking speech, as seeing eye, as hearing ear, as understanding mind (*manas*); all these are only names for his effects."[3]

[1] *sup.* p. 111 f.

[2] cp. 3. 3 :—"men live even without manas, for we see fools," and so in what follows.

[3] Bṛih. 1. 4. 7.

In Bṛih. 1. 3. 2–6 all five are filled with evil by the demons, and then by the vital breath in the mouth (*âsanya prâṇa*) are led beyond evil and death. But the true knowledge that every sensible perception is a work of the mind (*manas*), from which it follows that the rest of the organs of sense are subordinated to the *manas*, comes to the front in the Upanishads, appearing in the famous oft-quoted saying of Bṛih. 1. 5. 3.[1] "'I was elsewhere with my mind (*manas*), therefore I did not see; I was elsewhere with my mind, therefore I did not hear,' so it is said; for only with the mind do we see, and only with the mind do we hear. Desire, judgement, doubt, belief, unbelief, firmness, weakness, modesty, knowledge, fear,—all this is only manas. When then anyone is touched from behind, he knows it through the manas." This passage which is reproduced in Maitr. 6. 3, and countless times subsequently, and which all future ages regarded as authoritative, asserts that the manas, although only the organ of the âtman, is yet the central organ of the entire conscious life; which not only as "the primary root of the five faculties of knowledge"[2] shapes into ideas[3] the impressions of sight, hearing, taste, smell, touch, since we "see only with the mind, hear with the mind," but stamps these ideas further as resolves of the will (*saṅkalpa*, cp. Chând. 7. 4), so that in the latter sense the manas becomes the organ of the will and its expression by the five organs of action (speech, grasp, movement, evacuation, begetting). "For by the manas is a man impelled towards his wife, and begets with her a son, who is like him";[4] "And when a man directs his manas to the study of the sacred hymns and sayings, then he

[1] Forming a counterpart to the verse of Epicharmus:—νοῦς ὁρῇ καὶ νοῦς ἀκούει, τἆλλα κωφὰ καὶ τυφλά.

[2] *pañc'a-buddhi-âdimûlam*, S'vet. 1. 5.

[3] *saṅkalpa*="the definition of a presented object as black, white, etc."; S'aṅkara on Bṛih. 1. 5. 3.

[4] Bṛih. 4. 1. 6.

studies them; or to the accomplishment of works, then he accomplishes them; or to the desire for sons and cattle, then he desires them; or to the desire for the present and the future world, then he desires them."[1] Accordingly in Taitt. 2. 3 also, of the purusha consisting of manas (*manomaya*) "the Yajus is the head, the Ṛic′ is the right side, the Sâman the left side," etc.; because the sacrificial cult depends upon the Vedas, and this is founded on the selfish desires of the gods for offerings, and of men for the blessings of the gods. The superiority of manas to the indriyas is further expanded in Kâṭh. 6. 7:—"Manas stands higher than the senses"; and in Kâṭh. 3. 3, where the senses are represented as the horses yoked to the waggon of the body, but the manas as their bridle. This illustration is changed in a sense still more favourable to the manas in Maitr. 2. 6, where the organs of knowledge (*buddhi-indriyâṇi*) are the five reins, the organs of action (*karma indriyâṇi*) are the horses, the manas is the driver, and the prakṛiti his whip. By means of this manas drives the organs of action (speech, grasp, movement, evacuation, begetting) to their work, and they are then guided and controlled by manas by means of the organs of knowledge (sight, hearing, taste, smell, touch). Later passages which exhibit manas side by side with the *buddhîndriyâṇi* and *karmendriyâṇi* are Garbha 4 and Prâṇâgnihotra 4. Mention is made in Mahâ 1 of ten *indriyâṇi* with manas as an eleventh. Their ten functions are already named in the passage quoted above from Pras′na 4. 2. An enumeration of the ten corresponding organs is not found within our recollection earlier than Manu 2. 89 f.

5. *The Prâṇa and its Five Varieties*

Prâṇa also, like manas, is a word of very varied meaning, which only gradually attained its later technical

[1] Chând. 7. 3. 1.

significance. Originally prâṇa is the "breath"; then the "life" as connected with the process of breathing. In this character the prâṇa frequently becomes an empirical and consequently symbolical representation of the âtman. In the older period[1] all the vital powers (speech, breath, eye, ear, manas, etc.), like the life, were called the prâṇas. Only gradually manas and the indriyas as the forces of conscious life were separated from the prâṇa, which with its five subdivisions is incessantly active in waking and in sleep, and is consequently the especial vehicle of life as such. In sleep manas enters into the prâṇa,[2] and causes the soul "to guard its lower nest by the prâṇa."[3] It is from this perhaps that the later conception is derived that in sleep, while the organs of sense are absorbed into manas, the fires of prâṇa keep watch in the city of the body.[4] These fires of prâṇa, which are on the watch in sleep, are themselves five in number, viz. *prâṇa*, *apâna*, *vyâna*, *samâna*, *udâna*, and they are mentioned together both earlier and later numberless times, and employed in the most varied allegories, without its being possible to obtain a clear and consistent explanation of them. Sometimes only two (*prâṇa* and *apâna*) are named,[5] or three[6] (*prâṇa*, *apâna*, *vyâna*), or four[7] (*prâṇa*, *apâna*, *vyâna*, *udâna*), usually however all five.[8] This number is exceeded, as far as we know, only in Sarvopanishats. 10, where fourteen prâṇas are mentioned.[9]

[1] Occasionally also later, *e.g.* Pras'na 3. 4.

[2] Chând. 6. 8. 2. [3] Bṛih. 4. 3. 12. [4] Pras'na 4. 3.

[5] Taitt. Âr. 3. 14. 7; Atharvav. 11. 4. 13, Ait. Âr. 2. 1; Kâṭh. 5. 3; Muṇḍ. 2. 1. 7.

[6] Bṛih. 3. 1. 10, 5. 14. 3, Chând. 1. 3. 3, Taitt. 1. 5. 3, 2. 2.

[7] Bṛih. 3. 4. 1.

[8] Bṛih. 1. 5. 3, 3. 9. 26, Chând. 3. 13. 1–5, 5. 19–23, Taitt. 1. 7, Pras'na 3. 5, 4. 4, Maitr. 2. 6, 6. 4, 6. 9, 6. 33, 7. 1–5, Amṛitab. 34–35, Prâṇâgnih. 1. 4, Kaṇṭhas'ruti 1, Nṛisiṁhott. 9, etc.

[9] On their fourteen names, which the scholiast cites, cp. Vedântasâra 93–104.

Often as the five prâṇas are enumerated in the Upanishads, it is rarely that anything is found which serves to explain them. We propose to attempt to determine the several conceptions involved, so far as is practicable.

(1) *Prâṇa* and (2) *Apâna*. In the first place, it is certain from the witnesses cited on p. 264 that, according to S'aṅkara,[1] *prâṇa* denotes exspiration, *apâna* inspiration. The question is how this result is arrived at. Originally, in all probability *prâṇa* and *apâna* both denoted the same thing, viz. breath (without distinction of exspiration and inspiration) in general (whether with the slight difference that *pra-an* signifies "to begin to breathe," *apa-an* "to cease to breathe," in support of which view Ṛigv. X. 189. 2 is quoted, may be left undetermined considering the uncertainty of this passage). There is nothing in the prepositions to form the basis of a distinction, since *pra* (πρό) "forwards, onwards" is quite ambiguous, and *apa* (ἀπό, from) may just as well mean "from within outwards" as "from without inwards." *Prâṇa* however is by far the more usual expression, and therefore where it stands alone frequently denotes the sense of smell, consequently inspiration, as in the passage S'atap. Br. X. 5. 2. 15 quoted by Böhtlingk, or in Bṛih. 1. 3. 3, Chând. 1. 2. 2, Ait. 1. 3. 4. So very clearly in Kaush. 2. 5:—*yâvad vai purusho bhâshate, na tâvat prâṇitum s'aknoti.* Where however *prâṇa* and *apâna* stand side by side, there (apart from the conception of *apâna* as the wind of digestion, as to which see below), so far as a distinction can be recognised, *prâṇa* is exspiration and *apâna* inspiration. This is the case probably as early as Chând. 1. 3. 3, because it is said previously[2] "this is hot," and "as sound is it described."

[1] On Brahmasûtra, p. 723. 1–4, and on Chând. 1. 3. 3.

[2] In 1. 3. 2, where prâṇa only can be the subject, since apâna has not yet been named.

Both definitions apply better to exspiration than to inspiration. Though in Bṛih. 1. 3. 3 and Chând. 1. 2. 2 prâṇa as the vehicle of scent appears in its more general meaning of "breath" (inspiration and exspiration), in the parallel passage Tal. Up. Br. 2. 1. 16 the apâna takes its place :—"Its misfortune is that it inspires an evil odour by the apâna."[1] Here therefore apâna is certainly inspiration. So in Tal. Up. Br. 1. 60. 5 :—*apânena jighrati*, "a man smells with inspiration," not "one smells with exhalation (!)." The same argument applies in Tal. Up. Br. 4. 22. 2–3; the world-producing waters "*huss*" *iti eva prâc'îḥ prâs'vasan; sa vâva prâṇo 'bhavat. Tâḥ prâṇya apânan, sa vâ apâno 'bhavat.* The sound *huss* and the expression *prâc'îḥ prâs'vasan* point quite unmistakeably to prâṇa as exspiration, and consequently to apâṇa as inspiration. The principal passage is Bṛih. 3. 2. 2 :—*prâṇo vai grahaḥ; so 'pânena atigraheṇa gṛihîto; 'pânena hi gandham jighrati.* Everyone sees that the context requires the meaning faculty of smell and smell, and Böhtlingk need not have reproached me on the supposition that I failed to see it. He might have assumed that I had other reasons for my inability to accept his suggestion of a simple correction here in the desired sense. My reason was, that there existed here something in the background which exercised possibly a stronger attraction on the author or redactor of the passage than analogy or consistency, viz.—the wish to join prâṇa and apâna together here also as *graha* and *atigraha* in accordance with their usual association. *Apâna* therefore, inspiration as the vehicle of smell, represented the latter, and the explanatory addition (*apânena hi gandham*

[1] *pâpam gandham apâniti.* These words cannot signify, as Oertel maintains is possible, "exhaling bad odour," since it is said previously of the prâṇa, *i.e.* breath in the mouth according to the parallel passages, *na pâpam gandham apâniti.*

jighrati) was employed in order to justify the connnection, not as before and usually between *graha* and *atigraha*, but between *atigraha* and the object which it represented. That apâna being inspiration, prâna by its side (in its general meaning of "breath") could not at the same time denote the sense of smell, as so often elsewhere, would therefore be overlooked. That the original author of the paragraph caused this confusion, I find myself unable to believe; but the mistake, if we must so call it, is older than the separation of the Kâṇvas and Mâdhyandinas, and therefore not much less than three thousand years old,[1] and certainly would not have maintained its ground all this time if apâna had not already at that period denoted the faculty of smell, and therefore inspiration. The same conclusion follows from the symbolical treatment in Bṛih. 6. 4. 10–11, where the direction is given, if unfruitfulness is desired, *abhiprâṇya apânyât*, if fruitfulness, *apânya abhiprâṇyât.* The suppression of the vital power is symbolised by inspiration, its excitation by exspiration. Since however the emphasis lies not on the gerund but on the finite verb, *apânyât* signifies already in this passage "he inspires," *abhiprâṇyât*, "he exspires."[2] It is doubtful whether in Kâṭh. 5. 3 *ûrddhvam prâṇam unnayiti, apânam pratyag asyati*, exspiration and inspiration are to be understood as suggested by 5. 5, or not rather already as breath and the wind of digestion. In contrast, that is to say, to the accepted idea of prâṇa as exspiration, apâna as inspiration, a disposition was formed, and grew stronger as time went on, to see in prâṇa the breath (exspiration and inspiration), and in apâna the wind of digestion dwelling in the bowels. For this view the following passages are cited. The prâṇa

[1] cp. Deussen, *Upan.*, p. 377.

[2] In the translation I allow myself to be betrayed into regarding it *vice versâ*.

originates from the nose, the apâna from the navel of the primeval man;[1] Vâyu corresponds to the prâṇa, Mṛityu to the apâna;[2] the prâṇa smells the food, the apâna overmasters it.[3] So possibly in the passage quoted, Kâṭh. 5. 3. In Pras'na 3. 5, the prâṇa has its seat in eye, ear, mouth and nose, the apâna presides over the organs of evacuation and generation.[4] The prâṇa makes its exit upwards, the apâna downwards, and carries off the excrements.[5] The apâna serves for evacuation.[6] The prâṇa dwells in the heart, the apâna in the bowels.[7] The apâna is neighbour to the testicles.[8] This is the view adopted also by Vedântasâra 94–95, and the commentary on Chând. 3. 13. 3 and S'aṅkara's judgement on 1. 3. 3 maintains the same.

(3) *Vyâna*, "interspiration," is "the bond between prâṇa and apâna.[9] The conception of it is accommodated to that of apâna. If this is inspiration, then *vyâna* is the breath which sustains the life, when *e.g.* in drawing a stiff bow a man neither inspires nor exspires.[10] If, on the contrary, apâna is the wind of digestion, then vyâna is the bond of union between it and the prâṇa,[11] rules in the veins,[12] and sweeps like a flame through all the limbs.[13] So also in Vedântasâra 96.

(4) *Samâna*, "all-breathing," bears the name because, according to Pras'na 4. 4, it "leads to union" (*samam nayati*) exspiration and inspiration. On the other hand, according to Pras'na 3. 5 and Maitr. 2. 6, it assimilates the food, and according to Amṛitab. 34, 37 dwells white as milk in the navel. Cp. Vedântasâra 98.

[1] Ait. 1. 1. 4. [2] Ait. 1. 2. 4. [3] Ait. 1. 3. 4, 10.

[4] In Pras'na 4. 2–3, on the contrary, evacuation and generation are subordinated to the manas, not to the prâṇas; apparently therefore it follows the view first discussed.

[5] Maitr. 2. 6. [6] Garbha 1. [7] Amṛitabindhu 34.

[8] Sannyâsa 4. [9] Chând. 1. 3. 3. [10] Chând. 1. 3. 5.

[11] Maitr. 2. 6. [12] Pras'na 3. 6. [13] Amṛitab. 35. 37.

(5) *Udâna*, or "up-breathing," according to the usual view maintained also in Pras'na 3. 7, conducts the soul from the body at death, while according to Pras'na 4. 4 already in deep sleep it guides to Brahman; it is maintained however in Maitr. 2. 6 that udâna "either brings up again or swallows down that which is eaten and drunk." Elsewhere it is represented as dwelling in the throat.[1] Similarly also in Vedântasâra 97, where it is otherwise explained as the wind of exit.

5. *The subtle Body and its ethical Qualification*

As further companions of the soul on its wanderings together with the indriyas, manas, and the prâṇas, the later Vedânta reckons "the primitive substance" (*bhûta-âs'raya*), *i.e.* the subtle body, and "the foundation of works" (*karma-âs'raya*), *i.e.* the moral qualification which conditions the future life. On both we are able to adduce but little from the Upanishads.

In Chând. 6. 8. 6[2] it is said of the dying man:—"In the case of this man, my dear sir, when he dies, his speech enters into the manas, manas into the prâṇa, prâṇa into the heat, heat into the supreme godhead." Here, according to S'aṅkara,[3] as by speech the indriyas as a whole are to be understood, so by heat (*tejas*) the elements as a whole, as they constitute the subtle body in their character of vehicles of the organs on the departure of the soul. According to the words of the text however nothing further is implied here than the thought that the organs, manas, prâṇa and speech, as they have been derived according to Chând. 6. 5 by means of food, water, and heat from the "one being without a second," so in a similar way at death they are again resolved into it as the supreme godhead.

We may recognise a trace of the later theory of the

[1] Amṛitab. 34. [2] cp. 6. 15. 2. [3] Sûtra 4. 2. 8.

subtle body more clearly in the great transmigration text Chând. 5. 3–10,[1] where a description is given how the waters, having been five times in succession offered in sacrifice as faith, soma, rain, food and seed, in the sacrificial fires of the heavenly world, of rain, the earth, man and woman, "at the fifth sacrifice became endowed with human voice."[2] Here by the "waters" which were offered as faith, etc., may certainly be understood the still undivided unity of the two companions of the soul, which later were distinguished from one another as the subtle body and the ethical qualification.[3]

The same is true of the leading passage for both doctrines,[4] where it is said of the soul as it departs and hastens to a new birth:—"In truth, this self is Brahman, consisting of knowledge, manas, life, eye and ear, consisting of earth, water, wind and ether, consisting of fire and not of fire, of desire and not of desire, of anger and not of anger, of justice and not of justice, consisting of all. Exactly as a man in this life consists of this or of that, exactly as he acts, exactly as he moves, so will he be born; he who does good will be born good, he who does evil will be born evil, he becomes holy by holy deeds, evil by evil." If we leave out of consideration the addition "and not by fire" which is wanting in the Mâdhyandina recension, and from which a satisfactory meaning can only with difficulty be extracted, the passage enumerates as permanent companions of the soul the organs and five elements, as changing factors the moral qualities. We see here the theories of the subtle body and the ethical qualification growing up side by side. The following verse is appended:—

To this he clings, after this he aspires by his actions,
Whereby his inner man (*liṅgam*) and his desire (*manas*) abide.

---

[1] Bṛih. 6. 2.
[2] Chând. 5. 3. 3, 5. 9. 1.
[3] cp. below, Chap. XIV. 5.
[4] Bṛih. 4. 4. 5.

Here we meet, apparently already a technical term, the word *liṅgam*, by which the adherents of the Sâṅkhya were accustomed later to denote the subtle body.[1] It is perhaps to be taken in the same meaning further on in Kâṭh. 6. 8 and S'vet. 6. 9; where moreover the âtman is described as "lord of the lord of the senses," *i.e.* lord of the subtle body. A similar conception may underlie the description of the âtman as "higher than this highest complex of life."[2] The *liṅgam* makes its appearance precisely as in the later Sâṅkhya in Maitr. 6. 10, especially if we read[3] *mahad-âdi-avis'esha-antam liṅgam*, removing the anusvâra point, since the subtle body extends from the *mahân* to the subtle elements (*avis'esha*), not to the gross (*vis'esha*).[4] The *liṅgas'arîram* is described in Sarvopanishats. 16 as the vehicle of the organs, the prâṇas, the guṇas, and the ethical qualification, and accordingly is identified with the bands of the heart, of which we have put forward another explanation (*sup.* p. 270), referring to Bṛih. 3. 2. 1–9.

That finally the actions of the soul (the later *karma-âs'raya*) accompany it in the other world, and determine the formation of the next life, is often emphasized in the Upanishads, and will demand fuller consideration hereafter. The principal passages for this doctrine are Bṛih. 3. 2. 13, 4. 4. 5–6, Chând. 3. 14. 1, Kâṭh. 5. 7, Îs'â 17, etc.; above all Bṛih. 4. 4. 3:—"Then knowledge and actions take it by the hand, and its earlier formed experience." According to later belief also[5] the thoughts which occupy a man in the hour of death are of especial significance. This idea is found suggested in Pras'na 3. 10.[6]

[1] *sup.* p. 242.

[2] Pras'na 5. 5.

[3] As suggested, Deussen, *Upan.*, p. 337.

[4] Sâṅkhya-kârikâ 38–40.

[5] Bhag. G. 8. 6.

[6] cp. also Chând. 3. 14. 1, Bṛih. 4. 4. 5, and the prayer of the dying man in Îs'â 15–17=Bṛih. 5. 15.

6. *Physiological Conclusions from the Upanishads*

The gross body which the soul abandons at death as the mango fruit its stalk,[1] must be distinguished from the subtle body, which in its capacity as vehicle of the psychical organs accompanies the soul on its wanderings up to the time of its release. We propose here by way of appendix to collect all that the Upanishads have to say on the body, its organs and functions.

The body is the prâṇa's habitation, of which the head forms the roof, in which it is bound to the breath as posts by food as the rope.[2] It is the âtman "consisting of the juice of food," *annarasamaya*, in which is enclosed the *prâṇamaya* âtman, in this again the *manomaya*, in this the *vijñânamaya*, and in this as the innermost the *ânandamaya.*[3] Only later[4] is the *ânandamaya* âtman also described, like the rest, as a sheath *kos'a* of the soul.[5] Usually following Bṛih. 2. 5. 18, and especially Chând. 8. 1. 1, the body is described as the city of Brahman (*brahmapuram*), heavenly,[6] desirable,[7] the highest dwelling of Brahman,[8] in which as a house the lotus flower of the heart abides,[9] in which during sleep the fires of the prâṇa keep watch.[10] This city of the body has eleven,[11] or more usually nine gates,[12] viz., the nine openings in the body, to which when eleven are reckoned the navel and the Brahman orifice (*brahmarandhram*) are added. The latter is an imaginary orifice of the skull on the top of the head, through which, according to Ait. 1. 3. 12, Brahman entered into the body,

[1] Bṛih. 4. 3. 36.
[2] Bṛih. 2. 2. 1.
[3] Taitt. 2. 1 f.
[4] by Maitr. 6. 27–28.
[5] cp. Sarvopanishats. 9 f., where the *annamaya* âtman is still further divided into six sheaths consisting of food (according to the commentator of the Calcutta edition, these are,—bones, marrow, fat, skin, flesh and blood.
[6] Muṇḍ. 2. 2. 7.
[7] Brahma-Up. 1.
[8] Muṇḍ. 3. 2. 1.
[9] Chând. 8. 1. 1, Mahân. 10. 23, Nârây. 5, Âtmabodha.
[10] Pras'na 4. 3.
[11] Kâth. 5. 1.
[12] S'vet. 3. 18, Yogas'. 4, Yogat. 13, Bhag. G. 5. 13.

and by which the soul, or according to the more usual view only the souls of the emancipated,[1] having ascended by the hundred and first vein (subsequently named, following Maitr. 6. 21, *sushumnâ*), attains to union with Brahman.[2] Thus the conception is old. The name *brahmarandhram* is first found in Haṅsa Up. 3 in connection with the six mystical and imaginary regions on the body that occur there for the first time (the regions of the belly, loins, navel, heart, neck and eyebrows). It is perhaps an anticipation of this when, in Ait. 1. 3. 12, eye, manas and the ether of the heart (as the scholiast reckons them), are distinguished as special stations of the purusha, or in Brahma Up. 4, eye, throat, heart and head (in Brahma Up. 2, navel, heart, throat and head). From him who forms the light within men proceeds also, according to Chând. 3. 13. 8, the warmth of the body and the noises in the ear. The latter like digestion are ascribed by Bṛih. 5. 9 to the Vais'vânara fire in men, which when we bear in mind S'atap. Br. X. 6. 1 amounts to the same thing. The passages Mahân. 11. 10, Maitr. 2. 6, 6. 27, 6. 31 depend on a combination of the other two.

Descriptions of the body and its parts, usually with a pessimistic colouring, are first found at a later period. "In this evil-smelling unsubstantial body, shuffled together out of bones, skin, sinews, marrow, flesh, seed, blood, mucus, tears, eye-gum, dung, urine, gall and phlegm, how can we enjoy pleasure?"[3] "This body, originating from copulation, grown in the pit (of the mother's womb) and issuing forth through the passages of the excretions, is a collection of bones daubed over with flesh, covered with skin, filled full with dung, urine, phlegm, marrow, fat and grease, and to crown all with many diseases, like a treasure store crammed with

[1] Chând. 8. 6. 6=Kâṭh. 6. 16.

[2] cp. Brahmavidyâ 12, and especially Taitt. 1. 6.

[3] Maitr. 1. 3.

treasure."[1] A definition of the body is given by Âtma Up. 1:—"That self, in which are skin, bones, flesh, marrow, hairs, fingers, thumbs, spine, nails, joints, belly, navel, pudenda, hips, thighs, cheeks, brows, forehead, arms, sides, head, veins, eyes and ears, and which is born and dies, is called the external self."

The most complete elucidation of the body and its relations is furnished by the late and unfortunately very corrupt Garbha Upanishad. Its explanations are attached to a verse, which we quote, inserting the explanations that follow it:—"Consisting of five (earth, water, fire, wind, ether), ruling in these groups of five (the so-called five elements, or the five organs of knowledge, or the organs of generation and evacuation with buddhi, manas, and speech), supported on six (the sweet, sour, salt, bitter, acid and harsh juices of food), endowed with six qualities (unexplained), made up of seven elementary substances (the white, red, grey, smoke-coloured, yellow, brown, pale fluid in the body which is produced from the juice of the food), made up of three kinds of mucus (unexplained, probably the three *dosha*, humours, viz.,—*vâyu* wind, *pittam* gall, *kapha* phlegm), twice-begotten (from the father's seed and the mother's blood), partaking of various kinds of food (that which is eaten, drunk, licked and sucked up) is the body." On the parts of the body and their importance the Upanishad declares at the close:—"The head has four skull-bones, and in them there are (on each) side sixteen sockets. (In the body) there are 107 joints, 180 sutures, 900 sinews, 700 veins, 500 muscles, 360 bones, and $4\frac{1}{2}$ crore (45 million) hairs. The heart weighs eight pala (364 grammes), the tongue 12 pala (546 grammes), the gall a prastham (728 grammes), the phlegm an âḍhakam (2912 grammes), the seed a kuḍavam (182 grammes), the fat two prastha (1456

[1] Maitr. 3. 4.

grammes; the dung and the urine are indeterminate, depending on the quantity of food."

The head is compared in a verse from Atharvav. X. 8. 9 to a goblet tilted sideways, the opening of which is formed by the seven openings of the organs of sense as seven ṛishis. The same verse with the addition of speech as an eighth organ is repeated and explained in Bṛih. 2. 2. 3. According to this passage the eyes are two ṛishis, although immediately before the red black and white in the eye with the pupil, the humour, and the upper and lower lashes, had been inconsistently described as seven gods remaining in attendance on the eye. Of the purusha in the eye as the symbol of the âtman we have already spoken.[1] According to Bṛih. 4. 2. 2–3, Indra and Virâj dwell in the right and left eye; they are nourished from the heart through the veins *hitâḥ*,[2] and are, by virtue of their "union" in the ether of the heart, the individual âtman identical with the supreme.

As an appropriate punishment for arrogance in questioning or for the darkness of false knowledge there frequently occurs in the Upanishads the bursting of the head.[3] The expression may perhaps have its origin in the sensation of bursting which attends any excessive rush of blood to the head. This is indicated by Bṛih. 1. 3. 24 also, where the reference is to a bursting of the head caused by indulgence in soma. As a rule this punishment is only threatened.[4] Only once is it actually inflicted.[5]

The heart more than the head occupies the attention of the thinkers of the Upanishads. It is there that the

[1] *sup.* p. 114 f.

[2] cp. Maitr. 6. 2.

[3] The phrase is better translated in this way than by the falling off of the head; *vi-pat* might mean either.

[4] Chând. 1. 8. 6, 8, 1. 10. 9–11, 1. 11. 4–9, 5. 12. 2, Bṛih. 3. 6, 3. 7. 1.

[5] Bṛih. 3. 9. 26; cp. Atharvav. 19. 28. 4, S'atap. Br. 3. 6. 1. 23, 4. 4. 3. 4, 11. 4. 1. 9.

vital breaths reside.[1] Not only the five prâṇas, but also eye, ear, speech and manas originate from the heart.[2] The heart and not the head is the home of manas; [3] and the former therefore is the centre also of conscious life. In sleep the organs of the soul remain in the heart,[4] and there also they gather at death; [5] "through the heart we recognise forms," [6] through the heart we recognise faith, beget children, know the truth, on it speech also is based, while the further question on what the heart is based is angrily rejected.[7] Not the organs however alone, but all beings are based upon and supported by the heart; and even setting aside the actual definition of the heart as Brahman,[8] it is yet the empirical home of the soul, and therefore of Brahman:—"here within in the heart is a cavity, wherein he resides, the lord of the universe, the ruler of the universe, the chief of the universe." [9] The heart is called *hṛidayam*, because "it is he" who dwells "in the heart" (*hṛidi ayam*, Chând. 8. 3. 3), small as a grain of rice or barley; [10] an inch in height the purusha dwells in the midst of the body, as the self of created things in the heart.[11]

On the ground of Chând. 8. 1. 1 the heart is frequently in the later Upanishads compared with the hanging cup of a lotus flower,[12] or even with banana blossom; [13] and is more fully described in Mahânâr. 11. 8, Dhyânab. 14–16, Yogat. 9, Mahâ 3. In this lotus flower of the heart there is a small space,[14] in which, according to Chând. 8. 1. 3, heaven and earth, sun, moon and stars are enclosed, in which "the lights of the universe shine enclosed," [15] which

[1] Chând. 3. 12. 4. [2] Chând. 3. 13. 1–5. [3] Ait. 1. 2. 4.
[4] Bṛih. 2. 1. 17. [5] Bṛih. 4. 4. 1. [6] Bṛih. 3. 9. 20.
[7] Bṛih. 3. 9. 21–25. [8] Bṛih. 4. 1. 7. [9] Bṛih. 4. 4. 22.
[10] Bṛih. 5. 6, Chând. 3. 14. 3. [11] Kâṭh. 2. 20, 4. 12, 6. 17, etc.
[12] Mahânâr. 10. 23, Nâr. 5, Maitr. 6. 2, Brahmab. 15; Âtmab, cp. *Upan.*, p. 751; Haṅsa 6.
[13] Dhyânab. 14. [14] Or ether, *âkas'a*. [15] Muṇd. 3. 2. 1.

is "the strong support of this universe."[1] Into this space the soul enters in sleep,[2] in it the immortal golden purusha abides.[3] It is the cavity (*guhâ*), so often referred to, in which Brahman lies concealed,[4] and from which he issues in the meditation of yoga, when he pushes on one side the ether of the heart,[5] or forces his way through it.[6]

Several accounts are found of the veins that originate from the heart and surround it, and these are related in a peculiar and hardly definable way.

Bṛih. 4. 2. 3:—The veins called *hitâḥ*, fine as a hair a thousand times subdivided, have their home in the heart, and nourish the individual soul. A special vein leading upwards is the path on which it travels.

Bṛih. 4. 3. 20:—The veins called *hitâḥ*, fine as a hair a thousand times subdivided, are filled with white, grey, brown, green and red fluid. They are the abode of the soul in deep sleep.

Bṛih. 2. 1. 19:—The veins called *hitâḥ*, 72,000 in number, ramify from the heart outwards into the pericardium (*purîtat*). They are the abode of the soul in deep sleep.

These passages are in essential agreement; and Kaush. 4. 19 appears to be derived from a combination of them:—"The veins called *hitâḥ*, fine as a hair subdivided a thousand times, surround the pericardium They are the abode of the soul in deep sleep. They are filled with brown, white, black, yellow and red fluid." All this is like the passages from Bṛih., only that the succession and names of the colours[7] agree with Chând. 8. 6. 1.

Chând. 8. 6. 1 connects the idea of the brown, white,

[1] Brahma Up. 4. [2] Bṛih. 2. 1. 17. [3] Taitt. 1. 6. 1.
[4] Taitt. 2. 1, Kâṭh. 2. 12, 2. 20, 3. 1, S'vet. 3. 20, Muṇḍ. 2. 1. 10, etc.
[5] Maitr. 6. 27. [6] Maitr. 6. 38. [7] Up to *kṛishṇa* for *nîla*.

gray, yellow and red "veins of the heart" with the theory[1] of the rays of the sun similarly five coloured, which form the continuation of the veins unto the sun, thus uniting heart and sun, like two villages by a high road. In deep sleep the soul glides into these veins,[2] and through them becomes one with the heat.[3] At death the soul ascends to the sun by way of the veins and the sun's rays. The wise gain the sun, the ignorant find the entrance to it closed.

The verses Bṛih. 4. 4. 8–9 may perhaps be derived from this passage. They describe an ancient path, extending even to the individual man, which leads up to the heavenly world, and is white, gray, yellow and green. On this the soul of the wise man travels, after it has become heat, *taijasa*. The expression *taijasa* recalls the passages quoted from the Chândogya;[4] the colours are as in the Bṛihadâraṇyaka. In the main point all the passages hitherto cited agree.

A different view however seems to attach to the verse (perhaps derived from Bṛih. 4. 4. 2), which is appended to Chând. 8. 6. 6 and recurs in Kâṭh. 6. 16:—

> The veins of the heart are a hundred and one.
> Of these one leads to the head;
> By it he ascends who wins immortality.
> The others issue forth on all sides.

According to this verse only one vein leads upwards to immortality, while according to the preceding prose all the veins are connected with the sun's rays, and therefore lead to the sun, where first a separation takes place.

Later passages all depend on a combination of the theories of the 72,000 and the 101 veins. Thus on the

[1] Of which Chând. 3. 1–5 is an anticipation.
[2] Chând. 8. 6. 3.
[3] *tejas*, Chând. 6. 2. 3, 6. 8. 6, 6. 15. 2.
[4] cp. also however Bṛih. 4. 4. 7.

basis of them Pras'na 3. 6 enumerates 101 chief veins, each with 100 branch veins, to each of which again there are 72,000 tributary branch veins, making a total of $101 + 101 \times 100 + 101 \times 100 \times 72{,}000 = 727{,}210{,}201$, *i.e.* 72 crores, 72 lacs, and 10,201 as the commentary[1] correctly reckons. According to Maitr. 6. 30, countless white, not white, blackish yellow, gray, reddish brown, and light-red rays proceed from the heart, of which one leads to the sun, 100 to the abodes of the gods, and the rest downwards to the ordinary world. Kshurikâ 15–17 mentions the 72,000 veins, of which 101 are the most important. Through all these veins, which are grouped around the 101st, named *sushumnâ*, as round a cushion, the yogin forces his way, when conducted on the *sushumnâ* to Brahman. Similarly Brahmavidyâ 11–12 describes how the syllable Om (*i.e.* that on which he meditates) ascends on the vein of the head which is attached to the sun, and breaks through the 72,000 veins and the head, in order to unite with Brahman. These and other fancies depend upon a combination of the passages quoted from Bṛih. Up. with the verse cited from Chând. 8. 6. 6.[2]

The body consists on the usual hypothesis, which is traceable back to Bṛih. 4. 4. 5, of the five elements.[3] In Chând. 6. 5 also, where only three elements (food *i.e.* earth, water, and heat) are assumed, it is shown how the body and the psychical organs originate from the most dense, the medium, and the finest parts of them according to the following scheme:—

	Densest.	Medium.	Finest.
Food . . .	fæces	flesh	manas
Water . . .	urine	blood	prâṇa
Heat . . .	bones	marrow	speech

[1] According to the reading of the Ânandâs'rama edition.
[2] = Kâṭh. 6. 16.
[3] Garbha 1.

In this case, just as with the milk when churned to butter, the fine parts float to the top.[1] In proof of the statement that manas is composed of food, prâṇa of water, it is declared that if a man abstains from food but drinks water the life (*prâṇa*) is maintained, but thought (*manas*) fails.[2] In Bṛih. 4. 2. 3 also it is declared that the individual soul is nourished by the mass of blood in the heart, and that it therefore, as the bodily self, "has a choice food" (*pravivikta-âhâra-tara*). From this is derived the doctrine that the waking âtman "enjoys that which is gross" (*sthûlabhuj*), the sleeping on the contrary "enjoys that which is choice" (*pravivikta-bhuj*).[3]

Hunger and thirst, which according to Ait. 1. 2. 5 make their home in men as demoniac powers, are explained in Chând. 6. 8 on etymological grounds on the supposition that in hunger (*as'anâyâ*) the waters carry off (*as'itam nayante*) the food that is eaten (to build up the organism), while in thirst (*udanyâ*) the heat carries away (*udakam nayate*) the water that is drunk (likewise to build up the organism). When then in hunger and thirst the food becomes water, the water heat, they only return to the source from which according to Chând. 6. 2 they were derived.

The states of waking, dreaming, deep sleep and death will have to be discussed in the immediately following chapters. Here we propose merely to summarise the most important teaching of the Upanishads on the origin of organisms (which collectively are the wandering souls).

Organisms are divided according to their origin into four classes, viz.—born alive, born from an egg, born from moisture (insects and the like), and born from a germ (plants). This classification, which was universally

[1] Chând. 6. 6. [2] Chând. 6. 7.
[3] Mâṇḍûkya 3–4, interpreted differently in Vedântasâra 120.

adopted with a few modifications by later Indian writers,[1] depends solely upon two passages of the Upanishads. The first is Chând. 6. 3. 1:—"In truth, these beings have here three kinds of seeds, born from the egg, born alive, and born from the germ." In Ait. 3. 3 where a fourth class is added, and the enumeration is "born from an egg, born from the mother's womb, born from moisture, and born from a shoot," the impression is conveyed of a later origin and of apparent dependence on the former passage.

In harmony with the doctrine of transmigration, generation is not the birth of the soul for the first time, but is only its return from the moon, where it has received the fruit of the works of its earlier existence. According to the principal text of the doctrine of transmigration,[2] the stations through which the soul passes on its return from the moon are ether, wind, smoke, mist, clouds, rain, plants, seed and the mother's body. Hence is derived the description of Muṇḍ. 2. 1. 5; and the verses also of Kaush. 1. 2, in which the soul on its return from the moon directs its course through the bodies of father and mother, are connected with these ideas. Perhaps the obscure passage Prâṇâgnihotra Up. 2 is to be explained in a similar way. According to it the expiatory fire "by means of the brilliancy of the moon" effects generation.[3] The last receptacle of the soul on its descent from the other world to enter into a new body is the father's seed; this is the essence of men,[4] "the power gathered together from all the limbs,"[5] it is the pro-

[1] Manu 1. 43–48, Mahâbh. 14. 1136, 2543, etc.; cp. for the Vedânta, *Syst. d. Ved.*, p. 259; for the Sâṅkhya, Garbe, *Sâṅkhyaphilosophie*, p. 243; for the Nyâya, Colebrooke, *Misc. Essays*, I. p. 269 f.

[2] Chând. 5. 10. 5–6 = Bṛih. 6. 2. 16.

[3] Nârâyaṇa's explanation is different in the gloss quoted in *Upan.*, p. 615, Anm. 2.

[4] Bṛih. 6. 4. 1.

[5] Ait. 2. 1; on the expression *sambhṛitam tejas*, cp. Meghadûta 43.

pagation itself;[1] its home is in the heart;[2] Prajâpati created the woman as its dwelling-place;[3] into her the man pours forth his own self, and causes it thereby to be born:—"then enters he into the very essence of the woman, as though he were a limb of hers; therefore it is that he does her no harm; she however, after that this his âtman has come to her, cherishes it; because she cherishes it, therefore is she to be cherished."[4] According to this it is the soul of the father, which is born again in the child, while, according to the principal text of the doctrine of transmigration[5] quoted above, the child is a soul on its return from the moon, and consequently in its view both the father's seed and the mother's womb are only stations on the road. The myth ascribed to Yâjñavalkhya in Bṛih. 1. 4. 3–4 is not in agreement with either of these views, when it explains procreation as the desire for re-union of the two halves of one and the same being, originally belonging together, but divided by Prajâpati into man and woman. This myth, like that analogous to it in the Symposium of Plato, departs from the truth only to the extent that it places in the past what lies in the future. For the being that brings together man and woman is indeed the child that will be born (cp. Deussen, *Elements of Metaphysic*, 153).

To beget is represented as a religious duty. In Taitt. 1. 9 it is enjoined side by side with studying and teaching the Veda. Frequently it is allegorically described as an act of sacrifice.[6] In Taitt. 1. 11 the pupil dismissed from study is charged,—"After having delivered to the teacher the gifts of affection, take care that the thread of thy race be not broken." "He who in his lifetime rightly continues to spin the thread of posterity thereby transfers

[1] Bṛih. 6. 1. 6. [2] Bṛih. 3. 9. 22. [3] Bṛih. 6. 4. 2.
[4] Ait. 2. 2–3. [5] Chând. 5. 10. 5–6.
[6] Chând. 3. 17. 5, 5. 8–9, Bṛih. 6. 2. 13, 6. 4. 3.

his guilt to the fathers; for it (begetting) is the transference of his guilt."[1] By the son his continued life is assured in the world of men,[2] he is admitted to the fathers to consummate his righteous deeds;[3] "and if anything whatever has been committed perversely by him, his son will expiate all; therefore is his name 'son';[4] by the son that is to say he continues to exist in this world."[5] Particular directions are given in Bṛih. 6. 4 how to proceed in order to beget a son or a daughter of a definite disposition. This chapter forms the conclusion of the Upanishad, and therefore probably the close of the religious instruction imparted to the student at the end of his student life.

In contrast with these views, which include the act of procreation within the sphere of religious duties, an ascetic tendency gradually prevailed which rejected it altogether. In Bṛih. 1. 4. 17 the five natural objects of human endeavour (self, wife, child, kingdom, action) are replaced by five phenomenal forms of the âtman (manas, speech, breath, eye and ear, body). In Bṛih. 3. 5. 1 it is said of Brâhmans who have known the âtman that they hold aloof from the desire for children, possessions, and the world. Similarly in Bṛih. 4. 4. 22, where it has been said previously:—"This our ancestors knew, when they ceased to desire offspring, and said,—'What need have we of offspring, we whose soul this universe is.'" If these assertions are put into the mouth of Yâjñavalkhya, who nevertheless himself had two wives, this is only an additional proof that Yâjñavalkhya is a mere name, to which the loftiest and noblest thoughts of the school of the Vâjasaneyins were assigned. Whether in the wish also of Chând. 8. 14:—"May I not, the glorious of the

[1] Mahân. 63. 8. [2] Bṛih. 1. 5. 16. [3] Ait. 2. 4.
[4] *putra*, because he *pûraṇena trâyati pitaram*, S'aṅk.
[5] Bṛih. 1. 5. 17.

glorious, enter upon old age toothless," the expression "toothless, grey, slobbery" is to be understood of a fresh entrance into the mother's womb (as the scholiast takes it), or of a possibly long period of trial before old age and its troubles are reached may be left undecided. Of later passages only Mahân. 62. 7, 11, 63. 8, 13 need be cited, where self-renunciation is exalted above parentage, and Pras'na 1. 13, 15, where the *prajâpativratam* is still permitted on the condition that it is not practised by day, but the world of Brahman is promised only to those "who mortify themselves, in whom true chastity is firmly established." That the later Sannyâsa Upanishads are full of this spirit needs no proof. Sacrifice to Prajâpati, which is enjoined in them on the Sannyâsin at his entrance,[1] but is elsewhere forbidden,[2] appears to denote a symbolical release from the duty of propagation.

The length of the stay in the mother's body is estimated in Chând. 5. 9. 1 at "ten (lunar) months, or as long as it is." Detailed information on the development of the embryo is given in Garbha Up. 2–4 :—"The embryo is developed from the union of seed and blood, . . . from this union at the periodical time after one night a nodule arises, after seven nights a cyst, within half a month a lump, within one month it hardens, after two months the head is formed, after three months the parts of the feet, in the fourth month the ankle-bones, belly and hips, in the fifth the spine, in the sixth, mouth, nose, eyes and ears, in the seventh the embryo is furnished with the soul (*jîva*), in the eighth it is complete in all its parts. If the male seed is in excess a male is born, if the female a female, if both are equal a hermaphrodite; blind, lame, bent and dwarfed are the results of lack of power. If the seed on its entrance is

[1] Kaṇthas'r. 4. [2] Jâbâla 4.

divided by the pressure of the wind on either side into two parts, the body also becomes twofold, and twins are born. . . . Finally in the ninth month it is complete in all its parts, and also in knowledge; then it recalls (as long as it remains still in the mother's body, like Vâmadeva, Ait. 2. 4) its former births, and has knowledge of its good and evil deeds; . . . when however, arriving at the gates of the sexual parts, it suffers pain by the pressure, is with difficulty and in great anguish born, and comes into contact with the Vaishṇava wind (the wind of the external universe), it is unable any longer to bethink it of its births and deaths, and has no further knowledge of its good and evil deeds." Voltaire's mockery (Ep. XIII. sur les Anglais) has reference to similar ideas in the later Western philosophy, but it applies also to the Indian *a priori* imaginations:—je ne suis pas plus disposé que Locke à imaginer que, quelques semaines après ma conception, j'étais une âme fort savante, sachant alors mille choses que j'ai oubliées en naissant et ayant fort inutilement possédé dans l'utérus des connaissances qui m'ont échappé dès que j'ai pu en avoir besoin et que je n'ai jamais bien pu reprendre depuis.

XIII. The States of the Soul

1. *The Four States*

As the âtman, "becoming incarnate in bodily form,"[1] in space occupies the body as the aggregate of the organs "right up to the finger-tips,"[2] so also in time it passes in this its individual condition through a series of states, in which its real metaphysical nature becomes gradually more and more plainly visible. These states are:—(1) waking, (2) dream sleep, (3) deep sleep (*sushupti*), *i.e.*

[1] *sarîratvâya dehin*, Kâṭh. 5. 7.

[2] Bṛih. 1. 4. 7.

deep, dreamless sleep, in which the soul becomes temporarily one with Brahman and enjoys a corresponding unsurpassable bliss, and (4) the "fourth" state (*c'aturtha, turya, turîya*), usually called *turîya*, in which that disappearance of the manifold universe and the union with Brahman on which the bliss of deep sleep depends takes place not as before unconsciously, but with continued and perfect consciousness.

The theory of these four states took shape at first by degrees.

To begin with, it may well have been the loss of consciousness in sleep, and its return on waking which aroused attention and suggested such questions as in Bṛih. 2. 1. 16:[1]—"When he fell asleep here, where was that spirit consisting of knowledge (*vijñânamayaḥ purusha*), and whence has it now returned (on waking)?" This marvellous phenomenon of sleep was then explained as a transient immersion of the organs (speech, eye, ear and manas) in the *prâṇa*. This is the case in S'atap. Br. X. 3. 3. 6, and in the passage Chând. 4. 3. 3 which agrees with it almost verbally:—"For when a man sleeps, his speech enters into the prâṇa, the eye into the prâṇa, the ear into the prâṇa, the manas into the prâṇa." Chând. 6. 8. 2 is a mere amplification of this explanation of sleep (perhaps with a recollection of Bṛih. 4. 3. 19):—"Just as a bird tied to a string flies to this side and to that, and having found no resting-place elsewhere settles down on the spot to which it is tied, so also, my dear sir, the manas flies to this side and to that, and having found no resting-place elsewhere, settles down into the prâṇa, for the prâṇa, my dear sir, is the spot to which the manas is tied." The immediately preceding words of Chând. 6. 8. 1 are derived from a somewhat different conception:—"When it is said that the man is asleep, then has he, my dear sir, attained

[1] cp. Kaush. 4. 19.

to union with the self-existent (previously described in Chând. 6. 2 f.). He has entered into himself, therefore it is said of him "he sleeps" (*svapiti*), for he has entered into himself (*svam apîta*)."

None of these passages make any distinction between the sleep of dreams and deep sleep. Such a distinction is first found in Bṛih. 4. 3. 9–18, 19–33, then in Bṛih. 2. 1. 18–19,[1] and finally Chând. 8. 6. 3, 8. 10, 11–12.[2] This may well be the historical order. In Bṛih. 4. 3. 9–33 the distinction is not so fully carried out as in Bṛih. 2. 1. 18–19, where the name *sushupta* for the "deep sleeper," which is still wanting in Bṛih. 4. 3. 9–33, first makes its appearance, and from this are further developed the terms *sushuptam*[3] and *sushupti*[4] for "deep sleep." The amplifications of Chând. 8 seem to be the latest of all, and dependent already on Bṛih. 4. 3. 9–33; for when in Chând. 8. 3. 4[5] deep sleep is described (not as in Chând. 6. 8. 3 in connection with Chând. 6. 2. 3, 6. 8. 6 as a union with the *tejas*, but) as an entrance into the purest light, and an emergence therefrom as a necessary consequence in its own true form (*param jyotir upasampadya svena rûpeṇa abhinishpadhyate*), this peculiar conception may of course be referred back to Chând. 3. 13. 7, but it seems more natural to find in it a reminiscence of the "spirit consisting of knowledge, giving light within in the heart" of Bṛih. 4. 3. 7, which, as is there further expounded, "by virtue of its own brightness, its own light, serves as a light for itself" in waking, dreaming, and deep sleep. It is surely also a proof of dependence that the word *samprasâda*, which in Bṛih. 4. 3. 15, a passage that had probably already suffered interpolation, still has the meaning of the "perfect rest" of deep sleep, is used in

[1] cp. Kaush. 4. 20.
[2] cp. Chând. 8. 3. 4.
[3] From and after Mâṇḍ. 5.
[4] From and after Kaivalya 13. 17.
[5] =8. 12. 3.

Chând. 8. 3. 4, 8. 12. 3 directly of "the soul in deep sleep."

The brief notice of Ait. 1. 3. 12 is drawn from these older passages, and the more detailed discussions on dream sleep and deep sleep of Pras′na 4 are similarly dependent.

By the side of waking, dreaming and deep sleep, there is found a fourth and higher condition of the âtman, viz.—the *c′aturtham*, *turyam*, *turîyam* (sc. *sthânam*), or the *turîya* (sc. *âtmâ*). It occurs first in Mâṇḍ. 7, as compared with which the passages Maitr. 6. 19, 7. 11, which belong to the appendix, are probably later. Here also the three first states are denoted by the mystical names *Vais′vânara*, *Taijasa*, *Prâjña*. The waking soul is in this instance called *vais′vânara* perhaps because all men in their waking hours have a world in common,[1] but in dreams each has his own; the dreaming soul *taijasa*, probably because then the âtman alone is its own light;[2] the deep-sleeping soul *prâjña*, because in deep sleep the âtman, according to Bṛih. 4. 3. 21, is temporarily one with the *prâjña âtman*, *i.e.* Brahman.

The discussion of the four states severally may be introduced by the definition of them given in Sarvopanishatsâra 5–8 :—

"When using the fourteen organs of which manas is the first (manas, buddhi, c′ittam, ahaṅkâra, and the faculties of knowledge and action), that are developed outwards, and besides are sustained by deities such as âditya, etc., a man regards as real the external objects of sense, as sounds, etc., this is named the waking (*jâgaraṇam*) of the âtman."

"When freed from waking impressions, and using only four organs (manas, buddhi, c′ittam, ahaṅkâra), apart from

[1] As Heracleitus says, on Plut. *de Superstit.* 3.
[2] *svena bhâsâ, svena jyotishâ prasvapiti*, Bṛih. 4. 3. 9.

the actual presence of the sounds, etc., a man regards as real sounds dependent on those impressions, this is named the dreaming (*svapnam*, here neuter) of the âtman."

"When as a result of the quiescence of all fourteen organs and the cessation of the consciousness of particular objects, a man (is without consciousness), this is named the deep sleep (*sushuptam*) of the âtman."

"When the three states named have ceased, and the spiritual subsists alone by itself, contrasted like a spectator with all existing things as a substance undifferentiated, set free from all existing things, this spiritual state is called the *turîyam* (the fourth)."

2. *The Waking State*

"The *Vais'vânara*, that exists in a waking condition, recognising external objects, with seven limbs and nineteen mouths, enjoying that which is material, is his first quarter."[1] The âtman in the first of the four states, that of waking, is said to be "seven-limbed" because, according to Chând. 5. 18. 2, whence the name *vais'vânara* is derived, it consists of sky, sun, wind, ether, water, earth and (sacrificial) fire, and recognises this its cosmical being by means of its "nineteen-mouthed" (ten indriyas, five prâṇas, manas, buddhi, ahaṅkâra, c'ittam) psychical being. Thus it enjoys the world of "material" objects. Kaivalya 12 may be quoted in explanation:—

> When his soul is blinded by mâyâ,
> It inhabits the body and accomplishes actions;
> By women, food, drink, and many enjoyments,
> It obtains satisfaction in a waking condition.

As these passages already indicate, it is his own being alone which in the waking state the *vais'vânara* evolves

[1] Mâṇḍ. 3.

out of himself and enjoys as the world of material objects. On this the relation of waking and dreaming depends, which is already indicated when in Ait. 1. 3. 12 there are ascribed to the âtman "three dream-states" (*trayaḥ svapnâḥ*), by which, according to the commentators, waking, dreaming and deep sleep are to be understood. Even waking is a dream-state, because in it, as S'aṅkara remarks on this passage, "a waking of one's own real self does not occur, and a false reality is contemplated, just as in a dream."[1] This connection of waking with the dream-state is discussed in great detail by Gauḍapâda in the Mâṇḍûkya-kârikâ. Waking, like dreaming, is a delusion, since it reflects for us a manifold universe;[2] the perceptions of waking, just like those of a dream, have their origin solely within us,[3] and have no other existence than in the mind of him who is awake.[4] And as the reality of the dream is dissipated on awakening, so, on the other hand, the waking reality is dissipated by the oblivion of the dream.[5] The same thought may perhaps be traced as early as Bṛih. 4. 3. 7, where the knowledge and initiative of the âtman are first explained as merely apparent, and then the reason for this is assigned, that the âtman in the dream transcends the unreal phenomena of waking:—"it is as though he meditated, it is as though he moved about; for[6] in sleep he transcends this world and the forms of death." Just as a fish swims between two banks without touching them, so the âtman between the states of waking and dreaming;[7] from waking he hastens to dreaming, and from this again "back to the waking state; but by nothing which he sees therein is he affected; for nothing cleaves to this spirit."[8]

[1] On other expressions of S'ankara in this sense, cp. *Syst. d. Ved.*, pp. 297, 299, 372.

[2] 2. 5, 3. 29.

[3] 4. 37.

[4] 4. 66.

[5] 2. 7, 4. 32.

[6] *sa hi*, for which the Mâdhy. read *sadhîḥ*.

[7] Bṛih. 4. 3. 18.

[8] Bṛih. 4. 3. 16.

3. *Dream-sleep*

The principal passage on which apparently all others depend is Bṛih. 4. 3. 9–14:—

"When now he falls asleep, he takes from this all-comprehending universe the timber, cuts it down, and himself builds up of it his own light, by virtue of his own brilliance; when therefore he sleeps this spirit serves as light for itself. There are there no carts, no teams, no roads, but carts, teams and roads he fashions for himself; there is no bliss, joy or desire, but bliss, joy and desire he fashions for himself; there are no wells, pools and streams, but wells, pools and streams he fashions for himself; for he is the creator. To this the following verses refer:—

> Throwing off in sleep what pertains to the body,
> Sleepless he contemplates the sleeping organs;
> Borrowing their light he returns then back to his place,
> The golden spirit, the sole bird of passage.
>
> This lower nest he would have guarded by the life,
> And himself rises aloft immortal from the nest;
> Immortal he moves whither he will,
> The golden spirit, the sole bird of passage.
>
> In the dream-state he moves up and down,
> And fashions for himself as god many forms,
> At one time gaily sporting as it were with woman,
> At another again glowering as it were with terrible mien.
>
> Only his playground is seen here,
> He himself is not seen anywhere.

Therefore it is said,--he should not be wakened suddenly, for it is difficult to find a cure for one to whom he fails to find his way back. Therefore it is said also,—it (sleep) is for him only a waking state, for what he sees waking, the very same also he sees in sleep. Thus therefore this spirit serves for a light for itself."

In this passage two methods of conceiving the dream are poetically united. According to the one, the spirit remains in its place, and fashions from itself "by virtue of its own brilliance its own light," a new world of forms, using the materials of its waking hours. According to the other, the spirit in dreaming forsakes the body, and "moves whither it will," and consequently at times finds difficulty in returning to the body.

These two conceptions which are derived only from poetical imagination and do not essentially differ are taken up seriously in Bṛih. 2. 1. 18, and are reconciled with one another by limiting the wanderings of the dreamer to his own body:—"Where then he wanders in dreaming, these are his worlds; for he is as it were a great king or a great Brâhman; or he ascends as it were or descends.[1] And just as a great king takes his subordinates with him, and journeys throughout his land at will,[2] so he takes with him those vital spirits, and journeys about at will in his body." This extraordinary theory which has no natural foundation of a journeying about in the body during dreams, finds its explanation as an attempt to reconcile the different conceptions of the fundamental passage above quoted. The comparison also with the great king and great Brâhman seems to be based on the succeeding words of Bṛih. 4. 3. 20, which describes as follows the transition from the dreaming consciousness of being this or that to the deep sleep consciousness of being another:—"When now (in a dream) it is as though he were slain, as though he were flayed, as though he were trampled upon by an elephant (*vic'c'hâyayati*), or plunged into a pit,—everything of which he was afraid in his waking hours, that very

[1] *uc'c'âvac'am nigac'c'hati*, according to Bṛih. 4. 3. 13 *uc'c'âvac'am îyamânaḥ*.

[2] Recalling Bṛih. 4. 3. 37–38.

thing in his ignorance he regards as real; or, on the other hand, when it is as though he were a god or a king, on becoming conscious I alone am this universe,—this is his highest state." That is to say, as the paragraph goes on to state, it is the condition of deep sleep, in which a man knows himself to be one with the universe, and is therefore without objects to contemplate, and consequently without individual consciousness.[1] And when in Chând. 8. 10. 2 it is said of the dreamer:—"It is still however as though he were slain, as though he were trampled upon (*vic'c'hâyayanti*), as though he experienced hardship, as though he lamented," the connection with the passage quoted from Bṛih. 4. 3. 20 is obvious. The meaningless *vic'c'hâdayanti* of Chând. 8. 10. 2 was changed by M. Mûller[2] into *vic'c'hâyayanti*. An almost inevitable consequence of this change, bearing in mind the great rarity of this expression, is that Chând. 8. 10. 2 is immediately dependent on Bṛih. 4. 3. 20. The converse supposition, or even the idea of an interpolation of Bṛih. 4. 3. 20 from Chând. 8. 10. 2,[3] is scarcely probable in view of the general character of the two passages.

Pras'na 4. 5 is more certainly dependent on Bṛih. 4. 3. There, after it has been shown how in sleep manas absorbs into itself the ten indriyas, so that only the prâṇa fires keep watch in the city of the body, the dream is described as follows:—"Then that god (viz. manas) enjoys greatness, inasmuch as he sees yet again that which was seen here and there, hears yet again things heard here and there, perceives again and again in detail that which was perceived in detail in its surroundings of place and circumstance; the seen and the unseen, the heard and the unheard, the perceived and

[1] Bṛih. 4. 3. 21 f. [2] Followed by Böhtlingk and myself.
[3] The possibility of which was still in my mind in *Upan.*, pp. 464, 470.

the unperceived, the whole he views, as the whole he views it (*sarvam pas'yati, sarvaḥ pas'yati*)." The last words especially, when compared with Bṛih. 4. 3. 20 (*aham eva idam sarvo 'smi, iti manyate*), place the derivative character of this passage quite beyond doubt.

Of later passages we cite only Mâṇḍ. 4, where after the exposition of the waking state discussed above it is similarly said of dreaming:—"The *Taijasa*, existing in the dream-state, possessed of inner knowledge, with seven limbs and nineteen mouths, enjoying that which is excellent, is his second quarter." The expressions "seven-limbed," "nineteen-mouthed" are explained as above on waking. The dream-soul is said to be "enjoying that which is excellent" (*praviviktabhuj*) undoubtedly with reference to Bṛih. 4. 2. 3, where it is said of the individual soul that it in contrast to the body "has an excellent provision" (*pravivikta-âhâratara.*)

A discussion of the illusion of dreams with a view to elucidate the illusion of waking is furnished by Gauḍapâda 2. 1 f., 4. 33 f., where the same thoughts already appear, which later on S'ankara, a pupil of his pupil, has further expanded.[1]

4. *Deep Sleep*

Dream-sleep passes over into deep sleep, when by virtue of a nearer approach to the other world[2] the dreaming consciousness of being this or that, a god or king, etc., passes over, as is described in Bṛih. 4. 3. 20, into the consciousness of being the universe; and this, since there are no longer any contrasted objects, is no consciousness in an empirical sense, but a transient union with the *prâjña âtman*, the eternal knowing subject, *i.e.* with Brahman. These thoughts are expanded in the most important text that treats of deep sleep, and

[1] cp. *Syst. d. Ved.*, p. 371.

[2] Bṛih. 4. 3. 9.

which is probably also the oldest, Bṛih. 4. 3. 19–33:—"Just as there however in space a hawk or an eagle, after it has circled round, folds its wings wearied, and drops to the ground, so also the spirit hastens to that state in which fallen asleep it no longer experiences any desires nor sees any dream image." Then after a reference to the veins *hitâḥ*, in which according to Bṛih. 2. 1. 19, etc., the soul rests in deep sleep, and after the description of the transition from dreaming to deep sleep it is said:—"That is its real form, in which it is exalted above desire, free from evil and is fearless. For just as a man, embraced by a beloved wife, has no consciousness of outer or inner, so also the spirit embraced by the self consisting of knowledge (*prâjñena âtmanâ*, *i.e.* by Brahman) has no consciousness of outer or inner. That is his real form, in which desire has been laid to rest, he is himself his own desire, is without desire and free from pain. Then the father is no longer father, the mother no longer mother, the worlds no longer worlds, the gods no longer gods," etc., all contrasts are lost in the eternal One, "then is he unaffected by good and unaffected by evil, then has he overcome all the pangs of his heart. If he then sees not, yet is he seeing, though he sees not; since for the seeing One there is no interruption of seeing, because he is imperishable; there is moreover no second besides him, no other distinct from him for him to see." It is in this prolongation of existence as pure objectless knowing subject that the bliss of this state consists; an existence such as is seen in deep sleep, as is expounded later on in a continuation of the passage already discussed.[1] Bṛih. 2. 1. 19 might perhaps be regarded as a brief summary of the thought of this section:—"When however he is in deep sleep, when he is conscious of nothing, then the veins called

[1] p. 142 f.

hitâḥ, seventy-two thousand of which branch out from the heart into the pericardium, come into action; into these he glides, and rests in the pericardium; and just as a youth or a great king or a great Brâhman is at rest enjoying an excess of bliss,[1] so he also is then at rest."

Union with the *prâṇa* (which is identified with the *prâjñâtman*) is the essential element of deep sleep in Kaush. 3. 3 also:—"When a man has fallen so sound asleep that he sees no dream-image, then he has attained union with this prâṇa; then speech enters therein with all names, the eye with all forms, the ear with all sounds, the manas with all thoughts." Kaush. 4. 19–20 is a combination of the two last-quoted passages.

The passages of the Chând. Up. also which deal with deep sleep give throughout the impression of being of a derivative character. We quote them, referring as far as possible within parentheses to passages that have been employed as models.

"When a man has fallen so sound asleep, and has so completely and perfectly been lulled to rest, that he knows no dream-image, then he has glided into these veins (Bṛih. 2. 1. 19, 'into these he glides'); therefore no evil troubles him (Bṛih. 4. 3. 22, 'then is he untouched by good and untouched by evil'), for he has then become one with the heat" (Chând. 6. 2. 3, 6. 8. 6).[2] "When a man has fallen so sound asleep, and has so completely and perfectly been lulled to rest that he knows no dream-image, that is the Self, so he spake, that is the immortal, the fearless, that is Brahman."[3] The rejoinder is given:—"He has entered then into nothingness; herein I can discern nothing consolatory,"[4] and this is

[1] *atighnîm ânandasya*; this expression combines the ideas of Bṛih. 4. 3. 33, *sup*. p. 142.

[2] Chând. 8. 6. 3.

[3] Chând. 8. 11. 1.

[4] cp. the rejoinder of Maitreyî, Bṛih. 2. 4. 13,—"Therefore, sir, you have led me astray, in that you say that after death there is no consciousness."

met by a reference to wind and cloud, lightning and thunder, which emerge from the latent condition, and thereby reveal their true nature :—" so also this perfect tranquillity (*samprasâda*, in Bṛih. 4. 3. 15 'deep sleep,' here and Chând. 8. 3. 4 'the soul in deep sleep,' cp. Bṛih. 4. 3. 7 *sa hi svapno bhûtvâ*) emerges from this body (Bṛih. 4. 3. 11 :—'casting away in sleep what pertains to the body'), enters into the purest light, and issues forth through it in its own form (Bṛih. 4. 3. 9 :—'when he thus sleeps, then this spirit serves for its own light'); that is the supreme spirit, who wanders about there (Bṛih. 4. 3. 12 :—'Immortal he roves whither he pleases'), while he sports and plays and amuses himself, whether it be with women (Bṛih. 4. 3. 13 :—'at one time as it were gaily sporting with women'), or with chariots (Bṛih. 4. 3. 10), or with friends, and gives no thought to this appendage of a body, to which the prâṇa is yoked, like a team to the waggon (Bṛih. 4. 3. 35 :—'Just as a cart, when it is heavily laden, goes creaking')." It seems to be due to a misunderstanding of the verse Bṛih. 4. 3. 11–14 that here, as already in Bṛih. 4. 3. 15, that which belongs solely to dream-sleep is ascribed to deep sleep. In Pras'na 4. 6 also, as in Chând. 8. 6. 3, deep sleep is conceived as a union with the heat (*tejas*) :—" When however that god is overcome by the heat, then he sees no dreams, and then that joy rules in this body."

Finally the description of deep sleep in Mâṇḍ. 5 is entirely composed of reminiscences of other passages :— " The state in which he, fallen asleep, no longer experiences any desires, nor sees any dream-image (Bṛih. 4. 3. 19), is deep sleep. The *prâjña* that exists in the state of deep sleep, that has become one (Bṛih. 4. 4. 2), that consists entirely through and through of knowledge (Bṛih. 4. 5. 13), consisting of bliss (Taitt. 2. 5), enjoying bliss, having consciousness as its mouth (Bṛih. 4. 3. 21, 35), is his third quarter. He is the lord of all (Bṛih. 4. 4. 22), he is the all-knowing (Muṇḍ. 1. 1. 9), he is the inner guide (Bṛih. 3. 7), he is the cradle of the universe (Muṇḍ. 1. 1. 6), for he is the creation and dissolution (Kâṭh. 6. 11) of living beings."

5. *The Turîya*

Waking, dream-sleep and deep sleep are the only three states of the âtman which are found in the older Upanishads. According to their view, perfect union with Brahman, and therefore the highest attainable state, is reached in deep sleep. "This is his highest aim, this is his highest good fortune, this is his highest world, this is his highest bliss."[1] These words, which are used of deep sleep, exclude the thought of a yet higher state.

It was first later on, with the rise of the Yoga system, that in the yoga a state of the soul gained recognition, which was exalted above deep sleep, inasmuch as that union with Brahman and the supreme bliss associated therewith, which manifests itself in deep sleep apart from continued individual consciousness retaining its memory even after waking, is realised in the yoga together with complete maintenance of the waking individual consciousness. This distinction between the yoga and deep sleep is very clearly described by Gauḍapâda:[2]—

> As eternal changeless knowledge,
> Not distinct from that which is known,
> Brahman is ever known,—
> By the eternal is the eternal known.
>
> This process consists in this,
> The irresistible suppression
> Of all movements of the spirit,—
> It is otherwise in deep sleep.

---

[1] Bṛih. 4. 3. 32.

[2] Mâṇḍûkya-K. 3. 33 f.

The spirit gives light in deep sleep,
But when suppressed it gives no light,
It becomes Brahman, the fearless,
The sole and entire light of knowledge.

This suppression of consciousness of objects and union with the eternal knowing subject which is brought about by the yoga and is coincident with absolute wakefulness, is designated as the "fourth" state of the âtman by the side of waking dreaming and deep sleep; as *c'aturtha*,[1] or, adopting the ancient Vedic and therefore more formal word for *c'aturtha*, as *turîya*;[2] and in the latter case both "the *turîya*" (sc. *âtmâ*, masc.) and also "the *turîyam*" (sc. *sthânam*, neut.) were employed. Since this state forms in fact a part of the yoga system, we shall learn more of it in detail in our discussion of the latter in a later connection, and here we propose merely to cite the passages in which the doctrine of the turîya makes its first appearance. This conception is undoubtedly anticipated by the ancient doctrine of the four feet of Brahman in his character of Gâyatrî;[3] but the oldest passages in which the *turîya* is announced as a fourth distinct state of the âtman are Mâṇḍ. 7 and Maitr. 6. 19, 7. 11. Of these the passages from the Maitr. Up. (appendix) would seem to be the later, since they assume the *turîya* state as already known, which is not the case in Mâṇḍ. 7. In the latter also the technical term *turîya* is still missing, and in its place *c'aturtha* is once employed. This passage, of which later writers make much use, runs as follows:—

"Knowing neither within nor without nor yet on the two sides, nor again consisting throughout of knowledge, neither known nor unknown,—invisible, intangible, incomprehensible, indescribable, unthinkable, inexpressible, founded solely on the certainty of its own self, effacing the

[1] Mâṇḍ. 7.
[2] Also *turya*.
[3] Chând. 3. 12, 3. 18, 4. 5–8, Bṛih. 5. 14, where the very expression *turîya* is already found.

entire expanse of the universe, tranquil, blissful, timeless, —that is the fourth (*c'aturtha*) quarter, that is the âtman, that we must know."

The best exposition is given by the pertinent strophes of Gauḍapâda :[1]—

Neither of truth nor untruth,
Neither of itself nor another
Is *Prâjña* (deep sleep) ever conscious,
The fourth (*turya*) views everything eternally

In the refusal to recognise plurality
The *Prâjña* and the fourth are equal ;
Yet *Prâjña* lies in slumber like a germ,
The fourth knows no slumber.

Dreams and sleep belong to the two first,
A dreamless sleep is the possession of the *Prâjña*,
Neither dreams nor sleep does he who knows it
Ascribe to the fourth.

The dreamer's knowledge is false,
The sleeper knows nothing at all,
Both go astray, where all this vanishes
There the fourth state is reached.

In the world's illusion that has no beginning
The soul sleeps ; when it awakes
Then there awakes in it the eternal,
Timeless and free from dreams and sleep.

Assuming this doctrine of the *turîya* in its description of the yoga, the passage Maitr. 6. 19 urges the "keeping under of the individual soul called *prâṇa* in that which is called *turyam*"; and in 7. 11 assigns the four states of the âtman to the four feet of *purusha* (one of which is composed of all living beings, while three are immortal in heaven),[2] in such a way that waking, dreaming and deep sleep form the one foot, the *turîya* the three others :—

He who is in the eye, he who is in the dream,
He who is in deep sleep, and he who is supreme,—
These are his four varieties,
Yet the greatest is the fourth.

---

[1] 1. 12–16.

[2] Ṛigv. X. 90. 3.

A quarter of Brahman is in three,
Three-quarters are in the last;
In order to taste truth and delusion
The great self became twofold.

From later passages on the *turîya*[1] we propose to mention only the amplifications of Nṛisiṁhottaratâp. Up. 2. and 8, where the conception is further refined, and four degrees of turîya also are distinguished, viz.—*ota, anujñâtṛi, anujñâ* and *avikalpa* (pervading the universe, enlightening the mind, spirituality, indifference), of which the three first are still constantly affected by "deep sleep, dreaming and sheer illusion," and only *avikalpa*, the entire obliteration of all distinction, purified from every taint of the world is, as *turîya-turîya*, "the fourth of the fourth" pure, absolute thought.

[1] cp. Brahma Up. 2, Sarvopanishats. 8, Haṁsa Up. 8.

FOURTH PART OF THE SYSTEM OF THE UPANISHADS

ESCHATOLOGY, OR THE DOCTRINE OF TRANSMIGRATION AND EMANCIPATION, INCLUDING THE WAY THITHER (PRACTICAL PHILOSOPHY)

XIV. Transmigration of the Soul

1. *Philosophical Significance of the Doctrine of Transmigration*

What becomes of men after death? This question leads us to that doctrine which, if not the most significant in the Indian conception of the universe, is yet certainly the most original and influential, the doctrine of the transmigration of the soul, which from Upanishad times down to the present has held a foremost position in Indian thought, and exercises still the greatest practical influence.* Mankind, as S'ankara somewhere expresses it,[1] is like a plant. Like this it springs up, develops, and returns finally to the earth. Not entirely, however. But as the seed of the plant survives, so also at death the works of a man remain as a seed which, sown afresh in the realm of

* In Jaipur I met in December 1892 an old Pandit almost naked, who approached me groping his way. They told me that he was completely blind. Not knowing that he had been blind from birth, I sympathised with him, and asked by what unfortunate accident the loss of sight had come upon him. Immediately and without showing any sign whatever of bitterness, the answer was ready to his lips :—*kenac'id aparâdhena pûrvasmin janmani kṛitena*, "by some crime committed in a former birth."

[1] On Brahmasûtra 2. 1. 34, and frequently.

ignorance, gives rise to a new existence in exact correspondence with his character. Each life with all its actions and sufferings is on the one hand the inevitable consequence of the actions of a former birth, and conditions on the other hand by the actions committed in it the next succeeding life. This conviction begets not only a real consolation in the sufferings of existence, which are universally seen to be self-inflicted, but is also a powerful incentive to habitual right conduct, and the instances from Indian epic and dramatic poetry are numerous in which a sufferer propounds the question, What crime must I have committed in a former birth? and adds immediately the reflection, I will sin no more to bring upon myself grievous suffering in a future existence.

This conception, mythical as it is, nevertheless contains a germ of philosophical truth, which it is yet difficult to draw out in detail. For, properly speaking, the entire question "What becomes of us after death?" is inadmissible, and if anyone could give us the full and correct answer we should be quite unable to understand it. For it would presuppose an intuition of things apart from space, time and causality, to which, as forms of perception, our knowledge is for ever limited. If we determine, however, to do violence to truth, and to conceive in terms of space that which is without space, the timeless in terms of time, the causeless from the point of view of causality, then we may to the question, "What becomes of us after death?" (which is as it stands incorrectly put, because it assumes the forms of time) give three answers, inasmuch as we have only the choice between (1) annihilation, (2) eternal retribution in heaven and hell, and (3) transmigration. The first supposition is in conflict not only with a man's self-love, but with the innate certainty more deeply rooted than all knowledge of our metaphysical being as subject to no birth or dissolution. The second supposition, which opens up the prospect of eternal reward or punishment for an existence so brief and liable to error, so exposed to all the accidents of upbringing and environment, is condemned at once by the unparalleled disproportion in which cause and effect here stand to one another. And for the empirical solution of the problem (itself strictly speaking inadmissible) only the third supposition remains, that our existence is continued after death in other forms, other conditions of space and time, that it is therefore in a certain sense a transmigration. The well-known argument of Kant also, which bases immortality on the realisation of the moral law implanted in us, a result only attainable by an infinite process of approximation, tells not for immortality in the usual sense, but for transmigration.

Although therefore the doctrine of the soul's migration is not absolute philosophical truth, it is nevertheless a myth which represents a truth for ever inconceivable for us, and is accordingly a valuable substitute for the latter. Could we abstract from it the mental framework of space, time and causality, we should have the complete truth. We should then discern that the unceasing return of the soul is realised not in the future and in other regions, but here already, and in the present, but that this "here" is everywhere, and this "present" is eternal.

These views agree essentially with those of the later Vedânta, which clings to belief in transmigration. This belief, however, is valid only for the exoteric *aparâ vidyâ*; for the esoteric *parâ vidyâ*, the reality of the soul's migration falls to the ground with the reality of the universe.

We propose now to endeavour to trace the origin of this remarkable doctrine in the light of the Vedic texts. We must first, however, guard against a misunderstanding.

When it is said occasionally of the fathers that they "move along, adopting the external form of birds"; or when the soul of the Buddhist mother at death enters into a female jackal in order to warn her son on his journey of the unhealthy forest; when the dead pass into an insect that buzzes round the last resting-place of the bones; or when the fathers creep into the roots of plants;[1] these are popular representations, which are on a level with the entrance of the *Vetâla* into the corpse, or the yogin's animating of several bodies, but have nothing to do with belief in transmigration. They have as little to do with any such doctrine as the ancient Egyptian idea that the dead can return and assume any form at pleasure (which Herodotus in ii. 123 seems to interpret erroneously of the soul's migration), or the seven women in Goethe's poem, who appear by night as seven were-wolves. Superstitious ideas like these have existed amongst all peoples and at all times, but do not imply belief in transmigration, nor have they given rise to such teaching, least of all in India. Indeed, they have exercised scarcely any influence upon it; since, as we shall show, the theory of transmigration rests on the conviction of due recompense awarded to good and evil works, and this was at first conceived as future. Only later, for reasons which the texts disclose to us, was it transferred from an imaginary future into the present life. If therefore this recompense involves at times existence as an animal or plant, this is merely an incidental consequence on which no stress is laid from first to last; though it is true that this circumstance appeared to the opponents of the doctrine from the very beginning to be its especial characteristic, and has called forth their derision since the times of Xenophanes.[2]

[1] Oldenberg, *Religion des Veda*, pp. 563, 581 f.
[2] *Diog. L.* 8. 36.

2. *Ancient Vedic Eschatology*

In no Vedic text earlier than the Upanishads can the doctrine of the soul's transmigration be certainly traced, although the Upanishads themselves ascribe it even to the Ṛigveda. The artificial manner however in which this is done is in favour of the view that we have to do with a doctrine of recent origin, for which a confirmation was sought in the ancient sacred texts. Three passages have to be considered.

In Bṛih. 1. 4. 10 it is said of *Vâmadeva*, the poet of Ṛigveda IV., that he (by virtue of a *s'âstra-dṛishṭi*, an inspired conception, as Bâdarâyaṇa says,[1] quoting this instance) recognised himself as Brahman; and as a proof of his knowledge of Brahman alleged his acquaintance with his former births as Manu and Sûrya :—" Knowing this, Vâmadeva the ṛishi began :[2]—

I was once Manu, I was once the sun."

More clearly in Ait. 2. 4 the authority of Vâmadeva is invoked in order to prove that a third birth after death follows on the first birth (as a child), and the second birth (by spiritual education) :—" After he has completed what he has to do, and has become old, he departs hence; departing hence, he is once more born; this is his third birth. Therefore says the ṛishi :[3]—

While yet tarrying in my mother's womb,
I have learnt all the births of these gods;
Had a hundred iron fortresses held me back,
Yet like a hawk of swift flight I had escaped away.

So Vâmadeva spake though he still lay thus in his mother's womb." The quotation from the hymn of Vâmadeva admits of interpretation here only if we under-

[1] I. 1. 30. [2] Ṛigv. IV. 26. 1. [3] Ṛigv. IV. 27. 1.

stand by the hawk the soul, and by the iron fortresses the bodies through which it wanders.[1]

That neither quotation of Vâmaveda has anything to do with the doctrine of the soul's transmigration, needs no elaborate proof. In the first Indra glorifies his magical power, which enables him to assume all manner of forms.[2] In the second is depicted the cunning hawk of Indra already in his mother's womb, as he leaves his fortified dwelling-place, in order to fetch the soma from heaven; or perhaps the wise soma itself relates how it, borne away by the hawk from its iron strongholds, "as a hawk" (*i.e.* carried by it) comes down to earth.

At first sight the doctrine in question appears to be more closely related to a third quotation. In the great transmigration text it is said in a reference to the way of the gods:[3]—"And thou hast indeed failed to comprehend the word of the seer, who speaks thus:—

> Two ways, I heard, there are for men,
> The way of the fathers and the way of the gods;
> On the latter everything meets
> That moves between father and mother."

This translation is correct in the sense of the Upanishad, but not in the sense of the original, which is found in Ṛigv. X. 83. 15 (overlooked by all former translators) in a hymn celebrating Agni in his twofold character as sun by day and fire by night. In view of this connection, it can hardly be doubtful that by the two ways that unite all that moves between earth and heaven day and night are to be understood, and thus the passage is to be rendered:—"I have heard from my forefathers that there are two ways alike for gods and men." They are all subject to the laws of day and night.

[1] cp. Bṛih. 2. 5. 18.
[2] cp. Ṛigv. VI. 47. 18, *Indro mâyâbhiḥ pururûpa' îyate.*
[3] Bṛih. 6. 2. 2.

The hymns of the Ṛigveda therefore know nothing yet of a migration of the soul, but teach for the good a continued existence with the gods under the control of Yama, for the evil a journey only dimly indicated into the abyss. The standpoint of the Atharva hymns and of the Brâhmaṇas is the same; only that the conception of a recompense for works is carried out in detail. This recompense however lies always solely in the future, and in the Upanishads for the first time is transferred into the present. A brief glance at the ancient Vedic eschatology will confirm this.

Immortal life with the gods is represented in many hymns of the Ṛigveda, especially the older, as a peculiar gift of the grace of the gods, to confer which Agni,[1] the Maruts,[2] Mitra-Varuṇa,[3] Soma,[4] and other gods are entreated, and which is offered in particular to the generous worshipper.[5] Later on it is Yama, the first man, who has found the way for many descendants to that glorious height, and who there sits enthroned as the gatherer together of men.[6] In order to attain to him, the soul must successfully pass by the two spotted four-eyed broad-nosed dogs of Yama,[7] which apparently guard the entrance to the heavenly world and do not admit everyone. Here is probably to be found the first trace of a judgement of the dead, as it is put into practice by Yama in the late Indian eschatology. Elsewhere[8] to these dogs is assigned the office of wandering up and down amongst men, and dragging off those appointed to die. According to X. 165. 4 the dove (*kapota*) is Yama's messenger of death. Mention is made also[9] of the fetters or the catch-net (*paḍbîs'am*) of Yama, so that for the

[1] I. 31. 7. [2] V. 55. 4. [3] V. 63. 2. [4] I. 91. 1.

[5] *yaḥ priṇâti sa ha deveshu gac'c'hati*, etc., I. 125. 5–6.

[6] *saṅgamano janânâm*, X. 14. 1 f.

[7] X. 14. 10. [8] X. 14. 12. [9] X. 97. 16.

singers of the Ṛigveda he already represents also the terrors of death. Usually however in these older times Yama is conceived as the ruler in the kingdom of the blessed, as he sits enthroned afar,[1] in the midst of heaven,[2] in the bosom of the ruddy morning,[3] in the highest heaven,[4] in eternal light.[5] There he sits, drinking with the gods, under a tree with fair foliage,[6] there the dead gather around him, in order to see Yama, or Varuṇa;[7] they leave imperfection behind them, and return to their true home,[8] to the pasturage of which no one will again rob them,[9] where the weak is no longer subject to the strong,[10] where in immortal life in association with Yama they "delight themselves at the banquet" with the gods.[11] Stress has frequently been laid on the sensuous character which is thus borne by the ancient Vedic pictures of the future life. But on this point it may be remarked that a conception of the joy of heaven on the analogy of that of earth is natural to man and inevitable (so far as he shrinks from an absolute denial of its existence); that even Jesus represents the kingdom of heaven as a festal gathering, where they sit down to table,[12] and drink wine;[13] and that even a Dante or a Milton could not choose but borrow all the colours for their pictures from this world of earth. In other respects great differences are shown in the ancient Vedic descriptions of the other world, varying indeed according to the individual character of the poet,—from the fancy of the poet of Atharvav 4. 34, that runs riot in a vulgar sensuality (who indeed already sufficiently reveals his disposition by

[1] I. 36. 18. [2] X. 15. 14. [3] X. 15. 7.
[4] Vâj. Saṁh. 18. 51, Atharvav. 18. 2. 48.
[5] IX. 113. 7. [6] X. 135. 1. [7] X. 14. 7.
[8] *hitvâya avadyam punar astam ehi,* X. 10. 8.
[9] X. 14. 2. [10] Atharvav. 3. 29. 3.
[11] *sadhamâdam madanti,* Ṛigv. X. 14. 10, Atharvav. 18. 4. 10, etc.
[12] Matt. 8[11]. [13] Matt. 26[29].

the manner in which he praises his rice-pap and the gift of it to the Brâhmans; the whole might almost be regarded as a parody), to the more spiritual perception of the beautiful verses, Ṛigv. IX. 113. 7–11, of which we give a rendering with the omission of the refrain :—

7. The kingdom of inexhaustible light,
Whence is derived the radiance of the sun,
To this kingdom transport me,
Eternal, undying.

8. There, where Yama sits enthroned as king,
Among the holiest of the heavenly world,
Where ever living water streams,
There suffer me to dwell immortal.

9. Where we may wander undisturbed at will,
Where the third loftiest heaven spreads its vault,
Where are realms filled with light,
There suffer me to dwell immortal.

10. Where is longing and the consummation of longing,
Where the other side of the sun is seen,
Where is refreshment and satiety,
There suffer me to dwell immortal.

11. Where bliss resides and felicity,
Where joy beyond joy dwells,
Where the craving of desire is stilled,
There suffer me to dwell immortal.

There also "the fathers" dwell in company with the gods, and like them are invoked to draw near and partake of the sacrifice. To the fathers as well as to the gods are ascribed the wonders of creation,[1] the adornment of the sky with stars,[2] the bringing forth of the sun,[3] etc. They therefore stand generally on an equality with the gods, and though occasionally there is found as early as the Ṛigveda [4] an indication of a different abode of the fathers, no distinction of different degrees of blessedness, such as a

[1] Ṛigv. VIII. 48. 13.
[2] X. 68. 11.
[3] X. 107. 1.
[4] X. 15. 1–2.

later text assumes for the fathers, the unbegotten gods and the gods of creation,[1] is as yet recognised.

Of the fate of the wicked obscure indications only are contained in the Ṛigveda. They are "predestined for that abyssmal place,"[2] are hurled by Indra and Soma into the pit,[3] or into bottomless darkness,[4] into the grave,[5] or into the outer darkness.[6] Perhaps also the expression should be quoted "the blind darkness" (*andham tamas*) frequently employed by the Upanishads,[7] into which already, according to Ṛigv. X. 89. 15, 103. 12, the demons are to be plunged. They however do not understand by the "joyless regions veiled in blind darkness" into which the ignorant pass after death an imaginary hell, but this world in which we live.

The eschatological views of the Ṛigveda meet us further developed in the hymns of the Atharvaveda and in the Brâhmaṇas. More exact accounts are given of the fate of the good and the wicked. Verses such as Atharvav. 5. 19. 3, 13 remind us already of the later descriptions of hell:—

Those who spit at Brâhmans,
Or cast on them the mucus of the nose,
They sit there in pools of blood,
Chewing their hair for food.

The tears that rolled down from his eyes,
Bewailing himself, tormented,
Which the gods quaff as their drink,
Such are appointed for thee, torturer of Brâhmans.

In greater detail the Brâhmaṇas describe "the world of the pious" (*sukṛitâm loka*).[8] These rise again in

[1] Bṛih. 4. 3. 33, Taitt. 2. 8.
[2] *idam padam ajanata gabhîram*, Ṛigv. IV. 5. 5.
[3] *vavra*, VII. 104. 3.
[4] *anârambhanam tamas*, *ib.*
[5] *karta*, IX. 73. 8.
[6] X. 152. 4.
[7] Bṛih. 4. 4. 10 f., Îs'â 3. 9. 12; cp. Kâṭh. 1. 3.
[8] The expression occurs only once in the Ṛigveda, X. 16. 4, but afterwards, characteristically, becomes more and more common, Vâj. Saṁh. 18. 52, Atharvav. 3. 28. 6, 9. 5. 1, 11. 1. 17, 18. 3. 71, etc.

the other world, their body complete with all its limbs and joints (*sarvatanu, sarvâṅga, sarvaparus*).[1] This new body is stronger, and in the other world in proportion to the faithfulness with which they have observed the rites of sacrifice, many of the pious need to take food once only in fourteen days, in four, six or twelve months, or a hundred years, or finally they are able altogether to dispense with it.[2] Thus they live in perpetual intercourse, in fellowship with the worlds and with living beings (*sâyujyam, salokatâ, sarûpatâ*), with the gods, with Âditya,[3] with Agni, Varuṇa and Indra,[4] or even with the impersonal Brahman.[5] In S'atap. Br. 10. 5. 4. 15 indeed it is said already of the wise:—"He himself is free from desires, has gained all that he desires, no longer does desire (entice) him to anything. Concerning this is the verse:—

By knowledge they climb upwards,
Thither, where desire is quenched,
No sacrificial gift reaches thither,
Nor penance of the ignorant.

For that world cannot be won by sacrificial gifts nor by asceticism by the man who does not know this; for only to him who knows this does that state belong." Here already in place of works and asceticism knowledge makes its appearance, and in harmony with this emancipation instead of the glory of heaven. Transmigration therefore is not presupposed,[6] for there is no mention of transmigration earlier than the Upanishads. Probably however the germs of it are latent already in the Brâhmaṇas, as we propose now to show.

[1] Atharvav. 11. 3. 32, S'atap. Br. 4. 6. 1. 1, 11. 1. 8. 6, 12. 8. 3. 31.
[2] S'atap. Br. 10. 1. 5. 4.
[3] Ait. Br. 3. 44, Taitt. Br. 3. 10. 9. 11.
[4] S'atap. Br. 2. 6. 4. 8.
[5] S'atap. Br. 11. 4. 4. 2.
[6] As Weber assumes, *Zeitschr. d. D. M. G.*, ix. 139.

3. *The Germs of the Doctrine of Transmigration*

The chief aim of the Brâhmaṇas is to prescribe the acts of ritual, and to offer for their accomplishment a manifold reward, and at the same time sufferings and punishment for their omission. While they defer rewards as well as punishments partly to the other world, in place of the ancient Vedic conception of an indiscriminate felicity of the pious, the idea of recompense is formulated, involving the necessity of setting before the departed different degrees of compensation in the other world proportionate to their knowledge and actions. Since however the oldest form of punishment among all peoples in a natural state is revenge, this recompense also consists originally in the doing to us in the other world of the very same good and evil which we have done to anyone in this. This theory is realistically expressed in the words of S'atap. Br. 12. 9. 1. 1:—"For whatever food a man eats in this world, by the very same is he eaten again (*praty-atti*) in the other." A second proof is furnished by the narrative in S'atap. Br. 11. 6. 1 of the vision of the punishment in the other world which was permitted to Bhṛigu; and we may entirely assent to the view of Weber,[1] who was the first to discuss this question, when he explains the liturgical interpretation of this vision as a subsequent addition of the Brâhman author. Removing this there is left as the kernel, that Bhṛigu in the different regions sees men shrieking aloud, by whom other men shrieking are hewn in pieces limb by limb, chopped up and consumed with the words:—"Thus have they done to us in yonder world, and so we do to them again in this world." When the vision concludes with the black man with yellow eyes and the judge's staff in his hand, at whose side stand beautiful and ugly women (good and

[1] *Zeitsch. d. D. M. G.*, ix. 237 f.

evil works), assuredly no doubt is left as to its original meaning.

From the primitive doctrine of retribution, as this extract preserved accidentally in a later Brâhmaṇa text exhibits it, the idea of an equalising justice may have been developed by degrees, as it appears in S'atap. Br. 11. 2. 7. 33:—"For they lay it (the good and evil) on the scales in yonder world; and whichever of the two sinks down, that will he follow, whether it be the good or the evil." Not all, according to a somewhat different view, find the way to the heavenly world:[1]—"Many a man may fail to find his place when he departs hence, but bewildered by the fire (at the corpse burning), and clouded by the smoke, he fails to find out his place." Others are kept at a distance from the world of the fathers for a longer or shorter time by their misdeeds:[2]—"Whosoever threatens (a Brâhman) he shall atone for it with a hundred (years); he who lays violent hands on him with a thousand; but he who sheds his blood shall not find the world of the fathers for as many years as the grains of dust number that are moistened by its streams. Therefore men should not threaten a Brâhman, or lay hands on him, or shed his blood, for there is involved in it so great an offence." Here the "world of the fathers" seems still, as in the Ṛigveda, to present itself before the mind as the highest goal. In course of time however a distinction arose between the way of the gods and the way of the fathers,[3] and similarly between the world of the gods as the abode of the blessed and the world of the fathers as the place of retribution. Precisely again as in the later doctrine of transmigration it is said that the entrance to the heavenly world lies in the north-east,[4] and the entrance to the world of the

[1] Taitt. Br. 3. 10. 11. 1.
[3] Atharvav. 15. 12, etc.
[3] Taitt. Saṁh. 2. 6. 10. 2.
[4] S'atap. Br. 6. 6. 2. 4.

fathers in the south-west,[1] a distinction which is of all the more importance because it is found in two different passages, and is therefore not to be ascribed to an incidental process of systematising. Every man is born in the world fashioned by himself.[2] We hear of an "immortality" which lasts only a hundred years;[3] and that he who sacrifices to the gods "does not gain so great a world as he who sacrifices to the âtman."[4] In another text it is said that "day and night (time) consume in yonder world the worth (of good works) for him who does not know this";[5] and Nac'iketas solicits as his second wish the imperishableness (*akshiti*) of good works.[6] With especial frequency do we meet with the fear that, instead of the hoped for immortality (*amṛitatvam*, the "not-dying-any-more-ness") a renewed death (*punarmṛityu*, death over again) may await man in the other world, and to avoid this all kinds of means are provided. "He who builds up or knows the Nac'iketas fire, he escapes renewed death."[7] "He who celebrates the day of the equinox, he overcomes hunger and renewed death."[8] "He therefore who knows this escape from death in the agnihotram is delivered from renewed death";[9] "The *yajamâna*, who builds up the fire, becomes the divinity of the fire, and vanquishes thereby renewed death."[10] "He who knows how hunger flees before food, thirst before drink, misfortune before happiness, darkness before light, death before immortality, before him all these flee, and he escapes renewed death."[11] A like escape is his who builds up the fire in the appointed way,[12] offers an appointed sacrifice,[13] in the appointed way studies the

[1] S'atap. Br. 13. 8. 1. 5.
[2] S'atap. Br. 6. 2. 2. 27.
[3] S'atap. Br. 10. 1. 5. 4.
[4] S'atap. Br. 11. 2. 6. 14.
[5] Taitt. Br. 3. 10. 11. 2.
[6] Taitt. Br. 3. 11. 8. 5.
[7] Taitt. Br. 3. 11. 8. 6.
[8] Kaush. Br. 25. 1.
[9] S'atap. Br. 2. 3. 3. 9.
[10] S'atap. Br. 10. 1. 4. 14.
[11] S'atap. Br. 10. 2. 6. 19.
[12] 10. 5. 1. 4.
[13] 11. 4. 3. 20.

Veda.[1] Thus "escape from renewed death" becomes finally a stereotyped formula,[2] which is occasionally employed even where it seems to give no meaning.[3] We meet it even in the texts of the older Upanishads:—He escapes recurrent death who knows that death is his own self,[4] that sacrifices to the âtman avail,[5] that there is a water to quench the fire of death,[6] that the wind is the sum and substance of all.[7] That this renewed death is to be understood of a repeated dying in the other world is taught especially by two passages:—"Accordingly he brings his fathers, who are mortal, to a condition of immortality, and causes them who are mortal to rise again from out of the condition of immortality; in truth, he who knows this averts renewed death from his fathers."[8] "They then who know this or do this work rise again after death, and when they rise again they rise to immortality; but they who do not know this or fail to do this work rise again after death, and become again and again its prey."[9] From the parallel which this passage draws between immortality and recurrent death it is clear that the latter also is not to be understood as transmigration, but only of a resurrection and repeated death in the other world. It was only necessary however to transfer that renewed death from an imaginary future world into the present in order to arrive at the doctrine of transmigration. This takes place first in the Upanishads, and the reasons that led to this last step will not evade us. Here it is only necessary to remark further that not all the Upanishad texts know or recognise a transmigration of souls, and when it is said in Bṛih. 1. 5. 16,—"The world of men is to be gained only through a son, not at all by works; by works the world

[1] S'atap. Br. 11. 5. 6. 9. [2] 10. 6. 1. 4 f. [3] 12. 9. 3. 11.
[4] Bṛih. 1. 2. 7. [5] Bṛih. 1. 5. 2. [6] Bṛih. 3. 2. 10.
[7] Bṛih. 3. 3. 2. [8] S'atap. Br. 12. 9. 3. 12. [9] S'atap. Br. 10. 4. 3. 10.

of the fathers is gained, by knowledge the world of the gods," this text also knows nothing as yet of a transmigration, unless it is to be considered as a protest against the new up-start dogma. Similarly passages like Bṛih. 1. 4. 15 (good works come at last to nought) and 3. 8. 10 (sacrifice and asceticism win only finite reward) are still to be understood of an exhaustion of the value of works in the other world.

4. *Origin of the Doctrine of Transmigration*

The chief text that sets forth the doctrine of transmigration, on which almost all subsequent texts are dependent, is found in a twofold recension for the most part in verbal agreement with one another. These passages are Chând. 5. 3–10 and Bṛih. 6. 2.[1] The Indian authorities call it the doctrine of the five fires (*pañc'âg-nividyâ*). It is a combination of two different parts,[2] the doctrine of the five fires (in a narrower sense)[3] and the doctrine of the two ways.[4] While reserving these two names for the two parts, we propose here and in the sequel to term the combination of the two briefly the chief text.

It is remarkable in the first place that a text of such supreme importance for all that follows is found in Bṛih. 6. 2 only in an appendix (*khilakâṇḍam*), and not in the two chief divisions of this Upanishad, the *madhukâṇḍam*[5] and the *Yâjñavalkhyakâṇḍam.*[6] When these two were collected, and later on combined with one another, it must surely have been still unknown; for why otherwise should it have been passed over, when later on it gained the admission which its importance demanded? This of

[1] cp. S'atap. Br. 14. 9. 1.
[2] cp. Deussen, *Upan.*, p. 137 f., where this has been already shown.
[3] Chând. 5. 4. 1–5. 9. 2=Bṛih. 6. 2. 9–6. 2. 14.
[4] Chând. 5. 10=Bṛih. 6. 2. 15–16.
[5] Bṛih. 1–2.
[6] Bṛih. 3–4.

itself proves that the text is of late origin and a secondary product; still more so do its contents.

This so-called chief text teaches a double retribution, once by reward and punishment in the other world, and again by rebirth upon earth. This feature is evidently primitive, and is nothing more than a combination of the traditional future recompense found in the Veda with the novel recompense of the transmigration doctrine. We must therefore look for the original doctrine where it appears by itself alone and apart from combination with the ancient Vedic recompense in the other world. This leads us again to the Yâjñavalkhya sections,[1] in which we have already so often found the earliest form of Upanishad doctrine. In them we can still observe the origin of the doctrine of the soul's transmigration, together with the motives prompting it. According to a conception which is likewise already ancient Vedic, existing by the side of that usually current and hardly reconcilable with it, the eye of a man at death goes to the sun, his breath to the wind, his speech to the fire, his limbs to the different parts of the universe. With these thoughts already expressed in Ṛigv. X. 16. 3, and further expanded in S'atap. Br. 10. 3. 3. 8, is connected the passage which we here quote in full, since it gives expression for the first time, as far as our knowledge goes, to the thought of the soul's transmigration, which it regards as a great mystery; and at the same time it enables us to recognise the motive which led to this transference of the retribution from the future world to the present.

"'Yâjñavalkhya,' so he (the son of Ṛitabhâga) spake, 'when after a man's death his speech enters into the fire, his breath into the wind, his eye into the sun, his manas into the moon, his ear into the pole, his body into the earth, his âtman into the âkâs'a (space), the hair of his

[1] Bṛih. 3–4.

body into herbs, the hair of his head into trees, his blood and seed into water,—where then does the man remain?' Yâjñavalkhya answered:—'Take my hand, Ârtabhâga, my good friend; on this matter we must come to an understanding alone by ourselves, not here in the company.' Then they two went aside, and conferred with one another; and what they said that was work, and what they commended that was work. In truth, a man becomes good by good works, evil by evil works."[1]

In the last words the motive which lies at the basis of the doctrine of transmigration is clearly expressed. It is the great moral difference of character, existing from birth, upon which the singers of the Ṛigveda had already pondered,[2] and which the philosopher explains in our passage on the hypothesis that a man has already existed once before his birth, and that his inborn character is the fruit and consequence of his previous action.

Yâjñavalkhya expresses himself more clearly still in another well-known passage.[3] Here immediately after the departure of the soul from the body has been described it is said:—"Then his knowledge and works take him by the hand, and his former experience (*pûrvaprajñâ*). As a caterpillar, after it has reached the tip of a leaf, makes a beginning upon another, and draws itself over towards it, so the soul also, after it has shaken off the body, and freed itself from ignorance (*i.e.* empirical existence), makes a beginning upon another, and draws itself over towards it. As the goldsmith takes the material from a piece of carving, and from it chisels out another newer, fairer form, so also this soul, after it has shaken off the body and rid itself of ignorance, fashions for itself another newer, fairer form, whether it be of the fathers or the Gandharvas, or the gods or Prajâpati, or Brahmân or other living beings, . . . in proportion as a man consists now of

[1] Bṛih. 3. 2. 13. [2] Ṛigv. X. 117. 9. [3] Bṛih. 4. 4. 2–6.

this or that, just as he acts, just as he behaves, so will he be born. He who does good will be born good, he who does evil will be born evil; he becomes holy by holy deeds, evil by evil. Therefore, in truth, it is said:[1]—'Man is altogether and throughout composed of desire (*kâma*); in proportion to his desire so is his discretion (*kratu*), in proportion to his discretion so he performs acts (*karma*), in proportion to his acts so does it result to him.' On this subject is the verse:—

> To that he clings, after that he strives with deeds,
> By which his inner man and his desire hold fast;
> He who has arrived at the final goal
> Of the deeds which he here commits,
> He returns from yonder world again
> Back to this world of work.

This is the experience of those who feel desire (*kâmayamâna*)."

This passage does not yet recognise a twofold retribution, in a future world and again upon earth, but only one by transmigration. Immediately after death the soul enters into a new body, in accordance with its good or evil deeds. This is shown not only by the illustration of the caterpillar, which as soon as it has eaten up one leaf transfers itself to another, but also by the fact that the sphere of transmigration is extended through the worlds of men, fathers and gods up to Prajâpati and the personal Brahmân, that consequently the worlds of the fathers and the gods cannot be set apart, as according to the later theory, for a recompense by the side and independent of that by transmigration. It would be otherwise if in the appended verse we were obliged with S'ankara to understand *prâpya antam* as *bhuktvâ phalam*:—"After that he has enjoyed (in the other world) the fruit of his deeds, he returns from that world to this world of action."

[1] cp. S'atap. Br. 10. 6. 3. 1, Chând. 3. 14. 1.

In that case the verse (which under any circumstances is a later addition) would be in contradiction with the preceding words. It may however very well mean :—" After that he has finished with one life-course (like the caterpillar with its leaf), he returns after death to a new life."

The eschatology therefore of Yâjñavalkhya[1] does not yet recognise a twofold retribution, in a future world and again by a new life, but as is natural, only one by a rebirth in the sphere of empirical reality (the worlds of men, fathers and gods). In place of the ancient Vedic recompense in the other world, there is found the recompense by transmigration. It is no longer said of the man who obtains deliverance,—" He escapes recurrent death," but " he does not return back again."[2]

5. *Further Development of the Doctrine of Transmigration*

The ancient element in religious faiths is wont, as we have often had occasion to emphasise,[3] to assert its traditionally consecrated right side by side with conceptions of later origin. Accordingly we see here also how by the side of the belief in a return to earth the ancient ideas of a recompense of good and evil in the other world persist, and become united with the doctrine of transmigration, so that now all good and evil actions experience a twofold retribution, once in the other world and again by a renewed life upon earth. And thus that which has already received a full recompense is recompensed yet again, and strictly speaking the entire conception of a recompense is destroyed. This is the case in the chief text of the doctrine of transmigration.[4] We

[1] Bṛih. 1–5.
[2] Chând. 4. 15. 6, 8. 15, Bṛih. 6. 2. 15, Pras'na 1. 10, etc.
[3] *Allgemeine Einleitung*, p. 180, *supra* p. 117.
[4] Chând. 5. 3–10=Bṛih. 6. 2.

have however, as already remarked,[1] to distinguish two parts in this chief text, an older part,[2] which we propose to call the doctrine of the five fires (in a narrower sense), and a later,[3] to which we give the name of the doctrine of the two ways. Two of the questions proposed at the outset refer to the former, the three others to the latter. The difference of the two parts is clearly shown by the fact that according to the doctrine of the two ways, faith, *s'raddhâ*, leads to Brahman without return, while according to the doctrine of the five fires it is this which above all constitutes the motive for the return to earth.

The first and older part, the doctrine of the five fires, apparently assumes, like the expressions of Yâjñavalkhya that have been already quoted, the absence of recompense in the other world; but depicts how the soul, after it has journeyed to heaven on the burning of the corpse "in radiant form,"[4] returns thence immediately, as it seems, through the three regions of the universe, heaven atmosphere and earth, and through the bodies of father and mother, these being the five transit stations, to a new existence. This is the reply to the question proposed at the beginning:—"Do you know how at the fifth sacrifice the waters come to speak with human voice?"[5] Just as with Yâjñavalkhya the doctrine of transmigration makes its appearance as a great mystery,[6] so here also it comes before us veiled in secrecy as something new, not to be profaned. And just as to the Christians, who bury the body, the comparison of it to a seed buried in the earth suggested itself,[7] so in India, where the corpse is burnt, it is natural to conceive of this burning as a sacrifice. As the libation poured into the fire (soma, milk, etc.) ascends

[1] cp. Deussen, *Upan.*, p. 137, where a fuller discussion of this point will be found.

[2] Chând. 5. 4–9 (Bṛih. 6. 2. 9–14).

[3] Chând. 5. 10 (Bṛih. 6. 2. 15).

[4] Bṛih. 6. 2. 14.

[5] Chând. 5. 3. 3, Bṛih. 6. 2. 2.

[6] Bṛih. 3. 2. 13, *sup.* p. 329 f.

[7] 1 Cor. 15.

in spiritual form to the gods, so the immortal part of man ascends to heaven from the funeral pyre. This immortal part is termed by Yâjñavalkhya *karman*, work,[1] and in our passage is described after the analogy of the sacrificial fluid as "water," and later on as "faith." These mystically veiled expressions cause the Vedanta theologians much trouble.[2] They signify however essentially the same, inasmuch as the peculiar essence and so to speak the soul of the work (*karman*) that ascends as the sacrificial vapour (*âpas*) is the faith (*s'raddhâ*) with which it is offered. This "work," in Yâjñavalkhya's phrase, this "faith," as our passage describes it, probably not independently of him, ascends to heaven as the immortal part of man, and is there five times in succession offered up by the gods in the sacrificial fires of the heaven, the atmosphere, the earth, the man, and the woman. By this means it is changed successively from faith to soma, from soma to rain, from rain to food, from food to seed, and from seed to the embryo; thus it is led to a renewed existence on earth.

The second half of the chief text, which we propose to call the doctrine of the two ways, marks a considerable further advance, and combining the ancient Vedic eschatology with the doctrine of transmigration, teaches a twofold recompense (a recompense therefore of that which has been already recompensed), on the one hand in the other world, and once again by a return to earth. To this end it represents the souls of the dead as ascending by two different ways, the *Devayâna* (way of the gods) and the *Pitṛiyâna* (way of the fathers). These lead through several stations, that at times appear strange but which yet admit of explanation, if we take into consideration the origin of the doctrine. As early as the Ṛigveda and the Brâhmaṇas mention is frequently made

[1] *sup.* p. 330. [2] cp. *Syst. d. Vedânta*, pp. 401, 408.

of the *Devayâna*, which was originally in all probability the way by which Agni bore the sacrificial gifts to the gods, or the latter descended to them. It was then also the way by which the pious dead ascended to the gods, in order to live in eternal felicity with them, or, as later times preferred to express it, with Brahman. A more detailed description of the way of the gods is given in Chând. 4. 15. 5. On the burning of the corpse the soul enters into the flame, thence into the day, thence into the bright half of the month, thence into the bright half of the year (the summer season), thence into the year, thence into the sun, thence into the moon, thence into the lightning, and so finally into Brahman. The use of periods of time here as divisions of space occurs elsewhere also,[1] and needs in India no further remark. The meaning of the whole is that the soul on the way of the gods reaches regions of ever-increasing light, in which is concentrated all that is bright and radiant, as stations on the way to Brahman, who is himself the "light of lights" (*jyotishâm jyotis*).

The *Pitṛiyâna* or way of the fathers was next explained after the analogy of this *Devayâna*. As everything that was bright and radiant was directed to the latter, so to the former the counterpart of darkness and gloom. The difficulty however arose here that it was impossible to omit the moon from the *Pitṛiyâna*, and that this already belonged to the *Devayâna*. For, according to an old somewhat obscure conception, the moon was the abode of the departed,[2] and thus later on[3] its waxing and waning were brought into connection with the ascent and descent of the souls. Maintaining therefore the moon as the final goal, the *Pitṛiyâna* was explained in other respects in analogy with the *Devayâna*, the soul entering into the

[1] S'atap. Br. 1. 3. 5. 11, Chând. 2. 10. 5.
[2] Kaush. 2. 8.
[3] Bṛih. 6. 2. 16, Kaush. 1. 2, but not Kaush. 2. 9.

smoke not the flame, the night not the day, the dark half of the month not the bright, the months of winter not of summer, the world of the fathers not the year, the âkâs'a [1] not the sun, and finally as in the Devayâna into the moon, not however as a transit station, but in order to remain there "as long as a remnant (of good works) yet exists.[2] Our text skilfully evades giving a description of the transitory blessedness in the moon. In its place the ancient idea of the soma cup of the gods makes its appearance, which, after they have drained it, is each time refilled.[3] As far as this repletion is possible by means of the souls,[4] the latter are enjoyed by the gods; and this is again interpreted in the later Vedânta of a mutual enjoyment of the gods and the pious dead in intercourse with one another. The felicity in the moon lasts *yâvat sampâtam* "as long as a remnant exists."[5] In this it is implied that the retribution there is complete. Nevertheless there follows a second recompense upon earth. The descent is here not, as in the doctrine of the five fires, a passing through the five sacrificial fires as faith, soma, rain, food and seed, but a progressive materialisation of the substance of the souls into ether, wind, smoke, mist, cloud, rain, herbage, food and seed, to which succeeds the entrance into the womb of a new mother and the renewed birth. By the side of the way of the gods, which for the wise and faithful leads to an entrance into Brahman without return, and the way of the fathers, which in requital for sacrifice, works of piety, and asceticism guides to the moon and thence back to earth, our text originally but only obscurely pointed to the "third place" as the fate of the wicked, who are born again as lower animals.

[1] Only in the Chând.

[2] Chând. 5. 10. 5.

[3] cp. Ṛigv. X. 85. 5 :—"when they drain thee, O god, thou dost thereupon well up again."

[4] Kaush. 2. 8, 1. 2.

[5] Chând. 5. 10. 5.

The additions which are wanting in Bṛih. 6. 2. 16, and inserted in Chând. 5. 10. 7 alone, take us a step further in the development of these ideas. In contrast with the original text of the doctrine of the two ways, a distinction is here drawn among the souls returning from the moon between those of "pleasing conduct" and those of "abominable conduct." The former are born again as Brâhmans, Kshatriyas or Vais'yas, the latter as dogs, pigs or c'aṇḍâlas. By this means the "third place" by the side of the ways of the gods and the fathers becomes now superfluous, and ought entirely to disappear, but is nevertheless allowed to remain.

This contradiction, like the above-mentioned incongruity involved in the position of the moon on the ways both of the gods and the fathers, seems to have been early noticed. Kaush. 1. 2 is to be regarded as an attempt to relieve both these disadvantages. Here it is emphatically declared, with the view of obviating the necessity for the "third place," that "all who depart from this world go without exception to the moon." There however their knowledge is put to the test, and according to the result they go either by the *Devayâna* [1] which leads to Brahman without return, or (the name *Pitṛiyâna* is not used) they enter upon a new birth, "whether as a worm or a fly or a fish or a bird or a lion or a boar or a serpent or a tiger or a man, or as something else." This enumeration seems to be an imitation of that found in Chând. 6. 9. 3, 6. 10. 2; for there it was justified by the context, while here it appears somewhat superfluous.

Of later passages, which all to a greater or less extent depend upon that already discussed, we propose in conclusion to cite only the most important. In Kâṭh. 2. 10 the transitoriness of the treasure of

[1] Kaush. 1. 3.

good works[1] is taught. In reference to the return it is further said :[2]—

> One goes into the womb of a mother,
> Becoming incarnate in bodily form ;
> Another enters into a plant,
> Each according to his deeds, according to his knowledge.

Muṇḍ. 1. 2. 10 exhibits more evidently its dependence on Chând. 5. 3–10 :—

> Having tasted joy on the summit of the heaven of works,
> They return back into this world, and even lower.

In a later passage also reference is made to the five fires of the *Pañc'âgnividyâ* :[3]—

> From it originates the fire, whose fuel the sun is,[4]
> From the soma the rain springs,[5] plants from the earth,
> The husband pours out the stream upon the wife,[6]
> Many descendants are born to the spirit.

The ways of the fathers and of the gods are described in Pras'na 1. 9–10 on the basis of Chând. 5. 10 (misunderstanding however the expression "*s'raddhâ tapa'*" *iti* of Chând. 5. 10. 1). For confirmation reference is made to the verse Ṛigv. I. 164. 12, which nevertheless has nothing to do with the subject.

XV. Emancipation

1. *Significance of the Doctrine of Emancipation*

Love of life is the strongest of all the instincts implanted in human nature. In order to preserve life we make any sacrifice. We desire a long life for ourselves and our friends ; we congratulate those who attain it,

[1] *s'evadhi*, as in Taitt. Bṛ. 3. 10. 11. 2.
[2] Kâṭh. 5. 7.
[3] Muṇḍ. 2. 1. 5 ; cp. Chând. 5. 4 f.
[4] Chând. 5. 4. 1.
[5] Chând. 5. 5. 2.
[6] Chând. 5. 8. 2.

and commiserate those who are called away before their time. And the reason of our mourning for one so prematurely deceased is (when once we give to ourselves a clear account of it) not so much that he is wanting to us, as rather that we are wanting to him. We pity him because he has been so early deprived of existence, as though this were a supreme good. When we console ourselves over the death of a relative by recalling the sufferings, perils and hardships, from which he has escaped, this is the voice of reflection. A purely natural feeling expresses itself differently. It tells us that the loss of life is the most serious by which a man can be overtaken; that the most severe punishment is always that of death. Indeed, so strong in us is the instinct for life, that our whole existence is nothing more than this desire unfolding itself in space as the body and in time as the life.

How is it possible under these circumstances that in the course of development there could arise repeatedly amongst men and become established a disposition to regard that craving for life, upon which our entire empirical existence depends, as something which ought not properly to be? So that man's true duty is conceived to be not the satisfaction of the natural craving, but its suppression, and therefore the highest goal appears as a release (*moksha*), and that not such a release as death brings from a definite existence, but release from existence in general, which as our innate consciousness shows is not to be attained simply through death.

This rarest of all changes of inclination may be traced nowhere more clearly than in India, where deliverance, unmodified by the play upon it of the accidental events of history, appears not as a ransom, an atonement, a propitiation, etc., but merely as a release from empirical existence with all its desires, these last being regarded as fetters (*bandha*, *graha*), as bonds (*granthi*), which bind the soul to the objects of sense. Even in India it was not always so, and a long period of development, a vast interval, separates the poets of the Ṛigveda, who, filled with a warm desire for life, shrink from death,[1] and wish for themselves and their posterity a life of a hundred years, from the words with which the greatest Indian poet closes his masterpiece :—

> May he, the god, who fashioned me by his almighty power,
> Himself avert from me and destroy my re-birth.

Yet the philosophy of the future will often turn its glance to India in order to study the doctrine of emancipation in the land of its birth. We propose now to do what we can to render intelligible this most remarkable of all doctrines.

2. *Origin of the Doctrine of Emancipation*

Albrecht Weber in one of his very remarkable expositions[2] gave utterance to the conjecture that the doctrine of emancipation is necessitated by the dogma of transmigration. The idea that for the deeds of this brief life either eternal reward or eternal punishment must follow in the other world would have jarred upon the gentle disposition and thoughtful mind of the Indian. From this dilemma he tried to save himself by the dogma of transmigration. In reality however he only became deeper entangled, since on the eternal retribution *a parte post* is imposed yet another *a parte ante.* He therefore eventually saved himself by "cutting the knot," by representing the destruction of the entire individual existence as effected in emancipation ; so that now that which in the olden time was reckoned as the severest punishment appears as the supreme reward of all endeavour. Apart however from the fact that the eman-

[1] Ṛigv. VII. 89.

[2] *Zeitschr. d. D. M. G.*, ix. 239.

cipation of pre-Buddhistic times was from beginning to end no annihilation, but rather the precise opposite, a transcending of that which was in itself worthless, this ingenious explanation fails to harmonise with the course of historical development, for the additional reason that, as we shall see, the doctrine of emancipation is older than that of transmigration, and cannot therefore be a consequence of the latter.

The attempt has often been made to understand man's longing for deliverance from another side as the result of the heavy pressure upon the Indian people of the Brâhmanical system. Thereby, according to the view suggested, the ancient delight in existence had been ruined and lost in consequence of the subservience of the mind to the Brâhmans, and the body to the Kshatriyas. But not to mention that the conditions of life in the rich valley of the Ganges were in all probability hardly worse than formerly in the Panjâb, and that the idea of emancipation had certainly arisen not in the circle of the oppressed but rather in that of the oppressors, a disposition to pessimism, such as the theory assumes, was not at all peculiar to the times in which the doctrine of emancipation arose.[1] It is true that by emancipation suffering also with all its possibilities was removed; but Buddhism was the first to transform that which was a mere consequence into a motive, and by conceiving emancipation as an escape from the sufferings of existence, to make selfishness the ultimate mainspring of existence,—even if not to the extent that was done later by Islâm, which is never weary of depicting to the people the glories of heaven and the terrors of hell.

The doctrine in question cannot be derived from these or any other motives that have their seat in the will, for the very reason that it is the abrogation of all desire

[1] *sup.* pp. 140 f., 254 f.

(*yatra kâmâḥ parâgatâḥ*), and that certainly as early as its very first appearance. Accordingly it remains to seek for its original motive in the sphere of the intellect; and here we shall find the doctrine of emancipation to be so entirely the necessary consequence and final consummation of the doctrine of the âtman, that it is to be regarded only as a personal and so to speak practical application of the Upanishad view of the universe as a whole, which we have hitherto been engaged in expounding. This we now propose to show.

It is a natural idea that finds expression in all the systems of philosophy, when men regard that which for them is the first principle of things and the ultimate basis of the universe as at the same time the highest aim of personal endeavour. In olden times this was the gods, and thus union with the gods after death was the supreme wish of the ancient Vedic ṛishis, in order to attain to fellowship (*sâyujyam*), companionship (*salokatâ*), community of being (*sarûpatâ*) with Agni, Varuṇa, Indra, Aditya, etc. Later on the (impersonal) Brahman was exalted above the gods. This then became the final goal; and the gods were only the doors, through whom Brahman might be attained. "By Agni as the door of Brahman he enters in. When by Agni as the door of Brahman he enters in, he gains fellowship (*sâyujyam*), and companionship (*salokatâ*) with Brahman."[1] In the final step the creative principle of the universe was conceived to be the âtman, the self, and as was to be expected union with the âtman became now the aim of all endeavour and longing. This took place before anything was yet known of transmigration, but only of a renewed death in the other world, as the following passages prove. "Only he who knows him (the purusha) escapes from the kingdom of death; by no other road

[1] S'atap. Br. 11. 4. 4. 1.

is it possible to go";[1] "He who knows him, the wise long-emancipated youthful âtman, no more fears death";[2] "The self (*âtman*) is his pathfinder, he who finds him is no longer stained by action, that evil thing."[3] The last expression in particular shows that here the thought of emancipation is already present in all its entirety. So also in the following passage, which has been already quoted above for another purpose:—"Himself (the âtman) is free from desire, in possession of all that he desires, no desire for anything whatever (tempts) him. With reference to this is the following verse:—

> By knowledge they climb upwards
> Thither, where desire is at rest;
> Neither sacrificial gift reaches thither,
> Nor the penance of the ignorant.

For yonder world cannot be attained by sacrificial gifts or by asceticism by the man who does not know this. For that state belongs only to him who has this knowledge."[4] The rejection of work and asceticism, the emphasising of knowledge, and the suppression of all desire, are proofs that this passage has in view emancipation as a union with the âtman. But this union is still represented in harmony with traditional ideas as an ascent to heavenly regions,—as though the âtman were to be sought elsewhere than in ourselves. Thus a few pages further on in the passage S'atap. Br. 10. 6. 3, already translated above,[5] which teaches that destiny in the other world is determined by the degree of insight (*kratu*) which men have attained here below; and which then as the deepest insight imparts the knowledge of the âtman, who, filling all space and pervading all the universe, is greater than heaven and earth, and yet smaller than a

[1] Vâj. Saṁh. 31. 18.
[2] Atharvav. 10. 8. 44.
[3] Taitt. Br. 3. 12. 9. 8.
[4] S'atap. Br. 10. 5. 4. 15.
[5] *Allgemeine Einleitung u. Philosophie des Veda*, p. 264.

grain of rice or millet, dwells in the inner self. In conclusion it is said :—"He is my soul (*âtman*) ; thither to this soul on my departure hence shall I enter in."[1] Who does not feel the inner contradiction of these words, and that if the âtman is really my soul, no further entrance into it is needed!

A slight barrier only remained to be thrown down in order to see that that which is ever being sought at an infinite distance is nearer to us than anything else, and that the emancipation desired as union with God, union with Brahman, union with the âtman, does not require to be attained for the first time in the future after death, but is actually attained already here and now and from the very beginning,—by him "who knows this."

It is Yâjñavalkhya of the Bṛihadâraṇyaka who meets us again as the man who drew this final consequence of the doctrine of the âtman.

3. *The Knowledge of the Âtman is Emancipation*

Emancipation is not to be regarded as a becoming something which previously had no existence. In the first place, because in the sphere of metaphysical phenomena to which emancipation belongs there is in general no becoming but only a being (as all metaphysical thinkers, not only in India but in the West also, from Parmenides and Plato down to Kant and Schopenhauer, have recognised). The law of causation rules without exception everything that is finite, but nothing that lies outside and beyond, or like emancipation leads beyond. But for a further reason also emancipation cannot be a coming into being of that which did not previously exist, since it could not then be *summum bonum.* For everything that comes to be is transient; that which from nothingness became something may also return back from being something

[1] S'atap. Br. 10. 6. 3.

into its nothingness. What the wave threw up it may sweep away again; τὸ μηδὲν εἰς οὐδὲν ῥέπει.

> If deliverance had a beginning,
> Then it could not but have an end,

as Gauḍapâda rightly says,[1] nor could it be *summum bonum*, or *id quo majus cogitari nequit*, for we might always think of as a higher good an emancipation which had not come into being, and therefore was not exposed to the danger of vanishing away.

Emancipation therefore (which we must not judge by our one-sided Western ideas which have been shaped from historical and therefore narrow conditions) is not properly a new beginning, a καινὴ κτίσις, but only the perception of that which has existed from eternity, but has hitherto been concealed from us:—

> All souls are originally
> Free from darkness and without stain,
> "Already awakened and delivered before the world was,
> They rise up," saith the Master.[2]

We are all emancipated already (how could we otherwise become so!), "but just as he who does not know the place of a hidden treasure fails to find it, though he passes over it constantly, so all these creatures fail to find the world of Brahman, though they daily (in deep sleep) enter into it; for by unreality are they turned aside.[3] This unreality is removed by the knowledge "I am Brahman," am in truth not an individual, but the âtman, the sum and substance of all reality, the first principle which creates, upholds and preserves all worlds. "And therefore to-day also he who knows this 'I am Brahman' becomes this universe; and even the gods have no power to prevent his so becoming; for he is its soul (*âtman*)."[4] This

[1] Kârikâ 4. 30.
[2] Gauḍap. 4. 98.
[3] Chând. 8. 3. 2.
[4] Bṛih. 1. 4. 10.

thought is briefly and strikingly expressed in Muṇḍ. 3. 2. 9 :—"In truth, he who knows that supreme âtman, he becomes Brahman," or more correctly "he is already Brahman" (*sa yo ha vai tat paramam brahma veda brahma eva bhavati*). For deliverance is not effected by the knowledge of the âtman, but it consists in this knowledge; it is not a consequence of the knowledge of the âtman, but this knowledge is itself already deliverance in all its fulness. He who knows himself as the âtman, the first principle of things, he is by that very knowledge free from all desires (*akâmayamâna*), for he knows everything in himself, and there is nothing outside of himself for him to continue to desire :—*âptakâmasya kâ spṛihâ?* "what can he desire who has everything?"[1] And further, he who knows himself as the âtman "is not inflamed by what he has done and left undone," whether it be good or evil,[2] his works consume away like the reed-stalk in the fire,[3] and future works do not cling to him, as water does not remain on the leaf of the lotus flower.[4] His individuality, the basis of all works, he has seen to be an illusion, in that he has gained possession of the knowledge of the âtman, and therein of emancipation :—

> He who beholds that Loftiest and Deepest,
> For him the fetters of the heart break asunder,
> For him all doubts are solved,
> And his works become nothingness.[5]

THE KNOWLEDGE OF THE ÂTMAN DOES NOT EFFECT EMANCIPATION, IT IS EMANCIPATION.—If we seek for the origin of this thought that runs through the whole of the Upanishad literature, we are referred back to the

[1] Gauḍap. 1. 9.

[2] Bṛih. 4. 4. 22, Chând. 8. 4. 1, 8. 13, Muṇḍ. 3. 1. 3, Taitt. 2. 9, Kaush. 1. 4, 3. 1, Muṇḍ. 3. 2. 9, Maitr. 2. 7, 6. 34, etc.

[3] Chând. 5. 24. 3; cp. Bṛih. 5. 14. 8.

[4] Chând. 4. 14. 3.

[5] Muṇḍ. 2. 2. 8.

discourses of Yâjñavalkhya that are presented in Bṛih. 3 and 4.[1]

We begin with Bṛih. 4. 2. Yâjñavalkhya addresses King Janaka, whom we are to consider as occupying the foremost position among the sages of his time (somewhat as Nârada in Chând. 7. 1):—"Since then you are now rich in attendants and goods, hast studied the Veda and hast listened to the mystical doctrine (art *adhîtaveda* and *ukta-upanishatka*), tell me, whither will you go when once you depart hence?" "I do not know, reverend sir, whither I shall go" (he does not know, in spite of *devayâna* and *devaloka*, of which assuredly mention was made in his Vedas and Upanishads; the king seems no longer to place absolute confidence in their revelations). Yâjñavalkhya rejoins:—"Then will I declare to you whither you will go." "Declare it, reverend sir." What are we to expect to hear? Something at any rate which could not be more forcibly indicated than by this introduction as absolutely new at that period.

To begin with, Yâjñavalkhya describes the individual âtman, how it dwells in the heart, Indra and Virâj like as it were its feelers reach to the two eyes, and together with them are nourished by the blood-clots of the heart. Suddenly while he is speaking in so gross and materialistic a fashion of the individual âtman, a mist as it were is removed from our eyes:—"The anterior (eastern) regions of the heavens are his anterior organs, the right-hand (southern) regions of the heavens are his right-hand organs," etc., "all the regions of the heavens are all his organs. He however, the âtman, is not so, not so. He is inapprehensible, for he is not apprehended, indestructible, for he is not destroyed, unattachable, for nothing attaches itself to him; he is not fettered, he stirs not, he suffers

[1] It is from the circle of his thought that the words of Bṛih. 1. 4. 10 also, already quoted above p. 345, are derived; cp. Bṛih. 1. 4. 3.

no harm. O Janaka, you have attained peace. Thus Yâjñavalkhya spake."

The last expression leaves no doubt on the point that herein the intention is to impart the highest instruction, in which we are to seek for the answer to the initial question, "Whither will you go when once you depart hence?" And the answer asserts that the soul after death goes nowhere where it has not been from the very beginning, nor does it become other than that which it has always been, the one eternal omnipresent âtman.

The doubts which in view of the abrupt form of the paragraph might be felt as to the correctness of this interpretation, are completely removed by the unmistakeable teaching which Yâjñavalkhya imparts to Janaka in Bṛih. 4. 3–4. After that return to a new existence upon earth has been taught here as the fate of the *kâmayamâna*, "consumed by desire" (one who therefore does not yet know himself as the âtman), there follow words than which deeper, truer, more noble were never uttered by human lips:—

"Now concerning the man free from desire (*akâmayamâna*). He who without desire, free from desire, desire being laid to rest, is himself his own desire, his vital spirits do not withdraw, but he is Brahman, and ascends to Brahman. On this subject is the following verse:—

> When every passion vanishes
> That finds a home in the human heart,
> Then he who is mortal becomes immortal,
> Here already he has attained to Brahman.

As the skin of a snake lies cast off and dead upon an antheap, so this body then lies. But the bodiless, the immortal, the life is pure Brahman, is pure light."[1]

We propose in the first place to use these passages to

[1] Bṛih. 4. 4. 6–7.

throw light upon certain other expressions of Yâjñavalkhya which in themselves are obscure.

"'Yâjñavalkhya,' thus he spake, 'when a man dies, do the vital spirits wander forth from him or not?' 'By no means,' said Yâjñavalkhya, 'but they remain gathered together at the very same place; his body swells up, becomes inflated, and he lies there dead and inflated."[1] In this passage, as has been already remarked,[2] no restriction to those who are already emancipated is implied, since inflation by the expanding gases may be observed in every body without distinction. Yet we are compelled, as seems to have been done already by the Mâdhyandinas, to interpret the words only of the emancipated, if we would not set ourselves in irreconcilable contradiction with the words of Yâjñavalkhya elsewhere:—"When the life departs, all the vital organs depart with it."[3]

Still more obscure is the following:—"'Yâjñavalkhya,' thus he spake, 'when a man dies, what is it that then does not leave him?' 'The name,' he answered, 'for the name is infinite, infinite are the *vis've devâḥ*, and he gains with it the infinite world.'"[4] Here we are compelled to understand by the name the infinite "objective world," as has been already shown.[5] As long as this continues to subsist, the knowing subject also that sustains it preserves its existence.

It is in harmony with this explanation that Yâjñavalkhya asserts in Bṛih. 2. 4. 12,[6] in answer to Maitreyî: —"After death there is no consciousness"; and explains this by saying that the imperishable indestructible âtman (*avinâs'in, anuc'c'hittidharman*[7]) has after death no further consciousness of objects, because as knowing subject he has everything in himself, nothing outside of himself, con-

[1] Bṛih. 3. 2. 11. [2] See Deussen, *Upan.*, p. 431.
[3] Bṛih. 4. 4. 2. [4] Bṛih. 3. 2. 12. [5] Deussen, *Upan.*, p. 431.
[6] = 4. 5. 13. [7] 4. 5. 14.

sequently "has no longer any contact with matter" (*mâtrâ-asaṁsargas tu asya bhavati*).[1]

The mystical declaration also of Bṛih. 3. 2. 10 concerning the water (of knowledge), which is able to quench the fire of death, is thus satisfactorily explained.

Yâjñavalkhya has therefore entirely anticipated Schopenhauer's definition of immortality as an "indestructibility without continued existence."[2] Just as for the wise there is no longer any reality in the universe or in transmigration, so immortality also as prolonged existence after death is a part of the great illusion, the hollowness of which he has proved.

From the numerous passages in the later Upanishads, which in a similar way to the speeches of Yâjñavalkhya hitherto discussed celebrate the knowledge of the âtman as emancipation, a few may here be set down.

> "Yet he who has in thought conceived himself as the Self,
> How can he still wish to bind himself to the ills of the body?
> Him who in the profound defilement of the body
> Has awakened to a knowledge of the Self,
> Him know as almighty, as the worlds' creator!
> The universe is his, for he himself is the universe.
>
> The man who has beheld God
> As his own self face to face;
> The Lord of that which was and is to be,
> He feels no fear nor hides himself in dread.
>
> At whose feet rolling on by days and years time advances,
> Whom the gods adore as light of lights, as immortality,
> On whom depends the fivefold host of living beings, together with space,
> Him know I as my soul, immortal the immortal.[3]
>
> The seer sees not death,
> Nor sickness nor fatigue;
> The All alone the Seer sees,
> The All he everywhere pervades.[4]

---

[1] 5. 4. 14 Mâdhy.; cp. Deussen, *Upan.*, p. 485 rem.
[2] *Elements of Metaphysics*, § 249.
[3] Bṛih. 4. 4. 12–13, 15–17.
[4] Chând. 7. 26. 2.

He before whom words recoil
And thought, failing to find him,
Who knows this bliss of Brahman,
He no longer fears aught.[1]

Only he who knows it not knows it,
He who knows it knows it not.
Unknown by the wise,
Known by the ignorant.

In whom it wakes to life,
He knows it and finds immortality;
Because he is it, manhood is his,
Because he knows it, immortality.[2]

The one Lord and inner self of all living beings,
He his one form expands in many ways.
He who, the wise, sees himself dwelling in himself
He alone, and no other, is eternally blessed.

Not by speech, not by thought,
Not by sight do we apprehend him;
"He is!" By this word is he apprehended,
And not in any other way.

"He is!" thus may he be apprehended,
So far as he is the reality of both;
"He is!" who has thus apprehended him,
To him his essential nature becomes manifest.

When all the suffering vanishes,
Which finds a home in the human heart,
Then he who is mortal becomes immortal,
Here already he attains to Brahman.

When all fetters burst asunder
That are woven around the human heart,
Then he who is mortal becomes immortal,
Thus far the doctrine extends.[3]

Yet he who here recognises again
All living beings in himself,
And himself in everything that lives,
He no longer is vexed by any.

---

[1] Taitt. 2. 9. [2] Kena 11–12. [3] Kâṭh. 5. 12, 6. 12–15.

Here where the knowing self
Becomes all living beings :—
How could error be, how pain,
For him who thus beholds the unity?[1]

The darkness vanishes, there is no longer day nor night;
Neither being nor not-being,—blessed alone is he;
He is the syllable Om, Savitar's beloved light,
From him knowledge flowed forth in the beginning.[2]

He who, his spirit purified by contemplation,
Plunges into the âtman,—what measureless blessedness he feels!
That for the expression of which words are of no avail
Must be experienced within in the inmost heart.[3]

He who still craves for his desires and clings to them,
Will through his desires be born here and there;
He whose desires are laid to rest, whose self is prepared,
From him all desires vanish here below.

He who beholds that Loftiest and Deepest,
For him the fetters of the heart break asunder,
For him all doubts are solved,
And his works become nothingness.

Like streams flow and disappear in the ocean,
Abandoning name and form,
So the wise, freed from name and form,
Enter into that supreme divine spirit.[4]

In the world's false show that has known no beginning,
The soul slumbers; when it awakes,
Then there wakes in it the Eternal,
Beyond time and sleep and dreams.[5]

(The emancipated soul speaks):—

That which as enjoyment, enjoyment's object,
And enjoyer knows the three states,
Distinct therefrom, O spectator,
Pure spirit I am ever blessed.

In me the universe had its origin
In me alone does the All subsist,
In me it vanishes, this Brahman,
The timeless, it is I myself.

---

[1] Îsâ 6–7. [2] S'vet. 4. 18. [3] Maitr. 6. 34.
[4] Muṇḍ. 3. 2. 2, 2. 2. 8, 3. 2. 8. [5] Mâṇḍûkya-Kârikâ 1. 16.

The smallest of the small I am, and none the less am I great,
I am the motley rich universe,
I am the Ancient, the spirit, the lord,
Altogether of gold I am, the blessed Manifestation.

Without hands or feet am I, yet infinitely powerful,
I see without eyes, hear without ears;
I am the wise, and beside me
None other is wise in endless years.

In all the Vedas I am to be known,
I am the fulfiller of the Vedas, learned in the Vedas,
Free from good and evil, imperishable,
Unbegotten am I, without body or sensation;
For me there is neither earth nor water,
Nor fire, nor yet wind or ether.[1]

On the basis of this and other passages we propose finally to attempt here to give a brief characterisation of those who have gained release.

The knowledge of the âtman does not effect emancipation, but it is emancipation; for he who possesses it has found the existence of the universe as well as his own bodily and individual existence to be an illusion (*mâyâ*). Everything else follows from this.

(1) The wise man is *akâmayamâna*. Every wish, craving, desire, all hope and fear have for him been destroyed; for all this presupposes an object to which it is related. Such an object however no longer exists for the wise man. "In truth, after that they have become conscious of this soul, Brâhmans abstain from desire for children and possessions and the world, and wander about as beggars. For desire for children is desire for possessions, and desire for possessions is desire for the world; for all together are vain desire."[2] "This the men of old time knew, when they ceased to long for descendants and said, 'What need have we of descendants, we whose soul this universe is.'"[3] Gauḍapâda sums this up briefly and

[1] Kaivalya 18–23. [2] Bṛih. 3. 5. [3] Bṛih. 4. 4. 22.

strikingly in the words :[1]—"What can he desire who has all?" The wise man therefore no longer experiences fear. "He who knows this bliss of Brahman is not afraid either now or at any time";[2] he is no longer vexed by anything";[3] "for wherefore should he fear? since fear assuredly is of a second."[4]

(2) The knowledge of the âtman transcends individuality, and therefore the possibility of pain. "He who knows the âtman overcomes sorrow."[5] "He who is in the body is possessed by desire and pain, for because he is in the body no safeguard is possible against desire and pain. He however who is free from the body is not affected by desire and pain."[6] "He therefore who has crossed this bridge is like a blind man who gains his sight, like a wounded man who is healed, like a sick man who becomes whole."[7]

(3) "And his works become nothingness."[8] All works, the good as well as the evil, become of no effect for him who has attained knowledge, as is often affirmed.[9] For the individuality which gave rise to them is for the wise only a part of that great universal illusion which he has succeeded in penetrating.

(4) For the same reason future works no longer cling to him, as the water does not cling to the leaf of the lotus flower.[10] For him to do evil is entirely excluded by his freedom from all desire. "Therefore he who knows this is tranquil, subdued, resigned, patient and self-controlled. He sees the Self only in himself, he regards everything as the Self. Evil does not overcome him, he overcomes all evil . . . free from evil, free from suffering, and free from doubt, he becomes a Brâhman, he whose universe Brahman

[1] Kârikâ 1. 9.
[2] Taitt. 2. 4.
[3] Kâṭh. 4. 5, 12.
[4] Bṛih. 1. 4. 2.
[5] Chând. 7. 1. 3.
[6] Chând. 8. 12. 1.
[7] Chând. 8. 4. 2.
[8] Muṇḍ. 2. 2. 8.
[9] cp. the passages quoted above, p. 345 f.
[10] Chând. 4. 14. 3.

is."[1] "Whereby does this Brâhman live? By living as chance may determine."[2] His future condition, as far as the bodily state is concerned, which he has cast off like the skin of a snake, is entirely without importance:—

> No matter whether a man wish for himself
> A hundred years, pursuing his work;
> Remain then, as thus thou art, not otherwise,
> The stain of work clings not to thee.[3]

(5) "He who has reached this state in truth feels no doubt";[4] "for him all doubts are solved";[5] "free from doubt he becomes a Brâhman."[6] Because the knowledge of the âtman does not depend on reflection (*tarka*),[7] but on immediate intuition (*anubhava*), therefore he can no longer be shaken by any doubt. The illusion, when once it has been penetrated, can no longer delude. The question of the possibility of a relapse is not and cannot be raised.

4. *The Doctrine of Emancipation in Empirical Form*

(1) The âtman is unknowable.
(2) The âtman is the sole reality.
(3) The intuitive knowledge of the âtman is emancipation.

In these three propositions is contained the metaphysical truth of the teaching of the Upanishads. Its further development consists in bringing down, though illegitimately, this metaphysical truth into the sphere where knowledge is possible (just as among the Greeks and in later philosophy), and clothing it in empirical form. (1) The âtman becomes an object of knowledge, which in truth it is not. (2) The reality of the universe is maintained, and the consequent contradiction is adjusted by the oft-repeated assertion that the universe is identical

[1] Bṛih. 4. 4. 23. [2] Bṛih. 3. 5. [3] Îs'â. 2. [4] Chând. 3. 14. 4.
[5] Muṇd. 2. 2. 6. [6] Bṛih. 4. 4. 23. [7] Kâṭh. 2. 9.

with the âtman. (3) Emancipation appears finally and wrongly in the phenomenal form of causality as a becoming something which previously had no existence, and in the phenomenal forms of time and space as the removal of a temporal and spiritual separation from the âtman, which never really existed and therefore does not need to be removed.

This is the origin of the empirical and therefore mistaken view that deliverance (which actually subsisted from the very beginning, and in the very instant of recognition becomes ours perfectly and consciously) is first attained fully with the dissolution of the body. "To him shall I enter in when I depart hence";[1] "to this (worldly sphere) shall I belong only until I am delivered; then shall I go home";[2] "and when he has been delivered from the body (or, after that he has been delivered through knowledge), then (first ultimately in death) is he delivered," *vimuktas' c'a vimuc'yate.*[3] The comparison (of life) to the potter's wheel which ceases turning when the vessel (deliverance) is finished belongs to a later period,[4] like the distinction between those who are first delivered in the hour of death (*videhamukti*), and those who are already delivered during their life-time (*jîvanmukti*). This distinction and the above comparison have their origin primarily from the realistic age of the Vedânta that finds itself drifting towards the Sâṅkhya. Neither of them meet us in the Upanishads (with quite late exceptions), and are opposed to the original meaning of the doctrine of emancipation. According to it, every man, as soon as he is in possession of the knowledge of the âtman, is *jîvanmukta.* The continuance or cessation of his bodily existence is to him, as everything else in the world, a matter of indifference. He gains

[1] Chând. 3. 14. 4. [2] Chând. 6. 14. 2. [3] Kâṭh. 5. 1.
[4] *Syst. d. Ved.*, p. 459; Garbe, *Sâṅkhyaphil.*, p. 182.

nothing by death of which he was not in possession already beforehand, and is released from nothing from which he had not been already released previously by knowledge.

As the theory of the *videhamukti* together with the passages of the Upanishads that anticipate it rests upon the false supposition that between us and the âtman a temporal separation exists; so the hypothesis of a spatial separation between the two, so that a departure hence is necessary in order to reach the âtman, is not less mistaken and depends upon an unwarranted application of the methods of empirical knowledge. Nevertheless this mode of representation also is not rare in the Upanishads, under the influence of the ancient ideas of a departure to the gods, to Brahman, to the âtman.[1] That the ideas which thus emerge are far from being consistent lies in the nature of things. We propose briefly to survey the most important passages.

In Bṛih. 3. 3 we have an altogether mythical description (though it is put into the mouth of Yâjñavalkhya) of the way by which the offerers of the *as'vamedha* as the highest sacrifice are led hence, between the two shells of the egg of the universe, into the other world where the wind receives them. The averting also of renewed death which is promised at the close to him who knows the mind as particular and universal (individual and cosmical prâṇa) proves that this chapter is still to be ascribed to the age preceding the Upanishad teaching. Bṛih. 5. 10 may be regarded as a continuation of it. Here a description is given of the reception of the departed (without distinction) by the wind in the other world, after which through the sun and moon they attain "the world that is free from heat and cold (*as'okam ahimam*, *i.e.* free from the contrasts of earthly existence),

[1] *sup.* p. 343 f.

in order to remain there "perpetual years." The dying man takes his way to the sun in Bṛih. 5. 15[1] also. There however he recognises himself as identical with the purusha in the sun, an idea that already contains a suggestion of the âtman doctrine, although it is subordinated to traditional mythological conceptions. The same is true of Chând. 5. 13, where in the first instance the five prâṇas together with the five corresponding organs of sense and the five nature gods are called the five "openings of the gods" (*devasushayas*), and are described as "the five ministers of Brahman and door-keepers of the heavenly world"; but then "the light which shines there on yonder side of heaven," which is to be reached through them, is identified with the light "which is here within in men." The eschatology also of Chând. 8. 1–6 exhibits this intermingling of mythological and philosophical ideas. Thus in Chând. 8. 6. 1–5 the way hence to the sun is described that leads by the veins and the sun's rays that join them, although previously in 8. 3 the world of Brahman had been shown to be not at an incalculable distance, but in the heart. That the fundamental view here is philosophical, and the mythical colouring a later embellishment, is proved quite unmistakeably by the fact that in 8. 5. 3 from the word *araṇyam*, the "solitude," into which he who seeks Brahman retires, are invented "two seas in the world of Brahman in the third heaven from here" with the names *ara* and *ṇya*. To this a later hand added further glories of the world of Brahman (the lake *Airammadîyam*, the fig-tree *Somasavana*, the mountain *Aparâjitâ*, and the palace *Prabhuvimitam*). Perhaps the still more detailed description of the world of Brahman in Kaush. 1. 3 is already derived from this passage. Here among other things not only does the palace *Aparâjitam* (in

[1] Îs'â. 15–18.

this place neuter) recur, and a tree *Ilya* appear, but mention is made also of "the sea *Âra*." This latter name might well be a secondary formation from the sea *ara* of Chând. 8. 5. 3; and it would then be evidence for the dependent character of this passage. A different view from Chând. 8. 6. 1–5 is represented in the appended verse, Chând. 8. 6. 6, which recurs in Kâṭh. 6. 16. Here the separation of the emancipated as they ascend by the 101st vein is made to take place not on entrance into the sun, but immediately on quitting the body. With this is connected the path of the emancipated by the crown of the head, by fire, wind and sun, up to Brahman, as is described in Taitt. 1. 6. All these passages are under the influence of the thought of the Upanishads, which they clothe in empirical forms, while blending it with the traditional mythological ideas. This becomes obtrusive in Ait. 3. 4; Vâmadeva having recognised himself as the âtman has "ascended from this world, in yonder world of heaven attained all his desires, and has become immortal,"—very unnecessarily after he had already realised himself to be identical with the âtman, the first principle of all things.

These conceptions are made clearer by the development of the theory of the *Devayâna*, as found in Chând. 4. 15. 5, and its connection with the analogous formation of the *Pitṛiyâna* in the doctrine of the five fires, the principal text of the doctrine of transmigration, which has been already discussed. We saw[1] how the souls of the emancipated were represented as attaining to Brahman through a series of bright stations (flame, day, bright half of the month, bright half of the year, year, sun, moon and lightning), whence "they no longer return on the downward path to this human existence." The Pitṛiyana was then next explained after the analogy

[1] *sup.* p. 335.

of the Devayâna by means of the corresponding dark stations;[1] this however involved, as was shown, the making the moon common to both ways. This drawback the author of Kaush. 1. 2 endeavours to remove by omitting or ignoring the preliminary steps on either side that lead to the moon, and bringing all thither, whence the ignorant return back, and the wise tread the Devayâna, to which by way of compensation for the omitted stages a series of new stations are assigned (moon, the worlds of fire, wind, Varuṇa, Indra, Prajâpati and Brahman). By the later Vedântists these are simply placed side by side with the previous stations.[2] In other respects also the theory of the less authoritative Kaushîtaki has won a consideration not inferior to that of the *Pañc'âgnividyâ* supported by the authority of Chând. 5. 3–10 and Bṛih. 6. 2. On it depend almost all the later representations of the Devayâna, for example those especially that are found in Muṇḍ. 1. 2. 11, 3. 1. 6, Pras'na 1. 10. By its side the thought of Yâjñavalkhya that the knowledge of the âtman is in itself emancipation continues to hold its ground, and is often associated without any attempt at accommodation with the theory of the Devayâna, giving rise as a consequence to abrupt contradictions; compare for example Kâṭh. 6. 14–15 with 6. 16, or Muṇḍ. 3. 2. 2 with 3. 1. 10.

An adjustment of this contradiction was sought by the later theory of the *kramamukti* or release by stages, according to which the souls that for their devotion ascend on the Devayâna to Brahman are not yet emancipated, since they still fall short of perfect knowledge; nevertheless they do not return back to earth, (for it is said:—"For such there is no return"),[3] but attain perfect knowledge and therefore eternal

[1] *sup.* p. 335 f.

[2] *Syst. d. Ved.*, p. 475.

[3] Bṛih. 6. 2. 15, Chând. 4. 15. 5, 8. 15.

deliverance in the world of Brahman before the end of the *kalpa*, when that world also is destroyed.[1] In the Upanishads the *kramamukti* appears to be already advocated by the S'vet. Up. 1. 4, 1. 11, 5. 7. The verse in Muṇḍ. 3. 2. 6 may however be still older :[2]—

> They who have grasped the meaning of the Vedânta doctrine,
> Perfectly resigned, penitent, of unsullied purity,
> In the world of Brahman at the end of time,
> Will all be set free by the Indestructible.

XVI. Practical Philosophy

1. *Introduction*

Every theory of the universe includes judgements on the relative value or worthlessness of objects, and thereby secures an influence on our practical conduct. Every philosophical system therefore has an ethical side, whether it be matured or not into a special ethical system ; and it is precisely this side to which our feeling attaches so great importance that we are inclined to estimate the value of a philosophical theory of the universe by the ethical consequences which have resulted or may be derived from it. We allow ourselves to be guided in these matters by the old adage,—" By their fruits ye shall know them." [3] Even this saying however cannot be taken without limitations. For to continue the illustration employed by Jesus, it may happen that a tree is good and yet bears no, or no good fruit,—possibly because its blossoms are prematurely touched by the cold breath of the knowledge of the truth.

This may in fact have been the case in India. Eternal

[1] cp. *Syst. d. Vedânta*, pp. 430, 472.
[2] cp. Mahânâr. 10. 22, Kaivalya, 3–4.
[3] Matt. 7^{16}.

philosophical truth has seldom found more decisive and striking expression than in the doctrine of the emancipating knowledge of the âtman. And yet this knowledge may be compared to that icy-cold breath which checks every development and benumbs all life. He who knows himself as the âtman is, it is true, for ever beyond the reach of all desire, and therefore beyond the possibility of immoral conduct, but at the same time he is deprived of every incitement to action or initiation of any kind; he is lifted out of the whole circle of illusory individual existence, his body is no longer his, his works no longer his, everything which he may henceforth do or leave undone belongs to the sphere of the great illusion, which he has penetrated, and is therefore of no account. Accordingly he lives *îdṛis'a eva*, "as it happens,"[1] and though he wish for a hundred years of life and enjoyment, no action will defile him, or will defile you, *evam tvayi*, "when you are thus," *i.e.* when the universe is for you plunged in the abyss of the divine being. Only painfully and artificially has the Bhagavad Gîtâ the skill to derive from these premisses a demand for heroic action, as we shall see in a later part of our work. When the knowledge of the âtman has been gained, every action, and therefore every moral action also, has been deprived of meaning.

Moreover moral conduct cannot contribute directly, but only indirectly, to the attainment of the knowledge that brings emancipation. For this knowledge is not a becoming something which had no previous existence, and might be brought about by appropriate means, but it is the perception of that which previously existed, existed indeed from all eternity. It is compared

[1] Bṛih. 3. 5. 1; he is *yâdṛic'c'hika*, Mâṇḍûkya-K. 2. 37, Paramahaṁsa Up. 4.

[2] Îs'a. 1. 2.

(as early as the later Upanishads) with awakening,[1] and like that follows of itself[2] and not by design :—

> In the infinite illusion of the universe
> The soul sleeps ; when it awakes
> Then there wakes in it the Eternal,
> Free from time and sleep and dreams.[3]

It was first at a later period, when the method of empirical knowledge took entire possession of the doctrine of emancipation, and conceived it as has been shown under the category of causality, that the knowledge through which deliverance is attained came to be regarded as a becoming something, as an effect of definite causes, which might therefore be brought about by promoting such causes. Thus emancipation was conceived, again empirically, in accordance with the external signs which it manifested. These signs were principally two :—

(1) The removal of all desire.

(2) The removal of the consciousness of plurality.

It was worth while therefore to produce or at least to expedite emancipation by artificial means, and the result was two remarkable manifestations of the culture of India, which are contained in germ in the older Upanishads, and in a series of later Upanishads pass through a complete development.

(1) The Sannyâsa.

(2) The Yoga.

The former seeks by artificial measures to suppress desire, the latter the consciousness of plurality, and thus to secure the attainment of the knowledge through which deliverance is wrought, as far at least as its external signs are concerned. Practical philosophy is comprised in these

[1] *prabodha*, Haṁsa Up. 1, Âtmaprabodha 1, Gauḍap. 1. 14, 3. 40, 4. 92, 98 ; cp. *pratibuddha*, Bṛih. 4. 4. 13 ; *pratibodha*, Kena 12 ; *jâgrata*, Kâṭh. 3. 14 ; *boddhum*, Kâṭh. 6. 4 ; *nityaḥ, s'uddho, buddhaḥ*, Nṛisiṁhott. 9.

[2] Kâṭh. 2. 23.

[3] Mâṇḍûkya-Kâr. 1. 16.

two manifestations of culture, which pursue their course on parallel lines, and often touch; and it has been developed out of the thoughts of the Upanishads (empirically conceived). This we have yet briefly to treat, as far as the materials afforded by the Atharva Upanishads will allow us. First however we propose to gather together here the most important ethical ideas which present themselves in the Upanishads, not so much arising from the âtman doctrine as holding a place by its side.

2. *Ethics of the Upanishads*

Europeans, practical and shrewd as they are, are wont to estimate the merits of an action above all by its objective worth, that is by the resultant profit for neighbours, for the multitude, or for all men. He who has obtained the greatest results by this standard passes for the greatest man of his time; and the widow's mite is never anything more than a mite. But this objective worth of a good action is too entirely dependent on the favourable or unfavourable character of environment, on mental endowment, on position in life, on the accessory forces of trade and other accidents, to be capable of serving as a standard of moral value. Such a standard must have regard rather to the subjective worth of an action, which consists in the greatness of the personal sacrifice which is involved, or more strictly speaking in the actor's consciousness of the greatness of the sacrifice which he believes himself to be making, and consequently in the degree of self-denial (*tapas*), and self-renunciation (*nyâsa*), which is exhibited in the action, whether in other respects it be of great or little or absolutely no value for others.

This distinction may save us from being betrayed into an unjust judgement when we note, at first with some surprise, that amongst the ancient Indians, whose consciousness of human solidarity, of common needs and interests, was but slightly developed, the sense of the objective worth of moral action (that is, the worth it possesses for others) is very inferior to ours, while their estimate of its subjective worth (that is, its significance for the actor himself) was advanced to a degree from which we may learn much. In this sense the ethical system of the Upanishads concerns itself especially with the subjective interpretation of moral action, and less with their external results; although this latter consideration is by no means absolutely wanting, but is merely subordinated to the first. This we propose to show in the first place by a few examples.

In Chând. 3. 17 life is regarded allegorically as a great soma festival. In this a miniature ethical system in five words is incidentally interwoven, when as the reward of the sacrifice (*dakshiṇâ*), which is to be offered at the great sacrificial feast of life, are named:—(1) *tapas*, asceticism; (2) *dânam*, liberality; (3) *ârjavam*, right dealing; (4) *ahiṁsâ*, no injury to life; and (5) *satyavac'anam*, truthfulness.

In Taitt. 1. 9 twelve duties are enumerated, by the side of each of which the "learning and teaching of the Veda" are constantly enjoined. These are:—Right dealing and truthfulness; asceticism, self-restraint, and tranquillity; and as duties of a householder,—Maintenance of the sacred fire and the agnihotram, hospitality and courtesy, duties to children wives and grandchildren.

In India also, as in other countries, men believed that they heard the voice of the moral law-giver (Prajâpati) in the roll of the thunder, whose *da! da! da!* is explained in the myth of Bṛih. 5. 2 as *dâmyata! datta! dayadhvam!* (be self-restrained, liberal, pitiful).

The beneficent results of good actions are beautifully expressed in Mahânâr. 9.[1] "As the scent is wafted afar from a tree laden with flowers, so also is wafted afar the scent of a good deed."

[1] In the Atharva Recension 8. 2.

On the other hand, the wicked act is sternly condemned in the verse preserved in Chând. 5. 10. 9 :—

> The thief of gold, and the spirit drinker,
> The murderer of a Brâhman, the defiler of his teacher's bed,
> These four perish, and he who associates with them as the fifth.

The fact that only special cases are cited here instead of universal prohibitions of theft, drunkenness, murder and adultery, thus showing lack of generalisation, as well as the rarity of such warnings in Upanishad literature, proves that offences of this character were not common, and that many an Indian chieftain might make in substance his own the honourable testimony which As'vapati Kaikeya bears to his subjects :—

> In my kingdom there is no thief,
> No churl, no drunkard,
> None who neglects the sacrifice or the sacred lore,
> No adulterer or courtesan.[1]

This is in keeping with the gentle humane tone which we see adopted in the Upanishads in the intercourse of husband and wife, father and son, teacher and student, prince and subject.

Where ethics found so little external work to do, they could give the more undivided attention to the internal, in the spirit of the proverb :—

> In thyself know thy friend,
> In thyself know thy enemy.[2]

The strife with this internal foe is *tapas* (asceticism), the victory over it *nyâsa* (self-renunciation), and in these are contained the two fundamental ideas, around which the ethical thought of the Upanishads moves. *Tapas* has been already discussed in detail ;[3] and we will only add

[1] Chând. 5. 11. 5. [2] Bhag. Gîtâ 6. 5. [3] *sup.* pp. 65–70.

here that in Mahânâr. 8 all virtues are quite correctly explained as *tapas*, while according to Mahânâr. 62. 11 "all these lower mortifications"[1] are surpassed by *nyâsa*, self-renunciation. More importance than to isolated expressions of this character attaches to the fact that in course of time the ancient traditional life-stages of the *brahmac'ârin* and *gṛihastha* had a third and a fourth added to them, in which these two supreme virtues were incorporated as it were, *tapas* as *vânaprastha*, and *nyâsa* as *sannyâsin*. These four life-stages of the Brahman—as student, householder, anchorite and wandering beggar—in which according to a subsequent view the life of every Indian Brâhman should be spent, were at a later time very significantly named *âs'ramas*, *i.e.* "places of mortification."[2] The whole life should be passed in a series of gradually intensifying ascetic stages, through which a man, more and more purified from all earthly attachment, should become fitted for his "home" (*astam*), as the other world is designated as early as Ṛigv. X. 14. 8. The entire history of mankind does not produce much that approaches in grandeur to this thought.

In the older Upanishads the theory of the four âs'ramas is seen in course of formation. Chând. 8. 15 mentions only the Brahman-student and householder, and promises to these in return for study, the begetting of children, the practice of yoga, abstinence from doing injury, and sacrifice, a departure hence without return. Chând. 2. 23. 1 names the *tapas* (of the anchorite) side by side with these as a third "branch of duty." There is still no progressive series. Rather according to this passage the Brahman-students, in so far as they do not

[1] A list of which is given like the similar series of virtues in Taitt. 1. 9, *sup.* p. 365, and Mahânâr. 8.

[2] First, as far as our knowledge goes, in the *atyâs'ramin* of S'vet. 6. 21, followed by Maitr. 4. 3, etc.

elect to remain permanently in the house of the teacher, appear to have devoted themselves partly to the householder's state, partly to the life in the forest. It is in harmony with this that in Chând. 5. 10 among the dying the anchorite in the forest and the sacrificer in the village appear side by side. Chând. 2. 23. 1 contrasts all three branches of duty with the position of the man who "stands fast in Brahman." So too in Bṛih. 4. 2. 22, those who practise (1) the study of the Veda, (2) sacrifice and almsgiving, (3) penance and fasting, are contrasted with the man who has learnt to know the âtman, and in consequence becomes a *muni* and *pravrâjin* (pilgrim). Both have attained the knowledge of the âtman, and therefore the supreme goal. In the cognate passage Bṛih. 3. 5, on the contrary the Brâhmaṇa is still distinguished from the *muni* as a higher grade. In Bṛih. 3. 8. 10 also the knowledge of the âtman as the highest aim is differentiated both from the sacrifices and benefactions (of the householder), and from the practices of *tapas* (of the anchorite). All these passages assume only the three stages of Brahman-student, householder and anchorite, and contrast with them the men who know the âtman. The last were originally "exalted above the (three) âs'ramas."[1] This very position however of exaltation above the âs'ramas became in course of time a fourth and highest âs'rama, which was naturally assigned to the end of life, so that studentship, and the positions of householder and anchorite (which stood side by side) preceded it as temporary grades in this successive order. Until a late period however the separation between the third and fourth âs'ramas, between the vânaprastha practising tapas, and the sannyâsin who has succeeded in attaining nyâsa, was not strictly carried out. An intimation of the fourfold number of the âs'ramas is perhaps already afforded by the

[1] *atyâs'ramin*, as it is said in S'vet. 6. 21, Kaiv. 24.

words of Muṇḍ. 2. 1. 7:—" mortification, truth, the life of a Brâhman, instruction." Otherwise the oldest passage, which names all four âs'ramas in the correct order, would be Jâbâla Up. 4 :—" When the period of Brahman-studentship is ended, a man becomes a householder; after he has been a householder, he becomes an anchorite; after he has been an anchorite, let him travel about on pilgrimage."

The further development of the theory of the four âs'ramas belongs to the later period of the dharmasûtras and dharmas'âstras. Here we propose merely to take a brief survey of the substance of the teaching of the Upanishads on this subject.

(1) The *Brahmac'ârin.* " S'vetaketu was the son of (Uddâlaka) Âruṇi. To him said his father, ' S'vetaketu, go forth to study the Brahman, for none of our family, my dear son, is wont to remain unlearned, and a (mere) hanger-on of the Brâhman order.' "[1] From this remark it seems to follow that at that time entrance upon the life of a Brahman-student, while it was a commendable custom, was not yet universally enjoined upon Brâhmans. The entrance also of Satyakâma upon studentship appears to be his voluntary determination.[2] It was possible for a man to receive instruction from his father, as S'vetaketu,[3] or at the hands of other teachers, as the same S'vetaketu.[4] The request to be received must follow duly (*tîrthena*, cp. *vidhivat*, Muṇḍ. 1. 1. 3), *i.e.* according to Bṛih. 6. 2. 7, with the words,—*upaimi aham bhavantam.* The student takes the fuel in his hand as a token that he is willing to serve the teacher, and especially to maintain the sacred fires.[5] Before receiving him, the teacher makes inquiry

[1] Chând. 6. 1. 1.

[2] Chând. 4. 4. 1.

[3] Chând. 5. 3. 1, Bṛih. 6. 2. 1, Kaush. 1. 1.

[4] Chând. 6. 1. 1, differing from the passages just quoted.

[5] Kaush. 4. 19, Chând. 4. 4. 5, 5. 13. 7, 8. 7. 2, 8. 10. 3, 8. 11. 2, Muṇḍ. 1. 2. 12, Pras'na 1. 1.

into his birth and family,[1] but yet, as this example shows, in a very indulgent manner. Sometimes instruction is given even without formal reception (*anupanîya*).[2] The duration of the period of instruction is twelve years,[3] or "a series of years."[4] S'vetaketu also begins to receive instruction at the age of twelve,[5] and continues his study for twelve years. During this time he has "thoroughly studied all the Vedas,"[6] namely the verses of the Ṛigveda, the formulas of the sacrifice, and the hymns of the Sâma,[7] apparently therefore only the saṁhitâs. In other instances there appears to have been at first no mention of study. In one example Upakosala has tended the sacred fires for twelve years, and yet the teacher can never make up his mind to impart to him "the knowledge."[8] Satyakâma is sent at first with the teacher's herds of cattle into a distant country, where he remains for a succession of years.[9] A further act of service on the part of the brahmac'ârin consists in his going to beg for the teacher.[10] On festival occasions also we find him in the train of the teacher and awaiting his commands.[11] Together with and after these acts of service "in the time remaining over from work for the teacher" (*guroḥ karma-atis'esheṇa*) the study of the Veda is prosecuted.[12] The consequence was sometimes rather darkening of knowledge than real enlightenment.[13] We further find the students wandering from place to place; "they hasten from all sides" to famous teachers, like water down the hill;[14] they roam as far as the land of the Madras (on the Hyphasis) "in order to learn the sacrifice."[15] As a rule however they live as *antevâsins* in the house of the teacher, and not a few found this manner of life so

[1] Chând. 4. 4. 4. [2] Chând. 5. 11. 7. [3] Chând. 4. 10. 1.
[4] Chând. 4. 4. 5. [5] Chând. 6. 1. 2. [6] Chând. 6. 1. 2.
[7] Chând. 6. 7. 2. [8] Chând. 4. 10. 1–2. [9] Chând. 4. 4. 5.
[10] Chând. 4. 3. 5. [11] Bṛih. 3. 1. 2. [12] Chând. 8. 15.
[13] Chând. 6. 1. 2. [14] Taitt. 1. 4. 3. [15] Bṛih. 3. 7. 1, 3. 3. 1.

congenial that they "settled permanently in the teacher's house."[1] The others were dismissed at the close of the period of studentship with advice[2] or admonitions:—"After he has studied the Veda with him the teacher admonishes his pupil,—'Speak the truth, do your duty, forsake not the study of the Veda; after you have presented the appropriate gifts to the teacher, take care that the line of your race be not broken.'"[3] Further admonitions follow, not to neglect health and possessions, to honour father, mother, teacher and guest, to be blameless in act and life, to honour superiors, to bestow alms in the appropriate manner, and in all doubtful cases to order himself according to the judgement of approved authorities.

(2) The *Gṛihastha.* "He who returns home from the family of the teacher, after the prescribed study of the Veda in the time remaining over from work for the teacher, and pursues the private study of the Veda in (his own) household in a pure neighbourhood (where Brâhmans are permitted to live), trains up pious (sons and pupils), subdues all his organs in the âtman, and besides injures no living thing except on sacred ground (at the sacrifice), he in truth, if he maintains this manner of life all his days, enters into the world of Brâhman and does not return back."[4] According to this passage, the householder may remain in that state all his life long without doing injury to his soul. According to Chând. 5. 10, on the contrary, for those "who in the village observe the rites with the words—'Sacrifice and works of piety are our service,'" for those therefore who continue in the householder's state to the end of life, the transient reward in the moon is appointed and a return to a new earthly existence. The most imperative duty of the householder is to establish a family and to beget a son to continue his

[1] Chând. 2. 23. 1.
[2] Bṛih. 6. 4.
[3] Taitt. 1. 11.
[4] Chând. 8. 15.

father's works. This subject has been already considered.[1] Several wives are permitted, as in fact Yâjñavalkhya himself had two.[2] Further duties of the gṛihastha are named,—sacrifice, study of the Veda, and almsgiving.[3] How far the obligation of sacrifice suffered prejudice through the ideas of the Upanishads has been already discussed.[4]

(3) The *Vânaprastha* and (4) the *Sannyâsin* (*bhikshu*, *parivrâjaka*). A distinction between these two periods of life was established at first gradually. Originally the solitary life in the forest existed as a special "kind of vocation" (*dharmaskandha*) side by side with the position of householder.[5] Later it may have become usual to retire into the solitude of the forest on the approach of old age, after the obligations of the householder had been satisfied. Yâjñavalkhya is an example, when he addresses his wife Maitreyî:—"I will now abandon this state (of householder), and will therefore make a division between thee and Kâtyâyanî."[6] With Yâjñavalkhya this step means the putting into practice of his teaching in Bṛih. 3. 5. 1:—"In truth, after that Brâhmans have gained the knowledge of this soul, they abstain from desire for children and desire for possessions and desire for the world, and wander about as beggars." Here the third and the fourth states are not yet distinguished. The case is otherwise with the king Bṛihadratha, who surrenders his kingdom, journeys into the forest, and gives himself up to the most painful mortifications, gazing fixedly at the sun and standing with arms crossed, and yet is obliged to confess:—"I am not acquainted with the âtman."[7] Here the anchorite, who devotes himself to ascetic practices

[1] *sup.* p. 293 ff.
[2] Bṛih. 2. 4, 4. 5.
[3] Chând. 2. 23. 1, 8. 5. 1–2, Bṛih. 4. 4. 22, 3. 8. 10.
[4] *sup.* p. 61–65.
[5] Chând. 2. 23. 1, 5. 10. 1–3.
[6] Bṛih. 2. 4. 1 (4. 5. 1–2).
[7] Maitr. 1. 2.

with meditation,[1] has not yet attained the highest goal; if anyone without knowing the âtman "practises asceticism for a full thousand years, to him it brings only finite (reward)."[2] Asceticism leads only to the Pitṛiyâna,[3] and the case is different only with those who can say:—"Faith is our asceticism."[4] Penance and fasting are only the means by which Brâhmans "seek to know" the âtman.[5] According to some, tapas is indispensable as a means to the knowledge of the âtman;[6] according to others, it is superfluous as far as any fruits of the system are concerned.[7] For as long as the goal was future the hope might be cherished of approaching near to it by severing by means of asceticism the tie that binds to this life. If however emancipation is the discovery of oneself as the âtman, and therefore something that only needs to be recognised as already existing, not to be brought about as though it were future, the asceticism of the vânaprastha becomes as superfluous as the gṛihastha's sacrifice and study of the Veda.[8] He who knows the âtman is *atyâs'ramin*, "exalted above the (three) âs'ramas."[9] He has attained that which the ascetic only strives after, complete release from his individuality and from all that pertains to it, as family, possessions and the world.[10] He is called *sannyâsin*, because he "casts off everything from himself" (*sam-ni-as*), because he "wanders around" homeless (*parivrâj*, *parivrâjaka*), because without possessions he lives only as a "beggar" (*bhikshu*).

3. *The Sannyâsa*

The *Sannyâsa*, which is originally only the rejection of the entire Brâhmanical mode of life with its three

[1] Chând. 2. 23. 1. [2] Bṛih. 3. 8. 10. [3] Bṛih. 6. 2. 16.
[4] Chând. 5. 10. 1. [5] *vividishanti*, Bṛih. 4. 4. 22.
[6] Maitr. 4. 3, *na atapaskasya âtmajñâne 'dhigamaḥ*.
[7] Jâbâla Up. 4. [8] Bṛih. 3. 5, 4. 4. 21. [9] S'vet. 6. 21.
[10] Bṛih. 3. 5, 4. 4. 22.

âs'ramas, assumed in course of time the position of a fourth and highest âs'rama, which as a rule, though not necessarily, would first be entered upon towards the close of life after passing through the stages of brahmac'ârin, gṛihastha and vânaprastha. It thus, however, gained a further meaning. If it was originally an apparent consequence of the knowledge of the âtman, it became now a final and most certain means by which it was hoped to attain that knowledge. The Sannyâsa accordingly is represented as such a means to the knowledge of the âtman and to emancipation in a series of later Upanishads (the most important are *Brahma*, *Sannyâsa*, *Âruṇeya*, *Kaṇṭhas'ruti*, *Paramahaṁsa*, *Jâbâla*, *Âs'rama*); and from these we propose to endeavour to sketch a picture of this most characteristic feature of Indian religious life. Remembering however the slight regard which the Sannyâsins, following the example of Yâjñavalkhya,[1] entertain for the Vedic tradition, and the lack of other authority, it is intelligible that the rules and formulas out of which the Sannyâsa Upanishads have been compiled are in details full of contradictions.

(1) *Preliminary conditions of the Sannyâsa.* A clear distinction between these four âs'ramas is found only in Jâb. 4 and Âs'r. 1–4. The latter Upanishad distinguishes the third and fourth stages by the fact that all four varieties of the vânaprastha continue to observe the sacrifice in the forest, while the four varieties of the sannyâsin are absolved from it. Jâb. 4 enjoins entrance into the sannyâsa only after passing through the stages of brahmac'ârin, gṛihastha and vânaprastha, but permits the transition direct from any stage. Similarly in Kaṇṭh. 1 the injunction is given to renounce the world "in the right order," while in Kaṇṭh. 2 a deviation from it is allowed. In Sanny. 1 renunciation is defined as an

[1] Bṛih. 3. 5, 4. 4. 21.

"advance beyond the stages of life" (therefore still not a fourth stage). According to the descriptions of Sanny. 2 and Kaṇṭh. 4 the transition is direct from the position of householder to renunciation; and the reason for this may be either that gṛihastha and vânaprastha are still placed side by side as preliminary stages of renunciation,[1] or that vânaprastha and sannyâsin are not yet definitely separated.[2]

(2) *Departure from life.* The Sannyâsa demands a surrender of all possessions, a resigning the seven upper and seven lower worlds, which on this occasion are enumerated,[3] an abandonment of sons, brothers, relatives,[4] of father, son and wife,[5] of teachers and relatives,[6] of children, friends, wife and relatives,[7] a leaving behind of family.[8] In one passage only[9] is permission given for him who renounces the world to be accompanied by his wife. The Sannyâsa is accordingly a complete separation from life; and therefore in this instance also, as at death, a purification (*saṁskâra*) by sacred text and ceremonies has to be observed.[10] In particular the candidate for renunciation has still to offer a sacrifice for the last time, in the description of which the texts greatly differ. In Sanny. 1 an offering is prescribed to the deceased and a sacrifice to Brahman (*brâhmeshṭi*); henceforth the man who has renounced the world lives without offerings to the deceased and sacrifices.[11] Kaṇṭh. 4 requires that in the first place for twelve successive days an agnihotram with milk shall be proffered, during which time the sacrificer himself shall live only on milk; then after selecting once again as before all the hitherto recognised sacrificial priests,[12] he is to offer a *vais'vânara* sacrifice (*i.e.* to Agni Vais'vâ-

[1] As in Chând. 2. 23. 1.
[2] As in Âs'r. 3–4, and later.
[3] Âr. 1.
[4] Âr. 1.
[5] Âr. 5.
[6] Kaṇṭh. 4.
[7] Par. 1.
[8] Âr. 2.
[9] Sanny. 2. 7.
[10] Sanny. 1.
[11] Par. 4.
[12] Kaṇṭh. 1.

nara, probably to be understood as in Chând. 5. 19–24),[1] accompanied by a mouse to Prajâpati (perhaps as ransom from the duty of begetting), and a cake of three layers to Vishṇu.[2] In Jâb. 4, on the contrary, the sacrifice to Prajâpati is disapproved of, and only that to Agni as Prâṇa is demanded (probably therefore the *vais'vânara,* sacrifice), but subsequently direction is given for a *Traidhâtavîya* offering to the three elements, *sattvam, rajas* and *tamas.* Thus too in Jâb. 4, in harmony with the separation of all four stages here carried out, he who enters upon the Sannyâsa is thought of as a vânaprastha; and this is the ground of the immediately following prescription, that the priests shall cause the fire to be brought from the village; if no fire is to be had, the offering shall be made in water, "for water is all the deities."[3] This offering is made with the words, "*Om!* I offer to all the deities, *svâhâ,*" where the word *om* implies all three Vedas;[4] and thereupon the sacrificer shall taste the fat and savoury meats of the sacrifice. According to Kaṇṭh. 1 he is to stretch his limbs symbolically over the sacrificial utensils, thereby signifying his renunciation of them. Kaṇṭh. 4 commands him to throw his wooden vessels into the fire, the earthen into water, and to give the metal ones to his teacher; elsewhere he is to throw the broken wood into the fire.[5] Thereby he symbolically takes the fire, which henceforth he will no longer maintain, into himself,[6] or into his body.[7] The sacrificial fire he takes up into the fire of his belly,[8] the Gâyatrî [9] into the fire of his speech.[10] It is probably this taking up of the sacrificial fire into his own body which is symbolically intended when he who has renounced the world, addressing

[1] Kaṇṭh. 1 and 4. [2] Kaṇṭh. 4. [3] cp. *sup.* p. 190 f. [4] Jâb. 4.
[5] Sanny. 1, Kaṇṭh. 4. [6] Sanny. 1. [7] Sanny. 2. 4.
[8] In which for the future he offers the prâṇa-agnihotram, *sup.* p. 124 f.
[9] *i.e.* the Veda, Chând. 3. 12. 1. [10] Âr. 2.

the fire, has to consume a handful of ashes from the embers,[1] or to smell the fire.[2] Besides this ceremony, mention is made of a special initiation (*dîkshâ*),[3] which must be completed by means of the hymn Atharvav. 11. 8:—"When Manyu chose himself a wife from out of the saṅkalpa," etc. Since this hymn expresses itself in depreciatory style of the origin of the body,[4] this application of it perhaps meant that a man thereby declared himself free from his own body. After thus separating himself from sacrificial duties, a highly significant act followed, upon which accordingly stress is laid by all the texts, namely the laying aside of the sacred thread, the token that he belongs to the Brâhmanical class,[5] and the lock of hair which indicates his family descent.[6] Henceforth meditation alone is to serve as the sacrificial cord,[7] and knowledge as the lock of hair,[8] the timeless âtman is to be both sacred thread and lock of hair for him who has renounced the world.[9] According to Kaṇṭh. 4 the sacred thread, according to Jâb. 6 this and the lock of hair, are offered in water with the words "*svâhâ* to the earth"; according to Âr. 2 the sacred thread and lock of hair are to be buried in the earth or sunk in water. The later systematising of Âs'r. 4, which distinguishes four grades of Sannyâsins, insists on the retention of the lock of hair and the sacred thread by the Bahûdaka, the lock of hair without thread by the Haṁsa, and allows only the Paramahaṁsa as the highest grade to dispense with lock of hair and sacred thread, or even to shave the head. On this point also difference of opinion exists. Kaṇṭh. 2, 3, 4 demands removal of the hair of the head, Jâb. 5 complete baldness,

[1] Kaṇṭh. 4. [2] Jâb. 4. [3] Sanny. 3, Kaṇṭh. 5.
[4] cp. the translation, *Allgemeine Einleitung*, pp. 270-277.
[5] Kaṇṭh. 2, 3, 5, Âr. 1, 3, 5, Brahma 3.
[6] *s'ikhâ*, Kaṇṭh. 2, 3, Âr. 1, Brahma 3, Par. 1.
[7] Kaṇṭh. 2, Brahma 3, Par. 2. [8] Kaṇṭh. 2, Brahma 3.
[9] Par. 2.

Kaṇṭh. 5 only a lesser tonsure, Sanny. 3 and Kaṇṭh. 5 removal of the hair on the privy parts and armpits. Last of all, the separation from the son takes place, who accompanies his father for a certain distance, after which with festive greetings both turn right round and go their way without looking back; and the son is not permitted to shed tears.[1]

(3) *Dress* and *Equipment*. On these also great differences of opinion exist. The robe should according to Sanny. 3, Kaṇṭh. 5 be dark red, according to Jâb. 5 colourless, according to Kaṇṭh. 2 torn or made of bark, according to Sanny. 4 patched. Âs′r. 4 permits the Bahûdaka to wear a loin-cloth and dark red robe, the Paramahaṁsa only rags and a loin-cloth. Par. 4 requires of the latter that space be his clothing, Jâb. 6 that he should live "naked as he was born." Together with the coat, girdle and thread, the staves also of palâs′a, bilva or as′vattha wood, which serve to distinguish the castes, must be laid aside.[2] In their place the triple staff, composed of three staves twisted together (*tridaṇḍam*, probably as a token of the reconciliation of caste differences), makes its appearance,[3] but even this is sometimes forbidden.[4] We have instead the single staff (token of complete reconciliation),[5] or the staff of bamboo.[6] Even this however is prohibited[7] with the remark that he who carries knowledge alone as his staff is rightly named a man with a single staff. Âsr. 4 introduces system again here by permitting the triple staff to the Bahûdaka, to the Haṁsa the single staff, and allows no staff to the Paramahaṁsa. Similarly in Sanny. 3 a sieve, in Kaṇṭh. 5 a ragged cloth is allowed for the straining of liquid, to prevent the destruction of any living thing; on the contrary, in Jâb. 6 and the verses of Kaṇṭh. 5 even cloth-strainers are forbidden. A covering is permitted by Par. 1, but Par. 2 prohibits this for the highest

[1] Kaṇṭh. 2 and 3. [2] Âr. 5. [3] Sanny. 4.
[4] Kaṇṭh. 5, Jâb. 6, Âr. 2. [5] Par. 1. [6] Âr. 3. [7] Par. 3.

grade. A summary in verse is given of the objects which a less strict observance allows to the Sannyâsin :—

Pot, drinking-cup and flask,
The three supports, a pair of shoes,
A patched robe giving protection
In heat and cold, a loin-cloth,
Bathing drawers and straining cloth,
Triple staff and coverlet.[1]

These same objects, the very verse being repeated, are elsewhere forbidden to the Sannyâsin,[2] and with this the enumeration in the prose of Jâb. 6 agrees. Another passage[3] allows them to the Bahûdaka, and forbids them only to the Paramahaṁsa. The direction of Âr. 5, that he who has renounced the world shall bear the syllable *om* on his limbs, is unique.

(4) *Food.* The Sannyâsin must live by begging,[4] only bread given in charity and broken fruits are to be his food,[5] or water, air and fruits.[6] Food should be asked of all four castes,[7] the distinctions of which have no longer any existence for the Sannyâsin. Âs'r. 4 distinguishes here also four grades; the Kuṭîc'aras are to beg in the houses of their children, the Bahûdakas of well-to-do Brâhman families, and the Paramahaṁsas alone of all four castes. In begging the Sannyâsin is to employ a clay or wooden vessel, or a gourd,[8] but elsewhere the rule is laid down that his belly should form his vessel,[9] his hand,[10] or his belly or hand.[11] He who has renounced the world "shall eat the bread of charity, but give no alms" (*bhikshâs'î na dadyât*, for which might be read with a very slight change *bhikshâs'î 'shad adyât*, "living on the bread of charity he shall eat little").[12] This would be in harmony with other passages, according to which he who has renounced the

[1] Sanny. 4. [2] Kaṇṭh. 5. [3] Âs'r. 4.
[4] Kaṇṭh. 5. [5] Sanny. 4, 5. [6] Sanny. 2, 4.
[7] Kaṇṭh. 2. [8] Âr. 4. [9] Kaṇṭh 5, Jâb. 6.
[10] Kaṇṭh. 2. [11] Âr. 5. [12] Kaṇṭh. 5.

world should use his food only as medicine,[1] should avoid eating sufficient to put on fat, but should remain thin.[2] Nevertheless, should he feel weak, he should not pursue these and other abstinences so far as to give rise to disorder:[3] if he is ill, he should practise self-mortification only in the spirit or by means of words.[4] Elsewhere it is said, extending the theory of the Prâṇâgnihotra:[5]—"That which he eats in the evening is his evening sacrifice, in the morning his morning sacrifice, at the new month his new moon sacrifice, that at the full moon his full moon sacrifice, and when he cuts (afresh) in the spring the hair of his head, his beard, the hair of his body, and his nails, that is his agnishṭoma (a kind of Soma sacrifice")[6]

(5) *Place of abode.* The essential characteristics of the man who has renounced the world are already implied in the three chief names which he bears. As *sannyâsin* he must "cast everything from him," as *bhikshu* live only as a "beggar," and as *parivrâj*, *parivrâjaka* must wander about homeless as a "pilgrim (vagrant)." He is no longer tied to any locality. He has no further interest in dying in *Avimuktam* (a place at Benares that ensures immediate salvation for those who die there), for he bears always with him the *Varaṇâ* and the *Asî* (two streams, between which Benares lies, and from which it derives its name *Vârâṇasî*), as the arches (*varaṇa*) of his eyebrows and his nostrils (*nâsâ*).[7] As a rule he is to make his home by the side of water,[8] on sand-banks in a river or before the doors of a temple,[9] or to sit or lie on the bare earth.[10] According to Jâb. 6, he should "remain homeless in a deserted house, or a temple of the gods, on a heap of grass, or an antheap, or among the roots of a tree, in a potter's

[1] Kaṇṭh. 2, Âr. 3.
[2] Kaṇṭh. 2.
[3] Kaṇṭh. 2.
[4] Jâb. 5.
[5] *sup.* p. 124 f.
[6] Kaṇṭh. 4.
[7] Jâb. 1–2.
[8] Kaṇṭh. 2.
[9] Sanny. 4, Kaṇṭh. 5.
[10] Âr. 4.

shed, by a sacrificial fire, on an island in a river, in a cave in the mountains, a glen, or a hollow tree, by a waterfall, or on the bare earth." He may tarry only one night in a village, only five nights in a town.[1] An exception is allowed in the rainy season.[2] During the four months of rain he may remain in a village or a town;[3] in the remaining eight he is to wander about either alone or in the company of another.[4]

(6) *Occupation.* The Sannyâsin, as we have seen, no longer offers sacrifices, the place of these being taken by the nourishing of his own body,[5] and similarly he continues to live without study of the Veda,[6] without the Vedic texts;[7] but he is to "recite the Âraṇyakam and the Upanishads from all the Vedas."[8] All the texts require of him "bathing, meditation, and purification by sacred waters,"[9] washings at intervals of three days,[10] washings and rinsing of the mouth "with water as the vessel" (*i.e.* without a vessel).[11] In particular there is also enjoined upon him silence,[12] meditation,[13] and the practice of *yoga*.[14] His chief virtues are described as "chastity, abstinence from doing injury, poverty and truthfulness."[15] He says:—"All living creatures are at peace with me, for by me everything has been created."[16] He must not accept gold, or touch it, not even once look at it.[17] He has abandoned all desire, knowledge is his staff, therefore is he rightly named "with a single staff"; he however who takes the wooden staff, because it gives him freedom "to eat of anything," is a false sannyâsin, and goes to hell.[18] He on the

[1] Kaṇṭh. 2; according to Âsr. 4, this rule first becomes binding at the Haṁsa stage.

[2] Kaṇṭh. 5.

[3] Kaṇṭh. 2.; a gloss makes only two of them, cp. Deussen, *Upan.*, p. 699.

[4] Âr. 4. [5] Kaṇṭh. 4. [6] Par. 1, Âr. 1. [7] Âr. 2.

[8] Âr. 2. [9] Sanny. 4, Kaṇṭh. 5. [10] Âr. 2. [11] Kaṇṭh. 2.

[12] Kaṇṭh. 3. [13] Âr. 2. [14] Sanny. 4. [15] Âr. 3.

[16] Âr. 3. [17] Par. 4. [18] Par. 3.

contrary who has truly renounced the world "should bid farewell to lust, anger, desire, infatuation, deceit, pride, envy, self-will, presumption and falsehood."[1] He is "free from the six surges (of saṁsâra :—hunger, thirst, vexation, error, old age and death), and leaves behind him censure, pride, jealousy, deceit, haughtiness, longing, hatred, pleasure, pain, desire, anger, greed, error, joy, disappointment, self-will and everything of the kind; and because his own body is regarded by him merely as a carcase he turns away for ever from this decaying body, which is the cause of doubt, perversity and error, and directs his mind steadfastly to that (Brahman), makes his home in him, and knows of him, who is tranquil, immutable,—'I am that timeless one, consisting wholly of bliss and knowledge, it is I myself, he is my highest state, my lock of hair, my sacred thread.'"[2] He is not elated by praise, does not curse when he is reviled.[3] "He does not attract and he does not cast off; for him there are no longer Vedic texts, or meditation, or worship, or visible and invisible, or joined and disjoined, or I and thou and the world, . . . steadfast in pain, in pleasure without desire, in longing self-restrained, in all things dependent neither on beauty nor ugliness, free from hatred and free from joy. The motions of every impulse have been stilled, he abides only in knowledge, firmly founded in the âtman."[4] "Then he may enter upon the great journey, by abstaining from nourishment, throwing himself into the water or the fire, or choosing a hero's death; or he may betake himself to a hermitage of the aged."[5]

4. *The Yoga*

Emancipation consists in the consciousness of unity with the âtman as first principle of all things. It is essentially on the one hand an annihilation of all desire,

[1] Âr. 4. [2] Par. 2. [3] Kaṇṭh. 5.
[4] Par. 4. [5] Kaṇṭh. 4, Jâb. 5.

and on the other an annihilation of the illusion of a manifold universe. The first, as we saw, is the aim of the *sannyâsa*; to effect the latter by preparatory artificial means is the function of the *yoga*. It is therefore, apart from excrescences and exaggerations, a perfectly intelligible consequence of the doctrine of the Upanishads. For if the highest end is contained in the knowledge of self-identity with the âtman, why should we not attempt to reach it by purposely dissolving the ties that bind to the illusory world of phenomena, and by self-concentration? That the external world derives little or no advantage from the practices of the Yoga does not enter into consideration for a truer ethical judgement.[1] The only real consideration that may be urged against the practices of yoga, which have always been highly esteemed in India, and are to this day widely spread (precisely as they may be urged against the self-imposed acts of penance among the Pietists of the West), consists in this, that they aim at bringing about in an artificial way that which is only thoroughly genuine when it originates naturally and without the assistance of our will. *Tout ce qui n'est naturel est imparfait*, as Napoleon would have said. In other respects the phenomena of yoga are akin not only, as has often been asserted, to certain diseased conditions that exist also among ourselves (hypnotism, catalepsy, etc., upon which we do not enter since the material to hand in the Upanishads does not suggest it), but also with the entirely healthy and joyous phenomenon of æsthetic contemplation. The more than earthly joy which we experience at the sight of the beautiful in nature or in art depends upon a forgetfulness of one's own individuality, and a union of subject and object, similar to that which the yoga endeavours to secure by artificial means. These means we propose now to consider.

[1] *sup.* p. 364.

In post-Vedic times the practice of yoga was developed into a formal system with its own text-book (the sûtras of Patañjali). The rise of this system, as its first beginnings in Kâṭh. 3 and 6, S'vet. 2 and Maitr. 6 show, belongs to the time when the original idealism of the Upanishad teaching began already to harden into the realistic philosophy of the Sâṅkhya. On this foundation, which was far from being adapted to its original conception, the later yoga system was raised. This system therefore lays the chief stress on external means (*sâdhana*), and the external results thereby attained (*vibhûti*); and regards the union with the only real âtman, which was the original aim of the yoga, as a separation (*kaivalyam*) of the purusha from the prakṛiti, dismissing entirely into the background that which was properly its chief concern, the meditation on the âtman by means of the syllable *om*. Only the theism was preserved over from the later Upanishads, in contrast to the chosen basis of the Sâṅkhya; and thus external support was secured for the system, although no real life could ever be fostered on this uncongenial ground.[1] A remarkable testimony to this theistic modification of the Sâṅkhya system in the service of the doctrine of the yoga is given by the C'ûlikâ Upanishad, which, starting from the twenty-five principles of the Sâṅkhya, ranks the Îs'vara with them on purely external grounds "as the twenty-sixth" (or probably by the insertion of âtman as twenty-seventh),[2] and recognises its difference from the purushas only in the freedom with which it drinks from the breasts "of its foster-mother Mâyâ":—

> The children indeed are numberless,
> That drink there of the world of sense,
> Yet one alone drinks of it as God,
> Freely following his own will.[3]

---

[1] *sup*. p. 238 f. [2] C'ûl. 14. [3] C'ûl. 6.

In the sequel we limit ourselves to the *yoga*, as far as we are able to follow it up through the Upanishads, and adopt from the post-Vedic system merely as the framework of our picture the "eight members" (*aṅga*), into which the yoga is divided on the practical side, and of which the five last (with *tarka* as a sixth) are already enumerated in two passages of the Upanishads, though not yet in the regular order.[1] The later eight *aṅgas* are as follows:—(1) *yama*, discipline (consisting in abstinence from doing injury, truthfulness, honesty, chastity, poverty); (2) *niyama*, self-restraint (purity, contentment, asceticism, study, devotion); (3) *âsanam*, sitting (in the right place and in the correct bodily attitude); (4) *prâṇâyâma*, regulation of the breath; (5) *pratyâhâra*, suppression (of the organs of sense); (6) *dhâraṇâ*, concentration (of the attention); (7) *dhyânam*, meditation; (8) *samâdhi*, absorption (complete union with the object of meditation).

These requirements we see already presented separately in the older Upanishads. Thus we have *pratyâhâra* in the direction of Chând. 8. 15, "to bring all his organs to rest in the âtman," and *prâṇâyâma*, when Bṛih. 1. 5. 23 enjoins as the "sole vow" to inhale and exhale. Here and in other passages[2] the regulated breath takes the place of the sacrifice, and seems thenceforward to have been adopted into the yoga as a symbolic act. The word *yoga* in a technical sense first occurs, exclusive of Taitt. 2. 4, in Kâṭh. 2. 12 (*adhyâtma-yoga*), 6. 11, 18, S'vet. 2. 11, 6. 13, Maitr. 6. 18, etc. The true explanation of it as "harnessing, arranging" is evident from the expression *âtmânam yuñjîta* occurring in Mahânâr. 63. 21 and Maitr. 6. 3; while in Maitr. 6. 25 the *yoga* seems to have been conceived as a "union" (between prâṇa and the syllable *om*). The Upanishads quoted contain also the earliest

[1] Maitr. 6. 18, Amṛitab. 6.
[2] *sup*. p. 124.

theory of the yoga practice. Kâṭh. 3. 13, recalling Sâṅkhyan ideas, requires that speech and manas "shall be restrained" (*yac'c'het*) in the buddhi, the buddhi in the mahân which is still distinguished from it, and the latter again in the *avyaktam.* Kâṭh. 6. 10–11 enjoins a fettering (*dhâraṇâ*) of the organs (senses, manas, buddhi), whereby the purusha thus separated from them all may be drawn forth from the body, as the stalk from the bulrush.[1] S'vet. 2. 8–15 discusses already the choice of place,[2] the manner of sitting,[3] the regulation of the breath,[4] the control of the senses and manas in the heart,[5] and mentions the phenomena that accompany and follow yoga.[6] To this is attached the recommendation of the syllable *om*, which occurs as a symbol of Brahman as early as Chând. 1. 1, Taitt. 1. 8, as a vehicle (*âlambanam*) of meditation,[7] as fuel,[8] as bow,[9] or as arrow,[10] in order to pierce the darkness, and to hit the mark in Brahman. The three *morae* (a, u, m), of which the syllable *om* consists, are mentioned first in Pras'na 5, Maitr. 6. 3, while the third and a half mora first occurs as the "moraless" part of the word in Mâṇḍ. 12, as the "head of the syllable om" in Maitr. 6. 23. To these anticipations are attached descriptions of the practice of yoga, which are found in Maitr. 6. 18–30 and in the Yoga Upanishads of the Atharva-Veda. The most important are,—Brahmavidyâ, Kshurikâ, C'ûlikâ ; Nâdabindu, Brahmabindu, Amṛitabindu, Dhyânabindu, Tejobindu ; Yogas'ikhâ, Yogatattva, and Haṁsa ; upon these we base our description, following the later order of the eight members (*yama, niyama, âsanam, prâṇâyâma, pratyâhâra, dhâraṇâ, dhyânam, samâdhi*).

1 6. 17. 2 2. 10. 3 2. 8. 4 2. 9.
5 2. 8, 9. 6 2. 11–13. 7 Kâṭh. 2. 17.
8 S'vet. 1. 14, Dhyânab. 20. 9 Muṇḍ. 2. 2. 4, Dhyânab. 19.
10 Maitr. 6. 24.

(1) *Yama*, restraint, and (2) *niyama*, self-restraint. These two divisions do not yet occur in the enumerations of Maitr. 6. 18 and Amṛitab. 6, possibly because they are tacitly assumed to be universal duties (objective and subjective). The remark of Yogat. 15 might be quoted here with many others to prove that the yogin affords protection to all beings, since he knows them to be his own self; and admonitions like the following :—

From fear, from anger, from indolence,
From excessive wakefulness, excessive sleep,
From too much food, and from starvation
The yogin should constantly protect us.[1]

(3) *Âsanam*, sitting. Stress is laid in the first place on the choice of the right locality. As early as S'vet. 2. 10 it is prescribed for the practice of yoga :—

Let the place be pure, and free also from boulders and sand,
Free from fire, smoke, and pools of water,
Here where nothing distracts the mind or offends the eye,
In a hollow protected from the wind a man should compose himself.

Elsewhere "a pure region,"[2] a "level surface of the ground, pleasant and free from faults,"[3] are required. According to Yogat. 15 yoga should be practised "in a lawful place, quiet, remote, and free from distractions." Kshur. 2, 21 ordains that "a noiseless place" should be chosen. In regard to the mode of sitting, the Upanishads are still free from the extravagant definitions of the later Yoga, which betray external influence. No less than eighty-four modes of sitting are there distinguished. S'vet. 2. 8 prescribes only a triple holding erect (of breast, neck and head), and symmetry of sitting posture. Amṛitab. 18 lays stress upon facing the north (the region of the way of the gods), and enjoins only three modes of sitting, viz.—the lotus seat (*padmâsanam*, *i.e.* sitting with the

[1] Amṛitab. 27. [2] Maitr. 6. 30. [3] Amṛitab 17.

legs bent underneath, the usual method of sitting in India), the cruciform seat (*svastikam*), and the auspicious seat (*bhadrâsanam*); the two last differ only slightly from the first. Yogas'. 2 directs the choice of the lotus posture "or otherwise as seems good to him," with attention concentrated on the tip of the nose, hands and feet closely joined. Amṛitab. 22 commands the yogin to sit firm and motionless, "from every side above and below his gaze turned fixedly on himself." Kshur. 2 lays stress only on "the right mode of sitting." Kshur. 4 speaks of a correct inclination of the breast, hips, face and neck towards the heart. A special kind of bodily posture is described in the concluding verse of Sanny. 4. *Âsanam*, like *yama* and *niyama*, is not yet reckoned in the Upanishads as an *aṅga* of the yoga, and the latter has therefore only six divisions (*shaḍaṅgo yoga' uc'yate*),[1] not eight as later on. They are enumerated in Maitr. 6. 18, viz.—*prâṇâyâma*, *pratyâhâra*, *dhyânam*, *dhâraṇâ*, *tarka*, *samâdhi*. The same list, but with the transfer of *prâṇâyâma* to the third place, recurs in Amṛitab. 6. It is strange that both lists place *dhâraṇâ* not before, but after *dhyânam;* this may be due to some other conception of these ideas than that which later became usual. Both lists name *tarka*, reflection, in the fifth place, and this in Amṛitab. 16 is defined as "meditation, which is not contrary to the teaching," and explained by the commentator in one place [2] as control of the *dhyânam*, but elsewhere as the knowledge free from doubt which proceeds from the *dhyânam*.

(4) *Prâṇâyâma*, regulation of the breath. This is distinguished into *rec'aka*, *pûraka*, *kumbhaka*.[3] In harmony

[1] Amṛitab. 6 and Maitr. 6. 18.

[2] On Maitr. 6. 18.

[3] They are mentioned also in the Yoga sûtras 2. 50, a fact which Garbe contests, since only other names are chosen, after a manner that the sûtras affect, as *vâhya-abhyantara-stambha-vṛitti*.

with the chief passage,[1] (1) *rec'aka* is exspiration, which ought to be prolonged;[2] (2) *pûraka* is inspiration, described in Yogat. 12, effected either through one nostril, the other being closed with the finger,[3] or through the mouth pointed like the stalk of a lotus;[4] (3) *kumbhaka*, retention of the breath in the lungs,[5] whence apparently it pervades all the limbs of the body by means of meditation.[6] *Rec'aka* should be accompanied with the thought of S'iva, *pûraka* with that of Vishṇu, *kumbhaka* with that of Brahmân.[7] *Prâṇâyâma* effects the destruction of all sins.[8]

(5) *Pratyâhâra*, suppression of the organs of sense, is mentioned as early as Chând. 8. 15. As the tortoise draws in its limbs,[9] so are all the senses withdrawn into the man together with the active manas, for these are only emanations of the âtman,[10] are checked,[11] are shut up in the heart,[12] and are reduced thereby to tranquillity.[13] The objects of sense in him are thus brought to rest,[14] and the senses are restrained as in sleep.[15]

(6) *Dhâraṇâ*, concentration, affects the manas, which as the organ of the will hinders emancipation, unless it is checked, locked up in the heart, reduced to ineffectiveness, and so deliverance from the manas is attained.[16] The manas should therefore be subjected to external restraint,[17] curbed in every direction,[18] immersed in the self,[19] until it is entirely dissolved therein.[20] The imprisonment of the manas in the heart is taught also in Kshur. 3; in other respects also this Upanishad derives its name from the fact that it teaches a *kshurikâ*

[1] Amṛitab. 10 f. [2] Kshur. 5. [3] Amṛitab. 19.
[4] Amṛitab. 13, Dhyânab. 11. [5] Amṛitab. 12, Yogat. 13.
[6] Kshur. 4, 6 f. [7] Dhyânab. 11–13. [8] Amṛitab. 7–8.
[9] Kshur. 3, Yogat. 12. [10] Amṛitab. 5. [11] Kâṭh. 3. 13.
[12] S'vet. 2. 8. [13] Kâṭh. 6. 10. [14] Maitr. 6. 19.
[15] Maitr. 6. 25. [16] Brahmab. 1–5, Maitr. 6. 34.
[17] Maitr. 6. 19; a higher kind of *dhâraṇâ* is described in what follows, 6. 20.
[18] Yogas. 3. [19] Amṛitab. 15. [20] Nâdab. 18.

dhâraṇâ, a concentration of the attention of the manas on the several limbs and veins of the body, whereby they are in turn cut off from it by the knife of manas, and thus freedom from desire is attained.

(7) *Dhyânam*, meditation. Although even *svâdhyâya* is found among the niyamas,[1] yet as a rule the study of the Veda is very lightly esteemed by the yogin. He is not proud of brâhmanical descent, or of knowledge of the Scriptures,[2] he has in the search for true knowledge thoroughly examined the books, and found in them only chaff instead of wheat.[3] Therefore he throws the books away, as though they burned him.[4] The sole wisdom is that which teaches how to reduce the manas to impotence in the heart, "the other is learned trash."[5] The place of knowledge of the Veda is taken by meditation on that word, which "all the Vedas proclaim to us,"[6] the *praṇava*, *i.e.* the sacred syllable *om*. It is the best support,[7] the bow off which the soul as the arrow flies to Brahman,[8] the arrow which is shot from the body as bow in order to pierce the darkness,[9] the upper fuel which with the body as the lower fuel is kindled by the fire of the vision of God,[10] the net with which the fish of prâṇa is drawn out, and sacrificed in the fire of the âtman,[11] the ship on which a man voyages over the ether of the heart,[12] the chariot which bears him to the world of Brahman.[13] Its three *morae* a u m are fire, sun and wind,[14] they are the essence of all things.[15] He who meditates on them by one mora gains the world of men, by two the pitṛiyâna, by three the devayâna.[16] Besides the three morae the word has a fourth "moraless" part,[17] which forms the crown of the

[1] *sup.* p. 385.
[2] Tejob. 13.
[3] Brahmab. 18.
[4] Amṛitab. 1.
[5] Brahmab. 5.
[6] Kâṭh. 2. 15.
[7] Kâṭh. 2. 17.
[8] Muṇḍ. 2. 2. 4.
[9] Maitr. 6. 24.
[10] S'vet. 1. 14.
[11] Maitr. 6. 26.
[12] Maitr. 6. 28.
[13] Amṛitab. 2.
[14] Maitr. 6. 3.
[15] Maitr. 6. 5.
[16] Pras'na 5.
[17] Mâṇḍ. 12.

syllable om,[1] and which later on is described as the third and a half mora.[2] It is this half mora which leads to the supreme goal;[3] it is represented by the point (*bindu*) of the anusvâra, the point of strength, which bears the deepest meaning,[4] and sounds in the echo (*nâda*), the toneless *m*-syllable (*asvara makâra*),[5] which in one passage is described as completely silent, without noise, tone, consonant or vowel,[6] but in another sounds like the echo of a tin vessel when struck, or of a bell,[7] or like the prolonged dripping of oil, or the after tones of the notes of a bell,[8] or again may be produced in ten different ways, of which the last is recommended, sounding like a peal of thunder.[9] Compare also on the mention of the echo Atharvas'ikhâ 1. With increasing exaggeration there are ascribed to the syllable *om* five morae,[10] three morae and three echoes,[11] three morae with a half mora anusvâra and an echo,[12] three morae and four half morae,[13] and finally in a different sense twelve component parts.[14] The Upanishads are never weary of offering interpretations of the three or three and a half morae in allegorical style as Agni, Vâyu, the Sun, and Varuṇa,[15] as the three worlds, three Vedas, three fires, three gods, three daily periods, three measures, or three guṇas;[16] so that meditation on the half mora (the point or the echo) was valued far above all these things.

Essentially it was the unknowableness of the first principle of the universe, the Brahman, thus early entering into consciousness, and the impossibility of

1 Maitr. 6. 23.
2 Nâdab. 1, Dhyânab. 17, Yogat. 7, etc.
3 Yogat. 7.
4 Tejob. 1.
5 Amṛitab. 4.
6 Amṛitab. 24.
7 Brahmavidyâ 13.
8 Dhyânab. 18.
9 Haṁsa 4.
10 Amṛitab. 30.
11 Pranou Up., *Upan.*, p. 863.
12 Râmott. 2.
13 Râmott. 5.
14 Nâdab. 8–11, Kshur. 3, Amṛitab. 23, Nṛisiṁhott. 2 (cp. Deussen, *Upan.*, p. 782 f.).
15 Nâdab. 6–7.
16 Brahmavidyâ 4–7, Yogat. 6–7, Atharvas'iras 5, Atharvas'ikhâ 1, etc.

expressing it by word, conception or illustration (*neti, neti*), which had compelled the choice of something so entirely meaningless as the syllable *om*; but it was precisely on that account especially fitted to be the symbol of Brahman. The same consideration however led to a further advance beyond even the syllable, first to the half mora, and then even beyond this :—

> Higher than the original syllable
> Is the point, the echo higher than this;
> The syllable vanishes with the sound,
> The highest state is silent.[1]

This highest state, which is not expressed by any word or combination of words,[2] cannot be meditated on by means of *om*, but only in absolute silence. By the syllable *om* a man may only "enter upon" the yoga.[3] It is the chariot, which is abandoned where the highway ends and the footpath begins.[4] *Om* is never more than the "Brahman word," beyond which lies still the Supreme.[5] "Here the word signifies the sound *om*; ascending by this man attains to nothingness in that which is not a word," like the sap of the flowers in the liquid honey.[6] Thus the eighth and highest stage of yoga is reached.

(8) *Samâdhi*, absorption. Meditation becomes absorption when subject and object, the soul and God, are so completely blended into one that the consciousness of the separate subject altogether disappears, and there succeeds that which in Maitr. 6. 20–21 is described as *nirâtmakatvam* (selflessness). The empirical and particularising view, with reminiscence of ideas like those in Chând. 8. 6. 5–6, Taitt. 1. 6, looks upon this union as an ascent of the soul that meditates from the heart through the vein *sushumnâ* and the *Brahmaran-*

[1] Dhyânab. 4. [2] Tejob. 7. [3] Brahmab. 7.
[4] Amṛitab. 3. [5] Brahmab. 17. [6] Maitr. 6. 22.

dhram to union with the Brahman who fills the universe. Numerous descriptions of this progress are given, not always mutually consistent. The heart is represented as a lotus flower, a view already prevalent from the time of Chând. 8. 1. 1.[1] "It hangs down, encompassed by the veins, quite (*â*) like the calyx of a flower," a hot fire burns in it, and from its midst a tongue of flame rises mounting upwards.[2] More detailed descriptions of this lotus flower of the heart are found in Dhyânab. 14–16, Haṁsa 8 and frequently. At the meditation on the *a* the lotus flower becomes bright, opens at the *u*, rings gently at the *m*, and with the half mora ceases to move.[3] In the body (in the heart) there is a sun, in this a fire, and in this a tongue of flame which is the supreme god.[4] This last in the meditation of the yoga pushes its way through the sun of the heart:—

> Then it winds upwards
> Through the gleaming gate of the *sushumnâ*;
> Breaking through the arch of the skull,
> It gazes finally on the Supreme.

According to Maitr. 6. 38, there is in the heart a sun, in the latter a moon, in this a fire, in this again the *sattvam*, and in this the soul, which forces its way through all the coverings named, bursts through the fourfold woven sheaths of Brahman (*annamaya, prâṇamaya, manomaya, vijñânamaya*),[5] voyages with the boat *om* over the ether of the heart,[6] and so finally attains to the vision of the Supreme. Compare also the description of the ether of the heart, and its penetration of it.[7] We should thus have to understand in Brahmavidyâ 8–10 also by *s'aṅkha* not as the scholiast does the valves of the brain but of the heart. In them, according to this passage, the *a* shines as sun, in the latter the *u*

[1] *sup.* p. 287.
[2] Mahânâr. 11. 8–12.
[3] Yogat. 9–11.
[4] Yogas'. 4–7.
[5] Taitt. 2, Maitr. 6. 28, 38.
[6] Maitr. 6. 28.
[7] Maitr. 6. 22, 27.

as moon, in this again the *m* as fire, while above this is the half mora as a tongue of flame.

With regard also to the ascent of the soul from the heart very numerous representations are given. According to Maitr. 7. 11, by meditation on *om*, the *tejas*, *i.e.* the individual soul (cp. the second of the verses quoted below) bursts forth, ascends on high like smoke rising in a single column, and spreads itself abroad like one branch after another (unceasingly). Amṛitab. 26 represents the prâṇa as ascending by means of the silent *om* "through the gates of the heart and of the wind, the gates which lead upward, and the portals of emancipation." According to Dhyânab. 22, the half mora like a rope draws the manas upwards from the fountain of the lotus of the heart by the path of the veins until between the eyebrows it is lost in the Supreme. Brahmavidyâ 11–12 describes how by means of *om* the sun of the heart and the 72000 veins[1] are penetrated, the journey upwards is made on the *sushumnâ* (the carotis), and the head is broken through, and the man continues to exist as the giver of health to all beings, pervading the universe. The conception of Kshur. 8 f. is similar, according to which the prâṇa climbs up from the navel to the heart on the *sushumnâ*, like the spider on its thread (the same illustration as in Maitr. 6. 22), and so further still from the heart upwards; whereupon with the knife of the power of yoga it cuts through all the limbs, divides the 72000 and the 101 veins with the exception of the (101st) *sushumnâ*, leaves behind there its good and evil states, and ascends upon it to its termination in Brahman. Thus the yogin according to Maitr. 6. 19 strips off from himself all ideas, all consciousness, the entire psychical framework which is already separated from the external world (the *liṅgam*

[1] Bṛih. 2. 1. 19.

nirâs'rayam, cp. Sâṅkhya-K. 41) and "is merged in the supreme, indescribable, ineffable Brahman":[1]—

> Yet the joy, which with the gradual decay
> Of the mind is content with its own witness to itself,
> Is Brahman pure and eternal,
> The true way, the true world.[2]

He who "in this way at all times duly prosecutes the yoga" after three months attains to knowledge, after four to the vision of the gods, after five to their strength, and after six their absolute nature.[3] After six months he "gains a part in the perfect might of yoga."[4] By continued meditation on the morae his body by a process of gradual refinement becomes composed in turn of earth, water, fire, air and ether, until finally he thinks only in and through himself (*c'intayed âtmanâ âtmani*).[5]

> He knows nothing further of sickness, old age, or suffering,
> Who gains a body out of the fire of yoga.
>
> Activity, health, freedom from desire,
> A fair countenance, beauty of voice,
> A pleasant odour, fewness of secretions,
> Therein at first the yoga displays its power.[6]

The thought of Yoga delivers from all sins,[7] though the sins were "like mountains rising many miles high":[8]—

> He who through thousands of births
> Does not exhaust the guilt of his sins,
> Sees finally by the yoga
> The destruction of the saṁsâra even here.[9]

---

[1] Maitr. 6. 22.
[2] Maitr. 6. 24.
[3] Amṛitab. 28 f.
[4] Maitr. 6. 28.
[5] Amṛitab. 30–31.
[6] S'vet. 2. 12–13
[7] Yogat. 1.
[8] Dhyânab. 3.
[9] Yogas'. 10.

XVII. Retrospect of the Upanishads and their Teaching

1. *Introduction*

The Upanishads (apart from the later and less important books) have been handed down to us as Vedânta, *i.e.* as the concluding part of the Brâhmaṇas and Âraṇyakas, which teach and expound allegorically the ritual of sacrifice. They are nevertheless radically opposed to the entire Vedic sacrificial cult, and the older they are the more markedly does this opposition declare itself. "He who worships another deity (than the âtman, the self) and says 'It is one, and I am another,' is not wise. But he is like a house-dog of the gods. Just, then, as many house-dogs are of use to men, so each individual man is useful to the gods. If one house-dog only is stolen it is disagreeable, how much more if many! Therefore it is not pleasing to them that men should know this."[1]

This antagonism of the âtman doctrine to the sacrificial cult leads us to anticipate that at the first it would be greeted with opposition by the Brâhmans. An instance of this is preserved to us in Yâjñavalkhya, who in Bṛih. 3–4 meets with jealousy and contradiction at the hands of the Brâhmans, but with enthusiastic assent from King Janaka. This antagonism may have been the reason why the doctrine of the âtman, although originally proceeding from Brâhmans like Yâjñavalkhya, received its earliest fostering and development in the more liberal-minded circles of the Kshatriyas; while among the Brâhmans it was on the contrary shunned for a longer period as a mystery (*upanishad*), and continued therefore to be withheld from them. The Brâhman Bâlâki does not know that the âtman is Brahman, and is instructed on the point by king

[1] Bṛih. 1. 4. 10.

Ajâtas'atru.[1] Six Brâhmans "of great learning" first gain from king As'vapati the knowledge that they must seek the âtman vais'vânara before all else in themselves.[2] Similarly the Brâhman Nârada is instructed by Sanatkumâra the god of war,[3] and three Brâhmans by king Pravâhaṇa.[4] While the same king Pravâhaṇa enlightens the Brâhman Uddâlaki Âruṇi on the subject of the transmigration of souls with the remark:—"This knowledge has never up to the present time been in the possession of a Brâhman."[5]

According to these testimonies, which carry all the greater weight because they have reached us through the Brâhmans themselves, the Brâhmans had received the most important elements of the science of the âtman first from the Kshatriyas, and then in course of time had attached them to their own Vedic curriculum, so that the Upanishads became what they now are, the *Vedânta.* The hostility towards the sacrificial cult was then by means of allegorical interpretations, in which each school struck out its own path,[6] concealed rather than laid to rest. That the Brâhmans later on asserted a claim to the doctrine of the âtman as their peculiar heritage seems to be asserted by the verse:—" Only he who knows the Veda comprehends the great omnipresent âtman."[7] In any case the progress and regular development of the âtman doctrine was in their hands. And the oldest Upanishads are to be regarded as the latest fruits of this activity, to which were added in course of time other works produced in the same spirit, which with more or less right bore the names of *Upanishad* and *Vedânta.* Probably only at a considerably later period did they assume a written form. It seems a fair inference from Kâth. 2. 7–9:

[1] Bṛih. 2. 1 (Kaush. 4).
[2] Chând. 5. 11–18.
[3] Chând. 7.
[4] Chând. 1. 8–9.
[5] Chând. 5. 3–10 (Bṛih. 6. 2); Bṛih. 6. 2. 8.
[6] *sup.* p. 120 f.
[7] Taitt. Br. 3. 12. 9. 7.

—"Without a teacher there is no access here,"—that the older Upanishads were at that time not yet committed to writing.

No satisfactory chronology of the Upanishads can be framed, since each of the principal Upanishads contains earlier and later texts side by side with one another. On the whole and generally, however, the classification and order here adopted[1] may be expected to correspond also to the historical succession. A more precise confirmation of this is to be inferred from the general course of our exposition. Of especial weight in our view is the proof advanced that Bṛih. 1–4 (not the appendix 5–6) together with S'atap. Br. 10. 6 is older than all other texts of importance, especially older than the Chândogya Upanishad. The last confessedly is dependent not only on S'atap. Br. 10,[2] but also on the Yâjñavalkhya texts,[3] as is proved by the fact that often thoughts of the latter are reproduced by the Chând. Up., and at the same time misunderstood.[4] Thus we shall have to look for the earliest form of the doctrine of the Upanishads above all in the Yâjñavalkhya discourses of the Bṛihadâraṇyaka.

2. *Idealism as the Fundamental Conception of the Upanishads*

In the conception of unity as it is expressed in the words of Ṛigv. 1. 164. 46:—*ekam sad viprâ bahudhâ vadànti*, "the poets give many names to that which is one only,"—the fundamental thought of the whole teaching of the Upanishads lay already hidden in germ. For this verse, strictly understood, really asserts that all plurality, consequently all proximity in space, all succession in time, all relation of cause and effect, all interdependence of subject and object, rests only upon words (*vadanti*) or,

[1] *sup.* pp. 23–26.
[2] Chând. 3. 14, 4. 3, 5. 11–18.
[3] Bṛih. 3–4 compared with 1. 4, 2. 4.
[4] cp. *sup.* pp. 205 f., 233 f., 105 f.

as was said later, is "a mere matter of words (*vâc'âram-bhaṇa*),[1] and that only unity is in the full sense real. An attempt was made in the first instance to conceive this unity in the mythological idea of Prajâpati, then in the ritualistic idea of Brahman, and finally without allowing the latter to drop, and by a mere strengthening of the subjective element already contained in it, in the philosophical idea of the âtman. But even the âtman idea is not at first free from definitions (of the gods, Prajâpati, and Brahman) that it has inherited from the mythology. Thus for example in S'atap. Br. 10. 6. 3, after the âtman has been described as pervading all worlds, and at the same time, inconceivably small, dwelling at the centre of a man's being, it is said in conclusion :—"He is my soul, to him on my departure hence, to this soul shall I enter in." Everyone feels the contradiction in these words, and that there is no need of entering in after death if the âtman really "is my soul." The first to recognise this, and to grasp the conception of the âtman in its complete subjective precision, who therefore laid the foundation of the Upanishad doctrine proper, is the Yâjñavalkhya (himself mythical throughout) of the Bṛihadâraṇyaka Upanishad.

The teaching of Yâjñavalkhya (whatever may lie concealed behind this name) is a daring, uncompromising, eccentric idealism (comparable to that of Parmenides), which is summed up in three propositions :—

(1) *The âtman is the knowing subject within us.* "In truth, O Gârgî, this imperishable one sees but is not seen, hears but is not heard, comprehends but is not comprehended, knows but is not known. There is beside him none that sees, there is none that hears beside him, there is none that comprehends beside him, there is none that knows beside him. In truth, in this imperishable one is space inwoven and interwoven."[2] Here the above funda-

[1] Chând. 6. 1. 4.

[2] Bṛih. 3. 8. 11.

mental proposition is clearly expressed. At the same time two further propositions are inferred from it, which other passages abundantly confirm.

(2) *The âtman, as the knowing subject, is itself unknowable.* "Thou canst not see the seer of seeing, thou canst not hear the hearer of hearing," etc.[1] "How could he know him through whom all this is known, how could he know the knower?"[2]

(3) *The âtman is the sole reality.* In it, as the above passage declares, space with all that it contains is inwoven and interwoven. "He who has seen, heard, comprehended and known the âtman, by him this entire universe is known."[3] "The universe is given up to him who knows the universe apart from the âtman."[4] Only "where there is as it were duality does one see another,"[5] etc. "There is however no second outside of him, no other distinct from him for him to see":[6]—

> In the mind should this be perceived,
> Here there is no plurality anywhere;
> From death to death is he led blindly,
> Who here gazes on a plurality.[7]

These three thoughts are the kernel of the Upanishad teaching, and with it became permanently the innermost kernel of the entire religious and philosophical belief of India. This kernel however was eventually surrounded by a husk which, growing ever thicker as time advanced, concealed it in many ways, until finally on the one hand the kernel utterly perished and only the husk remained (the Sâṅkhya), while on the other (the Vedânta) an attempt was made to separate absolutely the two elements by distinguishing between a higher esoteric knowledge (*parâ vidyâ*) and a lower exoteric (*aparâ vidyâ*). This

[1] Bṛih. 3. 4. 2. [2] Bṛih. 2. 4. 14. [3] Bṛih. 2. 4. 5. [4] Bṛih. 2. 4. 6.
[5] Bṛih. 2. 4. 14. [6] Bṛih. 4. 3. 23. [7] Bṛih. 4. 4. 19.

process is quite intelligible. For the ideas of Yâjñavalkhya, which depend upon immediate intuition, though they won a hearing in the consciousness of his contemporaries and of posterity, yet did not find this consciousness unoccupied, but already in the possession of two elements, to which they had to accommodate themselves. The first was the tradition bequeathed by the past, the second was the empirical view of the universe and its orderly constitution in space, time and causal relations, which is natural to us all. The entire subsequent development with its phenomena often apparently inconsistent is completely explained by a gradually increasing accommodation to these two elements. This we propose to show briefly in the following pages for the different parts of the teaching of the Upanishads.

3. *Theology* (*Doctrine of Brahman or the Âtman*).

The âtman is the knowing subject within us. This knowing subject is "the loftiest height of all that can be described as âtman" (*sarvasya âtmanaḥ parâyaṇam*).[1] To this height, attained in the teaching of Yâjñavalkhya, Indian thought has climbed, with a gradual intensifying of the subjective element, through conceptions of *purusha* (man), *prâṇa* (life), *âtman* (self), to which were attached the more symbolical representations of the first principle of the universe as *âkâs'a* (space), *manas* (will), *âditya* (sun), etc. In these conceptions the thought of the times preceding the Upanishads, and in part also of these times themselves, moves. Perhaps, therefore, it may be possible in the future to distinguish successfully those portions which belong to a period before the recognition of the âtman as knowing subject from those which, like all that succeeds, have come under the influence of the thought of Yâjñavalkhya. In the older texts the ultimate principle

[1] Bṛih. 3. 9. 10.

is still the *purusha-prâṇa*,[1] the *prâṇa*,[2] *âditya*,[3] the *âkâs'a*,—"It is the âkâs'a from which all these living beings proceed, and into which they again return, the âkâs'a is older than they all, the âkâs'a is the ultimate starting-point."[4] Combinations also occur. For example, when the âtman (still transcendentally conceived) is described as the "*prâṇasya âtmâ*," and as *mano-maya*, *prâṇa-s'arîra*, *bhâ-rûpa*, *âkâs'a-âtman*;[5] or when it is said:—"Brahman is life (*prâṇa*), Brahman is joy (*kam* = *ânanda*), Brahman is extension (*kham* = *âkâs'a*)."[6]

It is otherwise in the later texts. Now it is no longer the *purusha* that is the first principle, but the *âtman* that draws it from the primeval waters;[7] no longer the *âkâs'a*, but that which is in it;[8] no longer the *prâṇa*, but the *bhûman*, the "unlimited," reached by prolonged and deepening insight into the nature of the prâṇa, *i.e.* the knowing subject which comprehends everything in itself, nothing outside of itself:—"When no other (outside of self) is seen, no other is heard, no other is known, that is the infinite; when he sees, hears or knows another, that is the finite."[9] The revolution is very clearly seen when in Ait. 1 it is no longer the *prâṇa-purusha*[10] that makes its appearance as the ultimate principle, but the âtman, and the latter is then explained as the consciousness that comprehends all things in itself (*prajñâ*).[11] Still more clearly does it appear in Kaush. 3–4, where the equation "*prâṇa* = *prajñâ*," which is only intelligible as arising from a compromise between series of heterogeneous conceptions, is repeatedly emphasised. All these changes seem to have been carried out under the influence of the

[1] Ait. Âr. 2. 1–3.
[2] Bṛih. 1. 1–3, Chând. 1. 2–3, 4. 3, Kaush. 2.
[3] Chând. 3.
[4] Chând. 1. 9. 1.
[5] S'atap. Br. 10. 6. 3 (Chând. 3. 14).
[6] Chând. 4. 10. 5.
[7] Ait. 1. 1.
[8] *tasmin yad antar*, Chând. 8. 1; *te yad antarâ*, 8. 14.
[9] Chând. 7. 15–24.
[10] As formerly in Ait. Âr. 2. 1–3.
[11] Ait. 3.

thought, in its first original freshness in the discourses of Yâjñavalkhya, that the âtman is the knowing subject which, itself unknowable, is conceived as sustaining all things in itself. How entirely this thought dominated the whole succeeding development of Indian theology, a few examples may show.

(1) *The âtman is the knowing subject.* He is "the spirit, consisting of knowledge, *vijñânamaya*, shining within in the heart,"[1] the light that enlightens when sun, moon, stars and fire are extinguished,[2] the "light of lights,"[3] the light "which is here within in men," and at the same time shines on yonder side of heaven in the highest, the highest of all worlds,[4] the "supreme light," into which the soul enters in deep sleep, and "issues forth in its own form."[5] And of this light of consciousness, which first invests all with intelligibility, we are to think when it is said :—

> There no sun shines, nor moon, nor glimmer of stars,
> Nor yonder lightning, earthly fire is quenched;
> All other light is inferior to him who alone gives light,
> The whole universe shines with his brightness.[6]

This light that alone is self-shining is the "seer" (*vipas'cit*), who, according to Kâṭh. 2. 18, neither is born nor dies, the "all-beholder" (*paridrashṭar*),[7] the "spectator" (*sâkshin*), as the âtman is so frequently called in the later Upanishads.[8]

(2) *The âtman as the knowing subject can never become an object for us, and is therefore itself unknowable.* "Thou canst not see the seer of seeing," etc.[9] Whatever conception we may form of it, it is always said :—*neti, neti*, "it is not so, it is not so."[10] It is that "before which

[1] Bṛih. 4. 3. 7 f. [2] Bṛih. 4. 3. 2–6. [3] Bṛih. 4. 4. 16, Muṇḍ. 2. 2. 9
[4] Chând. 3. 13. 7. [5] Chând. 8. 3. 4, 8. 12. 3.
[6] Kâṭh. 5. 15, S'vet. 6. 14, Muṇḍ. 2. 2. 10. [7] Pras'na 6. 5.
[8] From S'vet. 6. 14 and onwards. [9] Bṛih. 3. 4. 2.
[10] Bṛih. 4. 2. 4, 4. 4. 22, 4. 5. 15, 3. 9. 26, 2. 3. 6.

words and thought recoil, not finding it;"[1] "not known by the wise, known by the ignorant."[2]

> Not by speech, not by thought,
> Not by sight is he comprehended;
> "He is," by this word alone
> And in no other way is he comprehended.[3]

The âtman therefore can only be defined negatively. He is "not big and not slender, not short and not long, not red and not fluid, not cloudy and not dark, not wind and not ether, not adhesive, without taste or smell, without eye or ear, without speech, without understanding, without vital force and without breath, without mouth and without size, without inner or outer;[4] invisible, incomprehensible, without pedigree, colourless, without eyes or ears, without hands or feet."[5] The threefold definition also as "being thought and bliss" (*sac'-c'id-ânanda*), by which a later age characterised the âtman, and to the separate elements of which reference is frequently made even in the older Upanishads,[6] is essentially only negative. For the "being" of the âtman is no being as revealed in experience, and in an empirical sense is rather a not-being; and similarly the "thought" is only the negation of all objective being, and the "bliss" the negation of all suffering, as this exists in deep dreamless sleep. On the observation of which last state, as was shown,[7] this description was originally based.

(3) *The âtman is the sole reality* (*satyam, satyasya satyam*); for it is the metaphysical unity which is manifested in all empirical plurality. This unity however is not to be found elsewhere than in ourselves, in our consciousness, in which, as with splendid elaboration Bṛih. 3. 8 shows, the whole of space with all that it contains, with earth atmosphere and heaven, is

[1] Taitt. 2. 4. [2] Kena 11. [3] Kâṭh. 6. 12. [4] Bṛih. 3. 8. 8.
[5] Muṇḍ 1. 1. 6. [6] *sup.* pp. 128–146. [7] *sup.* p. 142 f.

"inwoven and interwoven." Therefore with the knowledge of the âtman (the reference here is not to knowledge in an empirical sense) all is known,[1] as with the comprehension of the instrument all its notes are comprehended. He is abandoned by men, gods and all worlds, who knows a universe outside of the âtman.[3] All besides him exists only "as it were" (*iva*). There is really no plurality,[4] and no becoming, "change is a mere matter of words, a simple name."[5] The later Upanishads breathe the same spirit; the entire universe should be immersed in God (*i.e.* the âtman);[6] nature is a mere *mâyâ* (illusion);[7] and the striking remark is added that no demonstration of the existence of a duality is ever possible, and that only the timeless âtman (the knowing subject) admits of proof.[8]

4. *Cosmology and Psychology*

PANTHEISM.—Metaphysical knowledge impugns the existence of any reality outside of the âtman, *i.e.* the consciousness. The empirical view on the contrary teaches that a manifold universe exists external to us. From a combination of these antagonistic propositions originated the doctrine which in all the Upanishads occupies the largest space, and which may conveniently be described as pantheism (though in its origin very different from the pantheism of Europe),—the universe is real, and yet the âtman remains the sole reality, for the âtman is the universe. This identity of universe and âtman is already taught by Yâjñavalkhya (who is as little able as Parmenides to avoid placing himself again temporarily at the empirical standpoint), when he

[1] Bṛih. 2. 4. 5, Chând. 6. 1. 2, Muṇḍ. 1. 1. 3.
[2] Bṛih. 2. 4. 7–9.
[3] Bṛih. 2. 4. 6.
[4] Bṛih. 4. 4. 19, Kâṭh. 4. 10–11.
[5] Chând. 6. 1. 4 f., cp. 8. 1. 3.
[6] Îs'â 1.
[7] S'vet. 4. 10.
[8] Nṛisiṁhott. 9.

celebrates the âtman as the *antaryâmin*;[1] or when he describes how the âtman upholds and maintains sun and moon, heaven and earth, the entire universe and its frame;[2] or when the knowing subject in us is made suddenly to expand into the universe around us on every side.[3] The later passages are numerous and do not need to be repeated here, which identify the âtman as the infinitely small within us with the infinitely great outside of us; and in this way the identity of the two, the âtman and the universe, is incessantly emphasised, as though it were a matter which stood greatly in need of emphasis.

Cosmogony.—None the less the equation "âtman = universe" remained very obscure. The one âtman and the manifold universe, often as they were brought together, always fell asunder again. A natural step therefore was taken, when more and more as time went on instead of this unintelligible identity the familiar empirical category of causality made its appearance, by virtue of which the âtman was represented as the cause chronologically antecedent, and the universe as its effect, its creation; and thus a connection with the ancient Vedic cosmogony became possible. Such a connection is not yet to be traced in Bṛih. 1. 4, where the cosmological form merely serves to explain the dependence of all the phenomena of the universe on the âtman. It is present however in all probability in Chând. 3. 19, 6. 2, Taitt. 2. 6, Ait. 1. 1, etc. It is characteristic at this point that the âtman, after having evolved the universe from himself, enters himself into it as soul. "That deity resolved:—'Verily into these three deities (heat, water, food) I will enter with this living self'";[4] "After he had created the universe he entered into it";[5] "He reflected:—'How

[1] Bṛih. 3. 7.
[2] Bṛih. 3. 8. 9.
[3] Bṛih. 4. 2. 4.
[4] Chând. 6. 3. 2.
[5] Taitt. 2. 6.

could this subsist without me?' . . . accordingly he cleft here the crown of the head, and entered in through this gate."[1] The individual soul maintains even at this stage its identity with the âtman. It is not, like everything else, a created work of the âtman; but it is the âtman himself, as he enters into the world that he has created. A distinction between the supreme and the individual soul does not even yet exist.

THEISM.—Theism is a further and chronologically later stage of development, which first arises at the point at which the supreme and individual souls appear contrasted with one another. This was early anticipated;[2] but later on the individual soul became more and more definitely opposed to the supreme soul as "another."[3] At the same time a theory of predestination was established, as an inevitable consequence of theism:—

> Only by him whom he chooses is he comprehended;
> To him the âtman reveals his nature.[4]

The chief monument of this theism is the S'vetâs'vatara Upanishad. It must be remembered however that here all the earlier stages of development, the idealistic, pantheistic and cosmogonistic, continue to exist side by side; as indeed generally in the religious sphere the old is accustomed to assert its time-honoured right by the side of the new, the fruits of which are readily seen in far-reaching inner contradictions.

ATHEISM and DEISM (Sâṅkhya and Yoga Systems).—With the recognition of a real universe external to the âtman, and the division of the latter into the supreme soul and a multitude of individual souls, the preliminary conditions of the later Sâṅkhya system were satisfied.

[1] Ait. 1. 3. 11. [2] By passages like Bṛih. 4. 4. 22, Kaush. 3. 8 (*ad fin.*).
[3] First in Kâṭh. 1. 3, then S'vet. 4. 6–7, 5. 8, etc.
[4] Kâṭh. 2. 23 (Muṇḍ. 3. 2. 3).

For that division necessarily led to the destruction of the one branch, viz.:—the supreme soul, since from the very beginning this had in reality derived its vitality from the existing fact of individual souls. When powers of creation and movement were assigned to matter itself God became superfluous, and there were left only *prakṛiti* and the multitude of individual *purushas*,—the precise assumptions of the Sâṅkhya system, which admits probably of philosophical explanation in no other way than that we have followed. A reconstruction of theism was attempted in the Yoga system; which in harmony with its later origin builds upon the basis of the Sâṅkhya system, very little fitted as that was for the purpose, a yoga practice which depends upon the teaching of the Upanishads. While then it certainly reintroduces the idea of God, it finds it impossible to give to the conception any real vitality on such a basis as this. So that this theory (practically, if not on the ground of its origin) may be fitly placed in a line with the Deism of later philosophy.

5. *Eschatology* (*Transmigration and Emancipation*)

In proportion as Brahman usurped the place of the ancient Vedic gods, and was interpreted in harmony with the idea of the âtman, the hope also which finds expression in the Ṛigveda of entering in after death to the gods was transformed in course of time into a hope of attaining "community of world," "community of life" with Brahman, or later on with the âtman. At the same time the idea of the âtman also, by virtue of the continued influence of that which it had displaced, was at first still conceived in a transcendental way, and it is said:—"He is my soul (âtman); to him, to this soul, shall I departing hence enter in."[1] If however the âtman is really my soul, my self, no entering in is

[1] S'atap. Br. 10. 6. 3. 2.

necessary, but only the knowledge of this fact, in order to become partaker of a full and complete deliverance. He who has recognised that *aham brahma asmi*, "I am Brahman," he already is, not will be delivered; he sees through the illusion of plurality, knows himself as the sole real, as the substance of all that exists, and is thereby exalted above all desire (*kâma*), for "what can he desire who possesses all?"[1] This also Yâjñavalkhya is the first to teach in the words:—"He who without desire, free from desire, his desire laid to rest, is himself his own desire, his vital spirits do not journey forth. But he is Brahman, and to Brahman he ascends."[2]

Deliverance is not effected by the knowledge of the âtman, but this knowledge is itself already deliverance. He who knows himself as the âtman has thereby recognised the world of plurality and the desire occasioned by plurality to be an illusion, which can no longer lead him astray. His body is no longer his body, his actions no longer his actions; whether he still continues to live and to act or not is, like everything else, a matter of indifference.[3] But the semblance of empirical knowledge persists, and it is a consequence of this that deliverance appears to be first attained in all its completeness after the dissolution of the body. And a still more far-reaching influence of the empirical mode of thought combined with the traditions of the past caused this internal deliverance from the world, the fruit of the emancipating knowledge of the âtman, to be represented as an ascent from the world to a transcendent distance, in order there for the first time to become united with Brahman, with the âtman. The theory therefore was formed of the way of the gods (*devayâna*), on which the emancipated were led after death through a series of bright stages to union with Brahman, whence "there is no return."[4]

[1] Gauḍap. 1. 9. [2] Bṛih. 4. 4. 6. [3] Îsâ 2. [4] Chând. 4. 15. 5.

What becomes however of those who die without having known themselves as the âtman? The Brâhmaṇas set before them for their good or evil deeds a recompense of joy or suffering in the other world. To the evil-doers was assigned also "recurrent death" (*punarmṛityu*). In contrast with the immortality (*amṛitatvam*, literally the "no more being able to die") of the perfected there remained for others the prospect of enduring in the other world together with other misfortune a "renewed necessity of death"; and this, since it has to do with those who have already died, is not to be thought of as experienced in the body, but indefinitely as a state of sufferings, which are in store in the other world as a recompense for evil-doing. It is the Upanishads first—and again for the first time by the mouth of Yâjñavalkhya—that transfer this retribution with its threat of recurrent death from an imaginary future into the present, since they place before it a renewed earthly existence. This is the origin of the theory of the Indian doctrine of transmigration (*saṁsara*), which does not rest on superstitious ideas of the return of the dead in other forms, such as are found amongst other peoples and even in India itself, but as the texts prove, on observation of the variety of the character and fate of individual men, which were explained as resulting from the actions of a previous existence. "In truth a man becomes good by good works, evil by evil."[1] "Verily according as he acts, according as he lives, so is he born; he who does good is born good, he who does evil is born evil, he becomes righteous by righteous works, evil by evil . . . according to the work which he does, so is he rewarded."[2]

These words of Yâjñavalkhya (the oldest in which a doctrine of transmigration is found) substitute a recompense in this world for one in the other, and this takes

[1] Bṛih. 3. 2. 13. [2] Bṛih. 4. 4. 5.

place by means of a re-birth on earth, apparently immediately after death.[1] While this theory met with acceptance, the ancient Vedic conception of a recompense for all alike, good and evil, in the other world held its ground by its side; and finally the two were combined in the doctrine of a double retribution, the first in the other world, lasting *yâvat sampâtam* "as long as a remnant (of works) remains,"[2] after which everything is once again recompensed by means of a renewed existence upon earth. This recompense of those already recompensed contradicts so entirely the whole conception of recompense, that it is impossible to understand it otherwise than as a combination of ideas derived from various sources. This is the point of view of the "doctrine of the five fires" (*pañc'âgnividyâ*),[3] which constructs, on the analogy of the way of the gods (*devayâna*) that leads to Brahman without return, a way of the fathers (*pitṛiyâna*) that leads to the moon and then back again to earth; and this was subsequently still further modified,[4] and has become the permanent basis of the whole of the later development.

The clothing of the doctrine of emancipation in empirical forms involved as a consequence the conceiving of emancipation, as though it were an event in an empirical sense, from the point of view of causality, as an effect which might be brought about or accelerated by appropriate means. Now emancipation consisted on its external phenomenal side:—

(1) In the removal of the consciousness of plurality.

(2) In the removal of all desire, the necessary consequence and accompaniment of that consciousness.

To produce these two states artificially was the aim of two characteristic manifestations of Indian culture.

[1] cp. the illustration of the caterpillar, Bṛih. 4. 4. 3.
[2] Chând. 5. 10. 5. [3] Chând. 5. 3-10 (Bṛih. 6. 2).
[4] Kaush. 1.

(1) Of the *yoga*, which by withdrawing the organs from the objects of sense and concentrating them on the inner self endeavoured to shake itself free from the world of plurality and to secure union with the âtman.

(2) Of the *sannyâsa*, which by the "casting off from oneself" of home, possessions, family and all that stimulates desire seeks laboriously to realise that freedom from all the ties of earth, in which a deeper conception of life in other ages and countries also has recognised the supreme task of earthly existence, and will probably continue to recognise throughout all future time.

INDEX I

SUBJECTS

INDEX II

REFERENCES

The Index includes all passages quoted or translated in the text, and all of which important illustrative use is made.

CATALOGUE OF DOVER BOOKS

BOOKS EXPLAINING SCIENCE AND MATHEMATICS

General

WHAT IS SCIENCE?, Norman Campbell. This excellent introduction explains scientific method, role of mathematics, types of scientific laws. Contents: 2 aspects of science, science & nature, laws of science, discovery of laws, explanation of laws, measurement & numerical laws, applications of science. 192pp. 5⅜ x 8. S43 Paperbound **$1.25**

THE COMMON SENSE OF THE EXACT SCIENCES, W. K. Clifford. Introduction by James Newman, edited by Karl Pearson. For 70 years this has been a guide to classical scientific and mathematical thought. Explains with unusual clarity basic concepts, such as extension of meaning of symbols, characteristics of surface boundaries, properties of plane figures, vectors, Cartesian method of determining position, etc. Long preface by Bertrand Russell. Bibliography of Clifford. Corrected, 130 diagrams redrawn. 249pp. 5⅜ x 8. T61 Paperbound **$1.60**

SCIENCE THEORY AND MAN, Erwin Schrödinger. This is a complete and unabridged reissue of SCIENCE AND THE HUMAN TEMPERAMENT plus an additional essay: "What is an Elementary Particle?" Nobel laureate Schrödinger discusses such topics as nature of scientific method, the nature of science, chance and determinism, science and society, conceptual models for physical entities, elementary particles and wave mechanics. Presentation is popular and may be followed by most people with little or no scientific training. "Fine practical preparation for a time when laws of nature, human institutions . . . are undergoing a critical examination without parallel," Waldemar Kaempffert, N. Y. TIMES. 192pp. 5⅜ x 8. T428 Paperbound **$1.35**

FADS AND FALLACIES IN THE NAME OF SCIENCE, Martin Gardner. Examines various cults, quack systems, frauds, delusions which at various times have masqueraded as science. Accounts of hollow-earth fanatics like Symmes; Velikovsky and wandering planets; Hoerbiger; Bellamy and the theory of multiple moons; Charles Fort; dowsing, pseudoscientific methods for finding water, ores, oil. Sections on naturopathy, iridiagnosis, zone therapy, food fads, etc. Analytical accounts of Wilhelm Reich and orgone sex energy; L. Ron Hubbard and Dianetics; A. Korzybski and General Semantics; many others. Brought up to date to include Bridey Murphy, others. Not just a collection of anecdotes, but a fair, reasoned appraisal of eccentric theory. Formerly titled IN THE NAME OF SCIENCE. Preface. Index. x + 384pp. 5⅜ x 8. T394 Paperbound **$1.50**

A DOVER SCIENCE SAMPLER, edited by George Barkin. 64-page book, sturdily bound, containing excerpts from over 20 Dover books, explaining science. Edwin Hubble, George Sarton, Ernst Mach, A. d'Abro, Galileo, Newton, others, discussing island universes, scientific truth, biological phenomena, stability in bridges, etc. Copies limited; no more than 1 to a customer, FREE

POPULAR SCIENTIFIC LECTURES, Hermann von Helmholtz. Helmholtz was a superb expositor as well as a scientist of genius in many areas. The seven essays in this volume are models of clarity, and even today they rank among the best general descriptions of their subjects ever written. "The Physiological Causes of Harmony in Music" was the first significant physiological explanation of musical consonance and dissonance. Two essays, "On the Interaction of Natural Forces" and "On the Conservation of Force," were of great importance in the history of science, for they firmly established the principle of the conservation of energy. Other lectures include "On the Relation of Optics to Painting," "On Recent Progress in the Theory of Vision," "On Goethe's Scientific Researches," and "On the Origin and Significance of Geometrical Axioms." Selected and edited with an introduction by Professor Morris Kline. xii + 286pp. 5⅜ x 8½. T799 Paperbound **$1.45**

BOOKS EXPLAINING SCIENCE AND MATHEMATICS

Physics

CONCERNING THE NATURE OF THINGS, Sir William Bragg. Christmas lectures delivered at the Royal Society by Nobel laureate. Why a spinning ball travels in a curved track; how uranium is transmuted to lead, etc. Partial contents: atoms, gases, liquids, crystals, metals, etc. No scientific background needed; wonderful for intelligent child. 32pp. of photos, 57 figures. xii + 232pp. 5⅜ x 8. T31 Paperbound **$1.50**

THE RESTLESS UNIVERSE, Max Born. New enlarged version of this remarkably readable account by a Nobel laureate. Moving from sub-atomic particles to universe, the author explains in very simple terms the latest theories of wave mechanics. Partial contents: air and its relatives, electrons & ions, waves & particles, electronic structure of the atom, nuclear physics. Nearly 1000 illustrations, including 7 animated sequences. 325pp. 6 x 9. T412 Paperbound **$2.00**

FROM EUCLID TO EDDINGTON: A STUDY OF THE CONCEPTIONS OF THE EXTERNAL WORLD, Sir Edmund Whittaker. A foremost British scientist traces the development of theories of natural philosophy from the western rediscovery of Euclid to Eddington, Einstein, Dirac, etc. The inadequacy of classical physics is contrasted with present day attempts to understand the physical world through relativity, non-Euclidean geometry, space curvature, wave mechanics, etc. 5 major divisions of examination: Space; Time and Movement; the Concepts of Classical Physics; the Concepts of Quantum Mechanics; the Eddington Universe. 212pp. 5⅜ x 8. T491 Paperbound **$1.35**

PHYSICS, THE PIONEER SCIENCE, L. W. Taylor. First thorough text to place all important physical phenomena in cultural-historical framework; remains best work of its kind. Exposition of physical laws, theories developed chronologically, with great historical, illustrative experiments diagrammed, described, worked out mathematically. Excellent physics text for self-study as well as class work. Vol. 1: Heat, Sound: motion, acceleration, gravitation, conservation of energy, heat engines, rotation, heat, mechanical energy, etc. 211 illus. 407pp. 5⅜ x 8. Vol. 2: Light, Electricity: images, lenses, prisms, magnetism, Ohm's law, dynamos, telegraph, quantum theory, decline of mechanical view of nature, etc. Bibliography. 13 table appendix. Index. 551 illus. 2 color plates. 508pp. 5⅜ x 8.
Vol. 1 S565 Paperbound **$2.00**
Vol. 2 S566 Paperbound **$2.00**
The set **$4.00**

A SURVEY OF PHYSICAL THEORY, Max Planck. One of the greatest scientists of all time, creator of the quantum revolution in physics, writes in non-technical terms of his own discoveries and those of other outstanding creators of modern physics. Planck wrote this book when science had just crossed the threshold of the new physics, and he communicates the excitement felt then as he discusses electromagnetic theories, statistical methods, evolution of the concept of light, a step-by-step description of how he developed his own momentous theory, and many more of the basic ideas behind modern physics. Formerly "A Survey of Physics." Bibliography. Index. 128pp. 5⅜ x 8. S650 Paperbound **$1.15**

THE ATOMIC NUCLEUS, M. Korsunsky. The only non-technical comprehensive account of the atomic nucleus in English. For college physics students, etc. Chapters cover: Radioactivity, the Nuclear Model of the Atom, the Mass of Atomic Nuclei, the Disintegration of Atomic Nuclei, the Discovery of the Positron, the Artificial Transformation of Atomic Nuclei, Artificial Radioactivity, Mesons, the Neutrino, the Structure of Atomic Nuclei and Forces Acting Between Nuclear Particles, Nuclear Fission, Chain Reaction, Peaceful Uses, Thermoculear Reactions. Slightly abridged edition. Translated by G. Yankovsky. 65 figures. Appendix includes 45 photographic illustrations. 413 pp. 5⅜ x 8. S1052 Paperbound **$2.00**

PRINCIPLES OF MECHANICS SIMPLY EXPLAINED, Morton Mott-Smith. Excellent, highly readable introduction to the theories and discoveries of classical physics. Ideal for the layman who desires a foundation which will enable him to understand and appreciate contemporary developments in the physical sciences. Discusses: Density, The Law of Gravitation, Mass and Weight, Action and Reaction, Kinetic and Potential Energy, The Law of Inertia, Effects of Acceleration, The Independence of Motions, Galileo and the New Science of Dynamics, Newton and the New Cosmos, The Conservation of Momentum, and other topics. Revised edition of "This Mechanical World." Illustrated by E. Kosa, Jr. Bibliography and Chronology. Index. xiv + 171pp. 5⅜ x 8½. T1067 Paperbound **$1.00**

THE CONCEPT OF ENERGY SIMPLY EXPLAINED, Morton Mott-Smith. Elementary, non-technical exposition which traces the story of man's conquest of energy, with particular emphasis on the developments during the nineteenth century and the first three decades of our own century. Discusses man's earlier efforts to harness energy, more recent experiments and discoveries relating to the steam engine, the engine indicator, the motive power of heat, the principle of excluded perpetual motion, the bases of the conservation of energy, the concept of entropy, the internal combustion engine, mechanical refrigeration, and many other related topics. Also much biographical material. Index. Bibliography. 33 illustrations. ix + 215pp. 5⅜ x 8½. T1071 Paperbound **$1.25**

HEAT AND ITS WORKINGS, Morton Mott-Smith. One of the best elementary introductions to the theory and attributes of heat, covering such matters as the laws governing the effect of heat on solids, liquids and gases, the methods by which heat is measured, the conversion of a substance from one form to another through heating and cooling, evaporation, the effects of pressure on boiling and freezing points, and the three ways in which heat is transmitted (conduction, convection, radiation). Also brief notes on major experiments and discoveries. Concise, but complete, it presents all the essential facts about the subject in readable style. Will give the layman and beginning student a first-rate background in this major topic in physics. Index. Bibliography. 50 illustrations. x + 165pp. 5⅜ x 8½. T978 Paperbound **$1.15**

THE STORY OF ATOMIC THEORY AND ATOMIC ENERGY, J. G. Feinberg. Wider range of facts on physical theory, cultural implications, than any other similar source. Completely non-technical. Begins with first atomic theory, 600 B.C., goes through A-bomb, developments to 1959. Avogadro, Rutherford, Bohr, Einstein, radioactive decay, binding energy, radiation danger, future benefits of nuclear power, dozens of other topics, told in lively, related, informal manner. Particular stress on European atomic research. "Deserves special mention . . . authoritative," Saturday Review. Formerly "The Atom Story." New chapter to 1959. Index. 34 illustrations. 251pp. 5⅜ x 8. T625 Paperbound **$1.60**

THE STRANGE STORY OF THE QUANTUM, AN ACCOUNT FOR THE GENERAL READER OF THE GROWTH OF IDEAS UNDERLYING OUR PRESENT ATOMIC KNOWLEDGE, B. Hoffmann. Presents lucidly and expertly, with barest amount of mathematics, the problems and theories which led to modern quantum physics. Dr. Hoffmann begins with the closing years of the 19th century, when certain trifling discrepancies were noticed, and with illuminating analogies and examples takes you through the brilliant concepts of Planck, Einstein, Pauli, de Broglie, Bohr, Schroedinger, Heisenberg, Dirac, Sommerfeld, Feynman, etc. This edition includes a new, long postscript carrying the story through 1958. "Of the books attempting an account of the history and contents of our modern atomic physics which have come to my attention, this is the best," H. Margenau, Yale University, in "American Journal of Physics." 32 tables and line illustrations. Index. 275pp. 5⅜ x 8. T518 Paperbound **$1.50**

THE EVOLUTION OF SCIENTIFIC THOUGHT FROM NEWTON TO EINSTEIN, A. d'Abro. Einstein's special and general theories of relativity, with their historical implications, are analyzed in non-technical terms. Excellent accounts of the contributions of Newton, Riemann, Weyl, Planck, Eddington, Maxwell, Lorentz and others are treated in terms of space and time, equations of electromagnetics, finiteness of the universe, methodology of science. 21 diagrams. 482pp. 5⅜ x 8. T2 Paperound **$2.25**

THE RISE OF THE NEW PHYSICS, A. d'Abro. A half-million word exposition, formerly titled THE DECLINE OF MECHANISM, for readers not versed in higher mathematics. The only thorough explanation, in everyday language, of the central core of modern mathematical physical theory, treating both classical and modern theoretical physics, and presenting in terms almost anyone can understand the equivalent of 5 years of study of mathematical physics. Scientifically impeccable coverage of mathematical-physical thought from the Newtonian system up through the electronic theories of Dirac and Heisenberg and Fermi's statistics. Combines both history and exposition; provides a broad yet unified and detailed view, with constant comparison of classical and modern views on phenomena and theories. "A must for anyone doing serious study in the physical sciences," JOURNAL OF THE FRANKLIN INSTITUTE. "Extraordinary faculty . . . to explain ideas and theories of theoretical physics in the language of daily life," ISIS. First part of set covers philosophy of science, drawing upon the practice of Newton, Maxwell, Poincaré, Einstein, others, discussing modes of thought, experiment, interpretations of causality, etc. In the second part, 100 pages explain grammar and vocabulary of mathematics, with discussions of functions, groups, series, Fourier series, etc. The remainder is devoted to concrete, detailed coverage of both classical and quantum physics, explaining such topics as analytic mechanics, Hamilton's principle, wave theory of light, electromagnetic waves, groups of transformations, thermodynamics, phase rule, Brownian movement, kinetics, special relativity, Planck's original quantum theory, Bohr's atom, Zeeman effect, Broglie's wave mechanics, Heisenberg's uncertainty, Eigen-values, matrices, scores of other important topics. Discoveries and theories are covered for such men as Alembert, Born, Cantor, Debye, Euler, Foucault, Galois, Gauss, Hadamard, Kelvin, Kepler, Laplace, Maxwell, Pauli, Rayleigh, Volterra, Weyl, Young, more than 180 others. Indexed. 97 illustrations. ix + 982pp. 5⅜ x 8. T3 Volume 1, Paperbound **$2.25**
T4 Volume 2, Paperbound **$2.25**

SPINNING TOPS AND GYROSCOPIC MOTION, John Perry. Well-known classic of science still unsurpassed for lucid, accurate, delightful exposition. How quasi-rigidity is induced in flexible and fluid bodies by rapid motions; why gyrostat falls, top rises; nature and effect on climatic conditions of earth's precessional movement; effect of internal fluidity on rotating bodies, etc. Appendixes describe practical uses to which gyroscopes have been put in ships, compasses, monorail transportation. 62 figures. 128pp. 5⅜ x 8. T416 Paperbound **$1.00**

THE UNIVERSE OF LIGHT, Sir William Bragg. No scientific training needed to read Nobel Prize winner's expansion of his Royal Institute Christmas Lectures. Insight into nature of light, methods and philosophy of science. Explains lenses, reflection, color, resonance, polarization, x-rays, the spectrum, Newton's work with prisms, Huygens' with polarization, Crookes' with cathode ray, etc. Leads into clear statement of 2 major historical theories of light, corpuscle and wave. Dozens of experiments you can do. 199 illus., including 2 full-page color plates. 293pp. 5⅜ x 8. S538 Paperbound **$1.85**

THE STORY OF X-RAYS FROM RÖNTGEN TO ISOTOPES, A. R. Bleich. Non-technical history of x-rays, their scientific explanation, their applications in medicine, industry, research, and art, and their effect on the individual and his descendants. Includes amusing early reactions to Röntgen's discovery, cancer therapy, detections of art and stamp forgeries, potential risks to patient and operator, etc. Illustrations show x-rays of flower structure, the gall bladder, gears with hidden defects, etc. Original Dover publication. Glossary. Bibliography. Index. 55 photos and figures. xiv + 186pp. 5⅜ x 8. T662 Paperbound **$1.35**

ELECTRONS, ATOMS, METALS AND ALLOYS, Wm. Hume-Rothery. An introductory-level explanation of the application of the electronic theory to the structure and properties of metals and alloys, taking into account the new theoretical work done by mathematical physicists. Material presented in dialogue-form between an "Old Metallurgist" and a "Young Scientist." Their discussion falls into 4 main parts: the nature of an atom, the nature of a metal, the nature of an alloy, and the structure of the nucleus. They cover such topics as the hydrogen atom, electron waves, wave mechanics, Brillouin zones, co-valent bonds, radioactivity and natural disintegration, fundamental particles, structure and fission of the nucleus,etc. Revised, enlarged edition. 177 illustrations. Subject and name indexes. 407pp. 5⅜ x 8½. S1046 Paperbound **$2.25**

OUT OF THE SKY, H. H. Nininger. A non-technical but comprehensive introduction to "meteoritics", the young science concerned with all aspects of the arrival of matter from outer space. Written by one of the world's experts on meteorites, this work shows how, despite difficulties of observation and sparseness of data, a considerable body of knowledge has arisen. It defines meteors and meteorites; studies fireball clusters and processions, meteorite composition, size, distribution, showers, explosions, origins, craters, and much more. A true connecting link between astronomy and geology. More than 175 photos, 22 other illustrations. References. Bibliography of author's publications on meteorites. Index. viii + 336pp. 5⅜ x 8. T519 Paperbound **$1.85**

SATELLITES AND SCIENTIFIC RESEARCH, D. King-Hele. Non-technical account of the manmade satellites and the discoveries they have yielded up to the autumn of 1961. Brings together information hitherto published only in hard-to-get scientific journals. Includes the life history of a typical satellite, methods of tracking, new information on the shape of the earth, zones of radiation, etc. Over 60 diagrams and 6 photographs. Mathematical appendix. Bibliography of over 100 items. Index. xii + 180pp. 5⅜ x 8½. T703 Paperbound **$2.00**

BOOKS EXPLAINING SCIENCE AND MATHEMATICS

Mathematics

CHANCE, LUCK AND STATISTICS: THE SCIENCE OF CHANCE, Horace C. Levinson. Theory of probability and science of statistics in simple, non-technical language. Part I deals with theory of probability, covering odd superstitions in regard to "luck," the meaning of betting odds, the law of mathematical expectation, gambling, and applications in poker, roulette, lotteries, dice, bridge, and other games of chance. Part II discusses the misuse of statistics, the concept of statistical probabilities, normal and skew frequency distributions, and statistics applied to various fields—birth rates, stock speculation, insurance rates, advertising, etc. "Presented in an easy humorous style which I consider the best kind of expository writing," Prof. A. C. Cohen, Industry Quality Control. Enlarged revised edition. Formerly titled "The Science of Chance." Preface and two new appendices by the author. Index. xiv + 365pp. 5⅜ x 8. T1007 Paperbound **$1.85**

PROBABILITIES AND LIFE, Emile Borel. Translated by M. Baudin. Non-technical, highly readable introduction to the results of probability as applied to everyday situations. Partial contents: Fallacies About Probabilities Concerning Life After Death; Negligible Probabilities and the Probabilities of Everyday Life; Events of Small Probability; Application of Probabilities to Certain Problems of Heredity; Probabilities of Deaths, Diseases, and Accidents; On Poisson's Formula. Index. 3 Appendices of statistical studies and tables. vi + 87pp. 5⅜ x 8½. T121 Paperbound **$1.00**

GREAT IDEAS OF MODERN MATHEMATICS: THEIR NATURE AND USE, Jagjit Singh. Reader with only high school math will understand main mathematical ideas of modern physics, astronomy, genetics, psychology, evolution, etc., better than many who use them as tools, but comprehend little of their basic structure. Author uses his wide knowledge of non-mathematical fields in brilliant exposition of differential equations, matrices, group theory, logic, statistics, problems of mathematical foundations, imaginary numbers, vectors, etc. Original publication. 2 appendices. 2 indexes. 65 illustr. 322pp. 5⅜ x 8. S587 Paperbound **$1.75**

MATHEMATICS IN ACTION, O. G. Sutton. Everyone with a command of high school algebra will find this book one of the finest possible introductions to the application of mathematics to physical theory. Ballistics, numerical analysis, waves and wavelike phenomena, Fourier series, group concepts, fluid flow and aerodynamics, statistical measures, and meteorology are discussed with unusual clarity. Some calculus and differential equations theory is developed by the author for the reader's help in the more difficult sections. 88 figures. Index. viii + 236pp. 5⅜ x 8. T440 Clothbound **$3.50**

THE FOURTH DIMENSION SIMPLY EXPLAINED, edited by H. P. Manning. 22 essays, originally Scientific American contest entries, that use a minimum of mathematics to explain aspects of 4-dimensional geometry: analogues to 3-dimensional space, 4-dimensional absurdities and curiosities (such as removing the contents of an egg without puncturing its shell), possible measurements and forms, etc. Introduction by the editor. Only book of its sort on a truly elementary level, excellent introduction to advanced works. 82 figures. 251pp. 5⅜ x 8. T711 Paperbound **$1.35**

MATHEMATICS—INTERMEDIATE TO ADVANCED

General

INTRODUCTION TO APPLIED MATHEMATICS, Francis D. Murnaghan. A practical and thoroughly sound introduction to a number of advanced branches of higher mathematics. Among the selected topics covered in detail are: vector and matrix analysis, partial and differential equations, integral equations, calculus of variations, Laplace transform theory, the vector triple product, linear vector functions, quadratic and bilinear forms, Fourier series, spherical harmonics, Bessel functions, the Heaviside expansion formula, and many others. Extremely useful book for graduate students in physics, engineering, chemistry, and mathematics. Index. 111 study exercises with answers. 41 illustrations. ix + 389pp. 5⅜ x 8½.
S1042 Paperbound **$2.00**

OPERATIONAL METHODS IN APPLIED MATHEMATICS, H. S. Carslaw and J. C. Jaeger. Explanation of the application of the Laplace Transformation to differential equations, a simple and effective substitute for more difficult and obscure operational methods. Of great practical value to engineers and to all workers in applied mathematics. Chapters on: Ordinary Linear Differential Equations with Constant Coefficients;; Electric Circuit Theory; Dynamical Applications; The Inversion Theorem for the Laplace Transformation; Conduction of Heat; Vibrations of Continuous Mechanical Systems; Hydrodynamics; Impulsive Functions; Chains of Differential Equations; and other related matters. 3 appendices. 153 problems, many with answers. 22 figures. xvi + 359pp. 5⅜ x 8½. S1011 Paperbound **$2.25**

APPLIED MATHEMATICS FOR RADIO AND COMMUNICATIONS ENGINEERS, C. E. Smith. No extraneous material here!—only the theories, equations, and operations essential and immediately useful for radio work. Can be used as refresher, as handbook of applications and tables, or as full home-study course. Ranges from simplest arithmetic through calculus, series, and wave forms, hyperbolic trigonometry, simultaneous equations in mesh circuits, etc. Supplies applications right along with each math topic discussed. 22 useful tables of functions, formulas, logs, etc. Index. 166 exercises, 140 examples, all with answers. 95 diagrams. Bibliography. x + 336pp. 5⅜ x 8. S141 Paperbound **$1.75**

Algebra, group theory, determinants, sets, matrix theory

ALGEBRAS AND THEIR ARITHMETICS, L. E. Dickson. Provides the foundation and background necessary to any advanced undergraduate or graduate student studying abstract algebra. Begins with elementary introduction to linear transformations, matrices, field of complex numbers; proceeds to order, basal units, modulus, quaternions, etc.; develops calculus of linears sets, describes various examples of algebras including invariant, difference, nilpotent, semi-simple. "Makes the reader marvel at his genius for clear and profound analysis," Amer. Mathematical Monthly. Index. xii + 241pp. 5⅜ x 8. S616 Paperbound **$1.50**

THE THEORY OF EQUATIONS WITH AN INTRODUCTION TO THE THEORY OF BINARY ALGEBRAIC FORMS, W. S. Burnside and A. W. Panton. Extremely thorough and concrete discussion of the theory of equations, with extensive detailed treatment of many topics curtailed in later texts. Covers theory of algebraic equations, properties of polynomials, symmetric functions, derived functions, Horner's process, complex numbers and the complex variable, determinants and methods of elimination, invariant theory (nearly 100 pages), transformations, introduction to Galois theory, Abelian equations, and much more. Invaluable supplementary work for modern students and teachers. 759 examples and exercises. Index in each volume. Two volume set. Total of xxiv + 604pp. 5⅜ x 8. S714 Vol I Paperbound **$1.85**
S715 Vol II Paperbound **$1.85**
The set **$3.70**

COMPUTATIONAL METHODS OF LINEAR ALGEBRA, V. N. Faddeeva, translated by **C. D. Benster.** First English translation of a unique and valuable work, the only work in English presenting a systematic exposition of the most important methods of linear algebra—classical and contemporary. Shows in detail how to derive numerical solutions of problems in mathematical physics which are frequently connected with those of linear algebra. Theory as well as individual practice. Part I surveys the mathematical background that is indispensable to what follows. Parts II and III, the conclusion, set forth the most important methods of solution, for both exact and iterative groups. One of the most outstanding and valuable features of this work is the 23 tables, double and triple checked for accuracy. These tables will not be found elsewhere. Author's preface. Translator's note. New bibliography and index. x + 252pp. 5⅜ x 8. S424 Paperbound **$1.95**

ALGEBRAIC EQUATIONS, E. Dehn. Careful and complete presentation of Galois' theory of algebraic equations; theories of Lagrange and Galois developed in logical rather than historical form, with a more thorough exposition than in most modern books. Many concrete applications and fully-worked-out examples. Discusses basic theory (very clear exposition of the symmetric group); isomorphic, transitive, and Abelian groups; applications of Lagrange's and Galois' theories; and much more. Newly revised by the author. Index. List of Theorems. xi + 208pp. 5⅜ x 8. S697 Paperbound **$1.45**

Differential equations, ordinary and partial; integral equations

INTRODUCTION TO THE DIFFERENTIAL EQUATIONS OF PHYSICS, L. Hopf. Especially valuable to the engineer with no math beyond elementary calculus. Emphasizing intuitive rather than formal aspects of concepts, the author covers an extensive territory. Partial contents: Law of causality, energy theorem, damped oscillations, coupling by friction, cylindrical and spherical coordinates, heat source, etc. Index. 48 figures. 160pp. 5⅜ x 8.
S120 Paperbound **$1.25**

INTRODUCTION TO THE THEORY OF LINEAR DIFFERENTIAL EQUATIONS, E. G. Poole. Authoritative discussions of important topics, with methods of solution more detailed than usual, for students with background of elementary course in differential equations. Studies existence theorems, linearly independent solutions; equations with constant coefficients; with uniform analytic coefficients; regular singularities; the hypergeometric equation; conformal representation; etc. Exercises. Index. 210pp. 5⅜ x 8. S629 Paperbound **$1.65**

DIFFERENTIAL EQUATIONS FOR ENGINEERS, P. Franklin. Outgrowth of a course given 10 years at M. I. T. Makes most useful branch of pure math accessible for practical work. Theoretical basis of D.E.'s; solution of ordinary D.E.'s and partial derivatives arising from heat flow, steady-state temperature of a plate, wave equations; analytic functions; convergence of Fourier Series. 400 problems on electricity, vibratory systems, other topics. Formerly "Differential Equations for Electrical Engineers." Index 41 illus. 307pp. 5⅜ x 8.
S601 Paperbound **$1.65**

DIFFERENTIAL EQUATIONS, F. R. Moulton. A detailed, rigorous exposition of all the non-elementary processes of solving ordinary differential equations. Several chapters devoted to the treatment of practical problems, especially those of a physical nature, which are far more advanced than problems usually given as illustrations. Includes analytic differential equations; variations of a parameter; integrals of differential equations; analytic implicit functions; problems of elliptic motion; sine-amplitude functions; deviation of formal bodies; Cauchy-Lipschitz process; linear differential equations with periodic coefficients; differential equations in infinitely many variations; much more. Historical notes. 10 figures. 222 problems. Index. xv + 395pp. 5⅜ x 8. S451 Paperbound **$2.00**

DIFFERENTIAL AND INTEGRAL EQUATIONS OF MECHANICS AND PHYSICS (DIE DIFFERENTIAL- UND INTEGRALGLEICHUNGEN DER MECHANIK UND PHYSIK), edited by P. Frank and R. von Mises. Most comprehensive and authoritative work on the mathematics of mathematical physics available today in the United States: the standard, definitive reference for teachers, physicists, engineers, and mathematicians—now published (in the original German) at a relatively inexpensive price for the first time! Every chapter in this 2,000-page set is by an expert in his field: Carathéodory, Courant, Frank, Mises, and a dozen others. Vol I, on mathematics, gives concise but complete coverages of advanced calculus, differential equations, integral equations, and potential, and partial differential equations. Index. xxiii + 916pp. Vol. II (physics): classical mechanics, optics, continuous mechanics, heat conduction and diffusion, the stationary and quasi-stationary electromagnetic field, electromagnetic oscillations, and wave mechanics. Index. xxiv + 1106pp. Two volume set. Each volume available separately. 5⅝ x 8⅜. S787 Vol I Clothbound **$7.50**
S788 Vol II Clothbound **$7.50**
The set **$15.00**

LECTURES ON CAUCHY'S PROBLEM, J. Hadamard. Based on lectures given at Columbia, Rome, this discusses work of Riemann, Kirchhoff, Volterra, and the author's own research on the hyperbolic case in linear partial differential equations. It extends spherical and cylindrical waves to apply to all (normal) hyperbolic equations. Partial contents: Cauchy's problem, fundamental formula, equations with odd number, with even number of independent variables; method of descent. 32 figures. Index. iii + 316pp. 5⅜ x 8. S105 Paperbound **$1.75**

THEORY OF DIFFERENTIAL EQUATIONS, A. R. Forsyth. Out of print for over a decade, the complete 6 volumes (now bound as 3) of this monumental work represent the most comprehensive treatment of differential equations ever written. Historical presentation includes in 2500 pages every substantial development. Vol. 1, 2: EXACT EQUATIONS, PFAFF'S PROBLEM; ORDINARY EQUATIONS, NOT LINEAR: methods of Grassmann, Clebsch, Lie, Darboux; Cauchy's theorem; branch points; etc. Vol. 3, 4: ORDINARY EQUATIONS, NOT LINEAR; ORDINARY LINEAR EQUATIONS: Zeta Fuchsian functions, general theorems on algebraic integrals, Brun's theorem, equations with uniform periodic coffiecients, etc. Vol. 4, 5: PARTIAL DIFFERENTIAL EQUATIONS: 2 existence-theorems, equations of theoretical dynamics, Laplace transformations, general transformation of equations of the 2nd order, much more. Indexes. Total of 2766pp. 5⅜ x 8. S576-7-8 Clothbound: the set **$15.00**

PARTIAL DIFFERENTIAL EQUATIONS OF MATHEMATICAL PHYSICS, A. G. Webster. A keystone work in the library of every mature physicist, engineer, researcher. Valuable sections on elasticity, compression theory, potential theory, theory of sound, heat conduction, wave propagation, vibration theory. Contents include: deduction of differential equations, vibrations, normal functions, Fourier's series, Cauchy's method, boundary problems, method of Riemann-Volterra. Spherical, cylindrical, ellipsoidal harmonics, applications, etc. 97 figures. vii + 440pp. 5⅜ x 8. S263 Paperbound **$2.00**

ELEMENTARY CONCEPTS OF TOPOLOGY, P. Alexandroff. First English translation of the famous brief introduction to topology for the beginner or for the mathematician not undertaking extensive study. This unusually useful intuitive approach deals primarily with the concepts of complex, cycle, and homology, and is wholly consistent with current investigations. Ranges from basic concepts of set-theoretic topology to the concept of Betti groups. "Glowing example of harmony between intuition and thought," David Hilbert. Translated by A. E. Farley. Introduction by D. Hilbert. Index. 25 figures. 73pp. 5⅜ x 8. S747 Paperbound **$1.00**

Number theory

INTRODUCTION TO THE THEORY OF NUMBERS, L. E. Dickson. Thorough, comprehensive approach with adequate coverage of classical literature, an introductory volume beginners can follow. Chapters on divisibility, congruences, quadratic residues & reciprocity, Diophantine equations, etc. Full treatment of binary quadratic forms without usual restriction to integral coefficients. Covers infinitude of primes, least residues, Fermat's theorem, Euler's phi function, Legendre's symbol, Gauss's lemma, automorphs, reduced forms, recent theorems of Thue & Siegel, many more. Much material not readily available elsewhere. 239 problems. Index. I figure. viii + 183pp. 5⅜ x 8. S342 Paperbound **$1.65**

ELEMENTS OF NUMBER THEORY, I. M. Vinogradov. Detailed 1st course for persons without advanced mathematics; 95% of this book can be understood by readers who have gone no farther than high school algebra. Partial contents: divisibility theory, important number theoretical functions, congruences, primitive roots and indices, etc. Solutions to both problems and exercises. Tables of primes, indices, etc. Covers almost every essential formula in elementary number theory! Translated from Russian. 233 problems, 104 exercises. viii + 227pp. 5⅜ x 8. S259 Paperbound **$1.60**

THEORY OF NUMBERS and DIOPHANTINE ANALYSIS, R. D. Carmichael. These two complete works in one volume form one of the most lucid introductions to number theory, requiring only a firm foundation in high school mathematics. "Theory of Numbers," partial contents: Eratosthenes' sieve, Euclid's fundamental theorem, G.C.F. and L.C.M. of two or more integers, linear congruences, etc "Diophantine Analysis": rational triangles, Pythagorean triangles, equations of third, fourth, higher degrees, method of functional equations, much more. "Theory of Numbers": 76 problems. Index. 94pp. "Diophantine Analysis": 222 problems. Index. 118pp. 5⅜ x 8. S529 Paperbound **$1.35**

Numerical analysis, tables

MATHEMATICAL TABLES AND FORMULAS, Compiled by Robert D. Carmichael and Edwin R. Smith. Valuable collection for students, etc. Contains all tables necessary in college algebra and trigonometry, such as five-place common logarithms, logarithmic sines and tangents of small angles, logarithmic trigonometric functions, natural trigonometric functions, four-place antilogarithms, tables for changing from sexagesimal to circular and from circular to sexagesimal measure of angles, etc. Also many tables and formulas not ordinarily accessible, including powers, roots, and reciprocals, exponential and hyperbolic functions, ten-place logarithms of prime numbers, and formulas and theorems from analytical and elementary geometry and from calculus. Explanatory introduction. viii + 269pp. 5⅜ x 8½.
S111 Paperbound **$1.00**

MATHEMATICAL TABLES, H. B. Dwight. Unique for its coverage in one volume of almost every function of importance in applied mathematics, engineering, and the physical sciences. Three extremely fine tables of the three trig functions and their inverse functions to thousandths of radians; natural and common logarithms; squares, cubes; hyperbolic functions and the inverse hyperbolic functions; $(a^2 + b^2)$ exp. ½a; complete elliptic integrals of the 1st and 2nd kind; sine and cosine integrals; exponential integrals Ei(x) and Ei(—x); binomial coefficients; factorials to 250; surface zonal harmonics and first derivatives; Bernoulli and Euler numbers and their logs to base of 10; Gamma function; normal probability integral; over 60 pages of Bessel functions; the Riemann Zeta function. Each table with formulae generally used, sources of more extensive tables, interpolation data, etc. Over half have columns of differences, to facilitate interpolation. Introduction. Index. viii + 231pp. 5⅜ x 8.
S445 Paperbound **$2.00**

TABLES OF FUNCTIONS WITH FORMULAE AND CURVES, E. Jahnke & F. Emde. The world's most comprehensive 1-volume English-text collection of tables, formulae, curves of transcendent functions. 4th corrected edition, new 76-page section giving tables, formulae for elementary functions—not in other English editions. Partial contents: sine, cosine, logarithmic integral; factorial function; error integral; theta functions; elliptic integrals, functions; Legendre, Bessel, Riemann, Mathieu, hypergeometric functions, etc. Supplementary books. Bibliography. Indexed. "Out of the way functions for which we know no other source," SCIENTIFIC COMPUTING SERVICE, Ltd. 212 figures. 400pp. 5⅜ x 8. S133 Paperbound **$2.00**

CHEMISTRY AND PHYSICAL CHEMISTRY

ORGANIC CHEMISTRY, F. C. Whitmore. The entire subject of organic chemistry for the practicing chemist and the advanced student. Storehouse of facts, theories, processes found elsewhere only in specialized journals. Covers aliphatic compounds (500 pages on the properties and synthetic preparation of hydrocarbons, halides, proteins, ketones, etc.), alicyclic compounds, aromatic compounds, heterocyclic compounds, organophosphorus and organometallic compounds. Methods of synthetic preparation analyzed critically throughout. Includes much of biochemical interest. "The scope of this volume is astonishing," INDUSTRIAL AND ENGINEERING CHEMISTRY. 12,000-reference index. 2387-item bibliography. Total of x + 1005pp. 5⅜ x 8. Two volume set.
S700 Vol I Paperbound **$2.25**
S701 Vol II Paperbound **$2.25**
The set **$4.50**

THE MODERN THEORY OF MOLECULAR STRUCTURE, Bernard Pullman. A reasonably popular account of recent developments in atomic and molecular theory. Contents: The Wave Function and Wave Equations (history and bases of present theories of molecular structure); The Electronic Structure of Atoms (Description and classification of atomic wave functions, etc.); Diatomic Molecules; Non-Conjugated Polyatomic Molecules; Conjugated Polyatomic Molecules; The Structure of Complexes. Minimum of mathematical background needed. New translation by David Antin of "La Structure Moleculaire." Index. Bibliography. vii + 87pp. 5⅜ x 8½.
S987 Paperbound **$1.00**

CATALYSIS AND CATALYSTS, Marcel Prettre, Director, Research Institute on Catalysis. This brief book, translated into English for the first time, is the finest summary of the principal modern concepts, methods, and results of catalysis. Ideal introduction for beginning chemistry and physics students. Chapters: Basic Definitions of Catalysis (true catalysis and generalization of the concept of catalysis); The Scientific Bases of Catalysis (Catalysis and chemical thermodynamics, catalysis and chemical kinetics); Homogeneous Catalysis (acid-base catalysis, etc.); Chain Reactions; Contact Masses; Heterogeneous Catalysis (Mechanisms of contact catalyses, etc.); and Industrial Applications (acids and fertilizers, petroleum and petroleum chemistry, rubber, plastics, synthetic resins, and fibers). Translated by David Antin. Index. vi + 88pp. 5⅜ x 8½.
S998 Paperbound **$1.00**

POLAR MOLECULES, Pieter Debye. This work by Nobel laureate Debye offers a complete guide to fundamental electrostatic field relations, polarizability, molecular structure. Partial contents: electric intensity, displacement and force, polarization by orientation, molar polarization and molar refraction, halogen-hydrides, polar liquids, ionic saturation, dielectric constant, etc. Special chapter considers quantum theory. Indexed. 172pp. 5⅜ x 8.
S64 Paperbound **$1.65**

THE ELECTRONIC THEORY OF ACIDS AND BASES, W. F. Luder and Saverio Zuffanti. The first full systematic presentation of the electronic theory of acids and bases—treating the theory and its ramifications in an uncomplicated manner. Chapters: Historical Background; Atomic Orbitals and Valence; The Electronic Theory of Acids and Bases; Electrophilic and Electrodotic Reagents; Acidic and Basic Radicals; Neutralization; Titrations with Indicators; Displacement; Catalysis; Acid Catalysis; Base Catalysis; Alkoxides and Catalysts; Conclusion. Required reading for all chemists. Second revised (1961) eidtion, with additional examples and references. 3 figures. 9 tables. Index. Bibliography xii + 165pp. 5⅜ x 8.
S201 Paperbound **$1.50**

KINETIC THEORY OF LIQUIDS, J. Frenkel. Regarding the kinetic theory of liquids as a generalization and extension of the theory of solid bodies, this volume covers all types of arrangements of solids, thermal displacements of atoms, interstitial atoms and ions, orientational and rotational motion of molecules, and transition between states of matter. Mathematical theory is developed close to the physical subject matter. 216 bibliographical footnotes. 55 figures. xi + 485pp. 5⅜ x 8.
S95 Paperbound **$2.55**

THE PRINCIPLES OF ELECTROCHEMISTRY, D. A. MacInnes. Basic equations for almost every subfield of electrochemistry from first principles, referring at all times to the soundest and most recent theories and results; unusually useful as text or as reference. Covers coulometers and Faraday's Law, electrolytic conductance, the Debye-Hueckel method for the theoretical calculation of activity coefficients, concentration cells, standard electrode potentials, thermodynamic ionization constants, pH, potentiometric titrations, irreversible phenomena, Planck's equation, and much more. "Excellent treatise," AMERICAN CHEMICAL SOCIETY JOURNAL. "Highly recommended," CHEMICAL AND METALLURGICAL ENGINEERING. 2 Indices. Appendix. 585-item bibliography. 137 figures. 94 tables. ii + 478pp. 5⅝ x 8⅜.
S52 Paperbound **$2.45**

THE PHASE RULE AND ITS APPLICATION, Alexander Findlay. Covering chemical phenomena of 1, 2, 3, 4, and multiple component systems, this "standard work on the subject" (NATURE, London), has been completely revised and brought up to date by A. N. Campbell and N. O. Smith. Brand new material has been added on such matters as binary, tertiary liquid equilibria, solid solutions in ternary systems, quinary systems of salts and water. Completely revised to triangular coordinates in ternary systems, clarified graphic representation, solid models, etc. 9th revised edition. Author, subject indexes. 236 figures. 505 footnotes, mostly bibliographic. xii + 494pp. 5⅜ x 8.
S91 Paperbound **$2.50**

PHYSICS

General physics

FOUNDATIONS OF PHYSICS, R. B. Lindsay & H. Margenau. Excellent bridge between semi-popular works & technical treatises. A discussion of methods of physical description, construction of theory; valuable for physicist with elementary calculus who is interested in ideas that give meaning to data, tools of modern physics. Contents include symbolism, mathematical equations; space & time foundations of mechanics; probability; physics & continua; electron theory; special & general relativity; quantum mechanics; causality. "Thorough and yet not overdetailed. Unreservedly recommended," NATURE (London). Unabridged, corrected edition. List of recommended readings. 35 illustrations. xi + 537pp. 5⅜ x 8.
S377 Paperbound **$2.75**

FUNDAMENTAL FORMULAS OF PHYSICS, ed. by D. H. Menzel. Highly useful, fully inexpensive reference and study text, ranging from simple to highly sophisticated operations. Mathematics integrated into text—each chapter stands as short textbook of field represented. Vol. 1: Statistics, Physical Constants, Special Theory of Relativity, Hydrodynamics, Aerodynamics, Boundary Value Problems in Math. Physics; Viscosity, Electromagnetic Theory, etc. Vol. 2: Sound, Acoustics, Geometrical Optics, Electron Optics, High-Energy Phenomena, Magnetism, Biophysics, much more. Index. Total of 800pp. 5⅜ x 8. Vol. 1 S595 Paperbound **$2.00**
Vol. 2 S596 Paperbound **$2.00**

MATHEMATICAL PHYSICS, D. H. Menzel. Thorough one-volume treatment of the mathematical techniques vital for classic mechanics, electromagnetic theory, quantum theory, and relativity. Written by the Harvard Professor of Astrophysics for junior, senior, and graduate courses, it gives clear explanations of all those aspects of function theory, vectors, matrices, dyadics, tensors, partial differential equations, etc., necessary for the understanding of the various physical theories. Electron theory, relativity, and other topics seldom presented appear here in considerable detail. Scores of definitions, conversion factors, dimensional constants, etc. "More detailed than normal for an advanced text . . . excellent set of sections on Dyadics, Matrices, and Tensors," JOURNAL OF THE FRANKLIN INSTITUTE. Index. 193 problems, with answers. x + 412pp. 5⅜ x 8. S56 Paperbound **$2.00**

THE SCIENTIFIC PAPERS OF J. WILLARD GIBBS. All the published papers of America's outstanding theoretical scientist (except for "Statistical Mechanics" and "Vector Analysis"). Vol I (thermodynamics) contains one of the most brilliant of all 19th-century scientific papers—the 300-page "On the Equilibrium of Heterogeneous Substances," which founded the science of physical chemistry, and clearly stated a number of highly important natural laws for the first time; 8 other papers complete the first volume. Vol II includes 2 papers on dynamics, 8 on vector analysis and multiple algebra, 5 on the electromagnetic theory of light, and 6 miscellaneous papers. Biographical sketch by H. A. Bumstead. Total of xxxvi + 718pp. 5⅝ x 8⅜.
S721 Vol I Paperbound **$2.50**
S722 Vol II Paperbound **$2.00**
The set **$4.50**

BASIC THEORIES OF PHYSICS, Peter Gabriel Bergmann. Two-volume set which presents a critical examination of important topics in the major subdivisions of classical and modern physics. The first volume is concerned with classical mechanics and electrodynamics: mechanics of mass points, analytical mechanics, matter in bulk, electrostatics and magnetostatics, electromagnetic interaction, the field waves, special relativity, and waves. The second volume (Heat and Quanta) contains discussions of the kinetic hypothesis, physics and statistics, stationary ensembles, laws of thermodynamics, early quantum theories, atomic spectra, probability waves, quantization in wave mechanics, approximation methods, and abstract quantum theory. A valuable supplement to any thorough course or text.
Heat and Quanta: Index. 8 figures. x + 300pp. 5⅜ x 8½. S968 Paperbound **$2.00**
Mechanics and Electrodynamics: Index. 14 figures. vii + 280pp. 5⅜ x 8½.
S969 Paperbound **$1.75**

THEORETICAL PHYSICS, A. S. Kompaneyets. One of the very few thorough studies of the subject in this price range. Provides advanced students with a comprehensive theoretical background. Especially strong on recent experimentation and developments in quantum theory. Contents: Mechanics (Generalized Coordinates, Lagrange's Equation, Collision of Particles, etc.), Electrodynamics (Vector Analysis, Maxwell's equations, Transmission of Signals, Theory of Relativity, etc.), Quantum Mechanics (the Inadequacy of Classical Mechanics, the Wave Equation, Motion in a Central Field, Quantum Theory of Radiation, Quantum Theories of Dispersion and Scattering, etc.), and Statistical Physics (Equilibrium Distribution of Molecules in an Ideal Gas, Boltzmann statistics, Bose and Fermi Distribution, Thermodynamic Quantities, etc.). Revised to 1961. Translated by George Yankovsky, authorized by Kompaneyets. 137 exercises. 56 figures. 529pp. 5⅜ x 8½. S972 Paperbound **$2.50**

ANALYTICAL AND CANONICAL FORMALISM IN PHYSICS, André Mercier. A survey, in one volume, of the variational principles (the key principles—in mathematical form—from which the basic laws of any one branch of physics can be derived) of the several branches of physical theory, together with an examination of the relationships among them. Contents: the Lagrangian Formalism, Lagrangian Densities, Canonical Formalism, Canonical Form of Electrodynamics, Hamiltonian Densities, Transformations, and Canonical Form with Vanishing Jacobian Determinant. Numerous examples and exercises. For advanced students, teachers, etc. 6 figures. Index. viii + 222pp. 5⅜ x 8½. S1077 Paperbound **$1.75**

MATHEMATICAL PUZZLES AND RECREATIONS

AMUSEMENTS IN MATHEMATICS, Henry Ernest Dudeney. The foremost British originator of mathematical puzzles is always intriguing, witty, and paradoxical in this classic, one of the largest collections of mathematical amusements. More than 430 puzzles, problems, and paradoxes. Mazes and games, problems on number manipulation, unicursal and other route problems, puzzles on measuring, weighing, packing, age, kinship, chessboards, joining, crossing river, plane figure dissection, and many others. Solutions. More than 450 illustrations. vii + 258pp. 5⅜ x 8. T473 Paperbound **$1.25**

SYMBOLIC LOGIC and THE GAME OF LOGIC, Lewis Carroll. "Symbolic Logic" is not concerned with modern symbolic logic, but is instead a collection of over 380 problems posed with charm and imagination, using the syllogism, and a fascinating diagrammatic method of drawing conclusions. In "The Game of Logic," Carroll's whimsical imagination devises a logical game played with 2 diagrams and counters (included) to manipulate hundreds of tricky syllogisms. The final section, "Hit or Miss" is a lagniappe of 101 additional puzzles in the delightful Carroll manner. Until this reprint edition, both of these books were rarities costing up to $15 each. Symbolic Logic: Index, xxxi + 199pp. The Game of Logic: 96pp. Two vols. bound as one. 5⅜ x 8. T492 Paperbound **$1.50**

MAZES AND LABYRINTHS: A BOOK OF PUZZLES, W. Shepherd. Mazes, formerly associated with mystery and ritual, are still among the most intriguing of intellectual puzzles. This is a novel and different collection of 50 amusements that embody the principle of the maze: mazes in the classical tradition; 3-dimensional, ribbon, and Möbius-strip mazes; hidden messages; spatial arrangements; etc.—almost all built on amusing story situations. 84 illustrations. Essay on maze psychology. Solutions. xv + 122pp. 5⅜ x 8. T731 Paperbound **$1.00**

MATHEMATICAL RECREATIONS, M. Kraitchik. Some 250 puzzles, problems, demonstrations of recreational mathematics for beginners & advanced mathematicians. Unusual historical problems from Greek, Medieval, Arabic, Hindu sources: modern problems based on "mathematics without numbers," geometry, topology, arithmetic, etc. Pastimes derived from figurative numbers, Mersenne numbers, Fermat numbers; fairy chess, latruncles, reversi, many topics. Full solutions. Excellent for insights into special fields of math. 181 illustrations. 330pp. 5⅜ x 8. T163 Paperbound **$1.75**

MATHEMATICAL PUZZLES OF SAM LOYD, Vol. I, selected and edited by M. Gardner. Puzzles by the greatest puzzle creator and innovator. Selected from his famous "Cyclopedia of Puzzles," they retain the unique style and historical flavor of the originals. There are posers based on arithmetic, algebra, probability, game theory, route tracing, topology, counter, sliding block, operations research, geometrical dissection. Includes his famous "14-15" puzzle which was a national craze, and his "Horse of a Different Color" which sold millions of copies. 117 of his most ingenious puzzles in all, 120 line drawings and diagrams. Solutions. Selected references. xx + 167pp. 5⅜ x 8. T498 Paperbound **$1.00**

MY BEST PUZZLES IN MATHEMATICS, Hubert Phillips ("Caliban"). Caliban is generally considered the best of the modern problemists. Here are 100 of his best and wittiest puzzles, selected by the author himself from such publications as the London Daily Telegraph, and each puzzle is guaranteed to put even the sharpest puzzle detective through his paces. Perfect for the development of clear thinking and a logical mind. Complete solutions are provided for every puzzle. x + 107pp. 5⅜ x 8½. T91 Paperbound **$1.00**

MY BEST PUZZLES IN LOGIC AND REASONING, H. Phillips ("Caliban"). 100 choice, hitherto unavailable puzzles by England's best-known problemist. No special knowledge needed to solve these logical or inferential problems, just an unclouded mind, nerves of steel, and fast reflexes. Data presented are both necessary and just sufficient to allow one unambiguous answer. More than 30 different types of puzzles, all ingenious and varied, many one of a kind, that will challenge the expert, please the beginner. Original publication. 100 puzzles, full solutions. x + 107pp. 5⅜ x 8½. T119 Paperbound **$1.00**

MATHEMATICAL PUZZLES FOR BEGINNERS AND ENTHUSIASTS, G. Mott-Smith. 188 mathematical puzzles to test mental agility. Inference, interpretation, algebra, dissection of plane figures, geometry, properties of numbers, decimation, permutations, probability, all enter these delightful problems. Puzzles like the Odic Force, How to Draw an Ellipse, Spider's Cousin, more than 180 others. Detailed solutions. Appendix with square roots, triangular numbers, primes, etc. 135 illustrations. 2nd revised edition. 248pp. 5⅜ x 8. T198 Paperbound **$1.00**

MATHEMATICS, MAGIC AND MYSTERY, Martin Gardner. Card tricks, feats of mental mathematics, stage mind-reading, other "magic" explained as applications of probability, sets, theory of numbers, topology, various branches of mathematics. Creative examination of laws and their applications with scores of new tricks and insights. 115 sections discuss tricks wtih cards, dice, coins; geometrical vanishing tricks, dozens of others. No sleight of hand needed; mathematics guarantees success. 115 illustrations. xii + 174pp. 5⅜ x 8. T335 Paperbound **$1.00**

RECREATIONS IN THE THEORY OF NUMBERS: THE QUEEN OF MATHEMATICS ENTERTAINS, Albert H. Beiler. The theory of numbers is often referred to as the "Queen of Mathematics." In this book Mr. Beiler has compiled the first English volume to deal exclusively with the recreational aspects of number theory, an inherently recreational branch of mathematics. The author's clear style makes for enjoyable reading as he deals with such topics as: perfect numbers, amicable numbers, Fermat's theorem, Wilson's theorem, interesting properties of digits, methods of factoring, primitive roots, Euler's function, polygonal and figurate numbers, Mersenne numbers, congruence, repeating decimals, etc. Countless puzzle problems, with full answers and explanations. For mathematicians and mathematically-inclined laymen, etc. New publication. 28 figures. 9 illustrations. 103 tables. Bibliography at chapter ends. vi + 247pp. 5⅜ x 8½. T1096 Paperbound **$1.85**

PAPER FOLDING FOR BEGINNERS, W. D. Murray and F. J. Rigney. A delightful introduction to the varied and entertaining Japanese art of origami (paper folding), with a full crystal-clear text that anticipates every difficulty; over 275 clearly labeled diagrams of all important stages in creation. You get results at each stage, since complex figures are logically developed from simpler ones. 43 different pieces are explained: place mats, drinking cups, bonbon boxes, sailboats, frogs, roosters, etc. 6 photographic plates. 279 diagrams. 95pp. 5⅝ x 8⅜. T713 Paperbound **$1.00**

1800 RIDDLES, ENIGMAS AND CONUNDRUMS, Darwin A. Hindman. Entertaining collection ranging from hilarious gags to outrageous puns to sheer nonsense—a welcome respite from sophisticated humor. Children, toastmasters, and practically anyone with a funny bone will find these zany riddles tickling and eminently repeatable. Sample: "Why does Santa Claus always go down the chimney?" "Because it soots him." Some old, some new—covering a wide variety of subjects. New publication. iii + 154pp. 5⅜ x 8½. T1059 Paperbound **$1.00**

EASY-TO-DO ENTERTAINMENTS AND DIVERSIONS WITH CARDS, STRING, COINS, PAPER AND MATCHES, R. M. Abraham. Over 300 entertaining games, tricks, puzzles, and pastimes for children and adults. Invaluable to anyone in charge of groups of youngsters, for party givers, etc. Contains sections on card tricks and games, making things by paperfolding—toys, decorations, and the like; tricks with coins, matches, and pieces of string; descriptions of games; toys that can be made from common household objects; mathematical recreations; word games; and 50 miscellaneous entertainments. Formerly "Winter Nights Entertainments." Introduction by Lord Baden Powell. 329 illustrations. v + 186pp. 5⅜ x 8. T921 Paperbound **$1.00**

DIVERSIONS AND PASTIMES WITH CARDS, STRING, PAPER AND MATCHES, R. M. Abraham. Another collection of amusements and diversion for game and puzzle fans of all ages. Many new paperfolding ideas and tricks, an extensive section on amusements with knots and splices, two chapters of easy and not-so-easy problems, coin and match tricks, and lots of other parlor pastimes from the agile mind of the late British problemist and gamester. Corrected and revised version. Illustrations. 160pp. 5⅜ x 8½. T1127 Paperbound **$1.00**

STRING FIGURES AND HOW TO MAKE THEM: A STUDY OF CAT'S-CRADLE IN MANY LANDS, Caroline Furness Jayne. In a simple and easy-to-follow manner, this book describes how to make 107 different string figures. Not only is looping and crossing string between the fingers a common youthful diversion, but it is an ancient form of amusement practiced in all parts of the globe, especially popular among primitive tribes. These games are fun for all ages and offer an excellent means for developing manual dexterity and coordination. Much insight also for the anthropological observer on games and diversions in many different cultures. Index. Bibliography. Introduction by A. C. Haddon, Cambridge University. 17 full-page plates. 950 illustrations. xxiii + 407pp. 5⅜ x 8½. T152 Paperbound **$2.00**

CRYPTANALYSIS, Helen F. Gaines. (Formerly ELEMENTARY CRYPTANALYSIS.) A standard elementary and intermediate text for serious students. It does not confine itself to old material, but contains much that is not generally known, except to experts. Concealment, Transposition, Substitution ciphers; Vigenere, Kasiski, Playfair, multafid, dozens of other techniques. Appendix with sequence charts, letter frequencies in English, 5 other languages, English word frequencies. Bibliography. 167 codes. New to this edition: solution to codes. vi + 230pp. 5⅜ x 8. T97 Paperbound **$2.00**

MAGIC SQUARES AND CUBES, W. S. Andrews. Only book-length treatment in English, a thorough non-technical description and analysis. Here are nasik, overlapping, pandiagonal, serrated squares; magic circles, cubes, spheres, rhombuses. Try your hand at 4-dimensional magical figures! Much unusual folklore and tradition included. High school algebra is sufficient. 754 diagrams and illustrations. viii + 419pp. 5⅜ x 8. T658 Paperbound **$1.85**

CALIBAN'S PROBLEM BOOK: MATHEMATICAL, INFERENTIAL, AND CRYPTOGRAPHIC PUZZLES, H. Phillips ("Caliban"), S. T. Shovelton, G. S. Marshall. 105 ingenious problems by the greatest living creator of puzzles based on logic and inference. Rigorous, modern, piquant, and reflecting their author's unusual personality, these intermediate and advanced puzzles all involve the ability to reason clearly through complex situations; some call for mathematical knowledge, ranging from algebra to number theory. Solutions. xi + 180pp. 5⅜ x 8. T736 Paperbound **$1.25**

FICTION

THE LAND THAT TIME FORGOT and THE MOON MAID, Edgar Rice Burroughs. In the opinion of many, Burroughs' best work. The first concerns a strange island where evolution is individual rather than phylogenetic. Speechless anthropoids develop into intelligent human beings within a single generation. The second projects the reader far into the future and describes the first voyage to the Moon (in the year 2025), the conquest of the Earth by the Moon, and years of violence and adventure as the enslaved Earthmen try to regain possession of their planet. "An imaginative tour de force that keeps the reader keyed up and expectant," NEW YORK TIMES. Complete, unabridged text of the original two novels (three parts in each). 5 illustrations by J. Allen St. John. vi + 552pp. 5⅜ x 8½.
T1020 Clothbound **$3.75**
T358 Paperbound **$2.00**

AT THE EARTH'S CORE, PELLUCIDAR, TANAR OF PELLUCIDAR: THREE SCIENCE FICTION NOVELS BY EDGAR RICE BURROUGHS. Complete, unabridged texts of the first three Pellucidar novels. Tales of derring-do by the famous master of science fiction. The locale for these three related stories is the inner surface of the hollow Earth where we discover the world of Pellucidar, complete with all types of bizarre, menacing creatures, strange peoples, and alluring maidens—guaranteed to delight all Burroughs fans and a wide circle of advenutre lovers. Illustrated by J. Allen St. John and P. F. Berdanier. vi + 433pp. 5⅜ x 8½.
T1051 Paperbound **$2.00**

THE PIRATES OF VENUS and LOST ON VENUS: TWO VENUS NOVELS BY EDGAR RICE BURROUGHS. Two related novels, complete and unabridged. Exciting adventure on the planet Venus with Earthman Carson Napier broken-field running through one dangerous episode after another. All lovers of swashbuckling science fiction will enjoy these two stories set in a world of fascinating societies, fierce beasts, 5000-ft. trees, lush vegetation, and wide seas. Illustrations by Fortunino Matania. Total of vi + 340pp. 5⅜ x 8½. T1053 Paperbound **$1.75**

A PRINCESS OF MARS and A FIGHTING MAN OF MARS: TWO MARTIAN NOVELS BY EDGAR RICE BURROUGHS. "Princess of Mars" is the very first of the great Martian novels written by Burroughs, and it is probably the best of them all; it set the pattern for all of his later fantasy novels and contains a thrilling cast of strange peoples and creatures and the formula of Olympian heroism amidst ever-fluctuating fortunes which Burroughs carries off so successfully. "Fighting Man" returns to the same scenes and cities—many years later. A mad scientist, a degenerate dictator, and an indomitable defender of the right clash—with the fate of the Red Planet at stake! Complete, unabridged reprinting of original editions. Illustrations by F. E. Schoonover and Hugh Hutton. v + 356pp. 5⅜ x 8½.
T1140 Paperbound **$1.75**

THREE MARTIAN NOVELS, Edgar Rice Burroughs. Contains: Thuvia, Maid of Mars; The Chessmen of Mars; and The Master Mind of Mars. High adventure set in an imaginative and intricate conception of the Red Planet. Mars is peopled with an intelligent, heroic human race which lives in densely populated cities and with fierce barbarians who inhabit dead sea bottoms. Other exciting creatures abound amidst an inventive framework of Martian history and geography. Complete unabridged reprintings of the first edition. 16 illustrations by J. Allen St. John. vi + 499pp. 5⅜ x 8½. T39 Paperbound **$1.85**

THREE PROPHETIC NOVELS BY H. G. WELLS, edited by E. F. Bleiler. Complete texts of "When the Sleeper Wakes" (1st book printing in 50 years), "A Story of the Days to Come," "The Time Machine" (1st complete printing in book form). Exciting adventures in the future are as enjoyable today as 50 years ago when first printed. Predict TV, movies, intercontinental airplanes, prefabricated houses, air-conditioned cities, etc. First important author to foresee problems of mind control, technological dictatorships. "Absolute best of imaginative fiction," N. Y. Times. Introduction. 335pp. 5⅜ x 8. T605 Paperbound **$1.50**

28 SCIENCE FICTION STORIES OF H. G. WELLS. Two full unabridged novels, MEN LIKE GODS and STAR BEGOTTEN, plus 26 short stories by the master science-fiction writer of all time. Stories of space, time, invention, exploration, future adventure—an indispensable part of the library of everyone interested in science and adventure. PARTIAL CONTENTS: Men Like Gods, The Country of the Blind, In the Abyss, The Crystal Egg, The Man Who Could Work Miracles, A Story of the Days to Come, The Valley of Spiders, and 21 more! 928pp. 5⅜ x 8.
T265 Clothbound **$4.50**

THE WAR IN THE AIR, IN THE DAYS OF THE COMET, THE FOOD OF THE GODS: THREE SCIENCE FICTION NOVELS BY H. G. WELLS. Three exciting Wells offerings bearing on vital social and philosophical issues of his and our own day. Here are tales of air power, strategic bombing, East vs. West, the potential miracles of science, the potential disasters from outer space, the relationship between scientific advancement and moral progress, etc. First reprinting of "War in the Air" in almost 50 years. An excellent sampling of Wells at his storytelling best. Complete, unabridged reprintings. 16 illustrations. 645pp. 5⅜ x 8½.
T1135 Paperbound **$2.00**

SEVEN SCIENCE FICTION NOVELS, H. G. Wells. Full unabridged texts of 7 science-fiction novels of the master. Ranging from biology, physics, chemistry, astronomy to sociology and other studies, Mr. Wells extrapolates whole worlds of strange and intriguing character. "One will have to go far to match this for entertainment, excitement, and sheer pleasure . . . ," NEW YORK TIMES. Contents: The Time Machine, The Island of Dr. Moreau, First Men in the Moon, The Invisible Man, The War of the Worlds, The Food of the Gods, In the Days of the Comet. 1015pp. 5⅜ x 8. T264 Clothbound **$4.50**

BEST GHOST STORIES OF J. S. LE FANU, Selected and introduced by E. F. Bleiler. LeFanu is deemed the greatest name in Victorian supernatural fiction. Here are 16 of his best horror stories, including 2 nouvelles: "Carmilla," a classic vampire tale couched in a perverse eroticism, and "The Haunted Baronet." Also: "Sir Toby's Will," "Green Tea," "Schalken the Painter," "Ultor de Lacy," "The Familiar," etc. The first American publication of about half of this material: a long-overdue opportunity to get a choice sampling of LeFanu's work. New selection (1964). 8 illustrations. 5⅜ x 8⅜. T415 Paperbound **$1.85**

THE WONDERFUL WIZARD OF OZ, L. F. Baum. Only edition in print with all the original W. W. Denslow illustrations in full color—as much a part of "The Wizard" as Tenniel's drawings are for "Alice in Wonderland." "The Wizard" is still America's best-loved fairy tale, in which, as the author expresses it, "The wonderment and joy are retained and the heartaches and nightmares left out." Now today's young readers can enjoy every word and wonderful picture of the original book. New introduction by Martin Gardner. A Baum bibliography. 23 full-page color plates. viii + 268pp. 5⅜ x 8. T691 Paperbound **$1.50**

GHOST AND HORROR STORIES OF AMBROSE BIERCE, Selected and introduced by E. F. Bleiler. 24 morbid, eerie tales—the cream of Bierce's fiction output. Contains such memorable pieces as "The Moonlit Road," "The Damned Thing," "An Inhabitant of Carcosa," "The Eyes of the Panther," "The Famous Gilson Bequest," "The Middle Toe of the Right Foot," and other chilling stories, plus the essay, "Visions of the Night" in which Bierce gives us a kind of rationale for his aesthetic of horror. New collection (1964). xxii + 199pp. 5⅜ x 8⅜. T767 Paperbound **$1.00**

HUMOR

MR. DOOLEY ON IVRYTHING AND IVRYBODY, Finley Peter Dunne. Since the time of his appearance in 1893, "Mr. Dooley," the fictitious Chicago bartender, has been recognized as America's most humorous social and political commentator. Collected in this volume are 102 of the best Dooley pieces—all written around the turn of the century, the height of his popularity. Mr. Dooley's Irish brogue is employed wittily and penetratingly on subjects which are just as fresh and relevant today as they were then: corruption and hypocrisy of politicans, war preparations and chauvinism, automation, Latin American affairs, superbombs, etc. Other articles range from Rudyard Kipling to football. Selected with an introduction by Robert Hutchinson. xii + 244pp. 5⅜ x 8½. T626 Paperbound **$1.00**

RUTHLESS RHYMES FOR HEARTLESS HOMES and MORE RUTHLESS RHYMES FOR HEARTLESS HOMES, Harry Graham ("Col. D. Streamer"). A collection of Little Willy and 48 other poetic "disasters." Graham's funniest and most disrespectful verse, accompanied by original illustrations. Nonsensical, wry humor which employs stern parents, careless nurses, uninhibited children, practical jokers, single-minded golfers, Scottish lairds, etc. in the leading roles. A precursor of the "sick joke" school of today. This volume contains, bound together for the first time, two of the most perennially popular books of humor in England and America. Index. vi + 69pp. 5⅜ x 8. T930 Paperbound **75¢**

A WHIMSEY ANTHOLOGY, Collected by Carolyn Wells. 250 of the most amusing rhymes ever written. Acrostics, anagrams, palindromes, alphabetical jingles, tongue twisters, echo verses, alliterative verses, riddles, mnemonic rhymes, interior rhymes, over 40 limericks, etc. by Lewis Carroll, Edward Lear, Joseph Addison, W. S. Gilbert, Christina Rossetti, Chas. Lamb, James Boswell, Hood, Dickens, Swinburne, Leigh Hunt, Harry Graham, Poe, Eugene Field, and many others. xiv + 221pp. 5⅜ x 8½. T195 Paperbound **$1.25**

MY PIOUS FRIENDS AND DRUNKEN COMPANIONS and MORE PIOUS FRIENDS AND DRUNKEN COMPANIONS, Songs and ballads of Conviviality Collected by Frank Shay. Magnificently illuminated by John Held, Jr. 132 ballads, blues, vaudeville numbers, drinking songs, cowboy songs, sea chanties, comedy songs, etc. of the Naughty Nineties and early 20th century. Over a third are reprinted with music. Many perennial favorites such as: The Band Played On, Frankie and Johnnie, The Old Grey Mare, The Face on the Bar-room Floor, etc. Many others unlocatable elsewhere: The Dog-Catcher's Child, The Cannibal Maiden, Don't Go in the Lion's Cage Tonight, Mother, etc. Complete verses and introductions to songs. Unabridged republication of first editions, 2 Indexes (song titles and first lines and choruses). Introduction by Frank Shay. 2 volumes bounds as 1. Total of xvi + 235pp. 5⅜ x 8½. T946 Paperbound **$1.25**

MAX AND MORITZ, Wilhelm Busch. Edited and annotated by H. Arthur Klein. Translated by H. Arthur Klein, M. C. Klein, and others. The mischievous high jinks of Max and Moritz, Peter and Paul, Ker and Plunk, etc. are delightfully captured in sketch and rhyme. (Companion volume to "Hypocritical Helena.") In addition to the title piece, it contians: Ker and Plunk; Two Dogs and Two Boys; The Egghead and the Two Cut-ups of Corinth; Deceitful Henry; The Boys and the Pipe; Cat and Mouse; and others. (Original German text with accompanying English translations.) Afterword by H. A. Klein. vi + 216pp. 5⅜ x 8½.
T181 Paperbound **$1.15**

THROUGH THE ALIMENTARY CANAL WITH GUN AND CAMERA: A FASCINATING TRIP TO THE INTERIOR, Personally Conducted by George S. Chappell. In mock-travelogue style, the amusing account of an imaginative journey down the alimentary canal. The "explorers" enter the esophagus, round the Adam's Apple, narrowly escape from a fierce Amoeba, struggle through the impenetrable Nerve Forests of the Lumbar Region, etc. Illustrated by the famous cartoonist, Otto Soglow, the book is as much a brilliant satire of academic pomposity and professional travel literature as it is a clever use of the facts of physiology for supremely comic purposes. Preface by Robert Benchley. Author's Foreword. 1 Photograph. 17 illustrations by O. Soglow. xii + 114pp. 5⅜ x 8½. T376 Paperbound **$1.00**

THE BAD CHILD'S BOOK OF BEASTS, MORE BEASTS FOR WORSE CHILDREN, and A MORAL ALPHABET, H. Belloc. Hardly an anthology of humorous verse has appeared in the last 50 years without at least a couple of these famous nonsense verses. But one must see the entire volumes—with all the delightful original illustrations by Sir Basil Blackwood—to appreciate fully Belloc's charming and witty verses that play so subacidly on the platitudes of life and morals that beset his day—and ours. A great humor classic. Three books in one. Total of 157pp. 5⅜ x 8. T749 Paperbound **$1.00**

THE DEVIL'S DICTIONARY, Ambrose Bierce. Sardonic and irreverent barbs puncturing the pomposities and absurdities of American politics, business, religion, literature, and arts, by the country's greatest satirist in the classic tradition. Epigrammatic as Shaw, piercing as Swift, American as Mark Twain, Will Rogers, and Fred Allen. Bierce will always remain the favorite of a small coterie of enthusiasts, and of writers and speakers whom he supplies with "some of the most gorgeous witticisms of the English language." (H. L. Mencken) Over 1000 entries in alphabetical order. 144pp. 5⅜ x 8. T487 Paperbound **$1.00**

THE COMPLETE NONSENSE OF EDWARD LEAR. This is the only complete edition of this master of gentle madness available at a popular price. A BOOK OF NONSENSE, NONSENSE SONGS, MORE NONSENSE SONGS AND STORIES in their entirety with all the old favorites that have delighted children and adults for years. The Dong With A Luminous Nose, The Jumblies, The Owl and the Pussycat, and hundreds of other bits of wonderful nonsense. 214 limericks, 3 sets of Nonsense Botany, 5 Nonsense Alphabets. 546 drawings by Lear himself, and much more. 320pp. 5⅜ x 8. T167 Paperbound **$1.00**

SINGULAR TRAVELS, CAMPAIGNS, AND ADVENTURES OF BARON MUNCHAUSEN, R. E. Raspe, with 90 illustrations by Gustave Doré. The first edition in over 150 years to reestablish the deeds of the Prince of Liars exactly as Raspe first recorded them in 1785—the genuine Baron Munchausen, one of the most popular personalities in English literature. Included also are the best of the many sequels, written by other hands. Introduction on Raspe by J. Carswell. Bibliography of early editions. xliv + 192pp. 5⅜ x 8. T698 Paperbound **$1.00**

HOW TO TELL THE BIRDS FROM THE FLOWERS, R. W. Wood. How not to confuse a carrot with a parrot, a grape with an ape, a puffin with nuffin. Delightful drawings, clever puns, absurd little poems point out farfetched resemblances in nature. The author was a leading physicist. Introduction by Margaret Wood White. 106 illus. 60pp. 5⅜ x 8.
T523 Paperbound **75¢**

JOE MILLER'S JESTS OR, THE WITS VADE-MECUM. The original Joe Miller jest book. Gives a keen and pungent impression of life in 18th-century England. Many are somewhat on the bawdy side and they are still capable of provoking amusement and good fun. This volume is a facsimile of the original "Joe Miller" first published in 1739. It remains the most popular and influential humor book of all time. New introduction by Robert Hutchinson. xxi + 70pp. 5⅜ x 8½. T423 Paperbound **$1.00**

Prices subject to change without notice.

Dover publishes books on art, music, philosophy, literature, languages, history, social sciences, psychology, handcrafts, orientalia, puzzles and entertainments, chess, pets and gardens, books explaining science, intermediate and higher mathematics, mathematical physics, engineering, biological sciences, earth sciences, classics of science, etc. Write to:

Dept. catrr.
Dover Publications, Inc.
180 Varick Street, N.Y. 14, N.Y.